The Arab World

PAST, PRESENT,
and
FUTURE

The Arab World

Past, Present, and Future

by

Nejla Izzeddin

Foreword by

William Ernest Hocking

Chicago · HENRY REGNERY COMPANY · *1953*

FOREWORD

THERE are peoples in the wide world whom it is our bounden duty to know. There are also peoples whom it is a delight to know. There are peoples whom it is both a duty and a delight to know—and such by all counts are the Arabs.

Our Arab neighbors for centuries have given character, meaning, and flavor to the entire Middle East—a character never dull, never mean, never quite obvious, which some have called a trifle enigmatic, with its own dimensions of majesty and depth, its own capacities for that union of reason and passion which is the life of history. They hold the cross-roads of three continents, and their political decisions will affect the course of world-history—including our own history—for years to come. We need to know them from many angles—that of the scholar, the diplomat, the man of business, the man of letters, the artist, the philosopher—and that of the woman, who may be all of these things and surely more.

It has been centuries since the Arabs could be identified with a habitat or origin in the Arabian peninsula, as they were for the Greeks and Romans—centuries, too, since the Arab nomad with his camel could symbolize any large fraction of the Arab people. Yet the physical fascination of that difficult terrain, which has done so much to shield historic Arabia from interested intruders, favoring the quiet and immediate intercourse of the human solitaire with the infinitudes of distance and the deep mysteries of the night sky, can never be wholly severed from the suggestion of the word 'Arab': one is reminded of the saying which Walter Bagehot applies to the life of nations, that "all great things are prepared in secret," sheltered in some geographic womb from the vicissitudes of irrelevant world-affairs.

Neither can the Arab peoples be precisely identified with the Moslem faith, for three reasons: Islam has far outgrown the Arab world; the Arab peoples include many Christians and other non-Moslem Arabs; the Moslem of today is making his own accounts with the modern spirit and with the problems of strict observance. Yet it was the electric spread of Islam that created the classical Arab domain, and with the aid of the Arabic language—and a marvelous receptivity to foreign cultures—stamped its character and the spirit of its civilization on the entire area to this day. Not all Moslems and not all Arabs make the Pilgrimage; but for all Moslems and most Arabs, Mecca and Medina remain places of pilgrimage for the soul, and with a depth of regard measured by their austere refusal to tolerate the "tourist": one of the few truly dignified peoples of the world in this respect.

If, as someone has said, language is the house of the soul, the Arabic language is at once a house and a temple. When the Abbasid Caliphate made its center in Baghdad, and became neighbor to the Persians, the Arabs eagerly began merging Persian thought with their own philosophies (a mystical, poetic, doubtfully orthodox Sufism was the wonder-child of the merger), while the Persians with equal eagerness began to think and write in Arabic. Omar Khayyam wrote Arabic verse as well as his Persian quatrains. This language, perhaps today the most useful defining mark of "the Arabs," is one of the most beautiful and expressive tongues, and, with Latin, it was one of the universal languages in medieval times of scholarship and diplomacy. It is a language which has maintained its purity against a hundred temptations to degenerate into local patois, because it is the language of the Koran, and shares its sacredness; until recently, thousands of Chinese children in the province of Yunnan were learning by heart their Koran in Arabic! —and so in other remote parts of the Moslem world.

Is it an advantage or a disadvantage that these defining marks have so high a degree of stability, the language, the domain, the history, the Islamic law and, for a large majority, the orientation to Mecca, the religion of a sacred Book? If these defining marks are shaken, must the Arab world lose its character and its cohesion? The most important single fact about these peoples, for the political discussions of the moment, is their rendezvous with *Change*, the god of "modernity." They are in process of growth: and since this is so, they are no longer to be identified with what they were yesterday but rather with what they will be tomorrow. Nevertheless, the anchorage of Arab culture must hold fast; and you and I can never grasp the significance of that tomorrow unless we first appreciate—without nostalgia, if possible—the splendor of the past, and the profound dignity even of the disturbed present, out of which that future is to grow.

It is to their credit and to the enrichment of all of us that the Arab peoples have held to their own quality longer than any other comparable part of the accessible civilized world. Until about 1920, a visit to Palestine could still be in actual feeling a visit to the land of Saul and David—in some spots even reminiscent of Isaac and Rebecca—of the Prophets, of Mary and Joseph and their Son, the carpenter of Nazareth. This is no longer the case. Caught like the rest of us, only more ruthlessly and blindly, in the drive of all-intrusive world-forces armed with penetrating instruments of travel and communication (undoubtedly instruments of "progress"), they are beset with the necessity of making swift adjustment to new world roles. If we in America are reluctant, as we are, to involve ourselves in Europe-Asia-Africa to the extent that the times now demand of us, we may dimly appreciate the corresponding reluctance on the part of peoples far less enamoured of change. I, for one, am glad if change comes to the Arab world hard and slow: not that change is to be fended off—God knows it is needed—but that it should come with no joy of rejection, *no revolutionary repudiation,* devoid of honor to the present and gratitude to the past. For that Arab world, as we can still touch it, is and has been a world of rare nobility and charm. And when the noise of a secularized, self-vaunting modernity bursts in, something is in danger of *losing hold of itself,* something may pass which the world will not easily recover—if at all. Read the story of the Arabs—read it lovingly, not merely for the facts, but to recover the intuition of a great phase of human experience, read it to find yourself in the Arab world of spirit, imagination, and reflection.

Let me mention a detail or two which Dr. Izzeddin, herself an Arab and therefore breathing these things as native air, might not notice as saliently as a non-Arab.

I know and remember gratefully what Arab hospitality is, and also Arab superiority to the tyranny of our measures of time. To an American, tied to his watch (though he fancies the watch tied to him), the unperturbed leisureliness of his Arab host in the Beka' can be disturbing, but at the same time freeing and magnificent. I have told him that I have an engagement in three hours at Zahleh, a hundred miles away. "Ah yes," he replies: "We shall at once hunt up our schoolmaster; there are Roman remains hereabout that you will surely wish to see; the schoolmaster knows them well. If you would stay only a week we could examine them in detail . . ."

I am haunted by the grace of characteristic Arab architecture strung through the world from the Taj Mahal to the Alhambra, and not alone of that of the exquisite mosques of Damascus, Jerusalem, Cairo. . . . The city in all the world I most crave to revisit is the purely Arab city of Hama on the Orontes, where (with a bit of exaggeration) every gate and doorway to garden enclosures is different from every other, and every window individually designed and carved, and the music of ancient waterwheels fills the air day and night. In Hama, too, I have a friend, a Moslem Arab; the drawing room of his house is built directly over one of the smaller waterwheels. I have had, all told, just an hour with him in this mortal life. We spoke of the Koran, and of ideas which Islam has given to mankind; when we parted there was a bond between us that will never break. Among the Arabs, reality is not hidden under a hundred irrelevancies; man is immediately in the presence of man. Is this itself an irrelevance, a trivial personal detail? To my mind, it is close to the heart of the matter; for what is civilization if not the swift accessibility of thought to thought across every barrier of nationality and history?

*   *   *

Once we have gained an intimate sense of what Arab culture has been, both in its great days when it was custodian for the entire western world of the Greek classics, of Plato and Aristotle, and in its present continuance through the academies and schools of Riyadh, of Damascus, of Mosul and Baghdad, of Cairo (Al Azhar), of Tunis and other centers, we become deeply concerned for its future. We want the recent parts of the story, as they are here presented, not alone for the economic and political upheavals; not alone for the criss-crossing of the Arab domain by artificial lines of division due to the ambitions of European powers (once embodied in secret treaties that burst like bombs into the consciousness of President Wilson full of hope for the "self-determination" of peoples), and due also to the lava-flow from a European volcanic eruption that spread itself over Palestine; and not alone for the struggles, through these divisions, of an Arab national consciousness to win some unitary embodiment; but we want them for the major question, *What is to be the destiny of Arab culture?* What will happen to it as other types of life press upon it, as French life did in the Napoleonic era, with effects not in the main destructive but liberating, because French life and language had at that time a soul, in which the Arab soul could find shelter and sustenance.[1] To what extent are the Western powers, with whose financial and political interests the material development of Arab peoples if they resist the deadly seductions of the Octopus to the north, is likely to be bound up,—to what extent are these Western powers aware that there is an Arab soul? And that it is this soul that should dictate the political forms of the new Middle East, not the reverse, that it is not the composite conveniences, commercial and political, local-Arab and western, which should be allowed to impose their stamp of plurality, separation and secularism on the Arab soul?

But what can prevent the continued fragmentation of the Arab world through the outlining of artificial communities with national names under the drive of these external powers, if they are not aware of the Arab soul? There are two factors which, working together, may have some effect. The first, a firmer conception on all sides of what *constitutes a nation and the right of separate national existence:* seeing that the immense force we call "nationalism," now so much decried by internationalists, has an indispensable role to play in world order; that it is no mere subjective impulse (such as Wilson's "right of self-determination" at first seemed to suggest) but a concrete obligation; that it implies an historic mission expressing itself in a unique system of laws and customs—an experiment in living from which all mankind may benefit. The second factor, the emergence *from within Arab lands of prophetic voices* indicating what the Arab mission is to be—voices like that of George Antonius in "The Arab Awakening," or that of the blind scholar of Egypt, Taha Husain, who, with no disregard for the factual and economic bases of a modern society, sees that the glory and political justification for Arab national existence will lie in its unique cultural contribution, growing out of its historical rootages. When the Arab world speaks with decision from its own self-consciousness of mission, there is at least a chance that the external powers which today tend to shape Arab destinies through bargains, programs, condescensions and commands, will begin to realize that there is in the wealth of Arab or Iraqi oil nothing peculiarly Arabic; whereas there is everything peculiarly Arabic in, let us say, the Koranic union of law and faith, in the poems of Ibn al-Faridh, in al-Ghazali's "The Destruction of the Philosophers"—yes, in the Thou-

1. And it is still occasionally functioning in this way. See for example the little book of Arab poetry done into French by Wacyf Boutros Ghali of Cairo *Les Perles Éparpillées.*

sand and One Nights, and in the imperishable thoughts of such innovators and heretics as Husayn ibn Mansur al Hallaj, "the wool-carder," crucified at Baghdad in 922 because he taught the blasphemy "Anā 'l haqq,"—"I am the Real,"—a deviation from Islamic orthodoxy in the direction of religions of Incarnation, which developed a school of its own, and has an unmeasured future. The Arab cultural contribution to the world—formerly centered in its religious consciousness, its mystical insight and depth, its marvelous native springs of poetry by no means run dry—will continue, from whatever is eternal in these same sources, to yield laws, constitutions, social arrangements typically Arabic, as well as a great literature, just in so far as that national genius is recognized and encouraged from within and from without.

*   *   *

But of those external powers, it is the United States which in the recent past has especially known and cared for the soul of Arab lands; and for this country, the question whether it can still see this soul, and act in its behalf, is peculiarly pressing. We have been a friend of the Arab peoples, a friend both of the body and of the mind; we have been regarded by them as a sincere friend: our great schools at Cairo, Beirut and elsewhere have been welcome. I have been able to walk into village schools, like that of Kab Ilias on the eastern slope of Lebanon, and have friendly talk with teacher and children because I came from America: it was assumed in Arab lands at that time that American people cared and wanted to help. This tradition still holds good locally where our men and institutions can continue to speak for themselves; but in general, it is shaken, and in wide areas reversed. Why? Not long ago there was a political gathering in New York in which the proposed partition of Palestine was being discussed. I asked a friend who had been present why the Arab position on that question had been so feebly presented. His answer remains in my mind with a sense of deep shame: "You must not forget that there is *no Arab vote* in this country!" No Arab vote! Then is it the bribery employed by those who have a vote, the implicit pressure upon candidates for office, and not the merits of the case, that governs the public policies of this reputedly democratic nation? If so, our ability to help the new Arab peoples to find the new political expression which accords with their genius will be lost.

There is another side to the picture which, one may hope, will not be forgotten. I repeat an account of which I have only a verbal report, but which I believe to be substantially correct. It was the president of the American University in Beirut, Dr. Bliss, who called on President Wilson at Versailles when the mandate idea was being discussed, and the apportioning of the mandates by secret treaties was on the table. Dr. Bliss was able to tell the President of the great impression made throughout the Near East by the Allied posters to the effect that our governments were intending to give each people a voice—not the sole voice, but a voice in determining their own governing power. "I have only one thing to request," said Dr. Bliss, "namely, that we keep this promise." President Wilson, finding that the other three of the Four had no proposals for finding what the choices of the peoples of the ex-Turkish districts were, declared that the United States felt in honor bound to take steps to find out even if it had to act alone. Without the approval of his colleagues, he created the "King-Crane Commission" which during 1920 made inquiries on the spot. I do not say that this was the wisest course (I have discussed the matter elsewhere);[2] I say simply that it was an act of good faith toward the Arab peoples of the Near East and that the spirit of this action is still, I believe, the controlling motive of our Government. Deflections from that course are due to ignorance of the total circumstances rather than lack of good will, an ignorance which is first of all ours, as a people, and then that of our rulers. The remedy for that ignorance is the wide dissemination of such accounts as this book contains.

There are other recent and useful books in this field, but there is no full equivalent of Dr. Izzeddin's work. She knows the special and absolutely vital point of view of the Arab woman; of all human institutions the family is the most central and, in the case of the Arab family, most threatened by the secularizing forces which everywhere accompany the modern touch. She knows America and its educational institutions at first hand. It is not enough to say that she has a Ph.D. from the University of Chicago: she is the first woman Ph.D. in any Arab land. And she knows in her own person the present-day vitality of what I have been calling, for lack of a better phrase, the soul of Arabia; and that this indefinable vital spark has potencies for the age to come which the world can ill spare. It is not her purpose here to write an exhaustive treatise

2. Spirit of World Politics, 254–5, 260, 267.

for scholars; she has a higher aim, arising from her wide experience with this poorly informed public: to bring together what is
essential, first, for this public's appreciation of what the Arab spirit
has been and is, and then for the understanding of the issues affect-
ing the present and the future of Arab national life.

The reader will note that this book is written with feeling as
well as with responsible care; and I would especially urge his attention to this indispensable element of emotion, without which
no history is alive, and no book can stir with its message. It is only
in feeling that the vital spark of Arab life can be conveyed; and
only the feeling of one who greatly cares can initiate history-mak-
ing changes.

If you would know the Arab, read this record, to find yourself
in the Arab world of spirit, with that immediate and healing awareness of eternal things of which the contemporary world has even
more need than the medieval world which first felt the Arab
power.

WILLIAM ERNEST HOCKING

Madison, New Hampshire
March 30, 1953

Contents

Illustrations

The Arab World

CHAPTER I

The Environment

A LAND qualifies as part of the Arab patrimony if the daily speech of its inhabitants is the Arabic language. This is not an arbitrary or loose definition, for the historically valid reason that wherever Arabic is in common usage, the people who speak it share—across the vast expanses of earth which they occupy—a fund of common ideas, religious, social and intellectual. They live in a society where community of beliefs and practices, traditions and memories have been thirteen hundred years in the making. Besides, most of these lands at one time in Arab history formed a political unity as well.

The Arab lands occupy a position of marked significance in the geography of the world; they are at the gates of two great continents, Asia and Africa, and for centuries have been the link between East and West.

The eastern boundary of the Arab lands is the Zagros mountain range dividing Iraq from Iran; to the west it is the Atlantic Ocean off the Moroccan coast. In the north, the natural boundary is the Taurus range dividing Turkey from the Fertile Crescent; and in the south, the Indian Ocean, the African Jungle, and the Great Sahara.

The Arab lands in Asia comprise the Arabian Peninsula and the Fertile Crescent of which the eastern half is formed by Iraq, and the western half by Syria considered as a geographical, natural unity extending from the Taurus mountains in the north to the desert of Sinai in the south. Between the two horns of the Crescent lies the Syrian Desert, a continuation of the vast rectangle of desert and steppeland to the south, Arabia proper. In Africa the Arabs have made their home in the countries of the Nile—Egypt and the Sudan—and along the whole coast from Egypt to Morocco. North Africa is the Arab Maghreb—the western land—with Libya, Tunisia, and Algeria on the Mediterranean, and Morocco on the Atlantic, in the "far west."

Lands that cover such extensive areas naturally exhibit a wide range of variety with regard to climate, topography, soil, products, and natural resources. Within their framework, nature has woven a pattern rich in color and design; mountain and valley, desert and oasis, the Garden of Eden and a forbidding wilderness, plots of trimmed and disciplined soil closely nestled to areas that human hands have not yet subdued. And throughout the complex pattern runs one recurring theme, conspicuous not only on the fringes of the design, but winding itself into its very heart. This is the Desert, reaching everywhere.

It is well, therefore, to describe briefly each of the component parts of this vast design. The description may appropriately begin with the Peninsula of Arabia, the cradle of the Arab people.

The Peninsula is a huge rectangle covering a surface of a million and a quarter square miles. Its boundaries are the Persian Gulf and the Sea of Oman in the east, the Indian Ocean in the south, and in the west the Red Sea. In the north it merges imperceptibly into the Syrian Desert. The Arabs call it Jazirat-al-Arab, the Island of the Arabs, because, according to the Arab geographers of the Middle Ages, its northern frontiers were also bodies of water, namely the Tigris River, the great bend of the Euphrates, and the Mediterranean Sea. The unity of the Peninsula with the Fertile Crescent was recognized by classical writers many centuries before Arabic geography was born. Pliny, describing Arabia as an immense country inferior to none throughout the world, makes it extend to Mount Amanus, and places within its boundaries the cities of Edessa and Harran.[1] This definition, which places the Fertile Crescent within the boundaries of Arabia proper, is fully in harmony with the facts of both the physical and the human geography of the area. Physically, the northern block is one with the larger area of deserts and steppes to the south, with an intrusion of a fringe of fertile land around its rim. As for the people who made it their home from time immemorial, it is believed that their main stock came from the Peninsula, and through the ages continued to be replenished by wanderers seeping in from the desert in the south.

In our usage, however, the Peninsula will be treated as a unit apart from the Fertile Crescent.

1. Pliny: *Natural History*, BK. v. ch. 21 and BK. vi. ch. 32.

Arabia is part of the desert mass which spans the continents of Africa and Asia. The two bodies of water, the Red Sea on the west and the Persian Gulf on the east, are mere cuts in the Great Saharan desert surface. Arabia is a plateau, higher in the west and sloping gently towards the east. Hot and humid lowlands—the *Tihama*—lie along the Red Sea, backed by a mountainous range which runs for a thousand miles parallel to the coast, from the Gulf of Akaba at the head of the Red Sea to the hinterlands of the Straits of Bab-al-Mandeb at the entrance of the Indian Ocean. In the north, the Hijaz Chain reaches a height of nearly 9,000 feet; the central part of the range in Asir rises to about 10,000; and in Yaman the highest peak is 12,000 feet above sea-level.

Yaman, which has the highest elevation in the Peninsula, is a tilted plateau, with wide areas between 7,000 and 10,000 feet high. Although the country lies in the tropical zone, the winters are cold, and the summer heat is relieved by the high elevation. Rainfall averages 20 inches over most of the plateau, and may reach double that amount on the highest ridges.

The coastal region is barren, but the plateau has rich, fertile soil. Its extensive level areas and its neatly terraced slopes are highly cultivated. Besides cereals, wheat, barley, and millet, a variety of Mediterranean vegetable plants and fruit trees are grown. Among the fruits are grapes, figs, apricots, pomegranates, and walnuts. The celebrated Mocha coffee is still cultivated, though not as extensively as in earlier days. Livestock are raised. Their skins are the main export of the country. San'a, in the mountains, is the capital of Yaman. Hodaida and Mocha are small ports on the Red Sea.

There was a time, in ancient and medieval days, when the products of Yaman captured the markets of the world. In ancient times Yaman was the seat of a highly developed civilization, built largely on a flourishing trade. Its wealth was proverbial in the Graeco-Roman world and gained for it the envied name of *Arabia Felix*. The Romans spent vast sums of gold on the aromatic gums of Arabia and the spices and silks of the East which reached them through the Arabs. Pliny laments the treasure so lavishly spent on the Arabian trade to satisfy the luxury of the Romans and their women.[2] To control this lucrative trade, the Romans decided to bring Yaman under the sceptre of Rome. An army was dispatched from Egypt in the reign of Augustus Caesar. By the time it reached the northern extremity of Yaman its ranks had been decimated by fever,

2. Pliny, BK. XII, ch. 41.

heat, and thirst. The remnants of this ill-fated expedition returned with memories of desolate wastes, and the attempt at a conquest of *Arabia Felix* was not repeated by the Romans.

'Asir, to the north of Yaman, is also a plateau, most of it above 5,000 feet high. The uplands have a moderate precipitation, and for several months during the year short, fast-flowing streams run down the deep valleys. The higher slopes of the valleys are terraced and laid to cereals, coffee, dates, bananas, and vines. Thick vegetation provides pasture for livestock.

South and east of Yaman are the Aden Colony and Protectorates. The Colony includes the Port of Aden with its hinterland and two dependencies, Perim and Kuria Muria Islands, at the entrance of the Red Sea. The Protectorates extend to the District of Dhofar and include the lands of a score of chiefs bound by treaty to Great Britain.

Within the Eastern Protectorate lies Hadramaut, a land rich in historical memories. Like Yaman it traded with the Mediterranean world in ancient times, and maintained a prosperous and advanced civilization, as witness the ruins of its ancient cities and the remnants of elaborate systems of irrigation. Hadramaut is the land of the precious frankincense, a product so highly valued in the ancient world that it was worth its weight in gold. Its fame reached the eager ears of Herodotus who relates with his usual relish the varieties of Arabian spices, the ritual with which they were collected, and the legends woven around them, and concludes his description saying: "Concerning the spices of Arabia let no more be said. The whole country is scented with them, and exhales an odour marvelously sweet."[3] The fragrance of Arabia's gums has delighted the imagination of writers and poets since antiquity. Milton celebrates it in these lines:

> Off at sea North-East winds blow
> Sabaean odours from the spicy shore
> Of Araby the blest; with such delay
> Well pleas'd they slack their course, and many a league
> Cheer'd with the grateful smell old Ocean smiles.[4]

Hadramaut is a valley intersected with *wadis*, river beds that are dry in summer. The people make the most of the poor soil and the small quantity of water available. They grow cereals, vegeta-

3. Herodotus, Book III, ch. 113.
4. *Paradise Lost,* iv. 159 f.

bles, and fruits. Tobacco is cultivated, chiefly for export. Honey is
a major product; and livestock forms the Bedouin's wealth.

Hadramaut is famous for its enterprising inhabitants, who have
always been adventurous and keen traders. A large part of the population lives abroad, in East Africa, India, and Indonesia. Their
largest and most prosperous community is settled in Java. But invariably they return to Hadramaut for which they have a passion,
even those of them who are born abroad. The returning emigrants
have built garden cities in the valley, with bungalows and villas
equipped with electric lighting and modern sanitation, and swim-
ming pools in the gardens.[5]

East of Hadramaut lies the Sultanate of Muskat and Oman with
1,000 miles of coast on the Indian Ocean and the Gulf of Oman.
With such a large seashore, the inhabitants of Oman take readily
to sea-faring, as do indeed all the South Arabs, who have been
called the Greeks of the Indian Ocean.

The narrow littoral of Oman is backed by mountains, beyond
which the plateau merges into the desert. At the highest peak the
mountains rise to about 10,000 feet. Snow falls occasionally, and
rain is relatively abundant in the region of Jabal-al-Akhdar—The
Green Mountain, where the slopes are terraced and cultivated.
Dates are the main crop, and with dried fish they are the principal
exports of the country.

Muskat harbor, hemmed by mountains, is one of the hottest
spots on earth. Excessive heat and humidity are characteristic of
the whole coast around Arabia.

Between Oman and the head of the Persian Gulf, the coastal
region is an undulating plain with low hills. From south to north
lie Trucial Coast and the Peninsula of Katar—a chain of Shaikhdoms linked to the British Government by a permanent truce, and
Hasa, a province of Saudi Arabia. Kuwait, at the northeast extremity of Arabia, is almost entirely a sandy desert. Kuwait and
Hasa hold what is estimated to be the richest oil deposits in the
world. Oil has been struck in Katar, in the Island of Bahrein, and
under water off the Arabian coast of the Persian Gulf. Pearl fisheries, which before the days of oil were the principal source of
income of Kuwait and Bahrein, still provide world markets with
the finest pearls.

Leaving the coastal provinces we come to Najd, the plateau in

5. Philby, *Sheba's Daughters*, pp. 176–178; Harold Ingrams, Political Development in the Hadramaut, *International Affairs*, April 1945, pp. 236–252.

central Arabia. It is enveloped by deserts, of which the most for-
midable is the Empty Quarter, the Great Desert to the south extending to Hadramaut. Najd itself enjoys a healthy climate, dry
and invigorating. It is famous for two breeds, valiant tribesmen and
the noble Arab horse. In modern times it has given rise to Wahhabism, a movement of religious regeneration. It is the home of
Abd-Al-Aziz Ibn Saud, a great leader of men, who has brought
peace and unity to the tribes, welding together the greater part of
the Peninsula, with Najd as the core.

And last, but in some respects most important, is the province
of Hijaz. Barren and poor, it is yet held in honor by Arabs in the
Peninsula and outside it, and by over 400 million Moslems wherever they live. For Hijaz is the cradle of the Moslem faith, and in
it are located Islam's two holy cities, Mecca and Medina. Towards
Mecca scores of millions of worshippers turn their faces daily in
prayer and devotion. Hijaz is the repository of the earliest memories of the Arab nation, just as that nation emerged from the chaos
of tribal life, achieved its unity, and was seized with a consciousness of a great destiny to proclaim to the world the gospel of universal brotherhood and the dignity of man. It was fitting, therefore,
that the signal for Arab freedom in modern times came from Hijaz:
the first shot of the Arab Revolt against the Turks was fired in
Mecca in June 1916. Today Hijaz is a part of Saudi Arabia.

Most of Arabia is desert. The centers of settled life are concentrated along the seashores where their position captures for them
the clouds which distill their life-giving waters upon a parched
land. Moreover, proximity to the sea opened opportunities for trade
with the outside world. The interior of Arabia, apart from scattered oases, is the vast roaming ground of the Bedouin and his
flocks.

The chief product of the cultivated land is the date. It is grown
on 90 percent of the agricultural land, and is the staple food over
all Arabia. In especially favored spots, as on the hills of Yaman or
around T'aif in the mountains of Hijaz, fruits of the temperate climate are cultivated with success, producing a fine and abundant
yield, a striking contrast to the barrenness around.

Iraq, the eastern half of the Fertile Crescent, covers an area of
175,000 square miles. It is the land of the Twin Rivers, the Tigris
and Euphrates. The two rivers flowing through Iraq from its northern extremity to the south, follow separate courses until about a
hundred miles from the head of the Persian Gulf, where they con-

verge at al-Kurna to form Shatt-al-Arab, a broad and navigable stream. It is here, somewhere near the place where the two rivers meet, that legend has placed the Garden of Eden, the site of the fall of man, and the beginning of a long road of toil and suffering leading, we hope, not to his destruction into the atoms from which he came, but to the achievement of a way of life better than any we have around us yet.

Iraq is divided into two climatic and topographical zones. The northern part is mountainous in the east, cold in winter, cool in summer, and has a plentiful amount of rain. Remnants of forests cover parts of the Kurdish mountains, and a variety of fruit trees are widely cultivated. As the land progresses southward it slopes into uplands and foothills, and the rainfall decreases considerably. Sheep and goats graze on the slopes; livestock, wool, and hides are among the important exports of Iraq.

The plain occupies about two thirds of the country's area. It is flat, slightly above sea-level, hot and dry, and depends entirely on irrigation from the two rivers. Wheat and barley, rice, and to a lesser extent cotton are grown. Dates are the chief export. Four-fifths of the world's exports of dates come from Iraq. From Baghdad to the Persian Gulf, the banks of the Tigris and Euphrates are lined with the graceful, stately palm. Basra, famous for its dates through-out the world, is beautiful in the midst of its palm groves, through which flow myriads of irrigation canals forming a network of water. These same groves evoke memories of prosperity and pleasure, and are the scene of many adventures related in the Arabian Nights.

Iraq has rich oil deposits. The northern field—Kirkuk—has been in operation since 1934. Another field was recently discovered in the neighborhood of Basra.

The western half of the Fertile Crescent was for centuries known as Syria. Its unity was broken after the first World War. In a de-scription of the physical environment, however, the region is best treated as a unit.

A coastal plain borders the length of the eastern shore of the Mediterranean from the Gulf of Alexandretta to Sinai. The plain is narrow in the north and center, and is broken at intervals by foot-hills that rise straight out of the sea. It broadens as it progresses southward, and attains its greatest width of 20 miles in the Gaza area.

Parallel to the coast runs a chain of mountains. The northern section is the Ansariyeh range. Lebanon is the central range, sepa-

rated from the Ansariyeh by the plain of 'Akkar through which
flows al-Nahr-Al-Kabir, the ancient Eleutherus. Lebanon, the highest of the ranges, culminates in a peak over 11,000 feet high. It
slopes towards the south and passes without a break into the plateau of Galilee. The plain of Esdraelon divides Galilee from the
Judaean plateau, which merges into the Negeb, a tableland slightly
lower than Judaea.

Beyond this chain lies the rift valley, a great geological trench
extending from Turkey to the Gulf of 'Akaba. In north Syria, this
structure, known as the Ghab, is occupied by the middle Orontes.
The Beka' gorge is in the center, between the Lebanon and Anti-
Lebanon ranges. The Beka' is a plateau rising to 3,000 feet above
sea-level at its highest point, Baalbek. The mountains east and west
of the Beka' rise yet another 5,000 to 7,000 feet above Baalbek, and
are covered with snow a good part of the year. The rift continues
south and sinks to its lowest depth in the Jordan trough, the greatest inland depression of the earth. Between Lake Tiberias and the
Dead Sea, the region known as Al-Ghor is entirely below sea-level.
The lowest point, 1300 feet below sea-level, is reached at the shore
of the Dead Sea.

Mountains rise to the east of the rift valley. The highest are the
Anti-Lebanon and Hermon ranges, separated by a narrow defile
through which flows the Barada river. Hermon, rising to over 9,000
feet, is capped with snow almost the whole year round. Hence its
Arabic name, Jabal-Al-Shaikh.

Between the Anti-Lebanon and the desert the country is an undulating plateau. In the north, it slopes gradually to the Euphrates
basin. In the center, the fertile Ghuta of Damascus, irrigated by
the Barada, borders on the desert. South of Damascus is the Hauran
plateau rising to the hills of Jabal Druze. The plateau of Transjordan slopes east and south and merges into the Syrian Desert.

A number of rivers and smaller streams cut through the mountains, and flow down the hills and through the plains. The Orontes,
Litani, and Jordan rivers flow most of their length through the rift
valley. Apart from the Euphrates river which flows through Syria
for 420 miles, the Orontes is the largest river in the region. It has
its source on the eastern slope of the Lebanon, flows northward
through the plains of Homs and Hama, bends to the west, and rush-
ing down the defile between the Amanus and Ansariyeh ranges, it
empties in the Mediterranean a few miles west of Antioch.

The source of the Litani—the classical Leontes—is close to the headwaters of the Orontes. Flowing south, the Litani drains the Beka', then makes a sharp bend westward, plunges through the mountains in a deep gorge, and joins the Mediterranean near Tyre.

The Jordan, with its main tributary the Yarmuk, provides the chief water supply for Palestine and Transjordan.

The topography of the region being varied, the climate also shows a wide range of variation. Over most of the country the seasons are well marked. Rains fall between September and May. Rainfall is abundant along the coast and on the western ranges. It decreases rapidly from west to east, and to a lesser extent from north to south.

The average yearly rainfall on the Lebanon coast is 36 inches, twice the amount that falls in the interior. On the Palestinian coast it is 23 inches. In the mountains it is slightly less than on the nearby coast.

In the troughs, rainfall is moderate in some parts; in others, especially the Jordan valley, it is deficient. On the Anti-Lebanon uplands precipitation is adequate, but it decreases again on the inland plateaux until steppe-land is reached with an annual rainfall of 10 inches or less.

The weather is typically Mediterranean on the coast. The winters are mild and wet; the summers rainless, hot, and humid. In the mountains, winters are cold and summers cool and pleasant. Inland, the climate is of the continental type, with cold winters, hot summers, and a great diurnal variation of temperature. In spite of the higher temperatures, summers in the interior are more endurable than on the coast because of the refreshing night coolness.

The diversity of climate and the wide differences in elevation have given the region a large variety of flora. Tropical plants thrive in the Jordan depression, and vegetation of the cold climates grows on the mountain tops. Along the coast, citrus and bananas are widely grown. The mountain and hill slopes are carefully terraced and planted with fruit trees and garden vegetables. The inland plains, apart from patches laid to orchards and garden produce, are under an extensive system of cereal cultivation. Olive culture is widely spread. Olive trees grow in great numbers on the mountain slopes, on the coastal belt, and on the plains of the interior all the way from the Judaean hills to the lowlands of the upper Orontes. Because of the general lack of animal fat, olives and olive oil are an important source of food. The olive, in Arab tradition, is considered a blessed tree. It is called blessed in one of the most beautiful passages of the Koran.[6]

In ancient times the mountain slopes were covered with forests down to the sea. Today only small remnants are left. They include varieties of oak, pine, juniper and cedar.

The Syrian desert is rich in flora. Investigations, though incomplete, have recorded no less than 2,000 species of seed-bearing plants.[7]

The region is deficient in mineral resources. Apart from the chemical solutions of the Dead Sea, no minerals have been found in commercial quantities. The topography of the Jazira, in northeast Syria, is believed to be favorable to the presence of oil, but so far oil has not been struck.[8]

Egypt covers an area of 386,000 square miles. Of this, however, only a fraction—3.5 per cent—is suited for cultivation. The cultivable land is confined to the narrow strip on both sides of the Nile, the Delta, and the Fayyum Oasis. A hundred miles from the sea, the Nile valley broadens into the Delta. Elsewhere high cliffs confine the fertile area within a narrow band. The maximum width of the valley does not exceed thirty miles. In some places it is only two miles wide. Beyond it on either side, the barrenness of the desert is relieved by an oasis here and there. Rain is almost unknown in southern Egypt, and in the north it is very scanty. Irrigation depends wholly upon the Nile which overflows its banks in August and September, inundating the land on either side and depositing over it a layer of precious sediment carried by the floods.

The irrigated land is very intensively cultivated. The chief product is cotton which, with its by-products, constitutes over 80 per cent of the country's exports. In quality, most varieties of Egyptian cotton are superior to brands grown anywhere else. Other important crops include cereals, rice, and sugar-cane. Fruit growing and vegetable gardening have extended considerably in recent years.

Egypt's mineral resources are still in an early stage of development. Oil deposits have so far yielded a quantity sufficient to meet

6. "God is the LIGHT of the Heavens and the Earth. His Light is like a niche in which is a lamp—the lamp encased in glass—the glass, as it were, a glistening star. From a blessed tree is it lighted, the olive neither of the East nor of the West, whose oil would well-nigh shine out, even though fire touched it not. It is light upon light." 24:35.

7. E. B. Worthington: *Middle East Science*, London, 1946, p. 87.

8. The description of Syria is largely based upon W. B. Fisher: *The Middle East, A Physical, Social, and Regional Geography*, 1950.

Egypt's needs. Iron of a high quality is found near Assuan in upper Egypt. In the Red Sea region phosphates, manganese and copper mines occur.

To the south of Egypt is the Sudan, an immense territory of a million square miles. Physical conditions in the Sudan vary considerably. In the north a rainless desert stretches on both sides of the fertile Nile belt. Proceeding south, the desert becomes shrub steppe suitable for pasturage. The central Sudan is sub-tropical with ample rainfall and dense vegetation. Millet and maize are raised, and pasturage is excellent. Extensive forests supply the world market with gum Arabic. The southern belt of the Sudan lies within the tropical zone where rainfall is heavy and much of the land is swamp and savannah forest.

Everywhere in the Sudan the rains fall during summer. In the south, rainfall averages 60 inches a year. All over the country there is a pronounced dry season.

Cotton, grown mostly in the Gezira—the triangle between the Blue and the White Nile—is the most important crop. Other products are bananas and cassava, cereals, groundnuts, and sesame.

The western desert of Egypt continues into the plateau of Libya, a territory almost wholly desert except for parts of the coastal plain and a few scattered oases.

The two sections of Libya, Tripolitania and Cyrenaica, have similar topography and climate. The coastal plain is wider in Tripolitania. A range of hills, Al-Jabal, rises south of the coast. Beyond, the plateau slopes gradually to the desert.

Rainfall here is low and irregular. A hot south wind, the Ghibli, blowing in spring and summer, adds to the dryness of the region.

On the coastal belt of Tripolitania large areas of date palms are intercropped with vegetables and cereals. In Cyrenaica the plain is extensively ploughed for barley, with some garden-vegetables and orchard produce. Date palms and fruit trees grow in the oases.

Parts of the northern slopes of Al-Jabal carry good woodland. Steppe, however, is the typical vegetation regime of Tripolitania and Cyrenaica. In Tripolitania, livestock are kept under a semi-nomadic system. In Cyrenaica, pastoralism is the principal activity, and animal products are its chief wealth.

Tunisia and Algeria have many similarities in climate, topography, and resources. Tunisia is by far the smaller of the two countries, with an area of 48,000 square miles to Algeria's 847,500. The Sahara, however, covers most of Algeria's territory. Both countries have fertile coastal belts where a variety of fruit trees grow and garden vegetables are raised on a large scale. Broad plains are under barley and wheat. In Algeria, vineyards and tobacco fields are characteristic of the landscape. Olives dominate the agriculture of Tunisia. About 20 million olive trees are planted in the plains and on the hill-slopes throughout the country. Millions of date palms grow in the oases.

The mountains are covered with forests of oak, pine, and cork-oak. Cork is the chief forest product. Expanses of esparto grass stretch for thousands of miles. Esparto is a valuable export used in the manufacture of high grade paper.

Livestock breeding is general. Millions of sheep graze on the hills and way into the Sahara. Meat, wool, hides, and skins are important exports.

The region has some mineral wealth; phosphate is the principal mineral. One-third of the world's phosphates comes from Tunisia, Algeria, and Morocco. Other minerals include iron, lead, zinc, copper, mercury, manganese, silver, and antimony.

With Morocco we reach the western limits of the Arab lands. The country has a frontage on the Mediterranean and Atlantic, and an area of 220,000 square miles of maritime plains, mountains, and desert. The population is concentrated in the fertile land of the plains. Agriculture is the chief occupation. Cereals, vegetables, and fruit trees are grown. The most numerous among the trees are the vine, olive, and almond. Date palms are a common feature of the African landscape.

Above the plain rise gradually the Rif mountains, and beyond them more abruptly the heights of the Atlas. Forests and alfalfa cover many million acres.

Millions of sheep and goats are pastured over the extensive ranges. Moroccan sheepskins and wool are of high quality. The country is rich in mineral resources. Coal deposits are abundant and of good quality. Morocco ranks fourth among the world's producers of phosphates, and is one of the few countries that produce cobalt. Manganese occurs widely; lead, zinc, and iron less frequently. There is also some production of gold and silver. Petroleum is found in small quantities, but is of a high grade.

This, in brief, is the physical environment in which the Arabs live.

About seventy million people live in the lands we have described. The largest concentration of them is settled in Egypt where twenty million[9] press on the narrow band along the Nile, making of Egypt one of the most densely populated countries in the world. The population of the Sudan has been estimated at eight million. About twenty million live in North Africa. Population figures for the Peninsula of Arabia are based on rough estimates which give some 3 million for Saudi Arabia, between 3 and 4 million for Yaman, about 750,000 for the Aden Colony and Protectorates, 500,000 for the Sultanate of Muskat and Oman, over one hundred thousand for the Trucial coast, and a hundred and fifty thousand for Kuwait. One hundred and ten thousand live on the Islands of Bahrain. In the Fertile Crescent, five million live in Iraq,[10] another five million in Syria and Lebanon, and about a million and a half in Palestine and Transjordan.

The name Arab does not denote a racial concept. It is rather a term of cultural association. The people who today are called Arabs are descended from several racial stocks, of which two are predominant, the Semitic in Western Asia, and the Hamitic in North Africa, both being branches of the Mediterranean race. The original home of the Semites is said by some authorities to be the Peninsula of Arabia. At intervals, when the land could no longer provide for its teeming denizens, waves of wanderers poured out of that desert ocean into the lands of the Fertile Crescent. These successive waves brought the Akkadians, later called Babylonians, to Mesopotamia, the Amorites to the northern plains of Syria, and the Phoenicians and Canaanites to the Syrian coast, the Aramaeans to central Syria, the Hebrews to the hills of Palestine, the Nabataeans to Arabia Petraea and numerous tribes to the east of the Jordan and south of the Dead Sea, among them the Moabites, Ammonites, Edomites, known mainly through their wars with the children of Israel. But even the earliest wave of Semites, which came in the fourth millennium B.C., found the land already settled by groups belonging to different racial backgrounds, the Sumerians in Mesopotamia and a people of an Armenoid type in the hills of Syria. Later, other strains were introduced, a Nordic element in North Syria, in the ancient Kingdom of Mitanni which flourished about 1500 B.C., whose descendants have been sought in the Kurds; and a wave of western sea-people that came down from the neighbor-

9. The 1947 Census gives 19,087,857.
10. The 1947 Census gives 4,799,500.

hood of the Aegean and settled on the Canaanite coast during the 12th century B.C. These were the Philistines after whom Palestine is named.[11]

Africa also had its Semites, a migration of them having reached Egypt in predynastic times. Here, however, it is the Hamitic stock that predominates, with some Negro infiltration from the south. In North Africa, on the Hamitic foundation was grafted a stock of blondes who came during the second millennium B.C. Tall, dolichocephalic, and of a light colored skin, they resemble the people of north-western Europe.[12]

Upon this background settled the Arabs, in the 7th century A.D., the last Semitic wave that came out of the Peninsula. Centuries earlier, Arab tribes had made their home in the Fertile Crescent; and Arab states—Petra, Palmyra, Hira, and Ghassan—had flourished in Syria and Iraq. But now, between 630 and 700 A.D. a new order emerged, and these many lands with their peoples and cultures were incorporated in the great Arab Society. And as the racial differences disappeared in a society that admitted no discrimination on the basis of race, so were the various cultures assimilated, producing a new and vigorous type whose dominant characteristic was formed by the broad sympathy and universal appeal of Islam.

11. Olmstead: History of Palestine and Syria, pp. 131, 257.

12. Carleton Coon, *The Races of Europe*, pp. 474–489; Toynbee, Survey of International Relations in the Islamic World, 1925, p. 92, n. 2.

CHAPTER II

The Cultural Heritage

THE Arab heritage has its roots in two divergent ways of life, the desert tradition, and the culture of a settled society old as the history of man himself. From the desert the Arab received a set of qualities of great human value, a love of freedom, a sense of equality, and a resolute self-reliance in meeting the hardships of his existence.

In the desert, life is on the level of mere subsistence. A bowl of milk, a handful of dates make the bedouin's usual meal. Camel's meat is an occasional repast; wheat and other cereals are a rare luxury. Water is so scarce, man calls the rain God's mercy.

The Bedouin's house is a tent of camel's hair, his possessions are barely a camel's load. He is constantly on the move in search of pasture for his flocks and the water-holes which are few and far between.

The physical environment is so hard it has weeded out the weaklings. Mediocrity does not thrive in such surroundings. Those who survive have a mark of distinction about them. They are lean of body, muscular and sinewy. Their regular features are carved on a hawk-like face. Their mind is keen, always on the alert, their talents are sharpened by the rigors of their life. Tenacious and patient in the extreme, they are of a temperament of steel, supple and resistant.

Since wealth is not known, class distinctions are also absent. This feeling of equality engendered self-respect, which in turn bred in the desert Arabs the dignity and poise so greatly admired by outsiders who come in contact with them. The ease and gentle manners with which the Arab greets total strangers and addresses men whatever their rank are the natural expression of his self-confidence, and his feeling of the equality of all men.

Tribal law is a code of honor rather than a set of rules. Chief among the virtues enshrined in it are courage and loyalty, hospitality to the point of sharing one's last possession, revenge for a wrong, and protection of the weak and all who seek refuge, be they yesterday's enemies or tomorrow's potential foes.

Authority rests with the elders of the tribe who elect the chief from the head clan, combining in this way the elective with the hereditary principle. All the tribesmen participate in deliberations and important decisions through the Majlis or tribal assembly to which the humblest of the tribe has access and where he freely speaks his mind.

Leadership is an arduous task and exacts a rare combination of qualities. The leader, or sayyid, is expected to embody the qualities of his people at their best and their ideals at the highest. In battle, his place is in the vanguard exposing his life to defend them. In peace he is always at their call, handling with wisdom and justice their affairs. His house is ever open and his table spread for all to partake of whatever he has. He must be watchful of himself not to indulge in any sign or appearance of superiority, but to treat his tribesmen as his equals and conduct himself with affability and consideration towards the old and young among them. And withal they are constantly reminding him that they elevated him to the leadership and made him their sayyid; that they are the source of his power, and authority rests with them. This philosophy they crystallized in the popular proverb: "A people's sayyid is their servant."

His authority over them rests upon moral force; it is exercised not through coercive measures but by persuasion. Hence the importance attached traditionally to the gift of speech and the ability to impress and convince the hearers. The assemblies of the tribe and the intertribal gatherings at seasonal fairs were frequent occasions for the display of eloquence. Tribes vied with one another over the number and excellence of their spokesmen. That tribe was considered luckiest which had the ablest orators and poets, mouthpieces of public opinion in the desert. For they sang its praises, vindicated its rights, and confused its enemies, spreading its fame far and wide throughout the land.

Poetry was esteemed more than prose. The Arabs rejoiced in its rhythmic cadence and melodious rhymes. Moreover it clung to the memory more readily than prose, an important consideration in a society where writing was hardly known. It became the repository of inherited wisdom, the vehicle through which the accumulated experience of the group was transmitted. They called it *diwan-al-'arab*, the record of the Arabs. It was also their school of honor, molding their character and impressing upon them the virtues which they revered.[1]

*   *   *

Besides the nomadic culture, a settled civilization developed in Arabia many centuries before Islam. Its seat was the southwest corner of the Peninsula, where it flourished for two thousand years, from about 1500 B.C. to 500 A.D., on a level comparable to the contemporary civilizations of the Mediterranean basin and the valley of the Tigris and Euphrates. From the records, which are not yet fully clarified, it seems that the Minaeans laid the foundations of settled life in this area, to be followed by their better known successors, the Sabaeans and Himyarites. These people overcame the difficulties of the terrain with remarkable energy and ingenuity, to which the remains of their constructions bear testimony. The dams for the storage of water and the extensive irrigation projects indicate a high degree of engineering knowledge and ability. Here also the earliest skyscrapers were developed and remain a striking feature of the landscape to the present day.

The South Arabs discovered that contact and trade with the outside world was necessary for the maintenance and improvement of their way of life. The trade routes which converged upon southern Arabia from India, Africa, and the Mediterranean played an important part in the civilization of the Mediterranean world. The south Arabs established colonies in Northern Hijaz and the northwestern desert which served as marts for their trade with the Mediterranean area. To these desert colonies they brought their enthusiasm for building and hewed in the rocky cliffs their houses and their temples, the impressive ruins of which remain to the present day.

Although the South Arab civilization broke down some centuries before written history among the North Arabs began, its memories continued to be cherished and inspired legends grew in wonders with the passing of time.

Before Islam also, a number of Arab kingdoms flourished outside the Peninsula, in the Fertile Crescent. The Nabataeans handled the overland trade between the Persian Gulf and the Mediterranean and were influenced by the civilizations of the countries at both ends of the trade routes, as the magnificent ruins of their capital

1. Henri Lammens: *Le Berceau de L'Islam.*

Petra testify. The Nabataean Kingdom, which at one time extended from Arabia Petraea to Damascus, was made a Roman province in the first years of the second century A.D.

The Palmyrenes who likewise thrived on the caravan trade, reached the height of their power and prosperity in the third century A.D. when their famous queen Zenobia ruled over a kingdom that extended from Asia Minor to Egypt. The stately ruins of Palmyra against the desert background are a memorable sight.

In the centuries immediately preceding the rise of Islam flourished the two kingdoms of Hira and Ghassan—the former in Southern Iraq within the orbit of Persian influence and civilization; the latter in the region corresponding to southeastern Syria and Transjordan, and in the sphere of Byzantine power. Thus before Islam, Arabs had penetrated into the Fertile Crescent not merely as nomadic wanderers but had succeeded in establishing strong and prosperous states.

Living in the parched desert, the Arab imagined and then believed that in bygone days his land was the most favored spot on earth where water was abundant and life plentiful. The people themselves of bygone times were cast on the heroic scale, approaching in height the stately palm. Their dwellings were tremendous, scores of cubits high, fit abodes for these giants of the earth. In the tradition of the son of the desert, the memory of a remote settled existence lived on, and in his heart lurked the longing for the good things of that life.

*   *   *

On the eve of Islam, there lived in Mecca a tribe, the Kuraish, already famous in pre-Islamic times but marked for a greater destiny under the aegis of Islam. Mecca was the religious center of the pagan Arabs, and the Kuraish derived great prestige from the guardianship of its holy places. But still greater power and substantial gains came to them from their well-organized and fairly extensive trade, when Mecca, located midway on the trade route between Yaman and Syria, succeeded to the traffic which the South Arabs had controlled for centuries. This trade carried the Kuraish southward to Yaman and across the Red Sea to Abyssinia. In the north they traded with Mesopotamia and more closely and regularly with Syria. Within Arabia itself they came in contact with most of the important tribes.

Trade necessitated the setting up of an elaborate organization, the management of which trained and prepared the Kuraish to assume the leadership of the Arabs when the feeling of national unity was instilled into them with the coming of Islam.

A sound political organization was already at work in Mecca, a veritable merchant republic. Here, as in the tribal majlis, authority was vested in the Mala', the people's assembly, where all matters of public concern were discussed and debated freely and at length.

At the dawn of the 7th century A.D. a social revolution was in preparation among the Arabs of Mecca. Its hero was a man from among them, born and raised in their midst, steeped in their tradition and sharing their qualities, but, unlike them, he was a man inspired, bearing a message from God. The message was Islam and the man, Muhammad, was the messenger of God.

With the acceptance of Islam, a sense of Arab solidarity transcending tribal rivalries and clannish loyalties came into being. It amounted to the birth of the Arab nation which the new faith infused with a purpose beyond and above themselves, and opened before them a high destiny leading to the regeneration of the world. Their gifts unfolded, their pent up energies were liberated, and the vitality stored for centuries at last found release in the fulfillment of a mission which raised the nation to immortality and carried the world a long step forward.

While the dawn of the 7th century witnessed the consolidation of a great people in the Arabian Peninsula, it presented a scene of weariness and moral disintegration in the surrounding world. Persia and Byzantium were the great powers of the time. They still maintained an imposing appearance when the Arabs knocked at their doors. Their lands were extensive, their armies trained, and their material resources infinitely greater than anything the Arabs possessed. But the huge structures were rotten at the core. Constant wars between the two powers had sapped their strength and nearly ruined their countries. The people were weighed down with taxes and exactions of all kinds to carry on wars, maintain extravagant courts, and support an idle upper class. Religion itself had lost its freshness and therewith its power to vitalize and infuse strength and hope into the life of its votaries. In Persia, the established Zoroastrian religion held hands with the people's rulers, and its priesthood formed another privileged class living off the people's toil and sorrow. In the provinces of the Byzantine Empire—western Asia and northern Africa—the beauty, vigor, and all-embracing charity of the early Christian religion were submerged under a rigid form of ritual and formulae which bred dogmatic arrogance among the clergy and hatred among the wrangling sects.

Into this world the Arabs came about 630 A.D. to overthrow the existing order. The first news of Arab incursions surprised but did not alarm the Persians and Byzantines, so lightly did they think of Arab strength. But when success accompanied those first inroads their apprehension grew. Still they believed a show of force would intimidate the Arabs, and a few gifts would turn them back to the desert from which they came.

A significant scene took place before one of the battles in southern Iraq in the tent of the Persian general, Rustum, between him and the messenger whom he had requested the Arabs to send. Rustum, crowned and robed with gold-embroidered clothes, surrounded by guards and officials of rank, sat on a magnificent throne in a tent resplendent with oriental luxury. A poorly dressed Arab walked in and straight to the throne where he seated himself beside Rustum. Forced to descend from this elevated place he calmly said: "Among us, the Arab folk, there is no distinction of rank, we are all alike; with us there is no master and no slave. I thought that you, like us, lived in equality among yourselves, but I see that you lord it one over the others." Then he warned: "Now I know that your order is destined to destruction and your end is near." Rustum bragged of Persia's might, reminded the Arab of the poverty and weakness of his people, and offered him and his comrades gifts of dates and clothes. And condescendingly he added: "For I do not wish to kill you." The Arab readily admitted that they were a poor and forgotten people—until God in his infinite mercy had sent them a Prophet who led them from darkness into light. And now they were the bearers of this message of light to the peoples of the earth.[2]

The countries into which the Arabs came were mellow with the fruits of an old history. They had witnessed the rise of man from the forest and the cave and followed his unbroken course since those remote days. For it was somewhere in these lands that early man first began his struggle to found a home for himself upon this earth. The epic takes its rise in the forests of the northern Nile valley and the swamps of the Tigris and Euphrates. The forests were cleared and the swamps drained, and fertile fields took their place. An ordered society gradually came into being, with arts,

2. Tabari, De Goeje's edition, Series I, V, 2267–2275.

writing, and the amenities of life. Then came the dawn of conscience and the unfolding of the moral law. In these lands God came near to man, making Himself known through a succession of revelations which have shaped the spiritual life of mankind.

Civilizations and empires succeeded one another on this crowded scene, first the Egyptian and the Sumerian, then the Babylonian and Assyrian, the Hittite and the Persian. Finally Hellenistic civilization came and brought together the genius and achievements of Greece and Rome with those of the eastern Mediterranean. But this world was now already weary with its age.

The Arabs came with the vigor and confidence of fresh, unburdened youth. They breathed a new life into the aging world, animated its members and revived its spirit. Here was a message full of hope and the promise of a better life. The peoples awoke, shaking off the dust of centuries and the shackles which had kept them down. A society was born which made no distinction between white and black, rich and poor, master and slave. All men were equal in the sight of God and all were made to serve His purpose and fulfill His plan. Peoples of all shades of color and all degrees and variety of culture joined hands and hearts and minds to build one of the most brilliant and beneficent of world civilizations.

It was definitely a Moslem society. Religion more than any other influence molded the lives of men. God was near, His presence was felt everywhere. To God so close, man had a direct, intimate relation. God is nearer to man than his jugular vein, said the Holy Book. The word Islam means surrender to the will of God. But it is a surrender that springs from an implicit trust and confidence in the purpose of a wise and loving Creator. For although God is the Almighty, the Transcendent, He is better known by His names the Merciful and Compassionate. This loss of self in God's will lent serenity and peace to the life of the believer. There is no need to fret and worry; God's purpose will be achieved and it will be the best for His servants. Suffering and hardships are borne patiently and with dignified resignation. Men accept but do not succumb under the chastisement of their Lord.

This concept of God resulted in a fellowship with and respect for all His creatures to whom He is equally near and who alike are the instruments of His will.

The good life is one of good works. The Moslem community is responsible for the well-being of its members. One of the pillars of the faith is *Zakat*, a tax levied on the rich for the benefit of the

poor. Sharing is a blessed act, and hoarding is hateful and repre-
hensible in the sight of God and man. Hence the many charitable
foundations, *awkaf,* and the varied purposes which they served.
Some of these fed the poor and provided homes for the destitute.
These gifts sprang from love and pity and went out unbounded
to the orphaned, the afflicted, and the weak. Others established
and endowed hospitals, schools, and libraries. Still others provided
wells of fresh water dug along desert routes, and caravanserais and
hospices built in large and small centers along high ways for travelers to rest and refresh themselves.

The common man fared well within this society. People moved
freely in its ranks, with no barriers to block their path, stunt their
growth, and prevent them from attaining their full stature. Opportunity was not the monopoly of a privileged class nor were the
rewards of work and talent the possession of a special caste. Numerous are the examples of those who rose from a lowly beginning
to positions of influence and distinction in the service of the state,
in the pursuit of learning, or in their quest after the things of the
spirit.

The broad humanity of Islam was responsible for its rapid success and its hold upon those who embraced it. It brought release
to the poor and oppressed, levelled down the barriers which hindered man's growth, endowed life with a meaning, and imparted
to it a sense of dignity and worth. "Wherever Mohammadanism
has gone, the value of the individual has been emphasized and men
stand upright in the strength of an unbreakable self-respect."[3]

Although the bond which held together this multitude of races
and cultures was religious and the community was an Islamic
brotherhood, the followers of other faiths were assured a recognized place within this world society. The People of the Book—
Jews and Christians—were not only left unmolested in the free exercise of their religions, but were allowed to organize themselves
in autonomous communities within the Moslem state. Islam as the
youngest of the three monotheistic religions considered itself the
continuation of the two older revelations and honored their scriptures and their prophets. The stories of the prophets are part of
the sacred literature of Islam. They occur frequently throughout
the Koran. Religious teachers and mystics drew upon them in their
teachings. Painters illustrated manuscripts with scenes and characters from the Old and New Testaments. The Koran speaks of

3. Harrison: *The Arab at Home,* p. 250.

Jesus as the word and spirit of God and of Mary as the blessed recipient of God's spirit. No pious Moslem mentions the names Jesus and Mary except in the terms "our Lord Jesus" and "our Lady Mary," always followed by the reverent invocation, peace be upon him or her.

Arab tolerance presented a sharp contrast to the sectarian bigotry of Byzantine rule, and was one of the causes which contributed to the ease and rapidity of the Arab expansion. A patriarch of the Eastern church, writing immediately after the conquest, says: "The Arabs, to whom God at this time has granted dominion over the world, are, as you know, among us. But they are not enemies of Christianity. On the contrary they praise our faith and honor the priests and saints of the Lord and confer benefits upon the churches and monasteries."[4] To the heterodox Christian sects, discriminated against and almost outlawed by the established Byzantine Church, the Moslems were a respite sent by God.

Christians and Jews held important positions at the courts of caliphs and princes. John of Damascus, the great theologian of the Greek Church, succeeded his father as counselor to the Omayyad Caliph Abd-al-Malik, a position which he held until his entry into the monastic life and his retirement to the Monastery of Mar Saba in the neighborhood of Jerusalem. While at court, John had joined in discussions between Christians and Moslems on the relative merits of their respective religions. Those friendly discussions with the people of the Book were enjoined by the Koran and encouraged by the enlightened attitude of the rulers. "Summon them to the way of thy Lord with wisdom and with kindly warning: dispute with them in the kindest manner."[5] "Dispute ye not, unless in kindliest sort, with the people of the Book, save with such of them as have dealt wrongfully with you: and say ye, 'We believe in what hath been sent down to us and hath been sent down to you. Our God and your God is one, and to Him are we self-surrendered.' "[6]

One of the most enlightened Moslem rulers was the Abbasid Caliph Al-Mamun whose qualities approached the description of Plato's philosopher-king. In his presence and under his direction religious and philosophical discussions were held. In 819 he presided over a meeting at which the Moslem and Christian doctrines were defended by their respective protagonists. That these discus-

4. Quoted in Philip K. Hitti: *History of Syria Including Lebanon and Palestine*, 1951, pp. 523–524.
5. Koran 16:126, Rodwell's translation.
6. Koran, 29:45.

sions were not confined to court circles is evidenced by the dia-
logues composed to guide the votaries of each faith in answering
the arguments of their opponents. Books on comparative religion
were also written, which, though definitely Moslem, show a remarkable breadth of vision and a deep knowledge of other faiths.

But Moslem society was not merely tolerant. It recognized the
values of diversity within the general pattern, and was hospitable to varieties of views and concepts. It encouraged and made
use of talent whatever its origin. In turn, the non-Moslem communities contributed to the enrichment of the common culture.
Their background fitted them for their role of carriers, transmitters,
and translators of the Mediterranean heritage. Christian schools
and monasteries where learned studies were pursued flourished
in Egypt, Syria, and Mesopotamia. Monks were busy translating
science and philosophy from Greek into Syriac, especially in the
two celebrated centers of Nisibin and Harran in northern Mesopotamia. When the Moslems were ready to study and assimilate
Hellenistic civilization, Christian scholars co-operated ably and
wholeheartedly in the translation of Greek learning. The most
prominent translators were two Christians, Hunain ibn Ishak and
his son Ishak.

Common activities were not limited to intellectual interests. On
the level of the ordinary life, relations were friendly also. Moslems
joined in celebrating some of the Christian feasts and the events
were occasions for great popular joy and gaiety. They honored
Christian saints and frequently visited their shrines to offer prayers
and gifts. The supposed remains of one of these saints, John the
Baptist, lie enshrined in the Omayyad mosque in Damascus, one
of the most venerated places of worship in the Moslem world.

*   *   *

The government of the state during the first century of Islam
was based upon the traditions inherited from pre-Islamic Arabia
and the teachings of the Moslem faith. Islam reinforced the heritage of the desert with regard to freedom, the distrust of hereditary
authority, and the equality of all men. "O men, verily we have
created you of a male and a female; and we have divided you into
peoples and tribes that ye might take knowledge one of another.
Truly, the most worthy of honor in the sight of God is he who

feareth Him most."[7] "Sovereignty belongs to God alone," says the
Holy Book, and the Prophet recommends the elective principle as
the ideal for the Moslem community. The Arabs were ever voicing
their suspicion of and dislike for autocratic rule, and their pity for
the nations who allowed themselves to be at the mercy of a single
man. Their poets, the journalists of the time, echoed their feeling
when they labeled those rulers whom they suspected of autocratic
tendencies with the hated names of Chosroes and Caesar, the ty-
rants of that age. Eloquence and the power to persuade through
reasoning continued to hold their important place in political life.
The Mosques became the forum where the people met with their
rulers. Here, even more than in the palace, important decisions
were made. The successful leaders were the great orators of the
age. In theory, at least, the caliphate remained an elective office;
every Moslem man with an upright character and sound judgment
qualified as an elector. The ceremony instating the caliph is known
as bai'a—contract—a term which signifies a voluntary act of recognition and allegiance. The Caliph was considered as first among
equals. In addressing the Caliph, although he was the powerful
and successful Al-Walid, the people called him by his name without title or ceremony. The Emperor of China was shocked by the
conduct of these proud and independent Arabs when a delegation
of twelve leaders was presented at his court. Chinese annals record
under the year 713 the visit of an Arabian embassy and the con-
sternation which it caused at the court by refusing to kowtow to
the Emperor.[8] So deeply ingrained was their sense of human dignity, the Arabs could not conceive of man humbling himself before
any one but God alone.

Participation by the people in the conduct of public life ceased
to be effective before the second Moslem century was far advanced.
One sect, the Khawarij, continued to hold to the concept that government should be controlled by the general body of believers.
The non-Arab elements of the Moslem community contributed to
the loss of this participation. They were constantly increasing in
numbers and influence; and they were peoples who, with all their
gifts and abilities, were accustomed to the rule of kings and des-
pots. The Arabs themselves became immersed in other interests
and pursuits, and turned their back upon the political phase of

7. Koran, 49:13.
8. Gibb, The Arab Invasion of Kashgar A.D. 715, *Bulletin of the School of Oriental Studies,* University of London, vol. II (1922), p. 469.

their society. But although political democracy receded into the background, the democratic way of life continued to flourish on the economic and social planes. And at all times there was one law for all, from which no one was immune, not even the Caliph himself.

*　　*　　*

For several centuries, vitality, creativeness, and enormous productivity characterized the endeavor of Arab society in all walks of life.

When the Arabs entered upon the intellectual heritage of the Mediterranean world and western Asia, they had no stock of learning to contribute, no system of philosophy, and no compendiums of law. But they possessed a keen mind, alive with curiosity and eager to explore and learn. They approached the study of ancient civilization with zeal and devotion, proving themselves apt pupils, and in time became masters and authors of the works of civilization in all its fullness.

Another asset of great value was the Arabic language. Rich and flexible, it was capable of infinite growth and adaptation, and was therefore eminently fitted as the vehicle of a great civilization. It surpassed in creativeness and power of assimilation the current languages of the time, which it found little difficulty in supplanting. Its expansion was rapid, and in those countries which formed the heart of the Moslem world its conquest was permanent. In the Middle Ages, Arabic was the medium of communication as well as intellectual expression from Central Asia to Spain. Its hold was such that in countries as far away as Transoxania on the borders of China, people were not only producing a rich harvest of literary, scientific, and religious works in the Arabic language, but were composing Arabic poetry of exquisite beauty and delicacy giving expression to intimate individual feeling in that most personal of poetic genres, the Lyric poem. In Spain, the popularity of Arabic among the Christian Spaniards drew a sad complaint from the Bishop of Cordova who watched the youth abandon Latin and the reading of religious literature for the poetry of the Arabs.

Poetry found a ready and wide response. A characteristic story is related in *Al-Aghani* of an Omayyad army sent to fight the

Khawarij. For a time the battle was suspended and hostilities forgotten while the combatants argued over the relative merits of Jarir and Al-Farazdak, the great poets of the day.

The Arabs are deeply attached to their language. They delight in its rhythms and revel in what seems to them its superb beauty. Enchanted, they call it "the lawful charm."[9] Today, the Arabic language is one of the strongest bonds of Arab unity.

The impetus to pursue and expand the domain of learning came from many sources. A great heritage was at hand, and the Arab mind was happily endowed with the gift to recognize its greatness, the will to borrow, and the capacity to learn. The Arabic language, hospitable to new ideas and concepts, was capable of growth and expansion to meet the demands of expanding knowledge and keep abreast with its ever moving frontiers. The Moslem religion taught men to seek knowledge even though it be in distant China. Since Islam had no organized priesthood, the individual had to be his own religious teacher and guide. It was thus essential that he should be able to read his Holy Book. Teaching a fellow man to read was considered a highly meritorious act. Numerous are the traditions attributed to the Prophet urging the faithful to seek knowledge and travel widely in the search.

Society set up the framework which supported the life of learning. Institutions devoted to the pursuit and furtherance of knowledge were numerous and well-endowed. Caliphs established "Houses of Wisdom," equipped them with libraries, and staffed them with the best available scholars whom they entrusted with the work of translating, writing, and collecting books. Schools and University mosques were founded by caliphs, sultans, and their viziers, or by ordinary citizens who, having a fortune on hand, wished to dispose of it in a way that was pleasing to God. It is said that in the reign of Harun al-Rashid, schools were so numerous that practically everyone was literate.[10] Madrasa is the name of a school of higher learning and is equivalent in some respects to the later medieval and early modern European university. There were scores of *madaris* all over the Moslem world. Baghdad alone had thirty, all richly endowed, according to Ibn Jubayr, the Spanish Arab traveler of the 12th century. The celebrated globe-trotter Ibn Batuta, passing through Egypt in 1326, remarked that the madaris

9. All other charms or magic (sihr) are unlawful and abhorrent.
10. Margaret Smith: *An Early Mystic of Baghdad*, p. 3.

in Cairo were so numerous he could not give their exact number. He also found them in the smaller towns of Egypt.[11]

These institutions generally carried endowments which provided for the support of the students as well as their education. Lodgings, kitchens, baths, and hospitals, as well as libraries were attached to the richer and larger of the madaris. The students received sufficient rations of food, new garments at certain seasons, writing equipment, and allowances. Their health and bodily cleanliness were looked after. A student did not have to be rich or belong to a particular class to attend a university. The opportunity for learning was within the reach of the humblest and the poorest.

Hospitals ministered to the sick and carried on the study of medicine in its various branches. They were equipped with libraries, laboratories, and clinics. Some of them were designed with as much care for the emotional and psychological needs of the patients as for their physical well-being. A lengthy description of the hospital built by the Mamluk Sultan, Kalaun, has been preserved. It was located in beautiful surroundings in the midst of gardens through which flowed rippling brooks. The rooms were spacious and bright. To the insane, particularly pleasant apartments were allocated. Music was played to soothe the pains of the inmates, and the morning call to prayer was sounded two hours before the appointed time to make the night seem short to those whose sufferings kept them awake.[12]

Libraries kept pace with the universities, both in numbers and in the services which they rendered in disseminating knowledge and making it accessible to any and all who were interested in acquiring it. The taste for books was widely spread and was common alike to the sovereign and the man on the street. Men spared themselves no trouble or expense to secure books, some of which they sought in far-off countries. There were several kinds of libraries. Some were established by caliphs. Of these the three most celebrated were the Abbasid Library in Baghdad, the Fatimid Library in Cairo, and the Omayyad Library in Cordova. There were private libraries, and libraries attached to mosques, universities, hospitals, and religious retreats. And there were libraries that stood by themselves, not connected with any institution, simply to serve the public. The books were catalogued and placed on shelves, and were

11. *Voyages d'Ibn Batuta,* 4 vol., texte et traduction par C. Defremery et B. R. Sanguinetti, 1853–1858, I, 70.

12. Joseph Hell: *The Arab Civilization,* translated by S. Khuda Bukhsh, 1926, pp. 117–118.

easily accessible to the readers who were supplied with paper and ink free of charge. Books were loaned on easy terms. The famous 13th century geographer and traveler Yakut, describing the libraries of Marw—of which there were ten—says that he always kept in his house two hundred or more volumes, without having to pay a deposit. One of these libraries, Yakut remarks, was founded by a man who started his life as a fruit and flower vendor.[13]

Some of the libraries were of a great size. The library of Tripoli (Syria), which the Crusaders destroyed, is said to have contained three million volumes.[14] Its destruction was only a prelude to what books suffered from the havoc wrought by the Mongols when they swept upon the lands of Islam.

Another interesting and characteristic institution was the bookshop. The booksellers (warraqun) were copyists, dealers in books and paper, and generally men of culture. Their shops were a meeting place of cultured people. Sometimes an avid scholar would rent a shop for the night and stay up reading and copying till the next day.

The manufacture of paper, invented by the Chinese, was taken over by the Arabs and developed. The cheapness of paper in comparison to parchment and other writing material made its use extensive and thus contributed to the popularization of knowledge.

The life of learning was held in high esteem. Rulers vied with one another in the generous patronage extended to scholars, whose presence enhanced the fame of their courts. Many among the dignitaries of state were themselves learned men.

People traveled widely and continuously over the extensive Moslem world and beyond in search of knowledge. Moving from one center to another, they sought teachers rather than institutions. Some seekers never ended the search, for there was always a famous and venerated master to travel to. This freedom of movement was made possible not so much by the political unity of Islam, a unity which soon broke down, as by the common language and culture which made the traveler feel at home wherever he went.

*   *   *

On the economic plane, we see the picture of an active and thriving community. Work was honored in all its forms. Here again the Koran and the sayings of the Prophet are the guide to the Moslem

13. Yakut, *Mu'jam al-Buldan,* ed. Wustenfeld, IV, 509–510.
14. Arnold and Grohman: *The Islamic Book,* p. 32.

concept of work. God gave the world to man to use and enjoy. A saying of the Prophet makes the quest of a livelihood, like the search for knowledge, a religious duty required of the Moslem. Even the mystics, the most unworldly of the believers, expressed the view that work was more acceptable to God than an unproductive life spent in prayer and the expectation to be maintained by the community. Material well-being was considered an aid to the life in God and obedience to His will, since it supplied the believer with means to spend in the service of God and for the welfare of His people.

The respect which Islam gave to work is reminiscent of the attitude of Calvinist Christianity, except that among the Moslems prosperity was not considered a mark of the elect as it tended to become with the development of Calvinism.

The Arab geographers of the Middle Ages, whose travels carried them far and wide throughout the lands of Islam, testify to widespread prosperity in a society alive with all kinds of productive activities. Agriculture was so diligently pursued that some countries presented the aspect of one continuous garden. For days on end travelers walked or rode in the cool shade of trees through lands well-groomed and carefully tended. Villages and rural settlements were strung along river banks like gems in an emerald necklace.

Towns grew like mushrooms, and markets covered the country side. In Egypt, says Ibn Batuta, the markets were linked in an unbroken chain from Alexandria to Cairo, and from Cairo to Assuan in Upper Egypt.

Industry also flourished and supplied with a rich variety of products a society that demanded quality and beauty in the articles of daily use. Artisans possessed the skill and leisure to produce them. They were often artists as well, and they brought to their work the love and devotion of the creative act. They also reaped in full measure the joy and pride of creation. Hence the refined beauty which made works of art of such things as bowls and lamps, tiles and rugs, and other common objects.

The industries and trades were organized in corporations or guilds. These corporations were of great social importance. They maintained the standard of craftsmanship and prevented underhand competition, thereby insuring a friendly society. Based on religious and moral foundations, they impressed upon their members a sense of duty towards the craft and towards one another.

Honesty and sobriety were characteristic qualities of the Moslem artisan. A tradition of mutual aid prevailed. Notwithstanding differences among the members in wealth and rank, social solidarity and social duty were emphasized, and the humblest member was assured a place in the social order.

The corporations were also centers of social and political effervescence. They were linked to the Karmathian movement with its emphasis upon social equality and its fight against oppression. In the ranks of the corporations, literati and cultured members were not rare. They participated with interest in the literary and theological discussions and controversies of the time. A number of books on crafts were written by artisans themselves.

The corporations were self-governing groups with regular statutes, chiefs, and tax assessments. They maintained discipline and order among their members and were thus an important pillar in the government administration. In return, governors respected the independence and traditional usages of the corporations.

The relative wealth of the crafts and trades corporations, their social solidarity, and their autonomous status, gave their members both as individuals and as an organized group a sense of dignity and independence of bearing, and a consciousness of their rights and the readiness to assert these rights. On many occasions their concerted action was a check upon arbitrary rulers.[15]

Trade even surpassed industrial and agricultural activity. It expanded far beyond the confines of the Moslem world. In Europe it reached the Baltic shores where great quantities of Arab coins have been uncovered. In the south, Arab traders penetrated to the heart of Africa. In the east, they maintained a lively trade with India and China by land and by sea.

Within the Moslem dominions, commercial activity was intense. Here again, the unity of a large portion of the earth resulted in freedom and facility of movement, and the consequent flow and exchange of commodities. Good roads, built and maintained for the postal service and other administrative purposes, contributed to the ease and security with which people and goods traveled. Travel was characteristic of this society in its various pursuits and occupations. An insatiable love of adventure made men brave hazards and overcome obstacles on land and sea. Religion, which re-

15. H. A. R. Gibb and Harold Bowen: *Islamic Society and The West*, London, 1950, pp. 276–278. Louis Gardet: *Humanism Musulman d'Hier et d'Auhourd'hui, Ibla*, Revue de L'Institut des Belles Lettres Arabes, Tunis, 1944, p. 32.

quired every able-bodied Moslem to make the pilgrimage to Mecca and Medina at least once in a life-time, set multitudes of people on the road in fulfillment of one of the five basic articles of their faith. They traveled slowly and leisurely, visiting not only the countries that lay on the pilgrim's route, but often extending their travels beyond their destination, and sometimes spending years before they returned home. Then there were the travelers who sought knowledge and, although they were less numerous than the pilgrims, there was always a steady stream of them flowing towards the centers of learning. And there were people who traveled for a livelihood, seeking gain and success in far-off lands. An anecdote recounted by Sa'di in his *Gulistan* gives an idea of the life of a busy and prosperous merchant in the 13th century. Sa'di met him in Kish on the Persian Gulf. The merchant, speaking of his trade, told the poet that he had a correspondent in Turkistan and an agency in Hindustan, and that he desired to make one more journey, after which he planned to retire. On this journey he would take Persian sulphur to China, China-ware to Greece, Grecian brocade to India, Indian steel to Aleppo, mirrors of Aleppo to Yaman, and striped Yaman cloth to Persia.[16]

Traveling, common as it was, brought some remarkable and enduring results. It strengthened the feeling of solidarity within the Moslem community by bringing people from its far-flung frontiers together at the cradle of their religion in Arabia. It increased the volume of knowledge and broadened its horizons, for it made possible the study and observation of men and the different environments in which they lived. It also contributed substantially to wealth and prosperity, and consequently to the elaboration and complexity of civilization with its ever increasing needs and requirements.

Finally, these constant journeys and wanderings from land to land gave rise to a mass of fascinating travel literature, much of which, based on fact and observation, is remarkable for its accuracy and wealth of information. Some accounts, however, though they have a basis in fact, have been highly colored by a rich fancy. To this latter category belong the tales of Sindbad the Sailor. Of the former class, the most famous are the travels of Ibn Batuta, which filled nearly thirty years of his life and took him from his home in Ceuta on the Atlantic to China, and from the Volga to Central Africa. The most striking note of Ibn Batuta's record is the

16. *Gulistan*, Ch. 3, Story 22.

deep human feeling that permeates it. The author himself was primarily interested in human beings and their society, and people reciprocated his feeling by their friendly treatment of him wherever he went.

* * *

The society which the Arabs founded over thirteen centuries ago has endured in the face of vicissitudes and disasters to the present day. Its permanence comes from certain fundamental concepts in which it is rooted. Chief among them is its broad humanity which embraced in the brotherhood of Islam all races and colors on a basis of equality. To those who remained outside the Moslem fold but adhered to revealed religions, it accorded wide tolerance, respecting their faiths and their ways of life. Had the Arabs organized themselves in a separate caste and withdrawn into a closed community, they would in time have disappeared like so many other conquering peoples before and since. Free from the stifling prejudices of class and race, they mingled with all peoples and, although numerically a minority in the midst of the native population, they succeeded in assimilating millions of people and a variety of cultures.

The lands on the periphery of the Moslem world, while clinging to Islam—with the exception of Spain—have broken away from the Arab community. The core, however, has remained Arab. It includes those lands which saw the rise and fall of the Babylonians and Assyrians, the Phoenicians and Aramaeans, and the ancient Egyptians. They saw conquerors come and go, Persians, Greeks, Romans, and Byzantines who, having remained alien to the life of the people, have disappeared from the scene.

The Arabs came and stayed. They have become as much and as permanent a part of the landscape as its mountains and plains and the life that grows on the soil. Serious shocks and calamities have come upon them as when the Mongols overran their lands, the Crusaders entrenched themselves in their midst, and the Ottoman Turks reduced them to subjection. They withstood the shocks and, recovering after each calamity, have maintained their society and preserved the identity of their culture.

CHAPTER III

The Arabs and the West in the Middle Ages

IN THE first half of the 7th century A.D., the Arabs appeared on the international scene as leading actors. During the hundred years that followed, they established themselves throughout a large part of the world of those days. In the east they reached the gates of China, in the west they thrust a wedge into Gaul beyond the Pyrenees, in the north they knocked at the gates of the capital of the Byzantine Empire, and in the south the limit of their expansion was the Indian ocean and the African desert.

Most of these lands were in the East. And in that age, the East counted far more than the West in the affairs of mankind. Hence the major part of Arab activities was carried on east of the Mediterranean.

Trade passed generally over the Indian Ocean, or moved back and forth across the face of Asia. So it was with relationships on the other levels of life: the interchange of ideas, the intermingling of the arts, and the give and take of social values.

This does not mean that Europe was out of the picture. On the contrary, parts of Europe came within the framework set up by the Arabs, and European civilization was influenced by Arab civilization to a greater extent than is generally realized. For with all their differences the two cultures have fundamental similarities. Both have roots in the Mediterranean heritage, and the Mediterranean has been since remote antiquity a passageway by means of which its shores on the continents of Asia, Africa, and Europe were linked.

The Romans drew those shores together within the orbit of Roman unity. Their predecessors, the Greeks, had established a unity of culture, the kind that lives on after empires have crumbled into dust. That culture known as Hellenism was the joint product of the Greek and Oriental mind and effort. Its chief centers of creativeness were located in the eastern countries of the Mediterranean, and in its development a large number of scientists and philosophers from Syria and Egypt took a prominent part.[1]

The Syrians carried Hellenistic civilization to the heart of Europe. In the early centuries of the Christian era, Syrians from the coastal regions and the interior of the country, Nabataens and Palmyrenes from the caravan cities of the Arabian and Syrian deserts, were settled in France, Italy, and Spain. In France the Syrians formed important colonies in Paris, Narbonne, Bordeaux, Tours, and Orléans. In Italy their largest communities were established in Ravenna and Rome. The presence of a large number of Syrians in Rome drew from a satirist of the second century, Juvenal, the remark that the Orontes river was emptying itself into the Tiber. In those centuries the Syrians were the commercial masters of Europe, to which they brought their wares and those of many countries beyond their own. With their wares the merchants disseminated their culture. The influence of the East is especially evident in religion and art.[2]

In the Moslem period, the westward flow of cultural influences was stimulated and its volume considerably enlarged. Thus, the terms Arab and Moslem are used interchangeably in this chapter, for the simple reason that during the period under review Arab and Moslem were practically synonymous terms. The Moslem religion, itself the great force welding the various races and cultures into one society, was originally revealed to the Arabs and through them it was propagated in the world outside Arabia. The Arabic language was the medium of expression and thought throughout the world of Islam, and over a large part of that world the language of daily use as well. Furthermore, the Arabs, nearest to Europe of the Moslem peoples, were the bearers and transmitters of Moslem civilization to the West.

To give a full description of Arab-Moslem civilization in the Middle Ages is beyond the scope of this chapter, as indeed of the whole book. An attempt is made merely to point out those aspects of it which have directly influenced contemporary Europe, and to mark the qualities and contributions which have become a permanent possession of all who share the Western heritage.

The Middle Ages are commonly represented as the dark ages.

1. Sarton, *The Unity and Diversity of the Mediterranean World*, Osiris, II, 1936, p. 430.

2. Sarton, Osiris, II, 427 ff; J. W. Thompson: *An Economic and Social History of the Middle Ages*, p. 156; W. Heyd: *Histoire du Commerce du Levant au Moyen-Age*, 2 vols., tr. Furcy Raynaud, 1923, I, 20–21.

This concept of the period takes no cognizance of the cultural activity in the Near East and its effects on Europe. It gives an erroneous and distorted picture of the development of Western civilization. When the Arab-Moslem phase of Medieval culture is studied, the Middle Ages stand out as luminous as any of the creative and productive periods of history.

Towards the illumination of this phase of human development George Sarton has shed brilliant and penetrating light. In his monumental work, *Introduction to the History of Science,* he traces with rare knowledge and insight the growth of ideas and the unfolding of men's minds all the way from China, across Asia and Europe, to Ireland, covering some 2000 years of history, from Homer through the 13th century A.D. In this universal survey, the intellectual achievements of Arab-Moslem civilization are placed in the foremost rank. The half-century periods into which his account is divided are named after the thinkers who made them significant to the progress of thought. Many of these periods bear the names of Arab-Moslem scientists and philosophers.

Already in the 8th century, barely a hundred years after the Arabs had left the desert, Iraq became the center of the greatest intellectual activity of the time. By the youthful vigor and exuberance of the new Arab society, science and learning were drawn from diverse and remote sources to the newly founded cities of Basra, Kufa, and Baghdad. The second half of the century is the age of Jabir ibn Haiyan, the half-legendary Gaber of the European Middle Ages, and one of the greatest personalities of medieval science. Through the thicket of legend and superstition that covers his person and his work, a scientific mind may be discerned which recognized more clearly than any other early chemist the importance of experiment, and set forth "remarkably sound views on methods of chemical research." His influence is evident on the whole course of European alchemy and chemistry.[3]

One of the greatest mathematicians of all times, Al Khwarizmi (from whose name is derived the word algorism), gives his name to the first half of the 9th century. "He influenced mathematical thought to a greater extent than any other medieval writer."[4] He brought into wider and more efficient use the Hindu system of

3. Sarton, *Introduction to the History of Science,* I, 532; Meyerhof, *The Legacy of Islam,* ed. by Sir Thomas Arnold and Alfred Guillaume, 1931, p. 327.

4. Sarton, *op cit.,* I, 545.

numeration, and was one of the founders of a thoroughly developed science of algebra.[5]

This is the period of the intellectual brilliance of Baghdad under the enlightened Caliph Al-Mamun, who established an academy of science comparable in scope and significance to the Museum of Alexandria founded in the third century B.C. Mamun sent his emissaries on a systematic hunt for manuscripts, and set the foremost scholars of the age to the task of translating the treasures of Greek learning into Arabic. Mathematics, astronomy, and medicine advanced considerably. The science of geography was enriched by travels and commercial activity.

Of the many brilliant figures who adorn this age, the philosopher Al-Kindi is outstanding. The 270 works attributed to him deal with mathematics, astronomy, medicine, physics, music, philosophy, and geography. Several of his writings were translated into Latin by the greatest of medieval translators, Gerard of Cremona. Cardan, a philosopher of the Renaissance, regarded Kindi as one of the twelve subtlest minds.[6]

The second half of the 9th century is named after Al-Razi, famous in Europe under the Latin form, Rhazes. For his all-embracing knowledge and the precision of his clinical observations, Al-Razi is ranked among the great physicians of all time. His encyclopedia of Greco-Arabic medicine, *Al-Hawi*—The Comprehensive Book—was printed several times in the Latin translation, and had a great influence on European medicine. His treatise on smallpox and measles gives the first clear account of these two diseases. It was translated into Latin, and later into several other languages including English, and was printed some forty times between 1498 and 1866. His clinical notebook, in which he describes very carefully the progress of his patients, is still preserved. The same empirical spirit he brought to bear on all the sciences which he studied.[7]

The 9th century is a Moslem century, according to Sarton, because of the overwhelming superiority of the works of Moslem scholars and scientists over anything produced in other countries.

5. *Ibid.*, p. 563; E. Wiedeman, *Al-Khwarizmi* in *E.I.*

6. De Boer, *The History of Philosophy in Islam*, pp. 97–106; and his article on Al-Kindi in *E.I.*

7. Meyerhof, *The Legacy of Islam*, pp. 323–5; Sarton, *op. cit.*, I, 609; De Boer, *op. cit.*, pp. 77–80; Kraus and Pines, Al-Razi in *E.I.*; Grunebaum, *Medieval Islam*, pp. 333–334.

This superiority continued throughout the 10th century. Books written in other languages—Latin, Greek, Hebrew—contained little that was new. "All the new discoveries and the new thoughts were published in Arabic" which was "the international vehicle of scientific progress."[8]

The 10th century is named by Sarton in its first half after the historian and geographer Al-Masudi, the "Pliny of the Arabs," and in its second half after the astronomer and mathematician Abu'l Wafa. It was a century of prodigious philosophical activity. The foremost philosopher of the age was Al-Farabi,[9] known as the second teacher, Aristotle being the first. Two great collections of knowledge belong to this period, *The Keys of the Sciences* by Mohammed Al-Khwarizmi, and the *Letters of the Brethren of Purity*,[10] both of which cover and reflect the knowledge of the age. A fascinating book, *Al-Fihrist,* is a catalogue of books which came to the knowledge of a widely-traveled bookseller.[11] The *Fihrist* is an impressive record of intellectual productivity, and a sad reminder of our loss, since many of the works known to its author have not survived, or have not yet been found completely or in their original form.

The vigor of the 10th century continued with greater intensity through the 11th, which marked the climax of medieval thought. Islam was in the vanguard of humanity. Passing from other cultures to the Arab-Moslem civilization "is almost like passing from the shade to the open sun and from a sleepy world into one tremendously active."[12] The great leaders of thought are so numerous that Sarton feels an embarrassment of choice in trying to select one name for his period title out of a galaxy of equally distinguished names. He decides to give the first half of the 11th century the name of Al-Biruni "one of the very greatest scientists of Islam, and, all considered, one of the greatest of all times."[13] His knowledge was all-embracing, for he was a philosopher, mathematician, astronomer, geographer, and traveler. More remarkable than the scope of his knowledge was his modern approach to learning, a process of rigorous criticism and investigation. With his critical approach he combined a broad tolerance of cultures other than his

8. Barton, *op. cit*, I, 543 and 619.
9. De Boer, *op. cit.*, pp. 106–128.
10. De Boer, *op. cit.*, pp. 81–96; and his article, *Ikhwan Al-Safa*, in *E.I.*
11. Grunebaum, *op. cit.*, p. 41.
12. Sarton, I, 695.
13. *Ibid.*, p. 707.

own. His love of truth and his intellectual courage are rare in medieval times and not very common in our own.

Biruni had two contemporaries almost as great as himself. One
was Ibn al-Haitham (Latin Alhazen), "the greatest Moslem physi-
cist and one of the greatest students of optics of all times."[14] His
principal work, the *Optics,* exerted a great influence upon western
science, especially upon Roger Bacon and Kepler.[15] "His researches
in geometrical and physiological optics were the most significant
to occur between ancient times and the sixteenth century."[16] The
other was Ibn Sina, the celebrated Avicenna, "the greatest physi-
cian of the time and one of the greatest of all times." To many
Moslems he is their most famous scientist, the prince of all learning. His two great encyclopedias, the one philosophical, *Kitab al-
Shifa,* the other, *Al Qanun,* medical, represent the culmination of
medieval thought. The *Qanun,* or Canon, had an overwhelming influence on European medicine. Translated into Latin by Gerard
of Cremona, it became a sort of medical bible and remained for
six centuries the supreme authority in Christendom as in Islam.
This enormous work was printed in Europe sixteen times in the
last third of the 15th century, and more than twenty times during
the following century. Commentaries on it in Latin, Hebrew, and
the vernaculars, both in manuscript and in print, and epitomes
of it are countless. It continued in use in Europe into the second
half of the 17th century and is still used in the East to the present
day. "Probably no medical work ever written has been so much
studied."[17]

The second half of the 11th century is the age of Omar Khayyam,
known and loved in the West for his Ruba'iyat, but to his countrymen better known as one of their greatest mathematicians and
astronomers.

In this period also lived Al-Ghazali, one of the noblest spirits in
Islam, and its most original philosopher. His life is as remarkable
as his work. It was dominated by a restless quest for knowledge,
and a burning desire to grasp the truth. In the early part of the
search, his soul, assailed by keen, deep-cutting doubts, suffered
severe torments. Having mastered the knowledge of his time as it
was understood and taught by the various religious sects and phil-

14. Sarton, I, 721.
15. Meyerhof, *Legacy of Islam,* pp. 333–335; De Boer, *op. cit.,* pp. 148–153.
16. Sarton, I, 698.
17. Sarton, I, 700–710; II, 66; Meyerhof: *The Legacy of Islam,* pp. 329–330;
De Boer: *op. cit.,* pp. 131–148.

osophical schools, he failed to find in it comfort and assurance. Yet
the quest was crowned with triumph, for it revealed to Ghazali the
weakness of philosophy and dogma, and the errors of the philosophers and theologians, and led him to an active approach to the
kind of certainty he was seeking.

Philosophy, as the term was used in Ghazali's day, meant the
theologically scholasticized Aristotelianism which was developed
in the Islamic world, adopted by medieval European Christianity,
and maintained in the somewhat modified form of Thomism as the
accepted ecclesiastical philosophy of a considerable section of the
Christian world to the present day. Theology in Ghazali's world
had become largely an ever expanding tissue of casuistic quib-
blings in canon law, spun over a petrifying core of automatically
authoritative dogmatic statements on God, man, angels, and devils.
Beside these two, and in large part intertwined with them, reverence for the family of the Prophet had merged with older religious
beliefs and movements into the belief in a personal, authoritarian,
infallible dictatorship of truth. All of these naturally failed to satisfy the keen mind of Ghazali in his deeply sincere quest for living
truth. His own search led him, on the one hand to renunciation of
a brilliant professorship at the court university of Baghdad, on the
other to a life resembling that of the late Mahatma Gandhi, alter-
nating between periods of worshipfully contemplative withdrawal
from society and periods of return to teaching and guidance for his
sorely confused fellowmen.[18] With this he found himself drawn
more and more into the company of sincere Sufis, similar to but
not to be confused with Christian mystics. There he found what
his heart desired, a living faith and a never ending quest to get
into ever closer touch with the creative source of truth, goodness,
and beauty which is God.

After the 11th century, the honors of intellectual leadership are
shared with the budding genius of Europe. Still the leaders of
the 12th century were predominantly Moslem. The dependence
of Europe on Moslem civilization is best symbolized by Europe's
representative man in this age, Gerard of Cremona the translator,
"who reminds us of the fact that progressiveness consisted to a
large extent in a wise gathering of the fruits of Muslim culture."[19]

During the 13th century, European leadership asserted itself, although in a number of sciences—astronomy and mathematics, bot-

18. Toynbee: A Study of History, III, 248–332.
19. Sarton, II, 279.

any and pharmacology, and certain branches of medicine, chiefly ophthalmology—the Arabs were still undisputed masters.

Scientific endeavor was only one aspect of the vigorous life of Arab society. Contact with the Arabs touched the life of Europe in countless ways. The means of transmission of Arab culture were numerous. Trade was one of the most effective and continuous. The stream of pilgrims to the Holy Land was seldom interrupted, although at times it dwindled to a mere trickle. The Crusades brought East and West more closely together, notwithstanding the violent fanaticism they engendered. The Crusaders who settled in the Levant were in daily contacts with the Arabs upon whom they depended for the needs of every-day life. Agriculture was maintained by native peasants; the arts, crafts, and industries were in native hands, as was local and international commerce. Furthermore, Arabs and Franks were drawn together at popular gatherings, festivals, tournaments, and other public events. Fanaticism was softened and gave room to mutual tolerance and appreciation. The difference between the resident Crusaders and new arrivals from Europe in their attitude toward the Moslems is noted in the contemporary Arab sources, as for example the Memoirs of Usamah ibn Munkidh.[20] It is evident also in the accounts of the Crusades written by Frankish historians living in the Levant, and those written by Europeans who did not know the East. While the chronicle of Jacques de Vitry breathes fire and hatred against the infidel, the history of William of Tyre shows an understanding of the Arabs and an insight into the world of Islam.

The Crusaders found in the Levant a culture in most respects superior to their own. Life on the whole was richer, brighter, and more varied. The land produced a rich variety of crops and fruits, many of them wholly unknown to the Europeans. Markets and bazars were stacked with all manner of goods, some made locally by native craftsmen and artisans, others imported from distant lands. The houses, in their structure and furnishings, were provided with comforts unfamiliar to Europeans. All sorts of wares and utensils served the daily needs of the people. Clothes were colorful and attractive, and food was prepared with infinite care.

Public cleanliness and sanitation were far ahead of conditions in Europe. Public baths were a principal feature of cities and towns. Hospitals, clinics, and apothecary stores were numerous. Public

20. Hitti, *An Arab-Syrian Gentleman and Warrior in the Period of the Crusades, Memoirs of Usamah Ibn Munqidh*, 1929.

health was safeguarded by means of elaborate and meticulous rules governing markets and public establishments of all kinds, and regulating the preparation and sale of foods, drinks, drugs and medicines. The duty of supervising and enforcing these laws was entrusted to the *Muhtasib,* Market Superintendent, a high ranking official of the government. The numerous books written on the duties and objects of the *hisba,* the office of the Superintendent, give a living picture of an active, well-regulated, and highly civilized town life.

It is difficult to assess the share of the Crusades in the transmission of Arab culture to Europe. The Crusades gave a strong impetus to trade. They stimulated the activities of the great commercial city-states of Italy: Venice, Genoa, Pisa, and others. During this period many of the products of Asia were introduced and disseminated in Europe. Sugar-cane, citrus fruits, and other trees and crops of the Levant were carried to the western lands of the Mediterranean. Fabrics, furnishings and all kinds of wares made their way to the European markets. New colors, dyes, and scents were introduced. The introduction of new articles was naturally accompanied by the diffusion of new fashions.[21]

The influence of the Crusades is evident in the public steam baths which began to make their appearance in Europe, and the foundation of hospitals on the pattern of those established by the Orders of the Holy Land.

If the Crusades failed to transmit the scientific and intellectual achievements of the Arabs, they nevertheless stimulated the intellectual life of Europe and its literary output by broadening the horizons of knowledge and imagination. They provided an inexhaustible source from which historians and story-tellers drew, and were an inspiration to artists, poets, and singers for many generations.

The most effective means of transmission, however, was provided by the bridgeheads which the Arabs established in Europe itself: Spain and Sicily.

The period of Arab rule in Sicily covered the 10th and 11th centuries, but the civilization brought by the Arabs lived on after their rule had ceased. Sicily was permeated with Arab-Moslem civilization. The Arabs settled not only in the towns, but in the countryside as well. Those of them who lived on the land brought to the island their knowledge of agriculture and introduced new

21. Ernest Barker: *The Legacy of Islam,* pp. 60–61.

crops. The artisans and craftsmen spread new designs and techniques, enriching industries and crafts. Daily contact with the Arab settlers left its mark upon the customs and manners of the native population. Intellectual life was stimulated by the impact of Moslem science and learning.

After the Norman conquest, Sicily continued to radiate Arab culture, and the Moslem community remained for some time a considerable element of the population. The Normans left the administration of the country very much as they found it, and kept Arabs in high posts. Trade and industry were largely in Arab hands. The Arabic language was used in official documents together with Greek and Latin; it was struck on coins and carved on buildings; and it was spoken by the polyglot population of the island.[22]

The Norman kings were patrons of science and art. They surrounded themselves with Moslem, Christian, and Jewish scholars. Under their enlightened patronage Arabic scientific books were translated, and through their connections with the rest of Italy and other parts of Europe, Arab ideas were widely disseminated.

Roger II, the most enlightened monarch of his age, owed the main scientific glory of his reign to his patronage of Al-Idrisi, a great Arab geographer born in Ceuta on the North African coast. Idrisi's book known as *Al-Kitab Al-Rujari* (The Roger Book) is the most elaborate description of the medieval world.[23]

Roger's grandson, Frederick II Hohenstaufen, inherited his ancestor's enlightenment as well as his kingdom. As King of Sicily, Emperor of the Holy Roman Empire, and King of Jerusalem, he was the most powerful ruler in Christendom. European politics revolved around his court, which was also a leading intellectual center of Europe. Frederick, who was a great statesman, was also a scientist of merit, a philosopher, and a patron of learning. His spirit was remarkably free and adventurous. Moslem influence was strong in his reign. He corresponded with scholars in various Arab countries, and during his travels in Italy, Germany, and the Holy Land he was accompanied by Moslem learned men. In 1224 Frederick founded the University of Naples and presented it with a unique collection of Arabic manuscripts. Under his patronage the works of Aristotle and Ibn Rushd (Averroes) were translated, and copies of the translations were sent to the universities of Paris and Bologne. He further promoted the diffusion of Arab civiliza-

22. Hitti, *History of the Arabs*, pp. 602–614.

23. Sarton: *op. cit.*, II, 140, 191.

tion by strengthening the political and economic ties between his kingdom and the Arab states in the Levant and in North Africa. Recognizing the futility of the Crusades, he tried to reconcile Christendom and Islam. His peaceful missions to the Holy Land accomplished more than the military expeditions of the Crusaders. Yet this man was ex-communicated at least five times during his life, and once more after his death.[24]

His son Manfred carried on the scientific activity of Frederick's reign. Manfred's conqueror, Charles d'Anjou, followed the tradition of the Norman kings in patronizing and promoting Arabic learning. In his reign the great medical encyclopedia of Al-Razi was translated into Latin.

Important as Sicily was as an outpost of Arab culture in Europe, it was surpassed by Spain where that culture came to full and abundant fruition. Conquered in 711, Spain became one of the finest Arab provinces, and for a time was the seat of a Caliphate which rivaled the Baghdad Caliphs at the height of their splendor. Arab rule in Spain lasted until 1492 when their last stronghold, Granada, fell on the second day of the year in which Columbus discovered America. After its fall the Moslems stayed on until they were expelled *en masse* in the early years of the 17th century.

The story of the Arabs in Spain is a chapter in their history upon which Arabs to the present day look with pride and love.

Soon after the conquest, victors and vanquished settled down to a life of fruitful and creative cooperation. The Arabs entered enthusiastically into the life of the country to which they brought a fund of energy and many skills. The land prospered and its population increased. Agriculture, industry, and trade flourished as they had never done before. A testimony to the advanced state of agricultural science and practice is given by Ibn al-Awwam, an Arab of Seville, who, in the 12th century wrote the most important book on agriculture in the Middle Ages. Here as in Sicily the Arabs introduced new plants, among them cotton, sugar-cane, rice, a variety of fruit trees—apricots, peaches, pomegranates—and a number of aromatic herbs and shrubs of which saffron was the most widely grown. The introduction of sericulture gave rise to a flourishing silk industry. The olive groves, known under the Romans, flourished anew. This wide and varied culture was made possible by the construction and maintenance of an intricate and widespread system of irrigation.

24. *Ibid.*, II, pp. 575–577; Haskins: *Studies in Medieval Science*, pp. 224–36.

Contemporary geographers represent Spain as a vast garden, covered with fruit trees and flowers. Their enthusiastic accounts are endorsed by modern historians.[25]

Reading the literature of the time one senses a pervading attachment to the land and a taste for life in the country even among the inhabitants of the cities. All the large cities had their rural suburbs, where the town dwellers kept country houses in the midst of gardens to which they repaired for rest in their quiet beauty and freshness. This love for the land inspired a type of poetry known as *nawriyyat* and *rawdiyyat,* flower and garden poems, which describe nature with a delicate sensitiveness to its beauties and a feeling entirely free of affectation.[26]

Industry did not lag behind agriculture. The skill which made the products of Damascus, Cairo, and Baghdad famous and widely sought, was part of the culture which the Arabs brought with them to Spain. A number of industries were established and they turned out products of high artistic value,—textiles, ceramics, metal-work, glass ware, book binding, and leather tooling, wood carving and inlay. From the silks woven in Spain were made the state-robes of Emperors and the vestments of church dignitaries. The celebrated ceramics industry, centered chiefly in Valencia, commanded a wide market. From Spain this industry was introduced to France. Imitations of it are found as far north as Holland. Toledo was famous for swords that rivalled those of Damascus, Cordova produced the celebrated leather work known as Cordovan. The minor arts flourished, and their products were the prized ornaments of the palaces and churches of Europe.[27]

The manufacture of paper, invented by the Chinese, owes to the Arabs its wide dissemination. Brought by them to Spain, it found its way to the rest of Europe, where its introduction made possible the development of book-printing in the Renaissance.

Trade kept pace with the thriving industry and agriculture; in a regular stream it flowed between Spain and the other Arab countries in the East. Merchants from as far as Khurasan in Central Asia brought their wares to Spain. On the other hand, Spanish products were known all the way from Europe to eastern Asia.

Prosperity was in evidence everywhere, in the towns as in the

25. Levi-Provencal, *L'Espagne Musulman au Xème Siècle,* pp. 164 ff.; Sarton, *op. cit.,* II, 56.

26. Levi-Provencal, *op. cit.,* pp. 174–175.

27. J. B. Trend: *The Legacy of Islam,* pp. 13–16.

country. An impressive evidence of prosperity was the great building activity, of which a few monuments, such as the Mosque of
Cordova, the Alhambra, and the Giralda tower at Seville, remain
to the present day to proclaim the glories of Arab rule in Spain.
Cordova, with its 3,000 mosques, 300 public baths, 70 libraries,
numerous free schools and bookshops, its magnificent palaces, its
paved and lighted streets, and its score of suburbs, was the ornament of the western medieval world. And Cordova was not unique
among the cities of Spain; it had worthy rivals in Granada, Seville,
and Toledo.

Material welfare was reflected in the manners and taste of the
people. Good manners were not confined to any one group but
were common to all classes of the population. Politeness among
the people was spontaneous and free of subservience. Their love
of beauty which delighted in nature was equally sensitive to beautiful objects made by the hands of men. Hence the care and fine
taste which went into the making of clothes, household furnishings, and other objects of common use.

Again, from the poetry of the time we glean impressions of a
joyous and contented life. To express the gayety and lightness of
heart which the Andalusians felt, a new form of Arabic poetry,
Al-Muwashshah, peculiar to Spain, was created and became widely
popular both in the colloquial *(Zajal)* and the classical style. It was
light, gay, and exquisitely delicate; and it was as close to music
as words can come. It was often set to music and sung. Poetry
seems to have been a passion with the people, and the ability to
improvise in poetry was common even among those with little or
no knowledge of reading. Music and dancing shared the popularity of poetry. To the present day, Spaniards celebrate "fiestas"
which have come down from the Arab period.

Races and cultures mixed freely in the Iberian Peninsula. Large
numbers of Goths accepted the Moslem religion and became in-
distinguishable from their fellow Moslems of other racial stocks.
Others held on to the faith of their fathers but lived close to
the Moslems and mingled with them in the routine of daily life.
These were called Mozarabs or Arabicized Christians because they
adopted the ways of the Arabs and spoke their language. By the
10th century the whole basis of life throughout Spain was profoundly influenced by Islam.[28] No better description can be given
of the enthusiasm of the Spaniards for Arab culture than the lament

28. J. B. Trend: *The Legacy of Islam*, p. 28.

of Alvaro, Bishop of Cordova, who wrote in the middle of the 9th century: "My fellow Christians delight in the poems and romances of the Arabs; they study the works of Mohammadan theologians and philosophers, not in order to refute them, but to acquire a correct and elegant Arabic style. Where today can a layman be found who reads the Latin commentaries on Holy Scriptures? Who is there that studies the Gospels, the Prophets, the Apostles? Alas. The young Christians who are most conspicuous for their talents have no knowledge of any literature or language save the Arabic; they read and study with avidity Arabic books; they amass whole libraries of them at a vast cost, and they everywhere sing the praises of Arabian lore. On the other hand, at the mention of Christian books they disdainfully protest that such works are unworthy of their notice. The pity of it. Christians have forgotten their own tongue and scarce one in a thousand can be found able to compose in fair Latin a letter to a friend. But when it comes to writing Arabic, how many there are who can express themselves in that language with the greatest elegance, and even compose verses which surpass in formal correctness those of the Arabs themselves."[29]

For centuries under the Arabs, Spain was the intellectual leader of Europe and one of the foremost centers of thought in the Arab-Moslem world. The caliphs of Cordova were great patrons of learning. They opened schools and collected books from distant lands. Among their subjects the taste for books and learning was widespread. It is told how people with little means went hungry and poorly clothed in order to buy books.[30]

In keeping with Moslem tradition, Spanish scholars took the long journey to the centers of learning in the East. Just as the exchange of material commodities between Spain and the eastern Arab countries was continuous, so scholars and ideas passed back and forth in a steady flow.

From Arab Spain, Moslem culture radiated to the rest of the Iberian Peninsula and to Europe. Mozarabs migrated north to the Christian kingdoms of Spain where their superior culture secured them high office at the court and in the ecclesiastical and civil administration.[31] Marriages between the Moslem rulers and the Christian royal houses were frequent. The carriers of Arab culture to Europe were a diverse crowd and included scholars, monks,

29. Dozy: *Spanish Islam*, p. 268.
30. Ribera, *Disertaciones y Opusculos*, I, 197 f.
31. Miguel Asin: *Islam and the Divine Comedy*, translated and abridged by Harold Sunderland, 1926, p. 243, n. 1.

merchants, soldiers, and captives of war, statesmen and ambassadors, singers and dancers. The great age of transmission was the 12th century; but about two hundred years earlier, Arabic learning had penetrated to the heart of Europe.

During the 10th century the Caliphate of Cordova was at the height of its power and splendor. Embassies were exchanged between the Caliphs and the Emperors of the Holy Roman Empire. In the middle of the century, Otto I the Great sent to Abd al-Rahman III an embassy under a learned monk[32] of the monastery of Gorza near Metz in Lorraine. The emissaries remained three years in Cordova where they most likely became acquainted with Arab learning, and upon their return brought back with them some scientific manuscripts. During this century the schools of Lorraine were famous throughout Europe, and the monastery of Gorza led the religious reform and scientific revival. To this center scholar monks came from Germany, Italy, France, England, Scotland, and Ireland. Here the seeds of Arabic science first germinated, and from here the knowledge radiated to other parts of Europe, especially England where Lotharingian churchmen found favor with Knut the Great and were appointed in various administrative positions. From his time on through many generations, Lotharingian scholars were given important positions in the churches and the schools of England. During the 12th century, Arabic science was taught in the Cathedral School at Hereford along with liberal arts and theology.[33]

England occupies a prominent position in the diffusion of Arabic science in Europe during the 12th century. Among a large group of English philosophers and translators from the Arabic, the names of Adelard of Bath, Michael Scot, and Roger Bacon are outstanding.

Adelard of Bath was one of the earliest and greatest translators. He seems to have learned Arabic during his visits to Sicily and Syria. He had a profound admiration for Arabic learning and acquired from it a secular and rationalistic attitude of mind.[34]

32. Probably Otto's brother, Bruno, Archbishop of Cologne and Duke of Lorraine who eagerly sought the company of learned foreigners.

33. J. W. Thompson: The Introduction of Arabic Sciences into Lorraine in the Tenth Century, Isis XII, 1929, pp. 184–193; Mary C. Wellborn, Lotharingia as a Centre of Arabic and Scientific Influence in the 11th Century, Isis XVI, 1931, pp. 188–199; J. C. Russell, Hereford and Arabic Science in England about 1175–1200, Isis XVIII, 1932–3, pp. 14–25.

34. Haskins, Studies in Medieval Science, pp. 10 ff; Sarton, op. cit., I, 563; Bernard Lewis: British Contributions to Arabic Studies, pp. 9–11.

Michael Scot received his training in Spain, and later entered the service of Frederick II of Sicily. He translated Arabic science and philosophy, and was one of the founders of Latin Averroism.[35]

Roger Bacon, like his predecessor Adelard of Bath, was a great admirer of Arabic science. He advised his students to abandon the schools of Europe for those of the Arabs.[36]

Toledo was the foremost center of dissemination of Arabic culture. A number of circumstances fitted it for this role. Both under Arab rule and after the Christian reconquest in 1085, Moslems, Christians, and Jews here lived together. Besides, a large French colony was established in a whole quarter of the town. The Moslems, known after the reconquest as Mudejars, pursued their accustomed occupations under their new rulers. In Toledo, as elsewhere in the reconquered provinces, Mudejar influence was predominant in agriculture, trade, arts and crafts, and municipal organization. The Mudejars took the place of the Mozarabs in transmitting Moslem culture. The Mozarabs themselves persisted in their Arab ways. Arabic continued to be the predominant language in Toledo until the end of the 12th century. It was still spoken and written two centuries later.

During the 12th century, Toledo became a great center of translation under the patronage of its learned Bishop Raymond I. Its schools of translation attracted scholars from other parts of Spain and from many European countries—France, Italy, and the Lowlands, England and Scotland, and Dalmatia.

The bulk of the translation was made from Arabic into Latin. A considerable amount was done into Hebrew, and some into the vernaculars, mainly Spanish and Portuguese.

The greatest of the translators was Gerard of Cremona, the father of Arabism in Europe. His activity was prodigious, for he is credited with the translation of nearly eighty works, some of them of immense size, such as the *Canon* of Ibn Sina. His translations included works of Kindi, Farabi, Khwarizmi, Farghani, Zarkali, Ibn-al-Haitham, El-Razi, and Ibn Sina.[37]

By the end of the 12th century most of the knowledge of the Arabs was available to Europe. It was a revelation to the Latins. Its impact is best illustrated in the rise of universities which had

---

35. Sarton, *op. cit.*, II, p. 491; 579–582.
36. Farmer: *The Legacy of Islam*, p. 371.
37. Haskins, *op. cit.*, pp. 14–15; Sarton, *op. cit.*, II, 338–344; Meyerhof: *Legacy of Islam*, p. 347.

not appeared at an earlier time for lack of a sufficient body of learn-ing. Arabic culture, with its rich content and its spirit of rationalism, supplied the universities with the necessary scope and opportunity. The interpenetration of the Moslem and the Christian civilization in the 12th century constituted the core of the new Europe. Hence the 12th century, may appropriately be called a Renaissance.[38]

In the 13th century, under the enlightened rule of Alphonso X called the Wise, the transfer of Arab culture to Christendom was furthered with vigor. Alphonso gathered around him Moslem, Christian, and Jewish scholars. With their cooperation, and under his patronage and supervision, vast works of translation and com-pilation were undertaken. An enthusiastic apostle of Arabic learn-ing, this Christian king had a school especially built in Murcia for a Moslem sage who lectured to Moslem, Christian, and Jewish disciples. He also founded a Latin and Arabic college in Seville where Moslem and Christian professors taught side by side.[39] A learned man himself, Alphonso wrote original works on physics and astronomy and composed the Songs to the Virgin Mary, *Can-tigas de Santa Maria,* one of the greatest collections of Medieval poetry. The *Cantigas* are written in the poetic form peculiar to Moslem Spain, the *Muwashshah* and *Zajal* type. The contemporary musical notation which accompanies the Songs is of Arabic origin, according to the Spanish scholar Ribera, and records a highly de-veloped musical art. A number of elements, harmony, the major and minor modes, and modulation, which are generally associated with much later developments in European music, are known to this 13th century document.[40]

The superiority of Moslem civilization was acknowledged by the intellectual leaders of Europe during the 13th century. Roger Ba-con attributed the defeat of the Christians by the Moslems to their ignorance of the Semitic languages and applied science of which the Moslems were masters.[41] The great teachers of Christendom were deeply influenced by Moslem thought. At the University of Paris, Averroistic Aristotelianism as introduced from Toledo was the foundation of learning. Like Roger Bacon, Albertus Magnus recognized the superiority of the Moslem philosophers and ex-pounded their works to the students who attended his lectures

38. Sarton, *op. cit.,* II, 2,285; Nordström: *Moyen Age et Renaissance,* p. 81.
39. Asin, *op. cit.,* pp. 245–246.
40. Trend: *The Legacy of Islam,* p. 35; Ribera: *Music in Ancient Arabia and Spain,* pp. 6–8.
41. Asin, *op. cit.,* p. 257.

in Paris and Cologne.[42] Among his students was Saint Thomas
Aquinas in whom medieval Christian thought reached its summit.
Saint Thomas himself sought inspiration in Moslem philosophy.[43]
His concept of the Beatific Vision is strongly influenced by the
ideas of the Moslem philosophers. Before Saint Thomas, Ghazali
had defined the Beatific Vision as a perfection of the understand-
ing. The spiritual concept of Paradise as visualized by Ghazali, Ibn
Rushd, and Ibn al-Arabi is echoed, at times almost literally, by the
Spanish scholastics Raymond Lull and Raymond Martin.[44]

The Crusades having failed, a peaceful approach to the Moslem
world was attempted in the form of religious missions. Training
for missionary work required an acquaintance with Islam, and thus
provided a further impetus for the study of Moslem culture. Friars
of the newly founded Dominican and Franciscan orders studied
the Arabic language and Moslem religion with the view of preaching to the Moslems. Chains of Arabic and other Semitic languages
were established in the new universities of Europe for the purpose
of preparing missionaries to the Moslem world.

In this age so imbued with Moslem civilization, Dante created
the Divine Comedy. It is not likely that Moslem learning, so widely
admired and eagerly sought by the intellectual leaders of Europe,
could have escaped Dante or left him untouched. The evidence
points to the contrary.

Moslem prototypes preceded the Divine Comedy by several
hundred years. The journey to the world beyond is a popular theme
in Arabic literature. The Prophet's nocturnal journey from Mecca
to Jerusalem and thence his ascension to heaven, mentioned in the
Koran and described more fully in the *Hadith*, inspired a crop of
legends. The journey to the beyond was not confined to the Prophet
but was shared by the Sufis who also rose to the Divine Throne
and experienced the contemplation of the Beatific Vision.

A comparison of the Divine Comedy with its Moslem prototypes
reveals striking similarities. The general architecture of the In-
ferno and Paradise are identical with the Moslem hell and heaven.
The plans of the infernal regions and celestial abodes appear, according to Asin, to be "drawn by one and the same Moslem architect."[45] Not only in the general outline, but in the many picturesque,

42. Sarton, *op. cit.*, II, 934.
43. Asin, *op. cit.*, pp. 160–161.
44. *Ibid.*, pp. 139–140.
45. Asin, *op. cit.*, Introduction, pp. xiii, xiv, and pp. 68–70 of the text.

descriptive, and episodic details, the two narratives are strikingly alike. Over and above the coincidence in form, a common spirit pervades the two legends. The same moral meaning that is conveyed by the Divine Comedy is imparted by the Moslem mystics. The celestial journey is symbolic of the regeneration of the Soul through faith and the practice of the theological virtues, and the attainment of the supreme bliss as represented in the Beatific Vision. In both narratives, the idealistic conception of heaven triumphs, where the blissful contemplation of the essence of God is the ultimate goal and final reward of the righteous.[46]

By the 13th century, Moslem religious legends, together with popular and philosophic conceptions of the after-life, had passed into the common stock of literary culture that was accessible to the best minds in Europe.[47] Dante's mind was receptive to the ideas of his age, and his age "was steeped in the learning and art of Islam."[48] Besides the literary sources available to him, Dante very likely learned about Islam from his teacher Brunetto Latini, a scholar of encyclopedic learning who acquired knowledge of Arabic culture at first hand during his residence in Toledo as ambassador of Florence to the court of Alphonso the Wise.[49] Under Alphonso, Toledo was permeated with Moslem civilization.

The glorification of Beatrice, the avowed object of the Divine Comedy, has precedents in the rapturous expressions of the Moslem mystics. The Spiritual Bride of the Sufi is the guardian angel and moral redemptress of her lover. From her abode on high, she keeps watch over him, leads him in the path of virtue, inspires him with the desire for perfection and a greater love for God, and throughout his life on earth imparts courage, comfort, and guidance in his struggle to attain righteousness. Finally, when death frees him from the earth and lifts him to heaven, he finds her, radiantly beautiful, waiting to receive him in Paradise. To the Moslem mystics, the beloved is the symbol of the Divine Wisdom. The passion felt for her is allegorical of the union of the mystic soul with God.[50]

The idealized concept of woman is not limited to the circles of the Sufis. We find it in Arabia in the early years of Islam, especially among a tribe of northern Hijaz, the Banu Odhra; hence the term

46. *Ibid.*, p. 74.
47. R. A. Nicholson: *The Legacy of Islam*, pp. 227–228.
48. Asin, *op. cit.*, Introduction, p. xvi.
49. *Ibid.*, pp. 252–254.
50. *Ibid.*, pp. 129–130; 274–275.

Odhri for the romantic attachment to an idealized and unattainable woman. The poetry of the age depicts the lover as dying of passion with no thought of touching the object of his love. This romantic interpretation of love found wide acceptance, and is reflected in the literature of the Arabs in the East and in Spain. In Kitab al-Zahra ("The Book of the Flower"), a 9th century philosopher and legist, analyzed and defended love in the spirit of the tradition attributed to the Prophet: "Whoso loves and conceals his love, remains chaste and dies, that one is a martyr."[51] Ibn Hazm, one of the foremost representatives of Arab civilization in Spain— for he was theologian, juriconsult, historian of religious and philosophical schools, and litterateur and poet of distinction—about 1022 A.D. wrote *The Dove's Neck-Ring*, a book on love which breathes the purest romanticism. Ibn Hazm illustrates his book with true stories of lovers drawn from all ranks of Moslem society in Spain. *The Dove's Neck-Ring* reflects a highly refined society, where love is a matter of the spirit, exquisitely delicate, tender, and sublime. Patience, restraint, and chastity are the qualities of the lover. He approaches his beloved with humility and reverence, and worships her with almost mystical adoration. Love effaces social differences. Kings are humbled before it. The ennobling effect of humility and suffering is the essential quality and mark of love. The essence of love is the union of souls. This union, in the glowing words of Ibn Hazm "is a sublime bliss, and a lofty rank, and a high degree, and an outstanding happiness, nay, it is the RENEWED LIFE and an exalted existence, and a permanent joy, and a great mercy of God."[52]

The spiritual and romantic love of woman, originating in Arabia and borne by the Arabs to Spain, inspired the troubadours of Provence and the Italian literary movement known as the "dolce stil nuovo." The troubadours owe to contacts with Moslem Spain the literary and emotional pattern of their songs. These poets who spread the cult of the lady and European chivalry, with its reverence for woman and its concept of love as an ennobling power, had as predecessors and models the poets and lovers of Arabia and their descendants in the East and in Spain.[53]

51. H. A. R. Gibb: *The Legacy of Islam*, p. 187.

52. Ibn Hazm: *The Dove's Neck-Ring*, tr. by A. H. Nykl, p. 86; Asin, *op. cit.*, p. 273.

53. Grunebaum: "The Arab Contribution to Troubadour Poetry," *Bulletin of the Iranian Institute*, Dec. 1946, pp. 138–151; Asin, *op. cit.*, 129, 271; Trend: *The Legacy of Islam*, p. 35.

Contacts with the Arabs stimulated other types of literary products. The border warfare inspired the *Chanson de Roland* and the legends of the Cid Campeador, whose name is the Arabic *Sid*—Sir. Merchants, pilgrims, and other travelers to Spain and the eastern countries of the Mediterranean brought with them stories of what they had seen and heard. The *chantefable,* a favorite form of medieval romance, was widely popular among the Arabs. The literature of adventure was influenced by the *Arabian Nights,* without which "there would have been no Robinson Crusoe, and perhaps no Gulliver's Travels."[54] The *Nights* have established themselves securely in the literary heritage of the West. They are among the most widely read popular classics, translated into all the languages of western Europe and published hundreds of times. They are read with equal eagerness by old and young, and are held in affection alike by the learned and the simple.

And finally, European music came under Arab influence. Music was a highly developed art among the Arabs, and one that was widely diffused. Although some religious schools frowned upon it, it was assigned a place in worship by no less an authority than Ghazali. Music was considered an aid to medicine because of its soothing effects upon the patients, and was brought into the hospitals for its therapeutic value. It formed an essential part of Muslim education. Above all, it was the art of the people. Public festivals were accompanied by music, as was the celebration of household feasts and family events. Reading the *Arabian Nights* or the *Book of Songs,* one gets the impression that music was always in the air.

Arab contributions influenced both the theory and the instruments of music. Europe received a number of musical instruments from the Arabs, the lute, guitar, rebec, naker, sonajas, tambourine, drum, trumpet, and zither, most of which have kept their Arabic names. The theory of music was developed by some of the foremost Muslim philosophers and scientists, who tested the theories which they had inherited in the light of their advanced mathematics and physics, and made considerable improvements.

Mensural music came from the Arabs to whom it was known as early as the 8th century. Later sources dealt with it fully, especially the *Book of Music* by Al-Farabi. In the 13th century, Safi-ed-Din,

54. Gibb, *The Legacy of Islam,* p. 201.

the greatest musical theorist of that age, founded the Systematist School which produced the most perfect scale ever devised.[55]

Arabic music accompanied the *Cantigas* to the Virgin Mary mentioned above. Another collection, the *Cancionero de Palacio*, consists of popular Spanish songs of the 15th and 16th centuries. Many of the melodies in the *Cancionero* are identical with the musical structure of the *Cantigas*. In both collections most of the songs are in the *zajal*, or strophic form, so popular among the Arabs of Spain. The *Cancionero* contains a number of Moorish songs. One of them, "Les Tres Morillas," appears in several versions; it was widely popular among all classes of Christian Spain. The melody of the "Three Maidens" has passed into the western classical music in the Fourth Symphony of Mendelssohn and in Meyerbeer's opera "L'Africaine."

The music of the *Cancionero de Palacio* is built on a completely developed harmony and written in clear notation. "The songs of the *Cancionero* clearly reveal well-developed major and minor scales with a regular harmonic basis and rapid, unprepared modulations, showing that this usage was already ancient."[56]

The theory and practice of Arabian music reached Europe through two channels. The popular form was carried orally with the songs and poetry which inspired the troubadours. The theory of the art was transmitted by the translators and studied as part of the quadrivium.

Thus the Arab-Moslem civilization, which for several centuries was a creative force, made fundamental contributions to the thought and life of Europe. The scientific spirit and intellectual curiosity of the Arabs, their eager search for truth and devotion to truth, their keen interest in the living and immediate world, and their buoyant vitality and joy in life foreshadowed the Renaissance with its interest and delight in the natural world as opposed to the medieval outlook, immersed as it was in the supernatural world and preoccupied with the life to come. "When at the Renaissance the spirit of man was once again filled with the zeal for knowledge and stimulated by the spark of genius, if it was able to set promptly to work, to produce and to invent, it was because the Arabs had preserved and perfected various branches of knowledge, kept the

55. H. G. Farmer, *The Arabian Influence on Musical Theory*, JRAS, 1925, pp. 3–22; Farmer, *The Legacy of Islam*, pp. 367–368; Sarton, *op. cit.*, II, 26.

56. Ribera, *op. cit.*, pp. 175–176.

spirit of research alive and eager and maintained it pliant and ready for further discoveries."[57]

The Arab-Moslem thinkers—Farabi, Ghazali, Ibn Sina, Ibn Rushd, Ibn Khaldun, and many others; the mystics—Ibn Al-Arabi, Al-Hallaj, Ibn al-Faridh; the works of the mathematicians, physicists, music theorists, biologists, physicians, geographers and travelers; the architectural monuments, the Dome of the Rock—"a symphony of lines and colors"; the Omayyad Mosque in Damascus, the Mosque of Cordova, Alhambra; all these and much besides are an integral part of the cultural effort of civilized humanity.[58]

The large number of words of Arabic origin in the European languages, words related to the many fields of intellectual activity, to architecture and the arts, to the various occupations, agriculture, industry, and commerce, to government and administration, and common words of everyday use, these terms testify to the enduring mark left by the Arabs upon all aspects of life.

Arab-Moslem influence is still alive and strongest in the West in Thomistic-Aristotelian scholasticism, which is the accepted philosophy of the Roman Catholic Church. Aristotelian scholasticism was fully developed in the Arab world; and Ibn Rushd (Averroes), the Arab "Commentator" of Aristotle, has been recognized by a great Arabist and a priest of the Church of Rome, Asin y Palacios, as the true forerunner of the Angelic Doctor, Thomas Aquinas. Another pinnacle of Western thought, *The Divine Comedy*, is permeated with Arabic thought and imagery.

The impact of the Arabs upon Medieval Europe was a leaven which liberated the spirit and awakened the dormant creative impulse. When supremacy passed to the West, the ideals of the Arab-Moslem civilization were not superseded, but assimilated and developed. "Thus the western victory did not imply for mankind a change of purpose or direction, but simply a change in leadership."[59]

57. Carra de Vaux: *The Legacy of Islam,* p. 377.
58. Gardet: *Ibla,* 1944, pp. 3–40.
59. Sarton, *op. cit.,* II, 2.

CHAPTER IV

Eclipse

FROM the 7th to the 13th century, Arab society throbbed with a vitality and creativeness that embraced every aspect of life. Arab capabilities found fruitful and abundant expression in religion, philosophy, science, art, and all other facets of civilization. Throughout these hundreds of years the Arabs were in the full stream of world events. And in the endeavor of mankind to reach goals of universal value, they were in the vanguard.

There followed a long period of stagnation during which the Arabs not only marked time but even lost touch with the creative and liberal values in their own tradition. Various causes have been offered to explain the quiescence and retrogression which befell Arab society close upon the age of exuberant creativeness.

The rise and fall of civilizations is a common phenomenon in history. It would seem that every civilization has its limits. Once they are reached, a younger society picks up the torch and continues the course until in due time its vitality ebbs away and a new and vigorous people resumes the human effort.

At any rate, the intellectual leadership and pre-eminence which Arab society had held during the greater part of the Middle Ages passed in the 13th century to Europe. From then on Europe progressed from strength to greater strength and from conquest to further conquest in the realm of thought. The Renaissance, the Reformation, the age of explorations and the discovery of the New World, the opening up of Asia and Africa, the Industrial Revolution, the triumph of Reason and Enlightenment over dogma and tradition, and the conquests of science and technology prepared and equipped western society for the position of dominance which it has held over the modern world.

Within Arab society, catastrophes succeeded one another. The Mongol invasion which broke upon the Moslem world in the middle of the 13th century battered the framework of society. The devastation it wrought is related by contemporary Arab historians with horror and sorrow. In Iraq, civil government broke down, and irrigation works collapsed. The bedouins, ever watchful for the weakening of authority, rose and added to the havoc. Baghdad, the city of culture and wealth, went up in smoke, and the fair cities and lands of Syria were laid waste. Schools and libraries, the nurseries of intellectual life, shared the fate of the cities which they adorned. Books were burned or thrown into the rivers. It is said, with very evident exaggeration, that the books dumped into the Tigris at Baghdad formed a bridge over which people walked from one bank of the river to the other.

During the next century, another scourge in the form of the Black Death swept twice over the Moslem countries, leaving a trail of misery in its wake. At the turn of the century, yet another visitation descended upon the survivors, no less appalling than the plague: Timulang and a second wave of Mongol hordes. The material basis of life was shaken not only by the wreckage of towns and farms, and the depletion of the population, but perhaps even more permanently by the deportation of skilled artisans and craftsmen to Samarkand, the Mongol capital in Central Asia. Age-old industries were left behind to languish for want of the skilled hand.

The Arabs partially recovered from the shock of the Mongol invasions, and the Mongols themselves settled down and gradually set up an ordered society which respected and encouraged arts and sciences. The *Pax Mongolia,* which covered China and all the lands westward to the Caucasus, contributed to material prosperity and resulted in a new efflorescence of trade and industry. With this Mongol world, the Arabs had close relations.

Yet even more devastating than the visitations which came from without was the drying up of the creative and adventurous spirit within Arab society itself. The keen intellectual curiosity which characterized the preceding period, the passionate and untiring search for knowledge, and the joy of adventure were smothered under a hard crust of dogma and fundamentalism. Free thought was banished, traditionalism reigned in its place. The unhampered pursuit of truth was branded as ungodly; the bolder and more adventurous of the thinkers of an earlier age were relegated to obscurity, and men's minds were set on the compilation of compendiums and commentaries on matters already known and not of the greatest consequence to human progress, instead of being applied to the fruitful task of breaking new paths of knowledge.

Arab society, however, was able to muster enough strength to expel the Mongols and Crusaders from its midst. After the expulsion of the foreign invaders, Egypt emerged as the strongest Arab state. Yet Egypt was exhausted by incessant warring among its rulers, the Mamelukes. The state, under the Mamelukes, seemed to have no reason for existence, and no occupation, other than war. The land itself was parceled out among the princes of this warring hierarchy and their retainers. Thus the state became a conglomeration of fiefs in the grip of overlords who constantly fought and dispossessed one another. Society on the level of the rulers was one of despoilment and pitched enmity, and to the common man it generally meant insecurity and oppression.

Still it would be incorrect to take an entirely somber view of this period. Life did not come to a standstill; it flowed on, at a slow tempo to be sure, and with waning vigor. Some phases indicating continued activity deserve to be noted.

While the rural population toiled in the feudal estates of the Mamelukes and was oppressed and insecure, urban life in Egypt was by contrast relatively prosperous and free. The relative safety and prosperity in the towns is largely due to the organization of the urban population in guilds or corporations whose protection and control embraced all classes of town dwellers. Contemporary authors and travelers testify to urban prosperity in this period. The 14th-century traveler Ibn Batuta, the 15th-century historian of Egypt Al-Makrizi, those stories of the *Arabian Nights* which belong to the Mameluke period, and numerous other accounts describe the busy markets and bazaars and the towns teeming with commercial and industrial activity.

The 13th to the 15th centuries were a time of very active and extensive trade from which the Arabs, as intermediaries between India and China on the one hand and Europe on the other, derived great wealth. Until the end of the 15th century they continued to command the Indian Ocean. Their ships busily plied its waters and were a familiar sight in its ports. When Vasco da Gama made his voyage to India in 1497, it was an Arab pilot, Ahmed Ibn Majid, who showed him the way. If the trade of the East came by land, a large part of it passed through Iraq on its way to the Syrian ports from which it was shipped to Europe. When it came by sea, as the bulk of it did, it touched the Arabian Peninsula at Aden and sometimes at Jedda, and was transshipped in Egypt where European traders picked it up. Commercial relations with Europe, especially with the Italian republics, were at their height. The merchant fleets of Venice and Genoa, Pisa, Amalfi, and other city-states competed feverishly for the trade of the Levant. The French cities Marseilles, Montpellier, Narbonne, and others, came in for their share of the lucrative enterprise. Spain did likewise. Her kings concluded commercial treaties with the Sultans of Egypt. In the eastern Mediterranean trade was exchanged with Cyprus and the Byzantine Empire.

This was also a time of intense industrial activity comprising, among other industries, weaving, metal-work, pottery, glassware, carpets, leather, and paper. Industry continued to be an art, and in all its lines produced objects of lasting beauty and worth. Many fine products of the Moslem minor arts belong to this period.

Architecture flourished. The Mamelukes were great builders, and had the means with which to gratify their desire for lasting monuments. Some magnificent mosques in Cairo were built in this age. Many of them were *madaris*—university mosques. This building activity kept up to the end of the 18th century.

The tradition of learning continued unbroken. In Egypt a school of history and religious studies flourished whose output was enormous. To Suyuti alone are ascribed 560 works. They ranged over a variety of subjects, Koran, Hadith, language, history, law, and philosophy, and were read throughout the Moslem world from India to Morocco. Those that have survived are 316 in number and include volumes of considerable size. Of the historians, Makrizi is the most celebrated for his painstaking researches and, on the whole, accurate description of the life of his time. Two famous works were written on the administration of Egypt, the *Zubdat Kashf al-Mamalik* by Al-Zahiri and Kalkashandi's 14 volume *Subh al-A'sha*. These sources give an impressive picture of the workings of government in the Mameluke period.[1]

This was the age of popular literature. The *Arabian Nights*, of various origins and dates, received their final form at this time. The romance of Antar, the desert hero, and the cycle of stories relating the adventures and heroic deeds of the Hilali tribes, together with the fables of Luqman, the pre-Islamic Arab Aesop, attained great popularity, making the story-teller a popular figure and his art a much appreciated accomplishment.

Another evidence of continued vitality is the expansion of Islam into Indonesia and the Malay Peninsula, and its penetration further into East and West Africa. Islam came into these regions with the

1. H. A. R. Gibb: *Arabic Literature, An Introduction*, 1926, pp. 105–106.

merchants who transmitted their culture with their wares and were diligent propagators of their faith.[2]

During this period, North Africa was an important center of Arab civilization. Its chief cities, Tunis, Fez, and Morocco, were comparable to centers of learning in the Arab countries of the East. The settlement of the Spanish Moors in North Africa after their expulsion from Spain stimulated cultural activities. One of the most important historical works was written by an Algerian as late as the 17th century. The author is Al-Makkari and his work, an immense historical and literary compilation, stands in the first rank of sources on Moslem Spain. Makkari's life, in keeping with the tradition of the scholar's calling, was one of constant travels to the sources of knowledge. After studying in Fez and Morocco, he went east, made the pilgrimage several times, and lectured at Mecca and Medina. He studied and taught in Cairo, Jerusalem, and Damascus. He finally settled in Cairo, where he died in 1632.

But the pride of North Africa and one of the greatest figures in Arab civilization is Ibn Khaldun who wrote his immortal *Prolegomena* near Tlemcen in Tunis in the latter part of the 14th century. Ibn Khaldun is the founder of the philosophy of history, and by 500 years the forerunner of Dürkheim and the creators of modern sociology. In the *Prolegomena* to his Universal History "he has conceived and formulated a philosophy of history which is undoubtedly the greatest work of its kind that has ever yet been created by any mind in any time or place."[3]

Another celebrated North African, the traveler Ibn Batuta, furnishes the most extensive source of information on the social and cultural life of the Moslem world in the post-Mongol period. His work embodies the accurate observations and an honest account of thirty years of travel within the Moslem world and beyond it.

* * *

Under the Turkish occupation which began early in the 16th century, the Arab countries steadily declined. The Turkish conquest coincided with the discovery of new trade routes which connected Europe directly with India and consequently reduced the role of the Arab countries as intermediaries in the lucrative trade of the East. This shift of the trade routes hit the townspeople hard

2. Gibb: *op. cit.*, p. 115.

3. Toynbee: *A Study of History*, III, 322. See also Charles Issawi: *Ibn Khaldun, An Arab Philosophy of History, Wisdom of the East*, John Murray, 1949.

and was one of the causes of the general decay under Turkish domination. Misrule was another. The oppression and rapacity of the rulers weighed heavily on the people, particularly the rural population who fled their villages to seek refuge in the towns. The countryside was depopulated and agriculture declined. The neglect of communications accompanied the economic dislocation and general misrule. All these elements together resulted in the sub-version of law and order and widespread insecurity.

Such was the state of decadence that at the time of Napoleon's invasion at the end of the 18th century Egypt had a population of barely two and a half million souls. Its cities had shrunk to the size of large villages. The famed industries of an earlier age were gone, and only a few rudimentary crafts survived in their place.

The intellectual life flowed along rigid paths from which there was no deviation. This traditional type of learning was pursued in a number of centers of which the thousand year old university-mosque Al-Azhar was the most celebrated. Al-Azhar has a unique place in Arab-Moslem culture, as guardian of the classical Arabic language and of Orthodox Islam. Since the Mongol invasion, Al-Azhar has been the chief center of learning in the Moslem world and has gathered within its precincts students from all over the wide world of Islam. About the time when Napoleon came to Egypt, Al-Azhar housed students from North Africa, Nubia, the Senegal country, and the Somali coast; from the holy cities of Mecca and Medina; from Yaman, Syria, and Iraq; from Turkey, Kurdistan, Khorasan, and Afghanistan, Java, Borneo, and India. And, of course, there were students from every part of Egypt.

In the holy cities Mecca and Medina, scores of thousands of Moslems gathered every year for the pilgrimage. Some of them stayed on and pursued religious studies for the rest of their lives. Well into the 19th century, circles of learning were a common sight at the Mosque of Mecca. The Dutch scholar and traveler Snouk Hurgronje, who lived in Mecca in 1884–85, was deeply impressed as he contemplated students of all the races of mankind gathered around professors of equally varied origins.

This was a long and dreary period, but it was not an age of slumber, nor was it terminated by a sudden awakening. It carried within it the seeds of regeneration and renewal, and nursed the reformers whose work and ideas deeply influenced the leavening of thought in the 19th century.

CHAPTER V

Stirrings within Arab Life

RELIGION provided the first promptings for the regeneration of society. Prior to the 19th century, all attempts at reform came from religious men. And during the 19th century, among all the forces and currents working for renewal, the religious reformers were the most influential.

This was natural enough. Religion, although it had lost much of its original purity and power, was still a strong force, perhaps the strongest, in men's lives. Among the men of religion, many had succumbed to the vices of their age; those of stronger metal, few to be sure, held fast to the dignity and duty of their calling. They stood without fear in the face of rulers, chastised them for their evil doings, and gave brave counsel regarding the duty and obligations of the ruler to the people.

A religious reformer of far-reaching influence came from Najd in Central Arabia. He was Mohammad ibn abd-al-Wahhab, founder of the Wahhabi doctrine. Abd-al-Wahhab lived in the 18th century and obtained his education in the traditional way, traveling far and wide in search of knowledge. His travels took him to Medina, Basra, Baghdad, Kurdistan, Hamadhan, Isfahan, and Qumm. Having studied theology, philosophy, and Sufism, he returned to his native province to preach the renovation of Islam. He preached a return to the faith in its original purity and simplicity, and the discarding of the innovations which had crept into it and, with the passage of time, had accumulated to the extent of obliterating its true form and meaning. His teaching aimed at the purification of the faith and the regeneration of the believer. It is comparable to the Protestant Reformation which also believed itself to be an attempt to return to the simplicity of early Christian times.

Though the Wahhabis, in their uncompromising creed, branded all other Moslems as unbelievers, and were in turn stigmatized as heretics, yet the revitalizing influence of Wahhabism gradually spread beyond the Arabian Peninsula, and its leavening effect was felt throughout the Moslem world.

Wahhabism reached India through Sayyid Ahmad who made the pilgrimage to Mecca in 1822, came under the influence of Abd-al-Wahhab's teaching, and returned to India to preach the new doctrine. The Ahmadyya movement has been a considerable force in Indian Islam.

Another religious leader who became acquainted with Wahhabism while on a pilgrimage to Mecca was Sidi Mohammad ibn Ali-al-Senussi, the Algerian. On his return from Arabia he settled in Cyrenaica where he founded the Senussi order, a religious brotherhood, and set up a theocratic state. In a time when the mind was cramped by *taklid*, the uncritical acceptance of authority, Senussi sounded anew the call to *ijtihad*, the exertion of personal effort to arrive at the truth. The Senussis have been the dominant element in the recent history of Cyrenaica.

Wahhabism also influenced the religious reform movement in Egypt through Mohammad Abdu, who made a strong plea for a return to the sources of religion and the reopening of the door of *ijtihad* closed by weak-minded ulema (religious leaders) who were willing to submit blindly to authority.

❋   ❋   ❋

The impact of Europe introduced new elements and quickened the pace of reform. The impact came with a shock when Napoleon invaded Egypt. The Mameluke army went out to meet the French. It was their first encounter with a modern army, far more effectively trained and equipped than they were. The Mamelukes were good fighters, and faced the invader with confidence and pride. However, the encounter soon turned into a disastrous rout. It was evident that superior training and arms carried the day.

But Napoleon's initial victory was offset by the resistance of the townspeople. Napoleon sought to win the Egyptians by claiming that he had come to expel the Mamelukes, foreigners to Egypt, and to establish an Arab state. He spoke of Egypt's glorious past and its great future possibilities. To this effect he distributed statements printed on the Arabic press which he had brought with him from France. But the people were not swayed by Napoleon's declarations. The Mamelukes, and their overlords the Turks, were Moslems and, therefore, not thought of as foreigners in an age when secular nationalism was still unknown.

Religious leaders were prominent in organizing and directing the people's struggle against the French. The combined forces of local resistance, the armies sent by the Sultan, and British navy and land forces—England having concluded an alliance with the Sultan against Napoleon—succeeded in driving the French out.

Napoleon had pinned high hopes on the conquest of Egypt. The successful outcome of the invasion was to make France the mistress of the Mediterranean, place at her disposal the wealth of Egypt, and undermine the power of England by threatening the route to India.

That Napoleon attached great importance to the Egyptian campaign is evident from his preparations for it. They were not only military, but included assembling a large staff of scientists entrusted with the work of surveying the country and studying its climate, topography, mineral resources, plant and animal life, historical monuments, and whatever else was pertinent to a thorough knowledge of the land and its potentialities.

The Scientific Mission included an array of distinguished experts. Among them were mathematicians, astronomers, geographers, geologists, mineralogists, chemists, botanists, zoologists, physicians, engineers, sculptors, musicians, and literary men. They were provided with a library and a collection of scientific instruments.

Napoleon put the scientists to work soon after his arrival in Egypt. He founded the Institute d'Égypte on the model of the Institute de France. Its members were the outstanding scientists of the mission and the ranking officers of the army who had a mastery of some branch of science. The purpose of the Institute was to advance knowledge about Egypt through studies and publications. It was divided into four sections, dealing respectively with mathematics, physical sciences, political economy, and arts and literature. The researches of the Institute are preserved in its monumental publication in several volumes, *Description d'Égypte*.

The scientific work was the most effective part of Napoleon's campaign. A number of the scientists remained in Egypt after the departure of Napoleon and his army, and helped in the work of modernization begun with vigor by Mohammad Ali. The Institute d'Égypte has survived to the present day.

With Mohammad Ali a new age dawned upon Egypt. Favorable

circumstances cleared his path to a great career, and his exceptional talents did the rest.

An Albanian soldier, Mohammad Ali, had come in 1801 with
the Turkish army to fight Napoleon. He witnessed the clash among
the various elements bidding for power in Egypt. He saw the disintegration of the Mamelukes, brought about by their incessant
fighting and plotting against one another, and by the arbitrariness
and rapacity of their rule which inflicted so much harm upon the
people. The Turks were weak and corrupt and remote from the
inhabitants of the country. Their constant quarrels with the Mamelukes added to the weakness of both.

There was a third element, and that was the people themselves.
We often hear that they were the victims of all sorts of exactions
and ill-treatment which they usually endured with patience and
resignation. We seldom see the other side of the picture in which
the people appear taking part in important events and at times
determining their outcome.

We have seen how among religious men there were always some
who bravely defended the people against injustice and tyranny.
The common people, on occasion, organized demonstrations, and
openly scoffed at and threatened their rulers. Tradesmen, artisans,
and other classes and groups of the town population were organized in powerful guilds, subject to their own rules and regulations
and conducted according to old inherited traditions. The guilds
had wide authority over their members. In some ways they were
autonomous units within the state, and were feared and respected
by the government. The townspeople made and possessed all kinds
of arms. They took part in the wars against the Crusaders and the
Mongols.

At the time of Napoleon's invasion, and later when the British
invaded Egypt in 1807, the people of Cairo and Alexandria and
other towns defended themselves against the invaders. The usual
manner in which defense was organized was for each guild to
collect money from its members and provide them with arms. The
richer members volunteered to pay for those who had no means,
and all exerted a united effort.

It was the people who, having rebelled against the Mamelukes
and the Turkish Wali (Governor), deposed the latter in 1805 and
raised Mohammad Ali to the position of governor of Egypt. The
pact which the leaders of the people made with Mohammad Ali is
evidence of an awakened sense of their importance and responsi-

bility. His acceptance of this pact shows to what extent he felt he needed, however temporarily, the people's support. The pact demanded of the Governor that he should rule in accordance with the precepts of the Sharia, that he should suppress injustice and unlawful practices, and that in all his actions he should seek the advice of the people's leaders. If he should fail to observe these conditions they would be free to depose him.

The appointment of the Wali was the Sultan's right and prerogative. It was unheard of that common people should depose the Sultan's viceroy and put one of their own choosing in his place. The deposed Wali, when informed of the people's decision said: "I am appointed by the Sultan and will not be deposed by order of the fellahin." But the Sultan bowed before the people's choice. The firman or royal decree, issued in Constantinople and investing Mohammad Ali with the governorship of Egypt, clearly stated that he was appointed to this office because the ulema (religious leaders) and the people wanted him.

Mohammad Ali's rivals continued their plotting. The Turks on the one hand, and the Mamelukes supported by the British on the other, sought to depose him. Great Britain, chief opponent of Mohammad Ali in later years, was even at this time uneasy about him. Her representatives in Constantinople negotiated with the Porte for his removal, and her emissaries to the Mamelukes entered into an agreement with them whereby, following the deposition of Mohammad Ali, the Turkish Pasha would be governor in name only, while authority would rest with the leader of the Mamelukes, Al-Alfi, Britain's ally. The Mamelukes attacked Cairo. The Sultan issued a firman deposing Mohammad Ali and nominating a new Wali. But Mohammad Ali's constant watchfulness, the continued support of the people, and the ever present dissension in the ranks of the Mamelukes, foiled these plots.

In this crisis Mohammad Ali had recourse to the people's leaders. They responded by issuing a proclamation summoning resistance against the tyrannous Mamelukes, and loyal support to Mohammad Ali whose conduct and acts they commended. Mohammad Ali sent this proclamation to Constantinople, accompanied with a handsome present or bribe. A firman came back reinstating him. In this as in the previous firman, the Sultan expressly stated that the people's support won for Mohammad Ali confirmation in his post.

Mohammad Ali was determined to eliminate the Mamelukes as

a force in Egypt's affairs. He fought and defeated them in the provinces. Those who were in Cairo he invited to a banquet in the Citadel and there had them massacred. With the destruction of the Mamelukes thus complete, Mohammad Ali was ready to direct his energy to the task of building a strong and modern state in Egypt.

Mohammad Ali's view of the state was paternalistic. He considered himself fully competent to run its affairs, and once firmly established, he brooked no interference with his actions. His remarkable abilities eminently fitted him to lead a state emerging from medievalism. His energy was untiring and was backed by perseverance. He was ever vigilant, and personally watched and supervised the many projects and plans which he launched. He toured the provinces for inspection and visited the numerous works of construction to see for himself how his orders were being carried out. Such was his vigor that at the age of seventy he made a long and arduous tour through the Sudan. His will was indomitable. Once he was determined on a course, there was no hesitancy or wavering about his actions and decisions. When he was considering the damming of the Nile at the Delta, the engineers, awed by the immensity of the project, expounded the difficulties which it entailed. To their objections Mohammad Ali made the answer: "This is a struggle between me and the Great River, and I shall come out of the struggle victorious."

His interests were keen and broad. He was ever eager to learn no matter what the source. An illiterate until the age of forty, he began to learn how to read and write after he had assumed full responsibility for governing Egypt. Though he was brought up in the old Ottoman tradition with no experience of the outside world, he grasped the importance of European progress, and worked feverishly to adopt European ways and methods. Throughout his long rule he sent missions of young Egyptians to study in Europe, appointed European experts to direct and manage his various enterprises, opened Egypt to European merchants and businessmen, and often spent his leisure hours conversing with Europeans, trying to learn whatever he could from them. The keynote of his life and work was discipline and organization, which he introduced into and impressed upon the government, the army, and other institutions and enterprises of the state.

To Mohammad Ali's mind, a strong army was the main support

of the state. Upon it also depended his own security and the permanence of his position. The experience of the Mamelukes and the Turks with the French army had opened his eyes to the need for adopting modern training and modern arms.

The Egyptian army created by Mohammad Ali was modeled upon the French army and trained by French officers. Its creation necessitated the introduction and development of industries for the manufacture of arms and ammunition. Several factories for cannons, muskets, and gun-powder were built; some of them were comparable to the most advanced arms factories in Europe in their organization and quality of output.

A strong navy seconded the army. Shipyards were constructed at Bulak in Cairo, and in Alexandria as well. Mohammad Ali was attached to his navy and felt a deep sorrow when it was destroyed in 1827 by the combined fleets of Great Britain, France, and Russia in the battle of Navarino during the Greco-Turkish war. A few years later the lost navy had been replaced by one constructed by Egyptian workers in Egyptian shipyards. Egypt in the time of Mohammad Ali was the strongest sea-power in the eastern Mediterranean.

The educational system established by Mohammad Ali was primarily designed to serve the interests of the army and provide the government with trained personnel.

A system of elementary, secondary, and technical schools was instituted. The educational pyramid started from the apex with the founding of the technical schools. The reason for this inverted procedure lay in Mohammad Ali's hurry to get trained officials. The students of the technical schools came from Al-Azhar. Later, secondary schools were established to prepare students for the technical schools, and last came the elementary schools.

The School of Medicine, the first technical school founded, opened in 1827 with a hundred students chosen from Al-Azhar and a teaching staff of eight physicians, all Frenchmen and officers in the army. The professors were assisted by interpreters who attended the courses and translated the lectures into Arabic. The program of the Paris Faculty of medicine was followed by the Cairo School. The same books were used as texts, and the course was six years as in Paris. The school was provided with a hospital, a library, a museum, and a botanical garden for medical plants and herbs.

Other schools dealing with the medical sciences, a School of Midwifery, a School of Pharmacy, and a Veterinary School, were founded within a decade.

The first medical mission, composed of twelve students, sailed for Paris in 1832 accompanied by Clot Bey, the director of the Medical School. The students spent eight years of study in Paris. Upon their return, some were appointed professors in the School of Medicine, others were placed in the army and hospitals. These first medical pioneers assiduously labored over the urgent task of translation. Within two decades several scores of important medical books were done into Arabic.

For the purpose of translation, a special school was founded in 1836. It was among the most interesting institutions established by Mohammad Ali. Under its enthusiastic and diligent director, Rifa'a Tahtawi, the School of Languages, as it was called, became the most important center for the dissemination of culture and learning in Egypt. Scores of books on a variety of subjects were translated, making the rich content of European thought available in the Arabic language.

Another important cultural institution was the Bulak Press, founded in 1821. Since the French carried back to France the Arabic press which they had brought with them at the end of the 18th century, the Bulak Press was thus the oldest press in the Arab world.[1]

Other technical institutions included schools of engineering, mineralogy, industrial arts, military and naval schools. A government department, the bureau of schools, was established in 1837 to supervise the working of the school system.

European learning was sought in the countries of Europe itself where successive missions of students were sent, beginning as early as 1813 and continuing until 1847, close to the end of Mohammad Ali's rule. Three hundred nineteen young Egyptians in all went to Europe on these missions. They studied medicine, law, civil administration, physical sciences, chemistry, mathematics, engineering, mechanics, printing, mineralogy, agriculture and irrigation, the textile and dye industries, military science and the manufacture of arms, navigation and shipbuilding. Most of the students were sent to France; the rest studied in England, Italy, and Austria. Mohammad Ali watched anxiously the work of this young brood of

1. A press with Arabic characters was set up in Aleppo in 1702, according to Hitti, *History of Syria*, p. 677.

potential experts. He required them to send regular reports of the progress of their studies, and personally read the reports and corresponded with the students. He told them exactly and emphatically what he expected of them, rebuked them when there was cause for rebuke, and urged them strongly to acquire all the knowledge they could and not waste a moment while they had the privilege of being in Paris, the city of "learning and light."

One of the fascinating personalities included in these missions was Rifa'a Tahtawi who accompanied as Imam the mission of forty students to Paris in 1826. Rifa'a came from a poor family in Upper Egypt and had gone through the traditional religious education terminating in Al-Azhar. Paris opened a new world before his eyes, a world which filled him with admiration and enthusiasm, and yet did not upset his values or loosen his traditional moorings. In his prodigious diligence and passion for study, he was a student entirely after Mohammad Ali's heart. Rifa'a plunged wholeheartedly into his work, reading and writing and translating incessantly. In Paris he met a number of its outstanding men of learning, among them the Baron De Sacy, leading orientalist of the time. He visited the various institutions and historical monuments of the French capital. He recorded his observations in a delightful account which reveals him as a keen and accurate observer, endowed with insight and an open mind. Rifa'a had a decided sympathy for liberal movements and constitutional government. He describes with enthusiasm the Paris revolution of 1830 and the triumph of the middle class. After his return to Egypt, Rifa'a maintained his habit of working persistently and with enthusiasm. He was an ardent patriot and understood patriotism as a life of service to the country.

Mohammad Ali attended to the material prosperity of the country with characteristic energy and ability. He developed agriculture, backbone of the country's economy, by the extension of irrigation and the introduction of new crops. The irrigation system was improved and expanded. Old works were repaired, new canals opened, barrages and regulators were constructed across the Nile in the Delta region. Trees were planted in great numbers, among them the olive and mulberry. Several hundred experts in silkworm raising were brought from Syria and Lebanon to launch sericulture in Egypt. Cotton, known to Egypt in earlier times, had been neglected and only a poor quality had survived. Mohammad Ali introduced new varieties, and since his time cotton has become the chief crop of Egypt. The cultivation of indigo, sugar-cane, and flax was expanded. These improvements resulted in a considerable increase in the country's wealth, and a marked growth of the population.[2] The same energy was directed to the development of industry. Machine industry was introduced, and modern, well-equipped factories were built. The arms factories, arsenals, ship-building and assembly yards held first place among the industrial projects of Mohammad Ali. Iron works were developed in the foundries which turned out looms, spinning jennies, carding machines, engine parts, and other machinery. A sugar refinery and a glass factory were set up in Alexandria. Textile factories handled all branches of the textile industry, woolen goods, silk, and cotton. There were forty-four cotton mills, some of them employing over a thousand workers. They absorbed one fourth of the cotton crop and supplied the home market with cheap goods. Locally manufactured cotton goods were exported to the Levant and the Balkans.

Egypt, throughout its long history, had been famed for its industries, but they had decayed in the general economic, political, and cultural deterioration which had preceded the 19th century. To revive and re-establish industry, Mohammad Ali brought to Cairo several hundred skilled artisans from Constantinople. He sent scores of young Egyptians to study the techniques of modern industry in Europe, and made European experts directors and managers of his industrial enterprises.[3] Trade also received an impetus as a result of the development of agriculture and industry, and because of the security which replaced the former chaos. The port of Alexandria was enlarged, Egyptian fleets plied the Red Sea and the Eastern Mediterranean, and the land route from Suez to Cairo was reopened and provided with stations along the way.

Mohammad Ali conceived an ambitious plan of an Arab state carved out of the Arab provinces of the Ottoman Empire, with himself at its head. He knew the weakness of the Government of Constantinople, and was well aware of the designs of the European powers on the moribund empire. As an Ottoman and a Moslem, and a man of great capabilities, Mohammad Ali deemed himself a worthy potential heir to at least part of the Ottoman dominions. At first he tried to render effective services to his suzerain, the Sultan, hoping that by his adequate and much needed support he

2. Crouchley: *The Economic Development of Modern Egypt*, p. 61.

3. Bonné: *State and Economics in the Middle East*, pp. 240–241; A. A. I. El-Gritly: *The Structure of Modern Industry in Egypt*, 1948, p. 364.

would earn the Sultan's gratitude and later recognition of his plans. Hence the Egyptian campaigns against the Wahhabis in Arabia and the wars against the Greeks when both Wahhabis and Greeks rebelled successfully against the Turks. But Mohammad Ali's power, instead of winning for him the good will of the Sultan, roused the latter's suspicion and fear. Conflict ensued and led to the wars of the eighteen thirties between the Governor of Egypt and the Porte. Mohammad Ali's eldest son, Ibrahim Pasha, led the campaigns. He easily drove the Turks out of Syria, won decisive victories over them in Anatolia itself, and was on his way to Constantinople when the European Powers intervened and called a halt to his victorious march.

Russia, ready to tear the Turkish Empire apart, offered her protection to the Sultan and sent her troops and battleships. Great Britain, anxious to obstruct Russia's designs and fearful of a youthful state in the eastern Mediterranean under an energetic and ambitious ruler, hurried to the support of the Porte and championed the maintenance of the integrity of the Ottoman Empire. War between Mohammad Ali and the Powers followed, and caused him the loss of Syria. In the treaty of London, signed in 1841, Turkey and the Powers recognized the autonomous and hereditary rule of Mohammad Ali over Egypt.

Mohammad Ali died in 1849, after having ruled Egypt for nearly half a century. In trying to estimate the significance of his rule it is well to keep in mind the spirit of his time and the circumstances which surrounded him.

Mohammad Ali was an autocratic ruler, motivated by strong personal ambitions. His wars in Asia and Africa and Europe were designed to secure him and his heirs power and glory and a permanent kingdom, but they exhausted Egypt and weighed heavily on the Egyptians. His economic policy was conceived primarily to assure the revenues needed for his military undertakings. Hence the monopoly imposed on practically all the resources of the country, whereby Mohammad Ali became the owner of the land and the only merchant and industrialist. Even his educational system was planned to meet the army's needs, and when military activity subsided, some of the schools were closed.

Mohammad Ali's wars failed to achieve the end for which they were waged, but they left a deep impression upon the Egyptian people. Service in the army evoked pride in the peasants and humble townsfolk. Victories over the Turks stirred their self-confidence.

Egyptian nationalism emerged out of the victories of peasants over their Turkish rulers.

The conquest of the Sudan opened up the country for exploration and contacts with the outside world. Khartum was founded and became the starting point for geographical expeditions. Three explorations were conducted during the time of Mohammad Ali. They studied unknown regions and prepared the way for the more extensive exploratory expeditions under Ismail.

The Egyptian campaigns in Syria were like a ferment which caused a great stir. The system of government was overturned. Modern regulations were introduced into the administration. Religious liberty was proclaimed, and adherents of the various religions were treated on a footing of equality. Democratic ideas were disseminated, and feudal chiefs were divested of their power. Improvements in agriculture were effected. Security prevailed, and trade revived. Facilities given to foreigners encouraged the coming of western merchants and missionaries. These opened schools which offered educational opportunities not available in the country. Although the Egyptian administration in Syria was short-lived and was a period of wars and rebellions, yet it fomented ideas and feelings which foreshadowed a new life.

Mohammad Ali was an admirer of European progress, and he eagerly sought to introduce European ways and methods into Egypt. He employed a large number of Europeans in all his enterprises, in the army, in education, in industry, in irrigation and other projects of construction. He also encouraged Europeans to settle in Egypt. But he never allowed Europeans to dictate to him. He was always master in his own house. European experts were employes like other government officials. Neither did he get entangled with foreign debts, much as his wars and development schemes required money. He was fully aware of the designs of European Powers on Egypt. When European financiers and diplomats approached him with regard to opening up the Suez canal, he answered that a canal cut across the isthmus of Suez would be another Bosphorus. He foresaw the international complications that were bound to follow, and rightly feared that with the opening of the Canal Egypt would pass under European control and his work would be undone. What he had the foresight and strength to forestall, his successors readily yielded.

CHAPTER VI

Cross Currents

URING the 19th century, Egypt loosened its ties with the Ottoman Empire and entered into closer relations with Europe. This course carried with it both advantages and dangers. On the one hand, Egypt was launched on the path of independence and the responsibilities which freedom entails, and in the process Egyptian nationalism came into being. Furthermore, Egypt had much to learn from Europe and could learn more freely if she was not tied to the cramping influence of the Porte. But on the other hand, the slackened ties to Turkey encouraged the designs of the European powers, and the reckless policy of Egypt's rulers in their eagerness to promote westernization prepared the way for European intervention, and eventually for the British occupation of Egypt.

Some aspects of modernization may be noted. Egypt was one of the first countries in the world to build a system of railroads. A network of telegraph lines was laid. Hundreds of bridges were built and thousands of miles of irrigation canals dug. The harbor of Alexandria was constructed. A million and a quarter acres were reclaimed from the desert and brought under cultivation. Improvements in irrigation and transport resulted in a marked increase in wealth and prosperity. Exports were double the value of imports, and included cotton, sugar, and grain.[1]

There were some noteworthy efforts in education. A number of schools—elementary, secondary, and technical—were founded. The first government school for girls was established in 1873. Foreign schools were opened under the auspices of various religious missions. The Public Library was founded in 1870, and the Geographical Society in 1875 for the purpose of promoting geographical science and exploration. Several printing presses were set up and made available the treasures of Arabic literature.

Egypt's progress was well thought of by contemporary Western

1. Rothstein: *Egypt's Ruin*, pp. 34–35; De Leon: *The Khedive's Egypt*, p. 119.

observers, among them De Leon, the American Consul General in Egypt. Writing about the public works constructed under Ismail, he describes them as "unequalled by any other country of quadruple the area and population of Egypt; and they have been of such a character as hereafter to enhance immensely the resources of prosperity of the country."[2] Of progress in education he says it "has been truly remarkable, and would be so considered in any country of the globe."[3] The *London Times* wrote in 1876: "Egypt is a marvellous instance of progress. She has advanced as much in seventy years as many other countries have done in five hundred."[4]

But modernization was accompanied by oppression of the people who paid with their sweat and blood for the public works. The prosperity evident in the reclamation of land, the increased production, and population growth, did not relieve the poverty and misery of the masses. Ismail borrowed recklessly from foreign financiers, and when hard pressed by his creditors, his government imposed heavy exactions upon the peasants. The misery in which the peasants toiled and lived roused their opposition to the regime responsible for this evil. During the 1870's a vigorous daily press appeared, and it attacked not only the European creditors and the Powers behind them, but assailed the principle of autocratic and irresponsible rule as well. Demands were raised for representative institutions. The presence of Afghani, the dynamic apostle of a reformed and invigorated Islam who arrived in Egypt in 1871, lent the movement moral and intellectual support. The promulgation of the Turkish Constitution in 1876 gave it further impetus. A Representative Assembly was convened in 1879. Its members considered themselves the spokesmen of the nation and the advocates of its rights.

After Mohammad Ali's death, foreign control steadily tightened its hold, culminating in British occupation in the year 1882.

European finance and business conceived plans far beyond Egypt's needs, plans which aimed at establishing the shortest and most convenient routes between Europe, which produced the finished products, and Africa and Asia, which provided the raw materials and the markets for Europe's goods. Hence the project for connecting the Mediterranean with the Red Sea, a project which Mohammad Ali had refused to countenance. A few years after his

2. De Leon, *op. cit.*, p. 368.
3. *Ibid.*, p. 160.
4. Rothstein, *op. cit.*, p. 34.

death a concession for opening the Suez Canal was granted to the French engineer De Lesseps. The inauguration of the Canal under Ismail was the occasion for the display of unrestrained extravagance, all the more glaring for the misery of the people whose sweat and blood made the canal possible. Once the canal was completed, it was bound to come under the control of Great Britain to assure the safety of the line guarded in the west and south by the British hold on Gibraltar and Bab-al-Mandeb respectively, and thus to safeguard imperial communications.

Mohammad Ali's successors lacked his qualities of mind and character. Mohammad Ali had used European experts because he recognized their technical superiority and his country's need for their services. But they were the servants of his ideas and projects. Under his successors, who had neither his capacity for work nor his shrewd insight and dominating personality, the Europeans became masters of the government and the country. Their influence reached its height under Ismail who, in his zeal for disseminating and promoting European ways in Egypt, spent a vast treasure and saddled his country with a heavy debt. His creditors were Europeans of a very unscrupulous type. They took advantage of Egypt's financial embarrassment to interfere in her affairs, promoting their illegitimate gains and growing fat on the land and its people. Economic confusion was the prelude to the loss of political control. The Powers forced upon Ismail two European ministers, one British, the other French, and obtained his acquiescence to their privileged position in the cabinet, with the power to annul any cabinet decision or action they did not approve. Thus the government came under the control of the British and French ministers whose chief interest lay in securing the necessary funds to pay the creditors. The Representative Assembly, limited though it was in power, was nevertheless a source of worry to the European ministers because of the opposition to their plans among its members. Accordingly, the Assembly was prorogued. These high handed measures of the foreign ministers called forth strong resentment. The movement for constitutional reform grew in strength, and was supported by Ismail as a counterweight to European interference. A constitution was drafted which stipulated ministerial responsibility before parliament, but before it was promulgated Ismail was deposed by the creditor powers.

Ismail's successor, Toufik, was a weakling who could not check the notorious influence and pressure of foreign bankers and money-lenders backed by their respective consuls in Egypt. A nationalist agitation was set afoot demanding a constitution that would provide safeguards for the country against the ever tightening grip of foreign exploitation. The Khedive wavered between submission to the Powers and granting the demands of the nationalists. The representatives of Great Britain and France sought to steady him by assuring him of the support of their respective governments should trouble break out. They urged him not to part with any of his power since they exercised that power themselves, using him as a mere puppet. When finally the convening of an assembly was forced by the nationalists, and a constitution was drafted, the European Consuls stood for reaction and demanded that the chamber be deprived of the right to debate or vote on the budget. The national movement, led by Arabi, represented the enlightened and liberal elements in Egypt. It was a struggle for freedom from foreign exploitation and an attempt to extract a constitution guaranteeing the people's rights and safeguarding their interests from a ruler who had become the helpless instrument for foreign and native reactionary intrigue. "It cannot be too strongly emphasized that the National movement of 1881 was essentially a fellah (peasant) movement, having for its object the emancipation of the fellahin."[5] That it expressed the wishes and needs of the people was made clear by the outburst of popular enthusiasm on the day when it was announced that the Khedive had promised to grant a constitution. A cry of jubilation rang throughout Egypt, and in Cairo strangers embraced each other on the streets.[6]

Sir Wilfred Scawon Blunt, who was in Egypt in 1881–2, knew Arabi well and sympathized fully with Egyptian aspirations. He describes Arabi as a liberal of broad humanity, possessed by an earnest desire for reform. His sincerity was above suspicion. He had no hatred for the British and the French; rather, his feeling for England was one of cordiality. He admired equally Byron's struggle for Greek independence and Gladstone's liberalism. Blunt's wife, Lady Anne, was Byron's granddaughter and had inherited her ancestor's enthusiasm and support for the cause of freedom. She accompanied her husband to Egypt and, like him, sympathized with the Egyptian movement. Blunt wrote: "It seemed to us, in presence of the events of 1881–2, that to champion the cause of

5. Blunt: *Secret History of the British Occupation of Egypt*, p. 110.
6. *Ibid.*, pp. 116–117.

Arabian liberty would be as worthy an endeavour as had been that for which Byron had died in 1827."[7]

The program of the National Party drawn up in 1881 is remarkable for its moderation and liberal spirit. The attitude to the Khedive was one of allegiance if his rule was just and subject to the law. With regard to the European Powers, the necessity of financial control by them was recognized, provided it was a temporary control. The heavy foreign debt, incurred at exorbitant interest rates, was accepted as a matter of national honor. The injustice of exempting Europeans living in Egypt from taxes and observance of the law of the country was to be remedied, but not by violence. The Nationalists had no quarrel with Europeans in Egypt if they were willing to conform to the laws and bear their share of responsibility to the state. The National Party was a political, not a religious organization, within its ranks were men of various creeds. It made no distinction on the basis of race or religion, but held that all men were brothers and all were entitled to equal rights. It was realized that a passive attitude could not secure liberty. To achieve freedom the Egyptians were resolved to complete their national education through the Parliament, freedom of the press, and the dissemination of knowledge among all the people. The last paragraph of their program deserves to be quoted in full; "Finally the general end of the National Party is the intellectual and moral regeneration of the country by a better observance of the law, by increased education, and by political liberty, which they hold to be the life of the people. They trust in the sympathy of those of the nations of Europe which enjoy the blessing of self-government to aid Egypt in gaining for itself that blessing; but they are aware that no nation ever yet achieved liberty except by its own endeavours; and they are resolved to stand firm in the position they have won, trusting to God's help if all other be denied them."[8]

It was at this time when Egypt was moving toward liberal reforms that England and France threatened intervention. Their violent attitude provoked Arabi's rebellion and diverted the course of the national movement from peaceful, constitutional development to war.[9] Vicious statements were made at the time in the British Parliament and circulated in the press, representing Arabi and his followers as fanatical, anti-Christian anarchists. This view,

7. *Ibid.*, p. 6.
8. *Ibid.*, pp. 383–5.
9. Khon: *Nationalism and Imperialism in the East*, p. 181.

however, was not shared by the editor of the *Times*, an Arab scholar of distinction who had a broad knowledge of Eastern affairs and readily grasped the truth of the situation. In 1881 he championed in his great paper the cause of Egyptian freedom. Not so the Liberal Premier Gladstone, who thundered forth his anger at the Egyptians struggling for their freedom. Thus British Liberalism lost the opportunity to sponsor and guide the infant Liberal movement in Egypt, whose leader was a peasant sprung from the heart of the people. The British at that time found it easier to bombard than to befriend. On the eve of the bombardment of Alexandria, May 19, 1882, the Swiss Consul wrote to Blunt: "My heart of an old Swiss patriot bleeds now at the most unjust of all international interventions. The country is entirely united in favor of its honest leader, sprung, like the fellahin, from the *limon du Nil* (the black mud of the Nile). The Egyptian people has loyally accepted its debt contracted for it by an unscrupulous despot—a peaceful revolution has been accompanied by and with the will of the nation. Not a single act unbecoming a scrupulous government has taken place during the great change effected. But Europe, interested more in the dealers in stocks and shares than in the aspirations of a people, sends her fleets. Why? Because the Chamber of Representatives found it proper to claim the right of discussing the Budget."[10]

A British fleet bombarded Alexandria and a British army defeated Arabi's peasants. Great Britain occupied Egypt in 1882, avowing openly that the occupation was a temporary measure. But British troops are in Egypt to the present day.

Political developments and the fight for constitutional government during the latter part of the 19th century were accompanied by efforts for religious and intellectual reform. The central figure and prime mover of the reform was Jamal-ed-Din al-Afghani. Though not an Egyptian nor an Arab, Afghani influenced like no other man the minds and lives of men who later became the leaders of modern Egypt.

Afghani, as his name denotes, came from Afghanistan where his family held a high political and social position. He traveled extensively through the Moslem world, and lived in Persia, India, Hijaz, and Constantinople. He came to Egypt in 1871 and stayed until 1879. This stay, forcibly terminated by the Khedive at the behest of the Powers, was a blessing to Egypt, for in these years

10. Blunt, *op. cit.*, pp. 213–214.

the seeds of freedom were sown by a man who had a burning passion for liberty and fought for its triumph wherever he went.

Afghani preached freedom not only from foreign rule, but also and even more from the obstructive force of rigid and wornout beliefs and practices. He struggled for freedom of thought, and urged the open and fearless proclamation of liberal ideas. He condemned tyranny and oppression whatever their form or source, equally denouncing Moslem rulers for betraying their trust by oppressing their subjects, and European imperialism for exploiting the peoples of Asia.

Afghani's vigorous and broad mind grasped the problems and conditions of the world around him. He deeply felt the decline of the Moslem peoples and worked for their spiritual and moral regeneration. He believed that spiritual rebirth was the basis of social and cultural progress, and the fundamental condition for the achievement by Moslems of their political emancipation and participation once again in the creative work of civilization.

Afghani was a religious reformer, an enlightened thinker, and a political leader.

Religious reform, to Afghani, meant a thorough understanding of Islam and a sincere conformity to its truths and fundamental principles. These truths, when fully grasped, are not at variance with scientific truths. Religion, then, is not a hindrance to scientific progress, but rather an impetus to the search for truth.

Intellectual reform was to be achieved by the liberation of the mind and its unhampered pursuit of truth. The free mind is in harmony with the world. This harmony restores balance to man, frees him of perplexity and doubt, and clears and illumines his path. And finally, political reform would follow as a necessary consequence of the reformed mind and spirit.

Afghani had a compelling personality which impressed itself upon all who knew him. His presence radiated strength and inspiration, and drew to him a large number of disciples who eagerly listened to his message. He disseminated his ideas by teaching and writing, by public conversation and discourse. Regular courses were held in his home where the Moslem classics were taught. In these courses he sought to broaden the intellectual horizon of the students, to open new avenues before them leading to a better understanding of the world, and to train them to seek knowledge and truth courageously. He aimed at forming thinking men, imbued with wisdom and discernment.

His more popular teaching was conveyed through talks in his home, in the houses of his friends, or in the coffee house. None was excluded from these talks, Afghani spoke alike to the intellectual elite and the man on the street, and all were captivated by his enthusiasm, strength of conviction, and courage.

In these discourses, as in all his work, his keynote was the achievement of freedom from bondage in all its forms. Afghani strove to create an informed public opinion, aware of its rights and duties. Such an awakened opinion would carry with it the belief in the people's right to rule themselves, and the determination to attain this right. Only then can representative institutions have meaning and significance, because they would not be the gift of the ruler bestowed from above, but well out of the conscious need of the people and their urge to share in the shaping of their destiny.

Afghani inspired a school of writers. He encouraged promising young men to found newspapers and infused them with ideas of national significance. Around him the nucleus of Arab journalism was formed and writers were trained to espouse the cause of the people and the nation.

His influence left a deep impression upon the trend of literature which until his time had been mainly occupied with praising princes and rulers however unpraiseworthy they might be. Afghani taught that the primary aim of literature was to serve the people by expressing their needs and defending their rights. A new literature developed which looked to the people for its matter and content, and dwelt on the subject of the people's rights and the duties of the ruler.

The rulers for their part found Afghani dangerous. They could not tolerate a man who taught the people to look upon themselves as the source of the ruler's power and wealth, who pointed out sharply and repeatedly the tyranny of rulers and the misery and poverty of the subjects, and who urged and incited the people to brace themselves and emerge from darkness into light.[11]

The forces of darkness, native and foreign, demanded Afghani's expulsion from Egypt. The Council of Ministers, in ordering his banishment, accused him of corrupting the youth, an accusation reminiscent of the judgment passed upon Socrates.

The termination of his stay in Egypt did not end Afghani's work for Egypt and the Arab and Moslem world. He went to Europe where he visited London, and then settled in Paris. In both capi-

11. Ahmad Amin: Zu'ama al-Islah fi l' Asr al-hadith, Cairo, 1948, pp. 57–121.

tals he became acquainted with men prominent in intellectual and public life. In Paris he founded *Al-Urwat-al-Wuthka* (The Indissoluble Bond), an Arabic periodical whose purpose was to awaken the Moslems to the reality of their state and guide them to face the facts of the age in which they lived. Afghani was joined in Paris by Mohammad Abdu, his disciple and friend, who assumed a large share in editing *Al-Urwa.*

Mohammad Abdu, a religious reformer with liberal views, came from a peasant family of a village in the Delta. He had received the traditional religious education culminating in Al-Azhar. Two influences shaped his life. One was his Moslem heritage, the other the liberal philosophy of 19th century Europe. Ghazali, with his emphasis on the personal experience in religion and his insistence on the right to individual judgment, was a determining influence and a source of inspiration. The teachings of Mohammad Abd al-Wahhab, calling for a return to the purity of early Islam, won the adherence of Mohammad Abdu, but he toned down the rigor of Wahhabism by his rationalist and liberal tendencies. Of his contemporaries, three men had a lasting effect upon him. One was Shaikh Darwish who led him to mysticism and at the same time drew him to the people by encouraging him to preach and teach, thus launching him on his career of reform. The other was Shaikh Hassan al-Tawil, a distinguished mathematician and a man of rare intelligence, with a broad knowledge of men and books. Shaikh Hassan was a courageous and outspoken critic of what he considered wrong, and for his boldness he was expelled from his professorship at Dar-al-Ulum. Left penniless, he was supported by the owner of a native coffee-house. When he resumed his work, he handed over his salary to the coffee-house keeper to maintain both their families, an interesting side-light on human relationships in those days. And finally, the man who influenced Abdu most was Afghani himself, to whom he was bound in a devoted and life-long friendship.

Mohammad Abdu's energy and talents ranged over a wide field of activity. He taught at Al-Azhar, at Dar-al-Ulum, and at the School of Languages. Like his teacher Al-Afghani, he attracted devoted disciples, some of whom were destined for a distinguished life of public service. As judge he strove for equity and justice and the reform of the religious courts. Journalism also came within his scope. The *Official Journal* became under his direction a platform for the dissemination of liberal views and ideas of social and politi-

cal reform. In the general enthusiasm which swept the nation at
the time of Arabi's revolt, Mohammad Abdu joined the rebellion
and was exiled. For a time, he lived in Beirut and pursued his favorite profession of teaching. Later he joined Afghani in Paris
where he was fully occupied editing and writing for *Al-Urwa.*

Al-Urwat-al-Wuthka, although it appeared only for a few
months, was nevertheless a great stimulus to enlightened Arabs
and Moslems. While it severely rebuked the peoples of the East for
their failings, it allowed no room for despair, but pointed out that
the present weakness was a temporary state, bound to pass away
when the people roused themselves in the determination to live
fully in their heritage and face the challenge of life in the contemporary world. Al-Urwa sought to diffuse hope among its
readers, spread knowledge of trends in the surrounding world,
strengthen the bonds between the Moslem countries, and urge religious, social, and political reform.

Al-Urwa was fought by reactionary forces, both native and foreign. It was not allowed into the lands under Turkish rule. The
British forbade its entrance to Egypt and India and punished those
who received it. And so once more the forces of eastern reaction
and Western imperialism were in accord.

Returned from exile, Mohammad Abdu continued his mission
of reform. In the meantime new elements had entered into the
public life of Egypt. The British occupation was firmly established.
Mohammad Abdu sought to befriend rather than antagonize the
British, in order to win their support for his program of reform.
This aroused the enmity of the Khedive, an impetuous young man
who chafed under the restraining hand of Lord Cromer, Britain's
representative in Egypt, and who yet did not cooperate sincerely
with the national and liberal elements in the country. More formid-
able opposition came to Mohammad Abdu from the newly constituted National Party under its fiery leader Mustapha Kamel. While
Mohammad Abdu believed that emancipation from British rule
could come only through education and public enlightenment,
and worked towards that end, the National Party was convinced
that there could be no thoroughgoing reform as long as Egypt was
under foreign occupation. The first step, therefore, was to get
rid of the British. Only then could positive, constructive work be
resumed.

Mohammad Abdu continued his work in the face of the Khedive's intrigues, the accusations of the National Party, and opposi-

tion among reactionary religious leaders. His life was dedicated to a three-fold mission comprising the reform of the Moslem religion, the Arabic language, and political institutions. He was a devout Moslem and believed that Islam was in harmony with modern science and thought, and that it satisfied the needs of modern life. The truths of Islam should be sought in their primary sources, where the faith would be found in its pristine purity before hard dogma and restrictive tradition set in. He was bent on the reform of Al-Azhar in the belief that if religious leaders were adequately trained in this great center of Moslem religion and thought, and were dedicated to a life of righteousness and service, they would be a leavening force throughout the world of Islam.

The Arabic language in Mohammad Abdu's time was in a bad state. Writers trained in Al-Azhar wrote a florid style of rhymed prose, verbose and pedantic, more concerned with the form than the meaning. Official publications were written in a corrupt and confused language, beset with barbarous expressions. Mohammad Abdu served the Arabic language as a journalist writing in the *Official Journal* and *Al-Urwat-al-Wuthka,* as a teacher of rhetoric and Arabic classics, and as author and translator. In all his literary activity he sought to propagate a simple and direct style and popularize a sound literary taste.

In the political field, Mohammad Abdu worked for the training of people in the knowledge and exercise of their rights and duties. He was one of the outstanding members of the Consultative Assembly.

Thoroughly steeped in the Moslem faith and in Arabic culture, Mohammad Abdu was an intelligent and informed admirer of European civilization. He visited Europe several times and every time was greatly stimulated by the experience. He visualized a modern Egypt resting on a firm and broad basis of the best in the Arab heritage enriched and fertilized by assimilation of the best in European thought and achievement.

❋　　❋　　❋

The British occupation interrupted the natural course of the country's evolution. Its immediate result was the disruption of constitutional development and education in self-government. The national and liberal forces were defeated and eliminated from positions of responsibility. A shadow Assembly was set up, and reactionary elements were installed under British control. The appearance of independence was maintained by the façade of Khedive, Council of Ministers, and General Assembly; but behind it ruled Britain's Representative, Cromer, and the British advisors assigned to the various government departments. Parliamentary government was not established until 1924 when the national revolution had achieved the partial independence of Egypt and secured a constitution which definitely established the principle of representative institutions.

The British administration succeeded in restoring the economic stability of the country and establishing its solvency. It introduced order and efficiency into the management of public affairs, and effected reforms in the system of justice. These benefits, however, were not a substitute for self-government, nor did they reconcile the Egyptians to British rule.

The failure of Arabi's revolt and the British occupation stunned the nationalist elements. For a time, opposition to foreign rule lay dormant. But before the close of the century the nationalist movement was revived.

In the first decade of the 20th century political agitation centered around the National Party and its leader, Mustapha Kamel. The dominant quality of Mustapha Kamel's life and work was his unshakable faith in Egypt and the Egyptians. In a time when despair overtook the spirits of men he worked with irrepressible enthusiasm for the restoration of self-confidence and the preparation of the nation to assume its responsibilities. He conveyed his message through his work in journalism and education. He founded a number of publications, a daily paper, a monthly journal, and a weekly, dedicated to a relentless struggle for the national cause. Two papers, one in English, the other French, sought to acquaint public opinion in Europe with Egypt's case. Mustapha Kamel carried his message to Europe in person, when, on his trips to European countries he lectured to the public, wrote articles for the press, and conversed and corresponded with European statesmen.

Mustapha Kamel took up the cause of education with characteristic ardor. He was fired by a passionate desire to spread education among all classes of the population. Public spirited men responded to his call and established schools. He was director of a school founded by two of his friends and presented as a gift to him. The club which he founded for the students and graduates of the schools of higher education became the center of educational and public welfare activities which included the founding of schools and the initiation of agricultural cooperatives. He conceived the idea of a national university upon his return from Europe in 1906, when a committee was organized to collect contributions for a gift to be presented to him as a token of appreciation of his work for the national cause. Mustapha Kamel responded to this gesture by suggesting that instead of a gift for him, funds would be more profitably collected for the establishment of a university open alike to the sons of the poor and the rich. The committee changed its function from collecting money for a gift to soliciting subscriptions for the founding of a university. Lord Cromer opposed the idea of a university for Egyptian youth and did not allow the project to be realized as long as he remained in Egypt. Soon after his recall in 1907, the Egyptian university was founded.

Mustapha Kamel's abundant life was cut short by an early death. When he died, there was a spontaneous outburst of national sorrow which demonstrated the fallacy of Cromer's judgment that nationalism was a "wholly spurious and manufactured movement."

To Mustapha Kamel as to other leaders, the restoration of constitutional government was a dominant issue. It was paramount to Lutfi al-Sayyid, a thoroughly cultured gentleman with progressive views, who has influenced generations of young people, first through his paper *Al-Jarida* and later as Chancellor of the Egyptian University. In *Al-Jarida,* founded in 1907, al-Sayyid repeatedly wrote on what he considered the pivotal question, the Constitution. He branded personal government as the most vicious of all governments since it can exist only among a humiliated and enslaved people. Under it morals are corrupted and material resources wasted. All classes of the Egyptian population, according to Lutfi al-Sayyid, strongly felt the need for constitutional rule, and the nation was unanimous in its demand for a constitution. This persistent and legitimate demand went unheeded by those in power, the Khedive on the one hand, the British on the other.

With the outbreak of the first World War nationalist activities subsided to be resumed with force after the cessation of hostilities.

*　　*　　*

While Egypt was breaking a new path outside the Ottoman Empire, the Arab provinces in Asia had followed their downward course under Turkish rule.

Syria's relations with Europe became less frequent after the discovery of the Cape route and the capture of the Indian Ocean trade by the Portuguese early in the 16th century. But at no time were they completely broken off. European merchants were still seen in the ports and other trade centers of the eastern Mediterranean. European pilgrims continued to make their way to the Holy Land. And in this period European cultural institutions began to be established in the East. The Italians were the earliest arrivals on the educational scene, as they had been the most active in trade. Next came the French. Lebanon was the chief center of their activity. During the 16th century a college for training Maronite priests was founded in Rome by Pope Gregory XIII. Several Lebanese Christians distinguished themselves in Europe teaching oriental languages, editing Arabic texts, and cataloging manuscript collections. Among the pioneers of oriental studies were four members of the Assemani family. One of them, Joseph Simeon (d. 1768), became librarian to the Vatican. The manuscripts which he brought to Rome after a journey to Syria and Egypt formed the nucleus of the celebrated Vatican collection of oriental manuscripts. He published several works, the most famous of them his *Bibliotheca Orientalis.* Another name, well-known to orientalists, is Ghaziri, among whose works is a catalog of the Arabic manuscripts in the Escurial. The French educational missions, of which the earliest came in 1625, became numerous in the 19th century, and exerted a strong and widespread influence.

The conquest of Syria by Egyptian armies under Mohammad Ali's son Ibrahim, the setting up of a modernized administration, and the proclamations of Ibrahim Pasha about Arab freedom, as well as the democratic conduct and unassuming appearance of Ibrahim himself stirred the people's minds and feelings and made them restless under Turkish rule. Egypt, no longer under Turkish control, became a refuge for Syrian patriots and liberal thinkers. Talented Syrians found in Egypt greater scope for their abilities. Syrians were prominent in the development of journalism. One of the earliest papers, *Al-Ahram,* founded in 1876, has kept to the present day a wide circulation and prestige throughout the Arab world.

The most prolific of the Syrian writers was Jurji Zaidan, an outstanding example of prodigious energy and wide knowledge. "The list of his works, and the variety of subjects of which they treated, is not likely to find a match in any modern literature."[12] He popularized Arab history and culture in a series of twenty historical romances. In this respect he is the Arab counterpart of Sir Walter Scott. For the more serious reader he wrote a *History of Moslem Civilization* in five volumes and another set of four volumes on the *Development of Arabic Literature*. Founder and editor of the monthly journal *Al-Hilal*, he used this influential organ for the propagation of Western thought and the study of current problems.

A very lovable Syrian who came to Egypt to breathe a freer air was Abd-al-Rahman al-Kawakibi, descendant of a noble and learned Aleppo family. The fine qualities which Kawakibi inherited were strengthened and enhanced by his upbringing. After his mother's death, his education had been entrusted to his maternal aunt, an able woman, cultured and wise. Favored by Providence, he responded by growing up to be a thoroughly just and good man.

In the course of his life, Kawakibi accumulated a wide experience. He tried government service, worked in commerce, practiced law and journalism, and traveled extensively in the Arabian Peninsula, Egypt, the east coast of Africa, and India. He read widely, and although unfamiliar with European languages, he was acquainted with European thought through translations. Traveling and reading, he became aware of the sad state of the Arab and Moslem peoples. He took up the fight on their behalf, and stood bravely in the face of tyranny and oppression. He was keenly sensitive to poverty and misery, treated the poor and weak with kindness and humility, and defended the oppressed by word and deed. The authorities suppressed the paper he founded in Aleppo because of his relentless attacks on despotic rule and corrupt rulers, and for the liberal views which he spread among the people.

Kawakibi wrote two books. In one he censured the Moslem governments, in the other he blamed the peoples themselves.

In the first book, entitled the *Attributes of Tyranny*, he analyzed the traits and tendencies of despotic government and their utterly ruinous effect upon the people. Under despotism, morals are corrupted. There is no love, either for country, for friends, or even for one's family. Fear and suspicion replace mutual confidence. Liberty is choked and thought corrupted. Pride, self-confidence, and manliness are suppressed. National resources are squandered,

12. Gibb: "Studies in Contemporary Arabic Literature," *Bulletin of the School of Oriental Studies*, University of London, IV, 759.

and misery and poverty are the lot of the people. Even religion is perverted. It is used as an opium to dull the people and divert their attention from their present ills to promises of happiness in a future life. Knowledge is barred because it is light, and despotism thrives only in darkness. Rulers are checked and restrained only if they are kept under strict and constant watch by a strong public opinion. Education should aim at awakening an awareness of misery and injustice, and should train people to resist tyranny. Kawakibi advocated a mild form of socialism under which the strong would help the weak and the rich share with the poor, and people would be brought closer to one another in all their relations.

The other book he called *Um-al-Kura* (The Mother of Towns) after the name of Mekka, scene of the story. It is the story of a group of Moslems gathered together for the pilgrimage from every part of the Moslem world. They are concerned over the general apathy which has overcome the Moslems and seek to find the cause. After an exchange of views, they agree that the causes are religious, intellectual, and political. Religion has ceased to be a living force in people's lives, belief in free will and personal exertion has been replaced by utter resignation and submission to fate, and religious men have become the tools of those in power. The people are steeped in ignorance, moral cowardice prevents them from demanding their rights, and despair has deadened their spirits. It is interesting to notice that the neglect of women's education and proper training is noted among the causes of the ills which afflict Moslem society. It is finally concluded that ignorance is at the root of all ills, and that the remedy lies in the enlightenment of the mind through education.

The two books are deeply thoughtful and are written with clarity and charm. They were published in Cairo, and were widely read and admired. Kawakibi's writings as well as the example of his personal life left a deep impression upon his contemporaries for he was a truly noble man with a heart as compassionate as it was brave.

In Syria, the second half of the 19th century and the early years of the 20th witnessed a cultural awakening, with the Arabic language its instrument and source of inspiration. Arabic, in the preceding centuries, had fallen upon hard times. Now this noble idiom was to be revived to give form and expression to the hopes of a new age. Poets and writers spread a cult of the Arabic language. They exulted in its wealth and beauty and the glorious literary treasures it possessed. Two Christian families from the Lebanon, the Yazijis and the Bustanis, are inseparably linked with the movement to restore to the Arabic language the qualities of its classical age. Nasif Yaziji and his son Ibrahim were poets with an almost mystical love for the pure classical Arabic; and to its revival they consecrated their talents and energies. They firmly believed that when the Arabs were made conscious of the treasures of their culture, found in the classical literature, they would bestir themselves to restore their glorious past. Both father and son belong in the first rank of Arabic scholars of their time; they produced an impressive amount of writings on language and literature, as well as their poetical works. From the Bustanis came a series of learned men; foremost among them was Butrus al-Bustani, author of an encyclopedia and a monumental dictionary, publisher of two reviews, one weekly, the other fortnightly, and founder of a national school. One great purpose dominated all his work, literary, political, and educational. This was the formation of an enlightened generation of men through the dissemination of knowledge drawn from the Arab heritage and from the modern culture of the West.[13]

In the meantime, a wider knowledge of Western culture was being spread by the educational activities of missionary organizations both French and American. The French had been established since 1625. The first Americans came in 1820, and ever since a keen competition has characterized the relationship of the two groups. Both opened many schools and each had one institution of higher learning. The Americans founded the Syrian Protestant College in 1866, later known as the American University of Beirut; the Jesuits established L'Université Saint Joseph in 1875, also in Beirut.

The foreign schools were not an unmixed blessing to the country. In some of them, sectarianism was encouraged, conflicting loyalties promoted, and a form of education fostered which was not suited to the life and cultural traditions of the people. These reservations being noted, the positive contributions of the foreign schools are seldom denied. For they provided an opportunity of education to many boys and girls who, but for them, would have gone without it. And it was education of a type far in advance of what the native schools of those days could offer. Moreover, the two higher institutions made their definite and lasting contributions, each in its own way. In the Syrian Protestant College—in its early years—instruction was given in Arabic throughout the whole medical and liberal

13. George Antonius, *The Arab Awakening*, London, 1945, pp. 47–51.

arts courses. To meet the need for text books and references, American scientists and educators collaborated with Arab scholars in translating English texts into Arabic. This fund of scientific Western thought enriched the modern Arabic language.

The scholars of the Jesuit University opened up the treasure of the old Arabic culture by their excellent editions of its classical texts and their original researches in the various fields of Arab history. For the publication of their work they had a perfect instrument in the Catholic Press in Beirut, whose Arabic type was, for a long time, the finest in the East.

An event of great significance and one which had wide repercussions throughout the Arab world occurred when the Turkish Constitution was proclaimed in 1908, putting an end to the tyranny of Sultan Abd-al-Hamid which like a hideous nightmare had weighed for over thirty years upon all Ottoman subjects. The event was hailed with frenzied jubilation all over the vast empire. To the Arabs it presaged the possibility of honest cooperation with the Turks and an honorable status within the Ottoman Empire. It was celebrated with a spontaneous and genuine outburst of literature, poetry and prose. It touched the hearts of the common people and they responded with a crop of popular poems and songs.

Reading the literature of those days and listening to contemporaries, foreign and native, who witnessed the behavior of individuals and of crowds one senses a dominant note of joyous hope and good will. Harmony and cordiality prevailed among the adherents of the various religions. Strangers meeting on the streets embraced each other, and a general feeling of brotherhood pervaded the atmosphere. The proclamation of the Constitution restored to the people a sense of dignity and self-respect. It created pride in Ottoman citizenship and kindled loyalty to the new Ottoman state and society upon which seemed to dawn an age of liberty and light.

These exuberant hopes were unfortunately short-lived. The chauvinistic policy of the Young Turks who held sway in Constantinople alienated the Arabs and deflected their loyalty and cooperation. The subsequent development of the Arab movement is the story of the Arab Revolt.

CHAPTER VII

The Arab Revolt

THE Arab Revolt broke out in Hijaz in the spring of 1916. It was neither an unheralded event nor a local outbreak. It was the expression of Arab national consciousness and awareness of an existence and a destiny apart from the Turks and outside the Turkish Empire. Trends and forces, slowly forming during the preceding hundred years, had gradually awakened Arab feelings of identity, and given shape to Arab nationalism, however vague and confused.

The years immediately preceding the first World War were years of agitation and ferment. Arab leaders, disillusioned by the outcome of the Turkish Revolution and robbed of the hopes they had pinned on cooperation with the Young Turks, intensified their efforts on behalf of Arab freedom and national existence. The proclamation of the Turkish Constitution provided opportunities for political activity. The Arab Provinces sent representatives to the Imperial Parliament in Constantinople, where they raised their voice vigorously in defense of Arab rights. Newspapers and journals multiplied and diffused national feelings among their readers. Political societies were formed and worked for the liberation of the Arab countries. Two of these organizations were secret, and they led the movement. One Al-Fatat, founded in Paris in 1911, drew its membership largely from the professional class. The other, Al-Ahd, was the organization of the army officers. Both societies had members in Iraq, Egypt, and Syria-Palestine.

The new Turkish regime, imbued as it was with Pan-Turanian tendencies was inimical to Arab aspirations. A policy suppressing Arab culture and nationalism was put in force. Following the dismissal of the Provincial Councils, a general strike was proclaimed in Damascus and Beirut. The strike closed down the two cities, stopped all communications, and brought out all classes of the people in mass demonstrations and a popular outburst of national feelings.

The Turkish Government expressed its recognition of the Arab national movement by sending an official representative to negotiate with Arab leaders meeting in Paris in 1913 as the first General Arab Congress. A Pact was concluded on the basis of decentralization whereby the Arab provinces would enjoy antonomy within the Ottoman Empire. Other terms of the Pact included the recognition of Arabic as the language of instruction in the public schools, and the allotment to the Arabs of an adequate number of seats in Parliament. The Turkish delegate assured the Arab leaders of the good will of the Turkish Government and its readiness to go to great lengths in meeting Arab demands, because of the religious and cultural bonds which linked Arabs and Turks.

The Pact was welcomed in the Arab Provinces. The Turkish Government, however, did not intend to put it into effect. With the outbreak of the first World War it was forgotten. It was then that a number of Arab leaders became convinced that their cause no longer lay in working for cooperation within a decentralized Turkish-Arab state, but in a complete break from the Ottoman Empire and the establishment of an independent Arab State.

Relations between the Arabs and the Turks were strained to the breaking point when the first World War was declared. The British, with a watchful eye on the Arab countries, approached their leaders to find out what the Arab position would be if Turkey should enter the war against the Allies. Immediately following Turkey's entry into the war, Lord Kitchener, Secretary of State for War, telegraphed a message to the British Agency in Cairo pledging England's support to the Arabs in their struggle for freedom if they came into the war on her side. Kitchener's message of October 31st, 1914 was conveyed to the Sharif Husain at Mecca.[1] A few months later, the Sharif received encouragement from another British source, the Governor-General of the Sudan.

The Arabs saw their chance but they did not take a head-long jump. Certain misgivings held them back. In the Sharif's house, Abdallah, the second son, favored the British alliance. Faisal, however, had suspicions of British and French designs on Iraq and Syria. The Sharif himself preferred not to declare his position until he had ascertained the attitude of Arabs outside Hijaz. He did not have to wait long before he was assured. An emissary came to him from Damascus bearing an oral message from the leaders in Syria

1. Antonius: *The Arab Awakening*, p. 133.

and Iraq, which said that political leaders and senior Arab officers
in the Turkish army favored a revolt for Arab independence, and
asked if the Sharif would lead it. The messenger arrived in Mecca
in January 1915. In the spring of that year Faisal visited Damascus
and was initiated into the secret nationalist societies. He found
their members apprehensive with the same fears and doubts about
European intentions that were troubling his own mind. But they
all endorsed an Arab revolt if the proper guarantee of Arab independence could be secured. The very same attitude had already
been expressed by the Arab leaders in Egypt when the British
authorities approached them on the subject of Kitchener's message
to Husain. In Mecca, Cairo, and Damascus, definite pledges were
insisted upon as the condition for Arab entry into the war.

The leaders in Damascus drew up a plan as the basis for alliance
with Great Britain and entrusted it to Faisal for transmission to his
father. This plan, known as the Damascus Protocol, stipulated:

The recognition by Great Britain of the independence of the
Arab countries lying within very specifically delineated frontiers
and covering all the Arab lands in Asia with one exception, the
Aden colony.

"The abolition of all exceptional privileges granted to foreigners
under the Capitulations.

"The conclusion of a defensive alliance between Great Britain
and the future independent Arab state.

"The grant of economic preference to Great Britain."

Husain now definitely declared himself. In his letter dated July
14, 1915, which opened the famous but ill-fated Husain-Mac-
Mahon[2] correspondence, he presented the Damascus Protocol as
the terms for the Arabs' entry into the war. It is necessary to stress
here, and keep in mind throughout, that Husain was recognized
as the spokesman of the Arabs on the basis of the Damascus Protocol; and this document clearly stated that the goal was independence. An alliance with Great Britain was conditional upon
her acceptance of Arab independence.[3]

MacMahon's answer to this first letter is a tangle of insincerity
and ambiguity. It confirms Britain's good intentions towards the
Arabs and her approval of an Arab caliphate whenever it should be
proclaimed. Then it goes on to say that it was hardly appropriate

2. MacMahon was British High Commissioner for Egypt.
3. Antonius, op. cit., pp. 157–158.

to discuss boundaries and frontiers in the heat of war, especially as some of the lands within these frontiers were still under the Turks.

Husain's answer expressed surprise at MacMahon's evasiveness, and explained that the proposed frontiers were the demands of the Arab people and not the suggestions of one individual. He insisted that upon the British decision on this issue depended the outcome of the negotiations.

MacMahon realized that his answer this time had to carry something more definite. Still it was hedged about with a number of limitations and reservations. In his letter of October 24, 1915, he excepted from the territories included within the frontiers laid down in the Damascus Protocol, the districts of Mersina and Alexandretta and portions of Syria lying to the west of the districts of Damascus, Homs, Hama and Aleppo, on the assumption that they were not purely Arab. With this modification and without prejudice to Great Britain's treaties with Arab chiefs, and without detriment to the interests of Britain's ally, France, the British government pledged "to recognize and support the independence of the Arabs in all the regions within the limits demanded by the Sharif of Mecca."[4]

Husain consented to the exclusion of Mersina but not to the alienation of a foot of land in Syria whose inhabitants are Arabs, though not all are Moslems. For he says, "There is no difference between a Moslem and a Christian Arab: they are both descendants of one forefather."[5]

Following these negotiations the Arabs came into the war on the side of the Allies. The first shot for Arab freedom was fired from Mecca on the 5th of June 1916. The Revolt was launched, and it came at an opportune time; the star of the Allies was not in the ascendant when the Arabs joined their cause.

The Arab Revolt made considerable contributions to the Allied victory on the eastern front. The Sultan of Turkey had declared the jihad or holy war as incumbent upon all Moslems. The Arab Revolt, led by the Sharif of Mecca, a descendant of the Prophet and Keeper of the Holy Cities of Islam, drew the sting of the jihad. The Revolt frustrated a Turko-German expedition to Arabia, which might have taken Aden by surprise. Entrenched in Arabia, the Germans could have blocked the Red Sea, and the Indian Ocean

4. Cmd. 5957. p. 8.
5. Cmd. 5957. p. 9.

would have lain open to their operations. The Arab Revolt brought these plans to naught.[6]

In the actual fighting, the Arabs shouldered a respectable share. When General Murray was advancing on Palestine in the spring of 1917, he "realized with a sudden shock that more Turkish troops were fighting the Arabs than were fighting him."[7] During Allenby's campaign in Palestine Faisal's army, now composed largely of Arabs from Syria, Palestine, and Iraq, was fighting east of the Jordan a nearly equal number of Turkish troops as were facing the British west of the river. To the south, the Arabs were holding in check another large Turkish force. Again in 1918, as in the preceding year, there were fewer Turks in Palestine to resist the British advance than were kept busy fighting the Arabs. Furthermore, the Turks and their allies the Germans, fighting on hostile soil, were harassed and exposed to perpetual annoyance and hindrance. "Unquestionably, the British campaign in the Near East owed much of its ultimate success to Arab aid."[8]

The crowning achievement of the Revolt came with Faisal's entry into Damascus in October 1918. The event reverberated throughout the Arab world. Damascus holds a place of special significance in Arab thought and imagination. It was the seat of the powerful and fully Arab Caliphate of the Omayyads and has throughout the ages treasured its Arab heritage. To the Arab of the Peninsula it is above all other places a symbol of bounty and beauty and grandeur, a veritable earthly paradise. And now after centuries of subjection it was freed by an Arab, in every sense a genuine and noble Arab, descendant of the Prophet, nurtured in the Arab tradition and the heritage of his native land, the Hijaz, and endowed with a personality fully qualified for leadership.

The Arab Revolt, immortalized in Lawrence's *Seven Pillars of Wisdom*, is generally regarded by English readers as Lawrence's show. That Lawrence was a prominent and splendid figure of the Revolt no one denies. His courage, endurance, and daring exploits won him the sincere and unstinted admiration of the Arabs who knew him. But Lawrence was not the organizer nor the spirit of the Revolt. No outsider could have been—however great his qualifications and honest his motives. When Lawrence arrived, the groundwork had been completed and the Revolt begun. The key

6. Antonius, p. 210.
7. Lawrence: *Seven Pillars of Wisdom*, 1935, p. 167.
8. Speiser: *The United States and the Middle East*, p. 51.

personality of the Revolt was Faisal himself. In Faisal, more than in any of his contemporaries, were united the qualities which marked him as a leader of men. He was strong without ostentation and brave without display. He led naturally and unconsciously, supported by inner strength and complete self-control. His relations with people were marked by unfailing tact. He fully shared the life of his followers, endured all the hardships to which they were exposed, was ever patient with their problems and needs, and always humble and gentle in his dealings with them.[9]

With the liberation of Damascus the Arabs believed that the aim for which they had fought was realized and independence was within their grasp. They had fully honored their share of the agreement concluded two years earlier with Great Britain. With the help of their Allies, they had freed the homeland of Turkish rule. Little did they know then—secure as they felt in the valor of their arms and the justice of their cause, and in their faith in the honor of their Allies—little did they know of the fate which these same Allies held in store for them.

Two agreements were concluded to dispose of the Arab lands over their heads and without their knowledge, at the very time when the inhabitants of those lands were dying so that their country might be free. And they were dying not only on the battlefield, but on the gallows and in exile, and in the famine brought upon them as a reprisal for their revolt.

The first of these two agreements was a secret affair concluded between England, France, and Russia in the spring of 1916 and known as the Sykes-Picot Agreement. It provided for the division, among the parties concerned, of the spoils of victory over the Turkish Empire. As Russia's share fell outside Arab territory, and as the whole treaty was later repudiated by the Bolsheviks along with other secret arrangements of the Tzarist regime, it was the two other parties to the treaty, Britain and France, who thwarted the Arabs' hopes and trampled upon their rights.

In this pact, England and France helped themselves to the Arab lands in the rectangle between Persia and the Mediterranean. France received the western part of Syria with the province of Mosul, and Great Britain appropriated Iraq from Baghdad to the Persian Gulf. In the desert between, the future Arab state was to be set up, the northern part of it under French control, the south-

9. T. E. Lawrence: *op. cit.*, pp. 122–123, 176.

ern part within the sphere of Britain. As for Palestine, the French insisted that the whole of Syria, including that southern portion of it known as Palestine, should be their share. The British, not desiring the presence of the French so close to the Suez Canal, pressed for its internationalization, reserving for themselves control over the ports of Haifa and Acre.[10] Thus the Arab lands were parceled out and the Arabs shut in the desert. The greater share of the responsibility for this immoral document must be laid at England's door. It was England and not France who, the year before, had pledged the independence of these lands which she now helped to dismember. And England withheld from France the terms of her alliance with the Arabs, and from the Arabs she kept any news of the Sykes-Picot Agreement.

Through the Russian disclosure of the secrets that lay in the Imperial Archives, the Arabs heard of this plot against their existence. Lawrence urged Faisal to put the British to shame by contributing his utmost to the course of victory and so make it impossible for them not to honor their pledges of Arab freedom. "I begged him not to trust in our promises, like his father, but in his own strong performance."[11]

Yet another plot was in the making. It issued in the Balfour Declaration of November 2nd, 1917, which promised a national home for the Jews in Palestine. The Arab leaders who heard of it made strong protests. Husain asked for an immediate explanation, and the British sent him a message of assurance borne by Hogarth, an official of high standing in the sphere of Arab affairs. Unlike the Balfour Declaration which guaranteed merely the civil and religious rights of the Arabs, the Hogarth message explicitly safeguarded the political and economic freedom of the Arab population.[12] A month later, in February 1918, the British Government again conveyed the confirmation of their pledges to the Arabs. This time it was in answer to a message from King Husain in which he had communicated to the British High Commissioner for Egypt the letters addressed by the Turkish commander-in-chief in Syria to Amir Faisal revealing the designs of the Allies on the Arab lands and people. The British note dismissed these rumors as Turkish intrigues to sow dissension between the Arabs and their

10. Antonius, pp. 244–251.
11. Lawrence: *op. cit.*, p. 555.
12. Cmd. 5964.

Allies "whose minds are directed by a common purpose to a common end. His Majesty's Government re-affirm their former pledge in regard to the liberation of the Arab peoples."[13]

Meanwhile Arab leaders were assailed with doubts and suspicions of the Allies' intentions, and they were gravely worried about the future of the Arab nation. Seven of those leaders, living in Cairo, submitted in the spring of 1918 a memorandum describing the situation and asking for a definite and comprehensive statement of policy by the British Government regarding the future of the Arab countries. The reply of His Majesty's Government, communicated to the Seven at a meeting convened on June 16, 1918, and known as the Declaration to the Seven, states:

1. With regard to the territories which were free and independent before the War, and those liberated from Turkish rule by the action of the Arabs themselves, "His Majesty's Government recognize, the complete and sovereign independence of the Arabs inhabiting those territories, and support them in their struggle for freedom." This category included the independent states of the Peninsula and Hijaz as far north as Akaba.

2. As for the territories occupied by the Allied armies, their future government "should be based upon the principle of the consent of the governed. This policy will always be that of His Majesty's Government." Under this category came Iraq from the Persian Gulf to Baghdad, and the Southern half of Palestine including Jerusalem and Jaffa.

3. Regarding finally the territories still under Turkish rule, namely northern Iraq and Syria "it is the desire of His Majesty's Government that the oppressed peoples in those territories should obtain their freedom and independence."[14]

The importance of this Declaration is twofold. In the first place, it is an official statement setting forth in clear terms the policy of the British Government with regard to those Arab lands comprised within the frontiers set down in the Husain-MacMahon correspondence. Secondly, it comes after both the Sykes-Picot Agreement and the Balfour Declaration, confirming Great Britain's earlier pledges to support the Arabs in their struggle not only for liberation from the Turks but for freedom and independence.

From America also came assurances of a better life. In President Wilson's Fourteen Points delivered before Congress on January 8,

13. Antonius, Appendix C, pp. 431–432.
14. Antonius, Appendix D, pp. 433–434.

1918, the Twelfth concerns the Arabs. "The other nationalities which are now under Turkish rule should be assured an undoubted security of life and an absolutely unmolested opportunity of autonomous development." And in his address on July 4 of that year, the President proclaimed that the basis for any settlement after the War should be the assent of those concerned.

The long series of promises and pledges closes with the Anglo-French Declaration issued on the 7th of November, 1918. By this time all of Syria and Iraq had been liberated, and the fighting Arabs as they settled down began to hear news and see signs which betrayed the insincerity of their Allies. Suspicion and restlessness were widespread, and a mutiny in the Arab army was barely averted. Faisal informed Allenby of the situation and asked for an immediate and authoritative declaration by the Allies of their intentions. The response came in the Anglo-French Proclamation issued as an official communique from General Headquarters. It was given wide publicity. The press was instructed to give it special prominence, and copies of it were posted in all the towns and many of the villages throughout the length and breadth of Palestine, Syria, and Iraq. The Declaration gives as the aims of France and Britain in their pursuit of the war in the East "the complete and definite freeing of the peoples so long oppressed by the Turks, and the establishment of National Governments and Administrations deriving their authority from the initiative and the free choice of the native populations."

"Far from wishing to impose any particular institutions on the populations of those regions, their only care is to assure by their support and efficacious assistance the normal working of the Governments which those populations freely shall have given themselves."[15]

At the Peace Conference which met in Paris in 1919, Faisal, at the head of the Hijaz Delegation, sat with the other Allied and Associated Powers. This was Faisal's first initiation into the ways of Western politics, and what he saw was not very edifying. About the statesmen of the Peace Conference he made the remark: "They are like impressionist pictures. The effect is excellent from a distance."[16]

It was clear from the outset that the Allies did not intend to keep their pledges. The French objected to Faisal's presence at the

15. Jeffries, *Palestine the Reality*, p. 238; Antonius, Appendix E. pp. 435–6.
16. Jeffries, p. 306.

conference and they took strong exception to his government in
Damascus. The British, occupied with getting strongholds for
themselves in the Arab lands, exerted strong pressure upon Faisal
to accept their plans.

President Wilson held to his principle of "the consent of the
governed" and proposed the appointment of an inter-Allied Commission of Inquiry to visit Syria and Iraq for the purpose of ascertaining the wishes of the population in those regions. The
French refused to collaborate in such an inquiry, knowing before
hand what the results would be for them. The British, after ap-
pointing their members, backed out. Wilson insisted that the American branch of the Commission set out alone if the others refused
to cooperate.

In the meantime, feeling in the Arab countries was inflamed as
the Conference disclosed the real intentions of Anglo-French policy. Responsible leaders in Syria decided to convoke a general assembly. They were the same men who in 1915 had drafted the
Damascus Protocol and sent it to King Husain as the basis of cooperation with the Allies. Now they organized the elections of the
first Arab Parliament, which met in Damascus on July 2nd, 1919,
and is known as the General Syrian Congress. Representatives were
sent from all parts of Syria, including the southern portion of Palestine. It is well to remember the resolutions passed at this meeting.
They called for the independence of Syria within its geographical
boundaries, and its organization as a constitutional monarchy with
broadly decentralized rule to safeguard the rights of minorities.
Faisal was to be king because he had striven so nobly for the cause
of Arab freedom. Iraq also was to be fully independent, and no
economic barriers to separate it from Syria. The unity of Syria
was stressed. No plan for its partition and dismemberment would
be countenanced. The claims of the Zionists in Palestine were
repudiated.

Political tutelage in any form was rejected. Economic and technical assistance would be acceptable if it was rendered for a limited
period and did not impair the independence or unity of the country. America was the first choice as the foreign power rendering
assistance. If she was not able to comply with the request, then
England would be asked. French assistance was not acceptable in
any form.

The Resolutions close with these words: "The basic principles
proclaimed by President Wilson in condemnation of secret treaties

cause us to enter an emphatic protest against any agreement providing for the dismemberment of Syria and against any undertaking envisaging the recognition of Zionism in southern Syria; and we ask for explicit annulment of all such agreements and undertakings.

"The lofty principles proclaimed by President Wilson encouraged us to believe that the determining considerations in the settlement of our own future will be the real desires of our people; and that we may look to President Wilson and the liberal American nation, who are known for their sincere and generous sympathy with the aspirations of weak nations, for help in the fulfilment of our hopes.

"We also fully believe that the Peace Conference will recognize that we would not have risen against Turkish rule under which we enjoyed civic and political privileges, as well as rights of representation, had it not been that the Turks denied us our right to a national existence. We believe that the Peace Conference will meet our desires in full, if only to ensure that our political privileges may not be less, after the sacrifices of life which we have made in the cause of our freedom, than they were before the war.

"We desire to be allowed to send a delegation to represent us at the Peace Conference, advocate our claims and secure the fulfilment of our aspirations."[17]

While the National Syrian Congress was in session, the American Section of the inter-Allied Commission of Inquiry, known as the King-Crane Commission, was touring the country in an effort to find out the conditions prevailing and the real wishes of the people regarding their future rule. Of the Programme of the Syrian Congress the American Commissioners say: "It is the most substantial document presented to the Commission and deserves to be treated with great respect. The result of an extensive and arduous political process, it affords a basis on which the Syrians can get together and as firm a foundation for a Syrian national organization as can be obtained. The Mandatory Power will possess in this Programme a commitment to liberal government which will be found to be very valuable in starting the new State in the right direction."[18]

The Commission which for six weeks toured the country, visiting the principal towns and many rural centers, interviewing peo-

17. Antonius: *op. cit.*, Appendix G, pp. 440–442.
18. Jeffries, *op. cit.*, p. 285.

ple, and reading hundreds of petitions, submitted its report to President Wilson and he communicated copies of it to the Allied governments.

Two recommendations were strongly urged in this report. One of them insisted on maintaining the unity of Syria, because "the territory concerned is too limited, the population too small, and the economic, geographical, racial, and language unity too manifest, to make the setting up of independent states within its boundaries desirable, if such division can possibly be avoided. The country is very largely Arab in language, culture, traditions, and customs."[19] The second point concerned the Jewish National Home. "The anti-Zionist feeling in Palestine and Syria is intense and not lightly to be flouted."[20] The Zionist program should be seriously modified because it could be carried out only by force of arms.

The King-Crane report is a document of unique value and importance. It is the work of men of high moral and intellectual standing who belonged to a nation which had no ambitions and designs upon the land which the report covers. It is objective and well informed. That its recommendations were based on correct knowledge of the situation and were the product of wisdom and insight was borne out by the events that followed when these recommendations were disregarded.

The Allied Supreme Council met at San Remo, in April 1920. England and France handed to each other mandates over the land and the people whose freedom and independence they had pledged. In Arab annals the year 1920 is known as the year of catastrophe; it brought the French to Syria, the British to Iraq, and the Zionists to Palestine.

This clearly was not what the Arabs had fought and died for. But Lawrence who accompanied the Arab Revolt foresaw and wrote: "If we won the war the promises to the Arabs were dead paper. Yet the Arab inspiration was our main tool in winning the Eastern war. So I assured them that England kept her word in letter and in spirit. In this comfort they performed their fine things; but, of course, instead of being proud of what we did together I was continually and bitterly ashamed."[21]

19. Antonius, *op. cit.*, Appendix H, p. 445.
20. *Ibid.*, p. 449.
21. *Seven Pillars of Wisdom*, p. 275–276.

CHAPTER VIII

Egypt Since 1918: The Political Struggle

THE national movement, which began in Egypt earlier than in the other Arab countries, received a setback when Great Britain occupied the country in 1882. Great Britain, as one of the signatories of the Treaty of London which recognized and guaranteed Egypt's independence under the nominal suzerainty of the Sultan, was committed to respect the status of Egypt under the treaty. Her occupation of the country was therefore an infringement of an international convention. Successive British governments, aware of the illegality of their position in Egypt, had repeatedly stated that Britain had no intention of annexing or securing a permanent hold on the country, that the occupation was only a temporary measure and would be terminated as soon as normal conditions within Egypt were reestablished. In the light of subsequent developments it became clear that these statements, rather than expressing a binding policy of His Majesty's Government, were intended, on the one hand, to allay sections of the British public, who troubled with doubts and misgivings were raising disturbing questions in Parliament; and on the other, to pacify European public opinion, particularly in France where Britain's action was received with widespread indignation and protest.

The first World War gave Britain an occasion to tighten her hold on the country. With the entry of Turkey, Egypt's suzerain, into the war against the Allies, Egypt was declared a British protectorate and the last ties with the Ottoman Empire were severed. The Legislative Assembly created in 1913, although merely consultative and debating body, was dissolved, and the country was virtually ruled by the British High Commissioner and the British advisors to the various government departments, who owed loyalty and responsibility to Britain's representative in Egypt and not to any local authority.

The British concept of representative government for Egypt, as expressed in the plan drawn up by the British Residency in 1918, showed how unsympathetic Britain was to the national aspirations of the Egyptian people. The scheme provided for a parliament with two houses; the lower house, composed of Egyptians, was to be purely consultative. Legislative power resided wholly in the Senate, of both Egyptian and foreign membership. A large number of Senators held their seats by appointment. The appointed members included Cabinet ministers, the British advisors to the various ministries, and other high ranking British officials. The elective members, of whom 30 were Egyptian and 15 were foreigners, were elected under a complicated and restricted procedure. This plan, which would have placed legislative power in the hands of foreigners, was submerged in the national revolution of 1919.

Popular unrest, already great, reached the breaking point when news came that the British Protectorate over Egypt was written into the Treaty of Versailles. The Egyptians had understood the Protectorate to be a war measure and expected it to terminate when the war ended. Instead it was made permanent by its insertion into an international treaty.

The Egyptian response to Britain's disregard of their rights and aspirations assumed at first the form of peaceful negotiation and protest. Later it turned into an open revolt. It began with the request by a representative delegation, headed by Sa'd Zaghlul, to visit London and put Egypt's case before the British Government and people. The Foreign Office refused the request. The delegation then submitted the case to the Peace Conference, and Sa'd proclaimed his program of national liberation. Political agitation followed, whereupon Sa'd and other leaders were arrested and deported to Malta. This was the signal for a widespread outbreak in which the cities and the countryside took part, and which enlisted the support of all sections of the population, including the women who appeared for the first time in public demonstrations.

A number of causes, political, economic, and social, combined to bring about the revolution. Politically, the Revolution of 1919 was a protest against the Occupation and all that it entailed by way of complete and widespread British control behind puppet native governments and arbitrary rulers over whom the people had no power. The hardships caused by the war added to the resentment against the existing order. The large number of foreign troops quartered in Egypt were a constant irritation. Egyptian peasants and workers were forcibly recruited and sent to labor on various fronts: Iraq, Palestine, the Dardanelles, and France. Beasts of burden were requisitioned and crops bought by the government at less than their market price. The economic life of the country was to a large extent in the hands of foreigners. Cotton, the main crop, was entirely controlled by foreign financiers and speculators.

The ground had been prepared for the revolution by the political parties—particularly the National Party led by Mustapha Kamel—and the press. The spirit of freedom was in the air in 1919. Wilson's principles and declarations gripped the hearts of subject peoples. Furthermore, the Allies had promised in official agreements independence to the Arabs of the Fertile Crescent and Arabia, and Egypt was an Arab country and no less advanced than those to whom promises of independence had been made.

The revolution was preceded by mass demonstrations which, in spite of the huge numbers taking part, were singularly well-organized and peaceful. All classes of the population joined: religious leaders both Moslem and Christian, notables, judges, lawyers, teachers and students, business men, merchants, artisans and other workers. Discipline was maintained by a police force recruited from the public and known as the national police. The people readily submitted to their own police who in turn were successful in eliminating lawless elements from among the crowds.

The British met the peaceful demonstrations with armored cars, and troops fired on the crowds even though at times these were not political demonstrations but groups of people leaving the mosques after the Friday noon prayer.

Strikes were another aspect of the revolution, and they were as widespread and well-organized as the demonstrations. The students were the first group to strike. They were followed by workers on street cars and railroads. Lawyers and even government officials went on strike, and the shops of Cairo closed down. Sabotage was the next phase of the revolution. Communications throughout the country were disrupted as a result of the damage to railways and telegraph and telephone lines.

Non-cooperation and boycott were the last step. Egyptians refused to take part in the formation of a government so that the

British, who anyway had the real power, would bear full responsibility for the events. British merchandise and business and the British community in Egypt were boycotted.

Sa'd Zaghlul, who had returned from his Malta exile, was arrested once more and with a group of collaborators deported to the Seychelles Islands near the equator in the Indian Ocean off the east coast of Africa, which have a wicked climate. Just as in India, those who remained continued the work and prepared themselves for future deportations by electing a series of substitute committees to replace those that might be arrested or deported. It was evident that the movement had a wide popular basis and could not be stopped by the removal of a few leaders at the top.

The revolution spread to the provinces and covered the entire country. In the provinces the British were guilty of unjustifiably severe acts of repression. Planes dropped bombs on crowds, taking a heavy toll of life, troops fired on any gathering, and even after the people had scattered, soldiers pursued them into the fields and killed indiscriminately. Villages were burned and looted, and crops destroyed. These seemed acts of vengeance and reprisal intended to terrorize the population, rather than measures necessary for the restoration of order.

The Egyptian population was unarmed. Few acts of bloodshed were recorded. There was no aimless destruction of life and property. Especial concern was given to the protection of the lives and property of the foreigners residing in Egypt.

It was a national revolution free of class hatred and religious fanaticism. Moslems and Copts cooperated wholeheartedly, and all classes of the population were united in support of a common cause.

British official opinion represented the revolution as an outbreak of chaos instigated by a few self-appointed and irresponsible leaders who were the tools of foreign mischief-makers—Turks, Germans, or Bolsheviks. Nevertheless, the British Government decided to send a Commission of Inquiry under the chairmanship of the Colonial Secretary, Lord Milner. The Commission arrived in Egypt in December 1919, and was received with hostile demonstrations and showered with telegrams and letters of protest. Its hearings were boycotted. So general was the feeling against it that when a foreigner happened to ask a peasant information about the road, the peasant thinking his inquirer to be a member of the Commission of Inquiry would answer: "Go to Sa'd in Paris, he will show you the way."

The Milner Commission reported a more serious situation than could be attributed to a few agitators or dismissed as the machinations of foreign agents. In the opinion of the Commission, the British Government was partially responsible for the revolution because it had failed to make good its repeated declarations that Britain was in Egypt only temporarily in order to help create the conditions under which the independence of the Egyptians would be secure. But, "After nearly forty years of British occupation, they seemed to be not nearer to, but distinctly further from, the goal at which Great Britain had professed to be aiming."[1] The leaders of the movement, continued the Report, were not extremists but had a record of moderate tendencies, for they belonged to the pre-war *Umma* Party which aimed at gradual constitutional growth. Continued frustration by the British had turned them into revolutionaries.

The Commissioners were impressed by the solidarity of the national movement, backed as it was "by the sympathy of all classes and creeds among the Egyptian population, including the Copts,"[2] and by the united popular support behind Sa'd Zaghlul, "the only man authorized by general acclaim to represent the Egyptian people."[3]

The Commissioners returned to England anxious to negotiate with the *Wafd* (Delegation) headed by Sa'd, the man who, in their opinion, had full control over the Egyptians. Sa'd and his companions had in the meantime been released from Malta and were living in Paris. They were invited to London for consultation in June 1920.

The *Wafd* proposed the idea of a treaty as a basis of relationship between Egypt and Great Britain. The suggestion was readily accepted by the British negotiators, and Milner presented terms for a proposed settlement. The *Wafd* decided to consult the nation about Milner's project. Sa'd sent a delegation to Egypt to lay before the country the draft proposals of the British negotiators. It was a sound precedent set by Sa'd: to return to the nation as the source of power and keep it informed of the progress of the *Wafd* in whom it had placed its confidence. It was also a shrewd move

1. *Cmd.* 1131, pp. 17–18.
2. *Ibid.*, p. 14.
3. *Ibid.*, p. 20.

on the part of Sa'd, inasmuch as it tended to emphasize the popular character of the movement and the unanimous support behind the *Wafd*. Upon the return of this delegation, Sa'd informed Milner that the nation had expressed certain reservations on his proposals, particularly with regard to the abolition of the protectorate and the unity of Egypt and the Sudan. Milner answered that his project was to be taken in its entirety without reservations. Thereupon the negotiations broke off and the *Wafd* left London.

Milner advised his government that the situation in Egypt could not be handled by a return to the old order. Nor was administrative reform alone adequate to solve the problem. He recommended the immediate conclusion of a treaty acceptable to both parties and its whole-hearted implementation as the only basis for sound relationship between Great Britain and Egypt.

But early in 1921, Milner resigned from the Foreign Office to be succeeded by Churchill. The settlement which the British Government saw fit to offer Egypt was not a freely negotiated and mutually acceptable treaty, but a unilateral statement issued by His Majesty's Government. This was the Declaration of February, 1922 whereby the Protectorate was terminated and the independence of Egypt recognized, subject to reservations with regard to British imperial communications, the defense of Egypt, the protection of foreign interests, and the status of the Sudan. The Egyptians welcomed the termination of the protectorate but they resented the Declaration both for its limited scope and its unilateral tenor.

Although the revolution did not immediately succeed in attaining its objectives its consequences were nevertheless significant. The abolition of the protectorate, however incomplete, is a direct result of the revolution. The principle of representative government, for which enlightened opinion in Egypt had struggled since Arabi's revolt, was firmly established as a result of the determining part which the mass of the people had taken in 1919. Above all, the psychological effect of the revolution was tremendous. Its spirit restored the self-confidence of the people, broke down the barriers among them, brought out the best in them, and inspired them with an ideal beyond themselves for which they were willing to die.

In Sa'd Zaghlul, the revolution had found a worthy leader, for he was a man wholly of the people and for the people, and has been appropriately likened in character to Abraham Lincoln. During Sa'd's lifetime the peasants rose twice against their rulers. In his youth, he had taken part in the peasant rebellion led by Arabi. In his old age, he led the people's fight for freedom from British rule.

Sa'd came from a thoroughly Egyptian background. His father, a peasant in a Delta village, was a prominent member of his community. Sa'd studied at Al-Azhar at a time when new ideas were stirring within this ancient university. He came under the influence of the two great reformers, Al-Afghani and Mohammad Abdu, who trained his innate intelligence and keen mind to logical and vigorous thinking, and imbued his spirit with ideals of renewal and reform. From his two great teachers he also learned the art of expressing himself with forcefulness and persuasion, and in the various callings of his abundant career as journalist, lawyer, and national leader, Sa'd was splendidly eloquent and convincing.

His French legal training gave him further preparation for public life. Sa'd became a great lawyer, distinguished by his unimpeachable integrity. He imparted dignity to the lawyer's profession, and as a judge—he was the first lawyer appointed to this office—his career was marked with probity and justice. As cabinet minister at a time when the British advisers were the real power in the government, Sa'd impressed his personality upon the ministry and all its officials including the British. His personality equally dominated the pre-war Legislative Assembly of which he was vice-president and leader of the opposition.

Sa'd was above all endowed with great human qualities. Perhaps his outstanding qualification was his complete identification with the people whose cause he undertook to lead and defend. His sincerity was beyond doubt. He believed in the people, the common people, kept ever close to them, was conscious of a popular will and responsive to it. A charming anecdote illustrates his faith in the people. During a visit to England, Sa'd was put up in one of the sumptuous palaces of the British nobility. His servant, a simple Egyptian who had accompanied him, was overawed with the magnificence of the place, and fearful lest the British were trying to tempt his master by the display of so much wealth and pomp, he shouted at Sa'd: "Pasha, beware for the country! This is something overwhelming!" Sa'd laughed. He calmed the apprehension of his companion and said: "A cause for which simple folk like this man have so much anxiety and concern is safe beyond all danger."

Unlike other public figures who sought to minimize the people's importance and override their will, Sa'd took pride in being the people's representative who draws his authority from their will.

Bravely and persistently he fought the people's battle, not only against the British but against tendencies within Egyptian ruling circles to vest authority in one man or a small group of men.

His courage was unflinching, his steadfastness and determination unshakable. His inborn self-confidence, a sort of peasant pride, was strengthened by the tremendous popular support which he succeeded in evoking. His power over the masses was unparalleled. Even in his exile, first in Malta and later in Seychelles, he controlled the people as no other person or authority could. When the British forbade the crowds to cheer for Sa'd, the people composed songs expressing their love for their leader. These folksongs, the spontaneous expression of popular feeling, were sung in towns and villages all over the country. The people lovingly called him "Father of the Egyptians."

Work on the Constitution began soon after the February Declaration had been proclaimed. The Constitution promulgated in April 1923 declared that sovereignty resides in the people, and established the principle of ministerial responsibility before parliament. Elections for the first truly representative Egyptian Parliament were held in January 1924 and, unlike some later elections, they were conducted with exemplary freedom and impartiality. The *Wafd* was returned with a 90 per cent majority; the government formed by Sa'd was known as the People's Government. In Parliament, Sa'd and the *Wafd* stood for complete independence. The February Declaration, as a unilateral statement, was considered not binding and its reservations were not recognized.

Sa'd was the champion of Egypt's independence from the British and the defender of the people's sovereignty against arbitrary individual rule. Both the British and the Palace were anxious to remove him. The opportunity to do so came with the assassination, in November 1924, of Sir Lee Stack, the British Governor-General of the Sudan. It was clear then and has since been established that the government had nothing to do with the assassination. On the contrary, Sa'd openly declared that it was a calamity for Egypt and a plot aimed directly against him and his government. Nevertheless, the British Government seized the occasion to issue a staggering ultimatum which demanded, among other things, the payment of a heavy indemnity by the Egyptian Government and the withdrawal of Egyptian troops from the Sudan; it announced the abrogation of the agreement concerning irrigation in the Sudan, and threatened that the Sudan Government would henceforth be free

MOSLEM SPAIN: The Hall of the Two Sisters in the Alhambra at Granada.

MOSLEM SPAIN: The Giralda in Seville, originally a minaret of the Moorish mosque
built in 1196 A.D.

Left. EGYPT: Crystal vessel, early Fatimid period, middle of the 10th century.

Below. IRAQ: Painted pottery bowl, "Samarra type," 10th century.

MOSUL: Large ewer, silver inlay work, middle of the 13th century.

EGYPT: The Citadel in Cairo with the Mohammad Ali Mosque.

Ewing Galloway

EGYPT: Modern office building, Cairo.

EGYPT—SUDAN: Mohammad Naguib of Egypt and Al-Sayyid Abd-al-Rahman al-Mahdi, Sudanese leader.

Ewing Galloway

SYRIA: The Omayyad Mosque in Damascus.

to increase the irrigated area to an unlimited extent, thereby endangering the water supply of Egypt. A show of force accompanied and followed the presentation of the ultimatum. British troops paraded in the streets of Cairo, warships appeared in the Alexandria harbor, and troops occupied the customs buildings.

Sa'd resigned. The new government accepted the British ultimatum and dissolved Parliament. The decade which followed was marked by a three-cornered struggle between the *Wafd* and the British, and the *Wafd* and the Palace.

The late king Fuad, a patron of learning and in some ways an enlightened ruler, was nevertheless an autocrat brought up in the tradition of absolute government and determined to be ruler in fact and not only in name. Since his status as ruler of an independent country was very much circumscribed by the presence of the British in Egypt, he tried to assert his authority at the expense of the people's sovereignty. Under Palace auspices, political parties with reactionary tendencies were formed. These parties had no following beyond a very narrow circle and in a country politically more developed than Egypt, they would have been of very little consequence. But in the as yet unstabilized condition of Egypt, they were a divisive element and an obstacle along the path of independence and constitutional development. The Palace-appointed governments were either weak or heedless of popular will. Under them parliaments were dissolved—one parliament was dismissed on the first day it met—and the Constitution was first mutilated by the introduction of reactionary amendments, later suspended, and finally abrogated altogether. While the absolutist regime was in power, the people stood by the *Wafd*. They returned *Wafdist* majorities to Parliament even though elections were conducted with pressure and interference in favor of government candidates. The people boycotted a restricted electoral law and forced the government to return to the earlier law which had established universal direct manhood suffrage without qualification.

The British reaped full benefit of the discord in Egyptian political circles, and it may safely be said that they did not discourage it. In fact, the British and the reactionaries were fellow travelers at least part of the way. The British could count on it that governments which had no popular support and little sympathy for ideas of people's sovereignty, would not push far and fast for the vindication of Egypt's rights versus the Occupying Power. These governments, in turn, could depend upon British support as long as their presence served British interests. It is a strange and incongruous thing but a fact nevertheless that the Egyptian Prime Minister who abrogated the Constitution was granted an honorary doctorate by a venerable British university while on an official visit to Great Britain.

The British were anxious to conclude a treaty with Egypt in order to legalize their presence in the country. But the treaty they had in mind was to be confined within the limits of the February Declaration. Negotiations between Sa'd and MacDonald's first Labor Government quickly broke down because of the wide divergence of the British terms from Egypt's demand for the evacuation of British troops, unity with the Sudan, and real independence. Later attempts, made at intervals between 1927 and 1930, also failed, and tension marked the relations between Egypt and Great Britain until 1935 when developments on the international scene, caused by the Italo-Abyssinian conflict, brought the two countries together. The Anglo-Egyptian treaty of 1936 was concluded amidst general good will. The treaty legalized Britain's status in Egypt and secured her interests. Egypt's obligations under the treaty consisted in the placing of ports, airports, and other means of communication at the disposal of Great Britain in time of war. England would withdraw her forces to the Canal Zone and maintain them until Egypt could ensure the liberty and security of navigation in the Canal. With regard to the Sudan, the Anglo-Egyptian condominium established in 1899 remained in force.

The treaty had certain advantages for Egypt. It relieved the constant friction with British authorities, and the consequent British interference in the internal affairs of Egypt. It recognized Egypt's sole right to protect the foreigners domiciled in the country. Provision was made to bring about the speedy abolition of the Capitulations. The term of the treaty was twenty years.[4]

The following year, capitulations came to an end when the Capitulatory Powers signed the Montreux Convention. The Mixed Courts established in 1879 with jurisdiction in all civil matters involving foreigners were abolished in October 1949. Thus for the first time the foreigners resident in Egypt came under the full jurisdictional and fiscal authority of the Egyptian Government, and the government was able to initiate much needed fiscal reforms.

During the second World War, Egypt was a major stronghold

4. Royal Institute of International Affairs, *Documents on International Affairs: 1936*, pp. 476–492.

of the Democracies. When the King tried to flirt with the Italians, the British forced upon him a Wafdist Government which fully discharged Egypt's obligations under the treaty. The resources of the country and all its communications were placed at the disposal of Great Britain and her Allies. In the time of greatest crisis, when Rommel was at the doors of Egypt and the outcome of the struggle hung in the balance, the support of a government backed by the people, was vital to the Allied cause. "Throughout the resulting period of anxiety the Egyptian public stood remarkably steady behind Nahhas Pasha and the Allies, and despite all past efforts of Axis propaganda in Egypt, there was no single case of sabotage of vital military communications across the Delta to Alamein."[5]

After the termination of the war, the revision of the 1936 treaty became a dominant issue in Egyptian politics. Public opinion was almost unanimous that the treaty had outlived its purpose and lost its usefulness. Those who disagreed with the general verdict, because their personal interests—political and economic—were linked with the continued presence of the British, were careful to conceal their views. Some of them even advanced the demand for revision in order to win popularity and deflect attention.

Great Britain, for her part, was willing to reconsider her relations with Egypt. Negotiations conducted during 1946 ended in the Sidqi-Bevin agreement which provided for the final evacuation of Egyptian territory by British troops by September 1949. But the agreement did not come into effect because the two parties held different opinions on the status of the Sudan and the question of joint defense.

In the summer of 1947, the Egyptian Government brought the case before the Security Council of the United Nations, which advised the continuation of direct negotiations between the contending parties.

Meanwhile, minority governments were in power in Egypt, appointed and dismissed by the king. Having no support in the popular will, they attempted to silence opposition by the methods of a police state. The opposition was not quelled, however, but rather intensified, especially after the Palestine disaster which in turn resulted in tightening the screws of arbitrary authority.

Such being the internal conditions in Egypt, the British could not entrust the settlement of their relations with Egypt to govern-

5. Royal Institute of International Affairs, *The Middle East: A Political and Economic Survey*, 1950, p. 164.

ments which were so remote from the people and rested insecurely upon force. Negotiations, therefore, were not resumed until a government was formed backed by a large majority in a parliament returned after duly conducted elections.

Upon assumption of office in January 1950, the Wafd Government officially declared that the 1936 treaty was no longer valid as a basis of relations between Egypt and England, and pledged to put an end to it. Negotiations were reopened and went on for eighteen months. They centered on the withdrawal of the British troops from the Suez Canal Zone and the union of the Sudan with Egypt. With regard to the withdrawal of her troops, Great Britain maintained that the defense of the Suez Canal was not a matter of concern only for herself and Egypt, but was closely linked with the security of the Western world on whose behalf she was discharging this international obligation. Egypt's attitude was considered impractical in view of the exigencies of a world situation which gave to the security of the area precedence over the question of Egyptian sovereignty. Egypt held to the position that her freedom and national honor—both jeopardized by the presence of British troops on her soil—mattered more than strategic considerations. Her foreign minister, Mohammad Salaheddin, echoed the general feeling when he said that Britain's alleged international responsibility in the Suez Canal was the latest of a long series of excuses whereby she has sought to justify her presence in Egypt. These excuses and explanations, offered by Britain throughout the seventy years of her occupation of Egypt, have varied to suit the spirit and exigencies of the time. In 1882, British troops had entered Egypt to protect the Khedive against his insurgent subjects. They had remained in the country to defend the foreigners, the minorities, or the peasants against their landlords. But the national revolution of 1919, which gave expression to the unity of purpose among the Egyptian people with regard to the Occupying Power, belied the claim that British troops were needed to defend one section of the population against another. A new claim was presently found in the need to safeguard the communications of the Empire. Now that Empires were outmoded and world opinion no longer interested in imperial communications, this claim was replaced by the supposed need to assure the security of the free world against a possible war with Russia. The danger of war, Egypt contended, would be greatly reduced and possibly eliminated if the big powers respected the rights of the smaller countries, and if these were strengthened and entrusted with their own defense.

As negotiations dragged on, public opinion in Egypt became increasingly impatient and suspicious of British intentions. The Egyptian Government, under pressure, announced on October 8, 1951 the abrogation of the 1936 treaty. It justified its unilateral action on the ground that the Anglo-Egyptian treaty conflicted with the spirit of the United Nations Charter which established the principle of equality in status among the member states, and with the United Nations resolution of December 1946 which specifically stated that no foreign troops may be stationed on the soil of a member country without its consent. The Egyptian Government charged that Great Britain had departed from faithful adherence to the terms of the treaty, for example with regard to the number of troops and the area in which they were to be stationed, and had failed to discharge her obligations to train and equip the Egyptian army. During the Palestine war, Britain withheld arms from Egypt when she was exposed to danger as a result of the British policy in Palestine which led to the establishment of a Jewish State. In the Sudan, the British authorities followed a policy inimical to the interests of Egypt.

The abrogation of the treaty was hailed with enthusiasm all over the country. Egyptian workers left the British camps by the thousands, and young men left their schools and universities to join the guerrilla war against the British troops which came out in full force. The British military authorities believed that the use of drastic measures would intimidate the resistance. The battle of Ismailiyeh, between lightly armed Egyptian militia and superior British forces supported by tanks and armored cars, was calculated to have this effect. Instead it called forth acts of superb heroism by the outnumbered and overpowered militia. News of the battle, which to the Egyptians was a needless massacre perpetrated by the British forces, so infuriated the public that on the following day, January 26, 1952 enraged mobs joined with discontented and destructive elements of various origins and tendencies in burning the business quarter of Cairo.

While the government was trying to cope with the British, its home front was insecure. Rumors intended to undermine confidence in the government were circulated. Misguided enthusiasts clamored for a government which would commit the army in the fight with Britain. Palace circles wove their plots and deployed their spies. The king and his associates found in the burning of Cairo the opportunity to dismiss the Wafd from office. Ali Maher, an able and trustworthy statesman, formed a government which tried to guide the ship of state through the troubled waters; but at the end of one month, he was forced to resign because of palace intrigue which seemed determined that the ship should founder. During the months that followed, the national struggle was shelved while politicians displayed their partisan spleen and courtiers pursued their intrigues. For the Egyptian people these months were a nightmare. But the dawn broke on the 23rd of July when Mohammad Naguib announced that the army was in control. Three days later, on the 26th, Farouk left the country after having abdicated in favor of his infant son.

Although Mohammad Naguib concentrated on internal reforms, he kept prominently in view the settlement of Egypt's relations with Great Britain. Of the two issues, the withdrawal of British troops and the future status of the Sudan, he tackled the latter first and settled it with remarkable statesmanship. A brief account of Egypt's connection with the Sudan is here given as a background of the present settlement.

After the Arab conquest of Egypt and North Africa, Arab merchants and settlers had found their way into the Sudan and brought their religion, language, and other facets of their culture. But it was during the 13th century, after a mass migration of Arab tribes, that the northern Sudan was Arabicized and its inhabitants converted to Islam. This penetration from the north has continued. Mohammad Ali conquered the Sudan around 1820 and annexed it to Egypt. A widespread revolt in the 1880's against the foreign-dominated Egyptian Government of the time resulted in the depopulation and ruin of the Sudan. Egypt, then in the grip of foreign money-lenders and under European political and financial control, was in no position to attempt the pacification of the country; and the Egyptian forces remaining in the Sudan evacuated upon the order of the British authorities in Egypt. A few years later, the British authorized the reconquest of the Sudan by an Egyptian army under British command; they did so to prevent the encroachment of other colonial powers, particularly France which was pushing towards the Sudan from her West African possessions. The Fashoda incident of 1898 nearly precipitated a war between Great Britain and France. The French were forced to withdraw on the grounds—among other considerations—that the Sudan was Egyptian territory. In 1899, an Anglo-Egyptian Condominium was established over the Sudan, a status confirmed by the 1936 Treaty.

The Condominium under partners so disparate in power has been little more than a fiction. Effective rule was in British hands, the Sudan in fact a British colony.

To Great Britain, the Sudan is important for strategic and economic reasons. It grows the cotton needed by British industry. The Gezira irrigation scheme, a joint project of the Sudan Government and British private enterprise, is one of the largest developments of its kind in the world, with a million acres of cotton under a system of planned rotation.[6] The Gezira scheme is only a prelude to the irrigation possibilities and agricultural development of the Sudan. Lumber and other forest products are among the economic assets of the country.

Strategically the Sudan is important as a junction of air routes across the continent of Africa from north to south and from east to west. The importance of the Mediterranean, until recently considered the life-line of the British Empire, has been challenged as a result of modern warfare which has proved the vulnerability of that line and the weakness of a system based only upon it. The British have therefore considered establishing a second line of defense to the south, thereby reinforcing the Mediterranean by an equatorial line across Africa from the Gold Coast to Kenya. As an essential part of this scheme, the Sudan has assumed new importance.

Furthermore, a great power established in the Sudan holds Egypt in her grip, since that power could have wide control over the Nile which is the very life of Egypt. The British are fully aware of this stranglehold, and in fact have on occasion—as in the ultimatum issued to the Egyptian Government upon Stack's assassination—used it as a threat.

After the war, Great Britain intensified her policy of isolating the Sudan from Egypt. The trend towards the development of a British-sponsored Sudanese Government was a step in that direction. The Sudanese Legislative Assembly, evolved from the nominated Advisory Council for the Northern Sudan, was a British dominated body with regard to both its membership and its functions. Through the fiction of self-government the British aimed

6. Douglas D. Crary: "Geography and Politics in the Nile Valley," *The Middle East Journal*, July 1949, pp. 266.

to eliminate Egypt, and at the same time remove the Sudan from the international supervision to which a dependency is subject under the terms of the United Nations Charter.

In the Bevin-Salaheddin talks, as in earlier Anglo-Egyptian negotiations, the Sudan figured prominently. The Egyptians claimed that to them the Sudan was not a foreign country. Apart from proximity, the geographical unity established by the Nile, and similarities in climate and topography, the inhabitants of Egypt and the Sudan share many characteristics which make for unity. They speak one language, profess the same religion, and through the community of language and religion, have basic cultural affinities. Egypt feared England's presence in the Sudan for reasons of national safety. The political and economic security of the country is inseparably linked with the Nile. Today as in the time of Herodotus, Egypt remains a gift of the Great River. Her increasing population makes imperative the expansion of cultivated land, and cultivation depends upon the quantity of water available for irrigation. The supply of Nile water available to Egypt at present is practically exhausted by the land already under perennial irrigation. Any further large-scale reclamation of land and extension of cultivation will require the construction of dams in the Sudan and the upper regions of the Nile. Hence, the question of who controls the sources of the Nile is a vital concern to Egypt.

In the Anglo-Egyptian controversy over the Sudan, each party claimed to be motivated by concern for the interests of the Sudanese. The welfare of the Sudanese was frequently mentioned in British pronouncements. The British pointed with satisfaction to their record of efficient administration under which the Sudan was evolving towards self-determination. The Egyptian negotiator stated that while Britain considered that tutelage was needed for a period estimated at from ten to twenty years before the Sudan could be granted self-government, Egypt was ready to recognize within two years home rule for the Sudan with union under the Egyptian Crown. Furthermore, the British authorities had worked towards separating the southern Sudan from the north, for which purpose they had left the inhabitants of the south in a primitive stage at the same level where they found them over half a century ago.

Where did the Sudanese stand in this controversy? It is hardly possible to speak of public opinion among the Sudanese, a people overwhelmingly illiterate and sparsely scattered over a vast territory. In the towns only, one encounters enlightened and articulate opinion. Leadership in the Sudan rests with the two great religious leaders, Sayyid Abd-al-Rahman al-Mahdi and Sayyid Ali al-Mirghani. Al-Mahdi has sponsored the *Umma* Party which had opposed union with Egypt. Al-Mirghani has always kept aloof from partisanship and involvement in politics but his followers, of whom the *Ashigga* are the politically vocal group, support the principle of union with Egypt and have boycotted the elections to the Legislative Assembly.

There were serious weaknesses in Egypt's position with regard to the Sudan. Union under the Egyptian Crown—the Crown being what it was—meant saddling the Sudan with the evils of the rule against which the Egyptians themselves were presently to revolt successfully. Among Egypt's claims upon the Sudan, one—the right of conquest—sounded incongruous with Egypt's demand for her own freedom from the British. Furthermore, few Egyptians in responsible positions had ever visited the Sudan and tried to ascertain on the spot what the wishes of all sections of the population were. And by stigmatizing all anti-unionists as British tools, they antagonized some able elements, at their head the influential and highly respected Al-Sayyid al-Mahdi.

The Sudan controversy was settled on February 12, 1953 when the Egyptian and British Governments signed the agreement on the future status of the Sudan. But the settlement was in reality effected when Egypt, through Mohammad Naguib, approached the Sudan directly. That was in October, 1952 when Mohammad Naguib received Al-Mahdi in Cairo as a friend and honored guest, and in an atmosphere of mutual trust and good will concluded with him and his party, *Al-Umma,* and other non-unionist parties the agreement which the Egyptian Government presented, on November 2nd, to Great Britain as Egypt's conditions, endorsed by the Sudanese, for settling the Sudan question. Meanwhile, representatives of the unionists, meeting in Cairo with Mohammad Naguib and under his guidance, united their parties in the National Unionist Party and affirmed their adherence to the agreement between the Egyptian Government and the other Sudanese parties.

The British Government was for a time doubtful about the general support behind the Cairo agreement. It raised questions and anticipated difficulties especially with regard to the Sudanization of the Civil Service and even more in relation to the southern Sudan. Less sympathetic still were the British authorities in the Su-

dan, among whom the officials in the provinces tried to stir up opposition to the agreement. Egypt's emissary, Salah Salem, toured
the Sudan and found the parties staunchly behind the Cairo agreement, which they confirmed with another document signed by
representatives of all the parties, in which they made their position
clear on the points raised by the British Government and affirmed
their intention of boycotting any elections unless conducted under
the terms of the agreement. Still the British insisted that the southern Sudan was so different from the north that in matters related
to it special powers should be reserved to the British Governor.
But the enthusiastic reception which greeted the Egyptian delegation during its visit to the south was of a nature to dispel doubts
about the attitude of its inhabitants towards the recent arrangement between Egypt and the Sudan. Tribal chiefs openly declared
that they did not need British protection against the north.

These are the terms of the February agreement. The right of the
Sudanese to determine their future status in full freedom is recognized. A transition period, not to exceed three years, during which
the Sudanese shall assume the full responsibilities of government
shall precede their determination of their future status. The Constitution shall be revised to assure the full and free functioning of
self-rule. The Governor-General—hitherto responsible to no one
in the Sudan—will henceforth practice his functions in collaboration with the Governor's Committee to be composed of two
Sudanese, an Egyptian, an Englishman, and a Pakistani—the Committee chairman. A seven-member Elections Committee, to be
formed under the chairmanship of the Indian member, with three
Sudanese, one Egyptian, one British, and one American, will prepare for and conduct elections to a parliament of two houses. The
electoral law shall be amended to provide for direct elections
whenever possible, their practicability to be determined by the
Elections Committee. The Sudanization Committee, with three
Sudanese, one Egyptian, and one Englishman, will be entrusted
with the process of Sudanizing the civil service, the police, and
the defense force. The British and Egyptian forces shall withdraw
from the Sudan before the election of the Constituent Assembly,
which shall determine the future status of the Sudan and draft the
new Constitution and electoral law. The unity of the Sudan is
stressed. Its future status shall take one of two forms, either complete independence or some form of union with Egypt.

The agreement was well received in Britain, both in Parliament and by the press. In Egypt and the Sudan, it was hailed as a great achievement and greeted with festivities and popular joy and enthusiasm. Mohammad Naguib announced that the agreement inaugurated a new relationship between Egyptians and Sudanese, a relationship firmly based upon mutual confidence and a love as between brothers. The agreement, he further stated, opened a new page in Anglo-Egyptian relations which by restoring confidence shall have its good effect upon the settlement of the questions still pending between the two countries.

On the question of the withdrawal of British troops from the Canal Zone, the position of Egypt is firm and unequivocal. Participation in Middle East defense is inacceptable as a condition for the evacuation of Egyptian territory by the British. Once foreign troops are gone, Egypt, in full freedom and without any external pressures, will determine its policy in relation to the world situation.

CHAPTER IX

Egypt: Social Aspects

THE political struggle has been the chief preoccupation of Egyptian leaders since the close of the first World War, with the consequence that much energy and thought have been diverted from the urgent task of social reconstruction. For, notwithstanding the modernization attempted during the 19th century and the many reforms introduced, Egyptian society remained basically medieval. The agricultural economy under which Egypt lived had none of the requisites to assure general prosperity and well-being, such as sufficient land per farmer, modern equipment, a system of cooperatives, and an enlightened peasantry. The land was concentrated in the hands of a few, largely irresponsible, absentee landlords, leaving the mass of a dense and prolific population in utter poverty, disease, and ignorance.

Some efforts were made, however, to remedy the social ills. Brave and devoted men and women tried to grapple with the staggering problems of widespread illiteracy, general ill-health, and destitution. Their achievements, however inadequate, deserve to be noted, all the more so because of the tremendous obstacles encountered at every step of the way.

More definite achievements have been recorded in education than in any other field. A review of the state of education during the forty years of British rule and the quarter of a century since Egyptian governments have been in control furnishes some enlightening facts.

The history of the British administration in Egypt records an utter and unjustifiable neglect of education. British historians and statesmen themselves have indicted this aspect of the British Occupation. "By whatever standard we judge the educational system devised for the youth of Egypt under British control, it has tended not at all to the salvation of the state. It is unquestionably the worst of our failures. At the end of nearly four decades illiteracy weighs down 92 per cent of the male population and over 99 per cent of the women of Egypt."[1]

It is true that England occupied Egypt at a time of financial chaos which dictated economy and made the balancing of the budget the most urgent task of the authorities. In the process, education and other social services were starved. During the first twenty years of the British Occupation, from 1882 to 1901, the amount spent on education and health combined was 1½ per cent of the total expenditure. In this same period public works received 8 per cent.[2] The stringency, therefore, was not entirely due to lack of funds. Public works were expected to make quick cash returns designed primarily to pay the European debtors and run the administration with its large and highly paid British personnel. Money spent on education was likely to yield thinking Egyptians, a possible embarrassment to their rulers.

Education deteriorated from the level it had attained under Mohammad Ali and Ismail. The British began their administration by abolishing free education. Twenty years later, when financial difficulties had been overcome and economic stability reestablished, the school fees, instead of being abolished, were raised. The allotment to education which during the first two decades of British rule was less than 1 per cent of the general budget, reached 3 per cent in 1910–1911, but again fell back to 1.7 per cent in 1920–1921. The deplorable state of education drew from the Milner Mission the pertinent remark: "Education, for which there is a real and crying demand among the people, remains atrophied."[3]

Nor was the paucity of funds the only handicap from which education suffered at the hands of the British. There were more serious ills, and they concerned the concept of education and its aims. On the elementary level, instruction was limited to a rudimentary knowledge of Arabic and arithmetic. What went by the name of higher education was designed merely to prepare its recipients for clerical jobs and subordinate government posts. Education was divorced from the people's background and environment. It was given in a foreign language, English, and was of a wholly theoretical nature, little concerned with the needs of the people. Arabic, which had been established as the language of instruction for all the courses given in the modern school system instituted by the

1. Sir Valentine Chirol. *The Egyptian Problem*, p. 221.
2. Charles Issawi: *Egypt, An Economic and Social Analysis*, p. 25.
3. Cmd. 1131, p. 10.

state during the 19th century, was relegated to a secondary position, thereby discouraging if not repressing the advancement of the national culture for which the native tongue is the only adequate medium of expression. Universal education for the masses as a preparation for citizenship was not in the British plan for Egypt. Nor was the training of responsible, effective leadership a part of their policy for that country. In fact, when the idea of founding a university occurred to some leaders it was promptly and vigorously opposed by Cromer. The university, established in 1908 after Cromer had left the country, was not a state institution supported by public money but a private enterprise the funds for which were collected from individual subscribers and donors.

Since an Egyptian administration has been in control, free and universal elementary education, written into the Constitution of 1923, has been the goal of successive governments. That today the actual achievement is still far from the goal is due to a number of causes. In the first place, work had to begin from the bottom, education, as we have seen, being atrophied when the national government assumed responsibility. Furthermore, Egypt has a large population with a very high birth rate, among the highest in the world. No sooner can school facilities be provided for a fraction of the children than a new generation has come along clamoring for admission. The training of teachers in adequate numbers has been a major difficulty. Other difficulties are the general political instability and partisan politics which have hindered the development of a continuous educational policy. Yet other difficulties have resulted from the fact that education in Egypt is still in an experimental stage where policies are initiated in good faith, and in good faith revoked, and new experiments are undertaken. Finally, when we remember that education is only one of the problems that demand a share of the national budget and make claims upon the available trained personnel, it becomes more understandable why illiteracy is still so high.

A few figures may be cited as a testimony to what has been achieved.

In 1921–1922, the last year of direct British control, the number of students attending government schools of all types was 105,405 out of a total population of about 13 million.[4] Nine years later, in 1930–1931, the number had almost quadrupled, with 409,039 students enrolled in the government schools. A decade later, in 1940–

4. The 1917 census gives 12,750,918 as the total population of Egypt.

1941, the figure had risen to 1,131,380. In 1949–1950 the total enrollment of students in all schools, including private schools, now subsidized by the government, reached 1,499,998. Thus, while after forty years of British rule there were slightly more than a hundred thousand students in school, the national administration has succeeded within less than thirty years in providing education for one million and a half of Egypt's population of about 20 million. The progress of women's education during this period is particularly noteworthy. In 1921–1922, only 24,316 girls attended the government schools. Of these 43 were in secondary schools and 653 in teachers training; the rest were in elementary and primary schools. No girls received higher education. By 1949–1950, the girls in school had increased over twentyfold, with 527,008 girls registered in the public and state subsidized private schools. Of these 19,511 were in secondary schools, 9,940 in vocational schools, 3,751 in teachers training, and 2,460 attended universities and other higher institutions. Appropriations for education increased from £.E.1,209,653, which amounted to 3.2% of the national budget, in 1921–22, to £.E.28,261,000 in 1949–50, about 14% of total expenditure.

The scope and aim of education have undergone fundamental changes. Until a few years ago, the first stage of the public school system consisted of two types of schools, the free elementary schools designed for the rural population and the poorer sections among the city dwellers, and the primary schools for the social classes who could pay fees. The first type was not integrated with the rest of the educational system, but ended in a blind alley. The student of the elementary school was debarred from enrollment in the secondary or technical schools and consequently deprived of the opportunities open to the better-trained youth. By contrast, the primary schools, where better instruction was given, led the pupils to the higher steps of the educational ladder. The danger of a dual system of education conceived on a class basis has been fully recognized, and measures to remedy the wrong have been put into effect. The program of instruction has been unified in the elementary and primary schools, and fees have been abolished for all the primary schools, both public and private, making them available to rich and poor alike. Private schools, to compensate for their loss, receive grants in aid from the government.

Unification on the first level of instruction has been followed apace by the diversification of the secondary schools—a further step towards the democratization and popularization of education since it provides a variety of educational opportunities to young people whose aptitudes do not lie along a purely scholastic line. After completion of the first stage of the secondary schools, students may transfer to vocational schools for commerce, industry, or agriculture, or may continue through the classical secondary course leading to the universities and other institutions of higher learning. Vocational instruction has been expanded considerably in recent years, and its standards raised. At the same time, the people's attitude towards vocational training has changed. They no longer equate education with the classical course only, but tend more and more to look upon vocations as worthy pursuits for educated youth.

Tuition fees for the secondary schools have been abolished. All teachers' training institutions are free, offering tuition, board, and lodging without charge.

Higher education is given in three state universities and a number of post-university institutions. Two of the universities are in Cairo, the third in Alexandria. Training in Moslem learning on a university level is given in Al-Azhar, the oldest university in the world.

The oldest of the modern universities, Fuad I, began as a private institution founded in 1908 and is known as the Egyptian University. Transferred to the Ministry of Education in 1923, it became, as the Faculty of Arts, the nucleus of the present university to which eight other colleges have been added. The School of Medicine, founded in 1827, consists of the Medical Faculty and the Cairo Institute for Health and Tropical Medicine, the Schools of Dentistry and Pharmacy, a School of Nursing and Midwifery, and a hospital. The School of Engineering goes back to 1831, the School of Law to 1868. Dar al-Ulum, founded in 1872 to train teachers of Arabic language and literature, was the first teachers' training school in Egypt. The College of Science was founded in 1925. In 1935 three pre-university schools for agriculture, commerce, and veterinary science were incorporated and have since become university colleges. Three post-university institutes, for archaeology, for oriental languages, and for writing, translation, and journalism are attached to the University. The University has a large central library, besides the separate college libraries, and a rich periodical section.

To supplement higher education available in Egypt, student missions are sent abroad for specialization. Several hundred young men and women are studying in the United States and Europe, most of them as government bursaries, others at their own expense but under the supervision of the Ministry of Education. The object for which students have been sent abroad has changed with the needs of the time. At first, the training of government servants, later the preparation of teachers was considered the most pressing need. At present the emphasis has shifted to specialization in science and the training of experts capable of developing the resources of the country and coping with its social and economic problems.

The diffusion of education among the masses is being pressed with ever increasing vigor and effectiveness. Under the Law to combat illiteracy, passed in 1944, all teachers in public and private schools are expected, whenever called upon by the Minister of Education, to take part in the campaign against illiteracy. Classes for illiterates are conducted in schoolhouses and other public buildings after regular school and office hours. Government departments are required to combat illiteracy among their employes, the prisons' department to teach illiterate prisoners, and the army to attend to the teaching of recruits. The Law makes owners of large estates and employers in industrial and commercial establishments responsible for providing elementary education for their workers. Youth organizations and women's societies are enthusiastically sharing in the campaign.

A step of significance and promise for the dissemination of education among adults was taken when the People's University—later known as the People's Cultural Foundation—was established in 1945. The aim of the Foundation is to raise the general level of culture among the people, encourage and develop individual talent through the acquisition of skills, strengthen individual personality through knowledge and the self-confidence which knowledge brings, and awaken a sense of social consciousness, thereby building from the grass roots social and national solidarity. There are no academic or financial requirements for attendance at the People's Cultural Foundation, an evening institution open to men and women. All that is required is ability to read and write, a nominal registration fee, and a minimum age of 16 years. No examinations are given and no certificates or diplomas granted. Education is pursued on a wholly voluntary basis with no immediate material rewards in view. The program of the Foundation offers a wide range of subjects from which the student may freely choose according to his individual taste and talent. Courses are offered in science, literature, modern languages, history, political science, social problems, health, journalism, commerce, industry, and agriculture. Art courses include painting, sculpture, music, drama, and decorative arts. Subjects of importance to women and the family are emphasized. Hygiene, child-care, home nursing, the family and its problems, sewing, cooking, and other aspects of home economics are taught. The Foundation has met a wide and enthusiastic response. In the few years since its establishment, fourteen provincial branches have been founded besides the two centers in Cairo and Alexandria.[5]

When Taha Husain, the celebrated blind scholar, teacher, and author was Minister of Education, he made a vigorous drive for the full implementation of universal elementary education, and the expansion of secondary and university education. To his critics who countered with the objection that sufficient facilities and adequate numbers of trained teachers were not yet available, and expressed the fear that the speedy enforcement of so wide a program was likely to lower the standard of education, he answered: Education is as essential to the human being as are air and water. Though the air and water may be impure yet people breathe the air and drink the water lest they suffocate or die of thirst. So it is important to provide education to all Egyptians, in the schools if enough schools can be found, otherwise, in the open air and on the bare ground; for ignorance is like a fire which consumes the soul and must be quenched by every means. The dissemination of education among the mass of the people is, according to Taha Husain, of the very essence of Arab civilization and not a mere imitation of the West: schools for children, known by different local names— Kuttab, Mulla, Fakin—and higher institutions—Madaris—for older scholars, were widely scattered all over the Arab world many hundreds of years before Western civilization provided education for its masses.

The achievements in education have been obtained under a system of strict centralization which left no freedom of choice to local authorities with regard to curriculum, texts, or any other eduational matters, all of which were prescribed by the Ministry of Education in Cairo. A rigid examination system was also enforced.

5. The material relating to education has been drawn largely from Sati' Al-Hosri: *Hawliyyat al-Thakafa al-Arabiyya*, a publication of the Cultural Section of the Arab League, Cairo, 1949; see also Matthews and Akrawi: *Education in Arab Countries of the Near East*, Washington, 1949.

This was necessary in view of the absence of local bodies, such as provincial councils, who were prepared to assume an appreciable share of the responsibility for education. The emphasis upon a uniform state examination as the sole criterion for promotion from one level of instruction to another was dictated by the need to maintain a respectable standard while the school system was being so rapidly expanded. The present trend is towards a loosening of central controls.

Among the problems with which the Ministry of Education under the new regime is trying to cope is the provision of school facilities for all children of primary school age. These number three million, and only half of them are in school. It is planned to increase the allotments to primary education, which have hitherto amounted to only 40 per cent of the education budget, and to establish three hundred new primary schools every year. With these provisions, it is hoped that within ten years facilities will be available to accommodate the whole school age population. Another objective is the further diversification of education on the secondary level, and the orientation of students to the type of training which will meet the demands of the expanding industrialization and agricultural development of the country. The problem of higher education needs to be faced. In the current school year, forty-three thousand young men and women are attending the three state universities, a tremendous strain upon the teaching staffs, and the laboratory and other equipment of these institutions. If the standard of education is to be maintained at proper university level, and the candidates for higher education are not to be turned away, then the establishment of new universities is urgent.

An important department of the Ministry of Education, the Department of General Culture, is charged with the task of disseminating and popularizing culture. It encourages writing and translation, publishes classics of Arabic literature, and gives aid to cultural organizations. Under its auspices outstanding works are translated from European languages and given to publishing houses to publish and sell at cost, the Department paying the publishers a legitimate profit. In 1948, the Department compiled and published the first *Cultural Register,* a record of all cultural activities in Egypt, books written and translated, daily papers, magazines, and periodicals, public libraries and publishing houses, lectures and radio broadcasts, conferences and cultural organizations, museums, art exhibits, the stage, and the cinema. The

Register, however incomplete—the gaps are due partly to the newness of the work—is nevertheless, a convenient source of information on the cultural life of Egypt.

Public libraries, so essential a medium for the dissemination of knowledge, are still too few. The National Library, founded in 1870, is the largest library in the Arab countries with its 600,000 volumes, of which 58,000 are manuscripts. The manuscripts constitute one of the richest repositories of unpublished and very significant material. The Library's department of research and publication has published a number of classical texts. The National Library has branches in Cairo and its suburbs. There is a municipal library in Alexandria, and about a dozen public libraries in the provinces.

The Archives Department, established in 1828, contains the State archives systematically arranged and classified, and easily accessible for purposes of research. Abdin Palace has a very valuable collection of archives, catalogued and at the disposal of historians and other research workers. The various museums and some government departments have specialized libraries.

A number of museums enshrine the monuments, arts, and relics of 6000 years of Egypt's unbroken civilization. The Museum of Egyptian Antiquities houses the treasures of Pharaonic Egypt, among them the famous finds of the Tutankh Amon tomb. In the Coptic Museum, unique of its type, the arts of the Coptic period are preserved. The Arab Museum, which has a fine and representative collection of Arab-Moslem art, publishes studies on Moslem art and archaeology.

The age-old artistic tradition of Egypt is finding expression in modern art, painting, sculpture, and decorative arts. Some works are kept in the Museum of Modern Art, others may be seen at the exhibits held at frequent intervals in Cairo. Egyptian painters have excelled in portraiture.

A number of learned societies participate in the advancement and dissemination of knowledge. The oldest is the Royal Geographical Society, founded in 1875 to promote geographical knowledge and the exploration of Africa. The Society has sponsored the publication of several monumental geographical studies on Egypt. One of them, *Monumenta Geographica Africae et Aegypti,* in twelve volumes, is a collection of all the maps and geographical texts concerning Egypt and Africa drawn and written throughout the ages, and reproduced in the original languages. The Society publishes a journal and helps in organizing expeditions of exploration in Africa.

The Society of Fuad I for Political Economy, Statistics, and Legislation studies all matters relating to the material and human resources of the country with the aim of developing the economic assets for the general welfare. The Society's journal, *L'Egypte Contemporaine*, carrying articles in Arabic, English, and French, is a valuable source for students of modern Egypt.

The Arab Academy whose membership is composed of Arab scholars and orientalists, watches over the growth of the Arabic language and its development to meet the needs of modern civilization. The Academy has studied and confirmed the use of some 10,000 terms relating to the sciences, arts, and various aspects of thought, or pertaining to matters of everyday life. Committees of the Academy are working on two dictionaries, one for general use, the other, a voluminous project, for more specialized purposes. Projects for the simplification of the Arabic language are under study with the object of facilitating the process of learning Arabic and narrowing the gap between the classical and the language of daily speech.

The process of modernizing, simplifying, and popularizing classical Arabic has been going on during the greater part of a century outside the halls of literary academies. Scientists, professional men, and technicians have made their contribution. The press, and the national movement which nourished the press and was in turn spurred on by it, were the chief instruments in molding the classical language into a form intelligible to the general public. Current and urgent problems could hardly be treated in flowery style and rhymed prose, the decadent form of latterday literary Arabic. National leaders, fully aware of the importance of persuasion in winning popular support for their cause, spoke and wrote with simplicity and precision. The press has attracted every notable writer. Leading thinkers, literary men, and even poets are active in the field of journalism as editors, proprietors, or regular contributors to the daily and periodical press.

There is a vigorous press in Egypt. In scope, quality, technical set up, and news coverage it compares favorably with the press in Western Europe and the United States. The two leading dailies, *Al-Ahram* and *Al-Misri*, have offices and reporters in the capitals of Europe and the United States, and in many countries of Asia. The partisan press was often violent, but carried at times incisive and thought-provoking articles.

Periodical literature displays a great variety of subjects and treatment. Science, philosophy, religion, literature and the arts, social and economic problems form the contents of the more serious publications. Weekly magazines abound. A striking feature of many of them is the excellence of their cartoons.

Apart from their occupation with journalism, Egyptian writers have produced a mass of purely literary works which, along with journalistic literature, have been instrumental in modernizing and simplifying the classical Arabic. Modern Arabic literature has been influenced by two sources, the early Arabic classics with their dignity and simplicity of expression, and the literatures of the Western world whose possibilities for the fertilization of thought are unlimited. The development of the novel and the drama, one of the fruits of literary contacts with the West, has done more than any other form of literature to simplify and popularize the literary language. In the first truly Egyptian novel, *Zainab,* a story of peasant life, the dialogue was written in popular Arabic, the rest of the story in the classical. The pioneer playwright Mohammad Taimur wrote his plays in the colloquial. The use of the dialect, however, was short-lived. Novelists and playwrights have developed a simple literary idiom, intelligible to the public. The classical language, thus simplified and enriched with the experiences of common life, has become a pliant and adequate medium of conversation. In so far as novelists and playwrights have described faithfully the life of contemporary Egypt with its manifold ills, they have also served a social purpose of great merit, for they have helped in spreading social consciousness and opening the eyes and minds of people to the problems of their society.

The trend in education during the last decade towards the unification of the system on the elementary level, and the implementation of the principle of free elementary education as the birthright of every child, coupled with the diffusion of knowledge and information through the press and the radio, have tended towards consolidating the nation, awakening awareness among the people, and instilling into the leaders a sense of social responsibility.

The task of social reconstruction, like the responsibility for education, rests largely upon the government. In education, private institutions have effectively seconded the government's efforts, while in the social service private organizations preceded government action. There are at present about 3000 welfare societies run by private groups. Their activities cover a wide range of social work. The haphazard, unorganized distribution of charity is gradually giving way to constructive aid administered, after careful study, through recognized agencies and institutions. Trained social workers are making their appearance beside the large number of volunteers. Cooperation between the government and private organizations is achieved through a department of the Ministry of Social Affairs—the Bureau of Welfare Societies—which consults with, orients, and coordinates the work of the various organizations. Government participation at times takes the form of subsidies, at other times the Government establishes an institution, partly finances it, and turns it over to a private society to run. Much of the social work is done by women, and a woman is at the head of the Bureau of Welfare Societies with a large staff of government officials under her direction.

Social services are receiving an increasing share of public expenditure. The establishment of Ministries for Social Affairs, Public Health, and Municipal and Rural Affairs is an expression of the growing concept of government as an agency to watch over and assure the welfare of the governed. The Ministry of Social Affairs, after extensive study and investigation, has recommended a number of bills which have become law. Under the Social Security Law, which came into effect February 1st, 1951, the state assumes its share of responsibility in relieving the hazards of life. All destitute people, those who cannot earn a living because of old age or some other incapacity, and widows with young orphans to support are entitled to a monthly pension paid by the government. The project extends beyond the distribution of the pay envelopes to the provision of social services for those covered by the law. Constructive work among the recipients of social insurance aid seeks to guide them to ways of improving their status and helping themselves. The personnel charged with the implementation of the Social Insurance Law are carefully selected and trained, and are impressed with the fact that the success of the project depends upon their good relations with the people and ability to win their confidence. Work on the preparation of a Health Insurance Bill, a necessary part of the Social Security Law has been completed.

Social Centers, of which one hundred and twenty, serving one

and a half million of the rural population, had been built by the
end of 1949, are a promising development in the direction of cooperation between the Government and the people. The Ministry
of Social Affairs establishes the Center at the request of the rural
community concerned, and provides the staff composed of an agricultural specialist trained in social work, a doctor, and a visiting
nurse. The local population furnishes the land and the labor for
putting up the buildings. The major units of the Center include
an out-patient clinic, a maternity and child section, halls for rural
industries and for social gatherings, a pumping station for the supply of pure water, and public baths and laundries. Simplicity and
economy are the main considerations in establishing the Center.
The staff work closely with the people who choose from among
them committees to help organize and manage the activities of the
Center. Medical services offered consist of vaccination and inocu-
lation of children and adults, isolation of epidemic cases, provision
of medical care and distribution of medicines, supervision of the
food market, and general improvement of community sanitation.
Especial care is given to children and expectant mothers. The agricultural work of the Center includes demonstrations and experiments conducted on local model farms and experimental fields.
Selected seeds and seedlings of choice qualities of fruit trees and
vegetables are distributed. Teaching better methods of cultivation
and pest control, the diversification of crops and introduction of
new varieties, the improvement of livestock, and reclamation of
waste land are among the agricultural activities of the Center.
Agricultural industries are encouraged to provide gainful occupations for the farmers whose work on the land occupies only a part
of their time, and to make use of the unmarketable products so
that no food is wasted in a land where there are too many mouths
to feed. Village industries include dairying, vegetable canning,
fruit drying and preserving, spinning and weaving of cotton and
flax, and weaving wool into rugs and blankets, and reeds and palm
branches into baskets and mats.

Among the social services of the Center, one of the most fruitful is the promotion of the cooperative movement. Cooperatives,
among their many virtues, are combating usury, the blight of
peasant life in Egypt. The educational and social program of the
Center consists of schools for the children, evening classes for
adults, vocational training, religious instruction directed against

superstitious beliefs and practices, plays with a social purpose, documentary films, songs, sports, and other entertainments.

Foreign experts who have visited the Centers have expressed unstinted admiration for the work done. Sir John Boyd Orr, a distinguished British agricultural scientist and President of the United Nations Food and Agriculture Organization in 1948 "was particularly impressed by the excellent combination of all the educational, medical, economic, and social services of the Center. The balanced vocational training of the children accompanied as it is by a comprehensive and fundamental program of adult education is worthy of study and emulation throughout the world."[6]

The Ministry of Public Health runs Health Units on the basis of a unit to every fifteen to thirty thousand people. By the end of 1949 about two hundred units had been completed. The Unit consists of an out-patient clinic, rooms for in-patients, a child and maternity center, a laboratory, and a pharmacy. A doctor is in charge of the Unit, assisted by a nurse and a midwife, a health inspector, a laboratory assistant, and other health workers. The services include a medical examination of the population and a health survey of the region, provision of pure water, construction of public baths and laundries, and village planning in accordance with the requirements of public hygiene. Popular health education seeks to spread knowledge of personal hygiene, proper nutrition, and simple and practicable health rules. Infectious diseases are combated by isolation of patients, vaccination, and disinfection. Mother and infant care are emphasized. There has been a marked improvement in health and a longer life expectancy among the people in areas served by health units.

Endemic diseases—bilharzia, ankylostomiasis, trachoma, malaria, and a host of others—plague the population of Egypt. Bilharzia, the most common disease, causes severe anemia, saps vitality, and so reduces the productivity of those infected with it. Since it is prevalent among three fourths of the population its effects on the nation are disastrous. The Ministry of Health, in cooperation with the Rockefeller Foundation, has been working on bilharzia control since 1928. The Bilharzia Snail Destruction Section of the Ministry fights the disease through research and surveys,

6. From a letter dated 17th February 1948 to the Minister of Social Affairs sent on behalf of Sir John Boyd Orr by the Administrator of the Near East Regional Office of FAO.

extermination of the snails, treatment of infected persons, and education in sanitary habits by means of posters, films, radio talks, and by enlisting the cooperation of village preachers and teachers.

Extensive research on endemic diseases is in progress at the research sections of the Ministry of Health and the Fuad I Research Institute and Hospital for Tropical Diseases. The health laboratories in Cairo, noted for technical perfection, include chemical, bacteriological, and pathological sections, and are provided with a large medical library.[7] Vaccines and serums are prepared in the pathological laboratories and the Pasteur Institute, and are also supplied to other Arab countries.

The extension of state hospitals, clinics, and traveling health units intended to reach small and out of the way villages, and the increasing number of privately endowed hospitals and free clinics are another phase of the fight against disease. The need for adequate hospital and other health facilities is still very great.

Poverty is another crushing burden that weighs down the Egyptian masses. It is partly due to the intense congestion of population on the agricultural land and the consequent land hunger and deficiency of food supplies. Egypt is the most densely populated country in the world, with 2,000 inhabitants to the square mile. The rural population density of 1,450 persons per square mile of cultivated land is more than twice as high as the level of the industrial countries of Europe, and ten times as high as the average density of their rural population.[8]

The cultivable land in Egypt, a mere 3.5% of the total area, is estimated at 8 million acres, of which just under 6 million are actually cropped. The growth of the Egyptian population, sixfold during the past hundred years, has by far outstripped the expansion of the cultivable area. That the population has not outrun the country's income is due partly to a great increase in the cultivated area, following upon the extension of perennial irrigation under which two or even three crops are grown annually on the same plot. Perennial irrigation, however, has its problems and disadvantages. There is the danger of soil exhaustion. The year-round use of the land has eliminated the deposition of the rich sediment carried by the Nile floods which, under basin irrigation, covered the fields for several weeks. Increase in soil salinity accompanies perennial irrigation and makes drainage a serious problem. Fur-

7. Worthington, E. B.: *Middle East Science*, London, 1946, p. 169.
8. Doreen Warriner: *Land and Poverty in the Middle East*, pp. 26, 32.

thermore, perennial irrigation is directly linked with the prevalence of bilharzia, since the incidence of the disease increases from 5% in basin irrigated land to 80% in areas under perennial irrigation.

The vast inequality in the ownership of property has aggravated the acute problem of land shortage and population pressure. While one half of one per cent of the landowners own about 40% of the cultivated land, about 70% hold less than one acre each and between them own a mere 12% of the area under cultivation. The large landowners are the wealthiest and most influential class in the country. Attempts to introduce bills limiting the extent of land holdings have been defeated by the large group of landowners within Parliament. Mohammad Naguib has tackled the problem with the decisiveness which it required. His land reform is described below.

The present irrigation system makes practically full utilization of the Nile waters in Egypt. The system consists of several major and auxiliary barrages, some for the storage of water for periods of low water, others for raising the river's level to command areas along either bank. In the Delta where, because of the low relief, barrages are difficult to construct, large pumping stations are installed and water is distributed by pumping.

A survey of the whole Nile system has been carried through under the auspices of the Ministry of Public Works by Egyptian and British scientists, with a view to establishing control schemes in the higher reaches of the Nile. The plans proposed include the construction of dams on Lake Tana in Abyssinia—the source of the Blue Nile, on Lakes Albert and Kioga, and at Owen Falls where the White Nile issues from Lake Victoria. These lake reservoirs will provide long-term storage facilities. The Main Nile Reservoir to be constructed at the Fourth Cataract is intended for annual storage. To save the waters of the White Nile, of which 50% are lost in the marshy Sudd region, the cutting of a canal to bypass the Sudd is being considered. These projects have been subjected to the most careful study and investigation and are now ready to be put into execution. The Owen Falls dam is already under construction. Collaboration between Great Britain, Egypt, and Abyssinia is essential for the success of these schemes. A precedent of co-operative effort has been established in the Anglo-Egyptian Nile Convention of 1929 which acknowledged Egypt's natural and historic rights in the waters of the Nile and its requirements for agricultural extension. The presence of men of high scientific ability, integrity, and tact at the head of the Physical Department of the Egyptian Ministry of Public Works has been recognized as the cause for the success of the present arrangements whereby Egypt has assumed responsibility for the hydrology of the whole Nile system.[9]

The Ministry of Agriculture runs well equipped laboratories where research on soils, crops, and livestock is carried on. It also maintains extensive plant and animal farms all over the country. Intensive research has been done on cotton, the mainstay of Egyptian agriculture, industry, and commerce. Research conducted in the Ministry of Agriculture and the Research Board, to which is attached the Cotton Spinning Laboratory, has improved the quality and yield of cotton to the extent that Egyptian cotton gives the highest yield per acre in the world and is at a premium over American, Indian, and Russian cotton. Between 60 and 70 per cent of the world's production of long staple cotton is supplied by Egypt, and in certain manufacturing processes, Egyptian cotton is used exclusively.[10] High cropping rates are characteristic of maize, wheat, and rice. The average yield of maize is the highest in the world. Wheat approaches the average of northwest Europe where the heaviest crops of the world are produced per unit acre.[11] Government control and research have greatly improved the strains of existing crops and introduced with success a number of new varieties. The area under rice has quadrupled during the past twenty years. As an article of export rice ranks next to cotton in importance and is known on the world markets for its fine quality. The cultivation of sugar-cane and flax has expanded. New brands of flax have been imported from Belgium and Ireland. Flax offers promising prospects for the manufacture of linen, an industry once widely spread in Egypt and developed to perfection. The extension and diversification of fruit culture, garden vegetables, and flowers are among the more recent developments. Egypt has practically untapped possibilities as the future garden of Europe for which she is marked by her proximity to Europe and the early maturing of garden and orchard produce in her warm climate.

An extensive program of animal breeding and improvement has been under way for some time. The quality and quantity of the meat and milk of cattle and sheep, of poultry meat and eggs, and of

9. Worthington: *op. cit.*, pp. 47–48.
10. Fischer, *op. cit.*, p. 467.
11. *Ibid.*, p. 465.

sheep's wool have been improved both by selection and by crossing of native stocks with imported breeds. Most progress has been made in disease prevention and cure. Veterinary departments and institutes with large staffs work on the production of vaccines and serums and the control and elimination of diseases.[12]

Fish breeding and fisheries are under the supervision of the Hydrobiological Institute. Facilities for research include a fine laboratory and aquarium at Alexandria, and a seafaring research ship.[13]

Agricultural research is conducted by the Colleges of Agriculture attached to the universities which like the Ministry of Agriculture are provided with modern laboratories and experimental farms. The Royal Agricultural Society has also taken part in agricultural investigations. The Society runs a model village near Cairo and maintains a large station for the breeding of pure Arab horses. The Cotton Museum established by the Society is the only one of its kind in the world.

The benefits of agricultural research are placed at the disposal of the peasant. Demonstration stations serve to popularize methods of cultivation and stock breeding. Agricultural and veterinary experts are stationed throughout the country, ready to offer guidance and practical help to the farmer. Cotton seed of pure bred nucleus stocks and seedlings from government nurseries are supplied at low cost. Information and instruction are disseminated over the radio and through freely distributed pamphlets.

Until recently, the economy of Egypt depended entirely upon agriculture. Even now, twenty years after the establishment of mechanized industry, agriculture still absorbs two thirds of the occupied population. There is a large surplus of farm labor which, even with present methods of cultivation, could be greatly reduced without causing a decline in production.

The industrialization attempted during the first half of the 19th century was short-lived. A host of unfavorable circumstances worked against the success of the industrial establishments set up by Mohammad Ali. Labor was not adequate, the peasants preferring work in the open fields to the atmosphere of a factory. The management was faulty. Skilled workers and trained overseers and foremen were few. Raw materials and fuel cost more than in Europe. There was no protection against imported goods. And finally,

12. Keen, *op. cit.*, p. 70, 90.
13. Worthington, *op. cit.*, p. 138.

the purchasing power of the population was too low to support an industry which, because it could hardly compete on foreign markets, had to depend entirely on the home market. Mohammad Ali himself was aware of the difficulties but, with a determination characteristic of his whole life and work, he believed the venture was well worthwhile for the purpose, as he put it, of "accustoming the people to manufacture."[14]

* * *

Nearly a century has elapsed between Mohammad Ali's venture and the establishment of industrialization in Egypt. Some of the causes for the industrial lag rest within Egyptian society itself, others lie at the door of foreign interests. The Egyptians lacked the managerial skill, the initiative, and the training for industrial enterprise. They preferred to invest their capital in land, a secure investment, rather than hazard into unfamiliar fields where foreign competition was strong. Foreign capital which flowed freely to Egypt during the second half of the 19th century was not invested in industry because European capitalists were unwilling to compete with the home economy. Their capital found ample and profitable investment opportunities in land and urban development, transport, mortgage banking, and the financing of the rapidly growing foreign trade.[15]

The British Occupation was a further hindrance to the development of industry. The economic interests of the British administration were centered primarily on the extension of cotton growing. Cotton, a cash crop in world-wide demand, provided the necessary foreign exchange for the payment of the large external debt. Moreover, Egyptian raw cotton fed the mills of Lancashire, and an unindustrialized Egypt was a convenient market for the manufactured cotton goods of England.

Obstacles were placed in the path of the country's industrialization. Imported raw materials and machinery were taxed at the same rates as finished products. Crippling excise duties were imposed on locally made goods, an 8% tax being levied on locally manufactured cotton goods. The entire economy of the country

14. A. A. I. El-Gritly: *The Structure of Modern Industry in Egypt,* 1948, pp. 364–365.

15. *Ibid.,* pp. 366–367.

was maintained in the shadow of the myth that an agricultural economy was the only kind suitable for Egypt.

The National Revolution of 1919 succeeded in shaking if not shattering this along with other myths about Egypt. The struggle for independence was accompanied by an urge to achieve an economic standing that was not tied hand and foot to foreign interests. The establishment of Bank Misr in 1920 broke the path towards economic independence. It was the first bank organized and managed by Egyptians and supported entirely by Egyptian capital. The Bank was received with an enthusiastic response, and immediately won the confidence and support of the middle class. Since its inception, Bank Misr has followed a policy of active participation in industry and trade. It has formed companies for transport, for insurance and trade, as well as a number of industrial concerns, the most important among them being spinning and weaving mills. In recent years new companies have been launched in partnership with foreign interests, a departure from the earlier practice which sought only Egyptian capital.

Nascent Egyptian industry struggled for several years without protection against an unrestricted foreign competition. The passage, in 1931, of the law protecting home industries marks the beginning of large scale industrialization in Egypt.

Spinning and weaving are the largest industries. Egyptian cotton is used although it is of too fine a quality for the manufacture of utility cloth. During the war the cotton industry nearly met the local need and supplied large orders to the British forces. For finer quality woolen textiles the thread is imported. Local wool is used in the manufacture of rugs and blankets. Locally made rugs, which use the wool in its natural colors, are popular in the markets of Europe. The weaving of linen has been known in Egypt since earliest times when linen textiles were as fine as silk, and were in common use even among the poorer people. At present the manufacture of heavy and medium cloth meets the local needs.

Glass and cement are other important industries. The glass industry supplies the home market with a variety of glass and porcelain ware. Two large cement companies meet the country's requirements and produce a surplus for export. Other industries include household furnishings, tanning and leather goods, paper, soap, chemicals, and cigarettes.

The cinema industry is represented by three companies with eight studios located in Cairo. Egyptian films have a wide market all over the Arab countries, and are shown in Abyssinia, Turkey, Pakistan and India, and in the United States and Argentina. Egypt's climate qualifies her as a first-class international film center.

Among the food industries sugar is the most important. The entire industry is in the hands of a multiplant firm which supplies local consumption and exports a surplus. Sugar-cane is grown, and raw sugar is imported and refined in Egypt.

A modern dairy industry is being developed. The canning industry, which at present satisfies 50 per cent of local requirements, is expected to grow as the area under fruit and vegetable cultivation expands.

A giant fertilizer factory, equipped with the most modern machinery and supplying one third of Egypt's need, has been established in Suez. Prior to its establishment, Egypt imported thirty million dollars worth of chemical fertilizers. The new plant uses the raw chemicals present in abundance in the country; it has relieved Egypt's dependence upon imported chemicals—such utter dependence had disastrous effects upon Egyptian agriculture during the war when transport was unavailable and markets inaccessible—and it has saved precious foreign currency.

Certain factors are essential to successful industrialization: easy access to raw materials, a cheap supply of fuel, availability of capital, labor, and trained personnel, and a market for the finished products. How far are these obtainable in Egypt?

The materials for light industries are available in the country itself. It is possible to attain self-sufficiency with regard to food and other agricultural industries. With the further development of agriculture, and the expansion and improvement of animal husbandry, their processed and manufactured products, after satisfying the country's needs, should be able to compete on world markets. This is especially true of cotton textiles because of their superior quality. Linen could become another Egyptian speciality when the industry recovers the standards of excellence for which it was celebrated in earlier periods. The presence of large deposits of iron ore of a high grade gives promise of a flourishing smelting industry.

For fuel, in the absence of coal, Egypt has depended on its oil resources which are adequate for local consumption. The generation of hydro-electric power from the Aswan dam will provide fuel for the industrialization of Upper Egypt. The power station on which work is already under way is expected to be working at full force during 1957. Another electrification scheme proposes to make use of the Qattara depression, located about 40 miles inland from the Mediterranean and halfway between the Nile valley and the border of Cyrenaica. It is proposed to carry water from the Mediterranean in canals and tunnels to the depression which at its lowest point is 450 feet below sea-level. A hydro-electric power station utilizing the difference in level between the Qattara depression and the Mediterranean could supply power to a large part of Egypt.

Labor is abundant. A rapid program of education is turning out trained personnel—industrial scientists, business experts, factory managers, and entrepreneurs. Capital is available in internal savings and sterling balances. Until recently savings were invested almost exclusively in land. The success of the industries already established, the growing spirit of enterprise, an awakening to the urgency of industrialization as an essential part of a program of national development, and finally the break-up of the big estates are diverting an ever increasing portion of internal capital towards industrial investments.

The sterling balances were accumulated during the war as a result of purchases by the British army in Egypt. The balances, except for a very small fraction, were frozen in London after the war. Protracted negotiations ended in an agreement releasing the greater part of the remaining balances over a period of nine years.

Foreign loans and investments may be another source of capital if Egyptian economy can offer enough inducements to attract capital from abroad.

Mechanized industry, although a recent development and as yet limited in extent, has nevertheless made its mark upon the economy of the country. Over a million and a half workers are employed in industry, communications, commercial and other business establishments—thus relieving, however partially, the extreme congestion in the rural areas. The path has been broken towards a more healthy economy and a more normal balance of trade, showing a steady increase in the import of industrial capital goods, a decline in imports of finished consumer goods, and a growing export of goods made in Egypt.[16] Government receipts from industry have become an important source of public revenue at a time when the

16. Alfred Bonne: *State and Economics in the Middle East,* pp. 296–297.

realization of large scale projects of social reconstruction requires vast funds. Above all, industrial development has released hitherto dormant forces within the nation, opened new fields of opportunity for talents and energy, and given rise to a new class of men, the industrial leaders, many of them self-made men, who have succeeded in winning for their enterprises the confidence of the public and have inspired the public with greater self-confidence and national pride. Industry seems to be securely established in Egypt, with Egyptian capital and enterpreneurship venturing into branches of production where severe foreign competition is likely to be encountered.[17] Agricultural Egypt is being industrialized, and the myth that Providence had decreed a peasant economy for the Egyptians is fading away.

Labor problems and a labor movement are natural concomitants of industrialization. Official concern for labor began to be felt in the 1930's when industrialization was begun as a necessary prop of Egyptian economy. Earlier there had been some attempts on the part of a few leaders and of the workers themselves to better their conditions. Before the first World War, societies for mutual aid were formed among the better paid workers. The National Party of Mustapha Kamel included among its activities night classes for workers. During the Revolution of 1919, a sense of brotherhood pervaded the entire population, and in the decade that followed the energies of labor as of all other groups were consumed in the political struggle. In 1930, the Government founded a labor office to initiate and administer legislation, and two years later it invited the Director of the International Labor Office to investigate labor conditions and recommend the necessary legislation. Most of the comprehensive program which he drew up has since become law.

During the 1930's, two developments were evident. On the one hand, there were attempts within the ranks of labor for better and more widespread organization; on the other, political parties and factions made an organized bid for the support and allegiance of labor. The competition between the *Wafd* and a buccaneering prince of the ruling family for the favor of the workers did much harm to the working class movement. Because of dissensions and also for lack of funds, many unions closed down. But before the end of the decade the labor movement began to reconstitute itself.

17. El-Gritly: *op. cit.,* p. 376.

In 1938, a Labor Congress, attended by representatives of forty unions, met in Alexandria and demanded the passing of laws regarding unions and social legislation.

Unions, although tolerated, were not recognized in law until the passage of the Trade Union Act of 1942, which allowed workers to organize and bargain collectively. But the Act was restricted in scope. It placed unions under strict government supervision, excluded from its provisions large sections of workers—state employees and agricultural labor—and prohibited the formation of a General Federation of Labor.[18] This law has recently been liberalized by an act which authorized agricultural workers to unionize.

The Higher Labor Advisory Council, under the chairmanship of the Minister of Social Affairs and with members representing the Government, employers, and employes, advises the government on labor and social legislation.

A number of circumstances combined to keep the workers down. An over-supply of labor, constantly replenished from an enormous surplus rural population, is largely responsible for the depressed wages. Monopoly and combinations have placed employers in a strong bargaining position. Labor legislation was held up by influential groups, among them the Federation of Egyptian Industries which alleged that such legislation would impose an intolerable strain on the still infant industry. The powerful landowning class which dominated Parliament opposed progressive labor legislation for fear it might extend to rural workers. In the absence of a labor party and of genuine labor spokesmen in Parliament, there was little check upon the conservative interests represented by the owners of large estates and big capital. And finally, the miserable condition of the working classes—abject poverty, wretched housing, ill-health, and the prevalence of illiteracy—left the workers little interest in or energy for organized work.

But a number of developments have helped to push the working class movement ahead. The expansion of industry during the war and the needs of the Allied armies based in Egypt resulted in a large demand for labor. Upon the termination of the war, the workers, fearing unemployment and insecurity, staged a series of strikes and joined with students in demonstrations and nationalist agitation. Recourse to police measures was one method of dealing with labor disturbances; another was the enactment of laws

18. Issawi: *op. cit.*, pp. 93–98; Al-Gritly: *op. cit.*, pp. 529–554.

prompted by the growing social consciousness among various groups of thinkers who carried out serious studies into social problems and the conditions of the working classes. Meanwhile, employers, with an awakened sense of responsibility, instituted social services for their employees. In the best instances, these services included adequate houses let to workers at a rent equivalent to no more than their upkeep, nutritious meals served at half their cost, free medical care, classes for adult illiterates, and recreational facilities.

An all important consideration is the developing sense of solidarity among the working class, their growing feeling of importance and their increased knowledge of their own problems and the world around them. In the words of a union leader: "The Egyptian worker today no longer puts his thumb print on any paper that is offered to him; but he reads, discusses, and makes suggestions, and is not prepared to accept anything unless he is convinced that it is right."

During the past thirty years Egypt experienced some real social change evident in the spread of education, the growing industrialization, the modernization of agriculture, and above all in the increasing awareness of rights among the mass of the people. But these developments, creditable as they were, fell far short of what was needed to reconstruct Egyptian society. As long as the old regime remained, no radical reconstruction was possible.

The army coup of July 1952, which removed Farouk from the throne, eliminated a major obstacle in the path of radical reform. General Mohammad Naguib immediately set to the task of cleaning up and reorganizing the army, the administration, and the political life of the country. He inaugurated a series of reforms. The most far-reaching among them is the land reform.

The Land Reform Act, issued in September 1952, fixes the maximum extent of agricultural property allowed to an individual at 200 feddans—acres—besides an allowance of 50 acres to each son provided the total does not exceed 100 acres. The excess is to be appropriated by the state over a period of five years, expropriation to begin with the largest estates. Compensation—equivalent to ten times the rental value of the land or seven times the land value as assessed for taxation, to which shall be added the value of any installations, fixed machines, and trees—will be paid in government bonds at 3 per cent interest and redeemable within thirty years. During the five year period, a special tax equivalent to five times the normal rate will be levied on the land earmarked for expropriation.

The expropriated land will be redistributed, also within five years, in lots not less than two nor exceeding five acres, depending upon the fertility of the soil, to landless peasants or peasants who own under five acres, preference to be given to the sharecroppers or tenants on the land and to peasants with large families.

The lands designated for gardens will be distributed among the graduates of the agricultural institutions in lots of not more than twenty acres, provided the beneficiary owns no more than ten acres of agricultural land.

The beneficiary pays in equal installments over a period of thirty years an amount equivalent to what the government paid in compensation, plus 15 per cent of the land value to cover the expenses incurred in expropriation and redistribution and a 3 per cent annual interest. Neither the beneficiary nor his heirs may alienate the land before the full payment of its price. Nor may the land be alienated within this period to pay off debts unless they are due to the Government, the Agricultural and Cooperative Bank, or the Cooperative Society.

The Land Reform Act provides for the formation of agricultural cooperative societies with a membership to be composed of the beneficiaries under the Act in one village or a group of villages. The functions of the society would involve procuring agricultural loans; extension of services needed for the development of the land, such as the provision of seeds, fertilizers, cattle, agricultural machinery, storage and transport facilities; organizing the cultivation of the land in the most efficient manner including the selection of seeds and grading of crops, combating pests, and digging canals and drains; sale of the principal crops on behalf of the members deducting instalments on the land, taxes, agricultural loans and other debts from the price of the crops; and rendering all other agricultural and social services to the members.

The agricultural cooperatives shall participate in forming general cooperative societies and cooperative federations.

The Act regulates the relations between landowners and tenants; agricultural land may not be rented except to those who cultivate it themselves; the rent may not exceed seven times the tax assessed on the land; in the case of share-cropping, the owner's share may not be more than one half after the deduction of all expenses; the lease for agricultural land cannot be made for less than three years and should be held under a written contract of which one copy will be kept with the proprietor, the other with the tenant.

The wages for agricultural labor will be fixed every year by a committee, formed by the Minister of Agriculture and presided over by a high official of the Ministry.

The Act authorizes the formation of unions for agricultural workers.

Although the benefits of the Land Reform Act will reach only a fraction of the rural population, perhaps not more than 150,000 families, its great significance lies in its psychological effect and its impact upon other aspects of reform. It struck at the bastion of reaction and vested interests, and the hitherto impressive structure collapsed.

This land reform is, in the opinion of its initiators, the instrument of a peaceful social, economic, and political revolution in Egyptian life. With the disappearance of the class which owned thousands of acres of the precious and all too scarce land, its depressing influence over the peasants has also disappeared. The peasant, now a landowner, has acquired a new sense of personal dignity and of value in the state. Politically, he is freed of the control of the landlord who had previously imposed his will at election time. No longer tenant or dispossessed laborer, the peasant will vote with greater freedom, and parliamentary life will in the future rest on a more secure basis than was possible so far. The land reform will have a healthy repercussion on Egyptian economy, for besides initiating a fairer distribution of wealth, raising the standard of living among the peasants and with it their purchasing power, it will divert the wealth hitherto directed to the accumulation of land— with its soaring land value, excessive rents, and high cost of living —toward investments in industrial and other development projects.

Simultaneously with the redistribution of the broken-up large estates, the reclamation of desert and waste land is being vigorously pushed ahead. One project of land reclamation on the borders of the Western Desert is expected to accommodate as many families as benefited under the Land Reform Act. At the same time, energetic efforts are directed to the full utilization of all other resources. A Permanent Council for the Development of National Production has been established to study and plan for development projects, supervise their prosecution, and evaluate the results achieved.

The leaders of today's Egypt, with Mohammad Naguib at their head, know what they want and are determined to attain it. They want national freedom, social justice, increased productivity, and wealth to be used for the people's welfare; and creative participation in the affairs of the contemporary world. They are applying themselves to the task with the devotion and zeal of men with a sense of mission. And they are spiritually and intellectually fit for the great task. They deserve to succeed.

CHAPTER X

Syria and Lebanon

FOR Syria, the outcome of the first World War was her immolation. The country extending from the Taurus mountains to Sinai and from the Mediterranean to the desert had been for centuries a cultural, economic, and political unity. The life and progress of the country, and the constructive role it was destined to play in the affairs of the Arab world, depended upon that unity being preserved. It was not preserved, but wantonly rent with flagrant disregard of the rights and interests of the country and its inhabitants.

The story of Syria's betrayal is painful to relate. But it must be told—for it reveals the cause at the root of much of the restlessness and confusion which have afflicted and continue to afflict not only Syria but the rest of the Arab world as well.

Syria, in all its parts, including Lebanon and Palestine, came out of the first war famished and exhausted. Yet it was full of hope. The hope expressed itself in the program of the National Congress assembled in Damascus in the summer of 1919. The program, presented to the American Commission of Investigation— the King-Crane Commission dispatched by President Wilson—won the respect and whole-hearted support of the Commissioners who, in their Report, stressed the necessity of preserving the unity of Syria as the indispensable basis for its existence as a stable and prosperous country, and who urged the speedy establishment of free institutions.

The fundamental interests of Syria and her well being, as conceived and expressed by her elected representatives and strongly endorsed by a neutral Commission, clashed with what Great Britain and France, the then two great powers, considered their interests in a region believed by them to be a key spot in their world position and their extensive empires. Syria and its inhabitants were sacrificed to the power politics of the day.

The disposal of Syria was not accomplished without disputes and bickerings between the two powers.

France considered herself entitled to Syria because of a historical connection with the country going back to the Crusades, a connection strengthened by the role which France assumed as protector of the Catholics in the Levant and maintained by the propagation of French cultural influence through numerous French religious and educational missions established in the country.

Great Britain was not willing to allow France a preponderant position in the Levant. She feared for her own position in Egypt if France held Syria, which included Palestine and extended dangerously close to the Suez Canal.

It was therefore decided to divide Syria. The northern part would go to France, the southern part, Palestine, would be internationalized. This was the first partition of the country inaugurated by the Sykes-Picot secret agreement of 1916.

But the Sykes-Picot agreement, unjust as it was to the Arabs, was revised upon the conclusion of the war to inflict still greater injustice upon them and to repudiate still further the repeated pledges and declarations made by the Allies, particularly Great Britain. Great Britain was not satisfied with the internationalization of Palestine. She strove for a British mandate over the country. She also wanted the oil of Mosul and succeeded in prevailing upon France to give up her claim, under the Sykes-Picot agreement, to the Mosul area. To make up for her losses, France tightened her hold on what was left of Syria.

Arab troops led by Faisal had entered Syria as part of the Allied forces under Allenby. The Supreme Command, upon protests from France, ordered Faisal to leave the Syrian coast to the French army. The country was divided into three military administrative zones, east, west, and south, occupied respectively by Arab, French, and British armies.

It was anomalous—this arrangement which treated Syria as occupied enemy territory in relation to the Arab administration under Faisal, and regarded the Arab army an army of occupation like the British and French. The National Congress, representing the various sections of Syria, and acting as Parliament and Constituent Assembly, decided to end this situation on March 8, 1920, by declaring the independence of Syria including Lebanon and Palestine, under Faisal as constitutional king, with political and economic union between Syria and an independent Iraq. At the same time, the independence of Iraq was proclaimed by the Iraqi leaders and army officers who had taken part in the Arab Revolt and were then with Faisal in Damascus. The proclamation was received with enthusiasm all over Syria and Iraq. It roused equally great indignation in British and French official circles. The British Government especially resented the inclusion of Palestine and Iraq in the declaration, and protested strongly against the action taken by the National Congress which they considered a rebellion against the Supreme Command. The French had at no time concealed their hostility towards Faisal, the Arab Revolt, and the whole Arab national movement. They now pushed even more strongly their policy of sowing dissension among the population of Syria and Lebanon, and intensified their campaign of defamation of Arab nationalism which they represented as a backward desert movement inspired by religious fanaticism.

In the following month, April 1920, Great Britain and France put their plans for the disposition of the Fertile Crescent through the Council of the League of Nations, meeting at San Remo. Great Britain received from the Council the mandates over Palestine and Iraq, and Syria was assigned to France. The British Secretary of State for Foreign Affairs expressed the official view with regard to the mandates when he announced in Parliament: "It is a mistake to suppose that the gift of the mandate lies with the League of Nations. It does not do so. It rests with the powers who have conquered the territories, which it then falls to them to distribute. In these circumstances the mandates for Palestine were given to England, and Syria to France."[1]

The situation in the spring of 1920 boded ill for the newly proclaimed Arab Kingdom of Syria. The Mandatory Power, France, was set on its destruction, and France which had come out of the first World War as the second world power had a strong army on the Syrian coast. Events moved rapidly towards the end which the French had in view. The two administrations in the one country, Arab in the interior and French on the coast, were mutually hostile and diametrically opposed in aim and purpose. Each released a virulent press campaign against the other. Minor clashes and border incidents were frequent. An issue created by the establishment of the Banque de Syrie et du Liban added to the tension. The Banque de Syrie, a French company, was given the right to issue notes which the Mandatory Power put into compulsory cir-

1. Philip Ireland, *Iraq*, p. 263.

culation as the official currency. The relatively stable Egyptian currency circulated by the Allied Forces during their occupation had to be exchanged for this new paper currency based on the depreciating French franc. The Banque de Syrie became the Mandatory's tool for the economic control of the country. Syria, aware of the economic danger inherent in the creation of such an institution, denied the French authorities the right to issue this currency, and prohibited its circulation. The position taken by the Government against the French Bank was one of the major grievances enumerated in the ultimatum which the French Military Governor, General Gouraud, sent to Faisal. Presently the Bank and the notes which it issued were to be forced upon Syria by fire and sword, and were to cause untold damage to the economy of the country.

Another grievance against Faisal and his government resulted from the relations between France and Turkey. French garrisons were occupying a number of Turkish towns near the Syrian border. The Turks, led by Mustapha Kamel, had risen against all the foreign invaders of their country. When the French tried to send reinforcements to their garrisons by the Syrian railway, the Arab Government refused their passage on the ground that Syria, being an independent state, was a neutral in the conflict. It may be stated here that while the Arabs had rebelled against Turkish rule, they felt the strongest sympathy and admiration towards Kemalist Turkey struggling to free itself from foreign occupation and the internal forces of reaction. Hence the position taken by Faisal and his government in the Franco-Turkish conflict, a position strongly resented by France and publicly spoken of by General Gouraud as constituting effective aid to the Turks and a blow against the French forces.

The ultimatum issued by Gouraud on July 14, 1920, if accepted, amounted to a military occupation of the whole country. Opinion around Faisal was divided, but the council which advised submission prevailed and Faisal, at the risk of personal humiliation and of exposing himself to the anger and resentment of the people, accepted the terms of the ultimatum. The popular reaction was violent. The populace of Damascus attacked the citadel to procure arms with which to fight the French, and crowds demonstrated before Faisal's residence accusing him of treason and calling for the dismissal of his ministers, these same ministers whose removal the French ultimatum had demanded. In accepting the ultimatum, the Syrian Government knew that they had no forces with which to oppose the French advance on Damascus, and Faisal planned to go to Europe where, with the support of his British friends, he hoped an understanding with the French could be reached.

How determined the French were to destroy Arab rule in Syria is evident from the events which followed the presentation of the ultimatum. Faisal sent a personal telegram to General Gouraud announcing his acceptance of the terms, and Gouraud replied thanking him and asking for an official confirmation enumerating the demands of the ultimatum. This second answer was duly dispatched but because of the turbulent conditions it was delayed a few hours beyond the time set. Thereupon Gouraud ordered French and Seneghalese troops to march on Damascus even though the ultimatum had been accepted and its terms were being faithfully carried out. The Arab army had been disbanded and the advancing French troops saw that Arab units had been withdrawn from the positions which they had occupied prior to the ultimatum. Still the advance proceeded, and it was accompanied by yet another ultimatum. To this the Arab Government answered that although they did not seek war, yet acceptance of the conditions of the new ultimatum was bound to expose the country to civil war. As the French troops kept advancing, the Government hastily collected a small force which met the enemy at Maisaloun, the pass guarding the entrance to Damascus. The Syrians fought gallantly and desperately and fell one by one under the fire of tanks, armored cars, and aeroplanes. Damascus was occupied, and Faisal left the country.

We have seen how determined the French were not to allow Arab freedom to live close to them. Yet the fall of the Arab state of Syria was due to other causes besides the hostility of the French. The Syrians, and for that matter the Arabs generally, had trusted implicitly and naïvely in the promises of the Allies. Reading statements made at the time by Arab leaders one is amazed at their naïveté and child-like faith in the utterances and declarations of Western statesmen and politicians. A sample taken from a statement of the Government read before the National Congress after the declaration of Syria's independence illustrates the general trend. It is a paean of praise to the Allied Powers who have defended justice and inaugurated a new era in which the rights and liberties of peoples shall be respected, who have rejected the policy of conquest and colonization, discarded secret treaties, and proclaimed the self-determination of nations. The statement goes on

to express the hope that the Allies, because they love the Arabs
and have helped them in their fight for freedom, will also help
them in their new life. In numerous speeches Faisal, touring Syria,
declared his faith in the disinterestedness of the Allies, their noble
motives and the high principles on which their acts were based,
and their particularly sincere intentions towards the Arabs. However, Faisal said, he found European statesmen in abysmal ignorance of the Arabs whom they knew only from the *Arabian Nights*.
This ignorance, he believed, was the cause of the disputes between
him and the Allied statesmen who confronted him at the Peace
Conference. Particular faith was placed in Great Britain whom the
Arabs, at the time, considered their friend and to whom they looked
for support in their struggle with the French. Had they been more
realistic they would have understood that not only would Great
Britain not quarrel with France for the sake of Arab freedom, but
that she had in fact tacitly agreed, in exchange for the oil of Mosul,
to give France a free hand in Syria. There was not a word of protest from Great Britain when the French occupied Damascus by
force and destroyed the last remnant of the Husain-MacMahon
agreement in which Great Britain had pledged her honor to support Arab independence.

Within the Arab State itself the framework for a stable and
effective administration was lacking. Economic life had been disrupted by the war and its aftermath, and there was a deficiency in
the funds wherewith to support a government and an adequate
army. Schools were few, and political education among the people was practically non-existent. Nor was the Arab State allowed
time to work out and develop in peace the requisites of a good and
strong government. Troubles and distractions followed in rapid
succession, and before it could recover from the shock of its birth
the Arab State was no more.

Yet the Arab State, though short-lived, was enduring in its significance for it created a tradition of independence which inspired
and nourished the subsequent struggle and revolts for freedom
from mandatory rule. It was the first modern national Arab State.
National and not religious ties formed its basis. In the first official statement Faisal issued on October 5, 1918, and in his public
speeches, he repeatedly emphasized the national character of the
new state and the national bonds which united all Arabs irrespective of their religious affiliation. Arabic was immediately established as the official language and the language of instruction in

all the schools, and forthwith work proceeded on the translation of school texts and the Arabization of the administration, classes being conducted for government officials to train them for the change from Turkish to Arabic. And it was a modern state in its form of government—a constitutional monarchy and parliament—and in its emphasis upon education. The Government reopened all the schools of the Ottoman period, among them the School of Medicine which had been transferred to Beirut during the war. It opened new schools, founded the Faculty of Law and the Arab Academy of Damascus. Faisal himself urged the founding of schools and the acquisition of learning as the essential need of the country. And Faisal was a thoroughly democratic ruler, bred in the desert tradition of freedom and equality, a refreshing contrast to the stuffiness of Ottoman rulers. He spoke of himself as the servant of the nation, and of the citizens as his brothers whom he asked to support the government with the filial loyalty due to a compassionate parent. And in the tradition of Omar the great Caliph, Faisal publicly declared: "If I err forgive me and point out to me my error."[2]

How different the subsequent history of Syria and Palestine would have been if the Arab State had been allowed to develop in peace the principles upon which it was founded. After the Battle of Maisaloun the course of the country's development was completely warped. Instead of peace there was conflict and unrelieved strain, and the energies of the people, diverted from constructive work, were consumed in opposition to the mandatory regime. For a wide gap separated the people of Syria from the Mandatory Power who assumed the mandate with the colonial spirit and mentality, and actually staffed the Syrian administration with French colonial officials.

France inaugurated her trusteeship by breaking up the already partitioned country. Syria and Lebanon were proclaimed separate states, and Syria was divided into four so-called states—Damascus, Aleppo, the Alawites, and the Druze Mountain—and the Sanjak of Alexandretta under a special status.

Over this conglomeration France established a military dictatorship. The first three High Commissioners were military men

2. An authoritative account of the Arab State is given by Sati' al-Hosri in *Youm Maisaloun*, Beirut, 1945. Al-Hosri was member of the Damascus Government since its inception, first as director and then as minister of education. He was Faisal's envoy during the negotiations with General Gouraud, and therefore was in the full stream of the events which he relates.

with a large army under their command. The High Commissioner ruled like an autocrat with unfaltered legislative and executive powers and influence over the judiciary. Civil liberty was sur-pressed under the martial law which continued in force until 1925. Self-government was denied; French officials swarmed all over the country. Education was given a strong French bias and orienta-tion. The nationalist press was repressed, and national leaders were subjected to a system of police supervision.

There were economic troubles as well. Syria had emerged from the war impoverished. Its economic life was dislocated by its de-tachment from the Ottoman Empire, its fragmentation into sepa-rate political and economic sections, and the barriers set up between it and other Arab states which had previously formed an economic unit. The French denied Syria the right of reverting to the stable currency which she enjoyed before the war, and established a monetary system based on the franc and subject to its fluctuations and uncertainties. Native industries were ruined so that French manufacture could find an undisputed market. Although under the terms of the mandate the Mandatory was committed to the open door policy, yet in practice there was discrimination in favor of French goods. Concessions were given to French companies, and French officials, acting on behalf of Syria, concluded agreements which served to enrich French speculators to the detriment of the country's interests.

Of all the grievances, the dismemberment of the country was the most bitterly resented, all the more as the divisions were based on sectarian differences. The French promoted religious antipathies and dissensions and played one group of the population against another, a policy destructive of the healthy growth of the country and in sharp conflict with the spirit and purpose of the mandate.

Uprisings and revolts broke out in various parts of the country; the most serious was the revolution of 1925–1927 which came close to throwing the French out of Syria. It started among the Druzes, a people passionately attached to freedom and proud of a tradition of valor and personal bravery. They had on several occasions re-belled gainst the Turks, although Turkish authority over the Druze Mountain was nominal and hardly touched the inhabitants. French rule was intolerable by comparison.

From the Druze Mountain the revolution spread northward to Damascus and central Syria and westward to the confines of Leb-anon. While its immediate cause was the high-handed policy of the French governor in the Druze district, its aim was a united Syria free of French rule. A proclamation was issued calling for:

1. The complete independence of Syria, one and indivisible;
2. The establishment of a national government and a freely elected Constituent Assembly for framing the Organic Law;
3. The evacuation of the French army and creation of a national army;
4. The application of the principles of the French Revolution and the Rights of Man.[3]

The French used excessive measures to meet the Revolution. Twice they shelled and bombed Damascus, traditionally known as the oldest city in the world. Villages were bombed without warning, trees cut down, and the waters cut off so that whole groves withered away. Villagers were gathered and indiscriminately shot. And in keeping with their policy of setting the different communities against each other, the French armed the Armenians and Circassians, and for a time allowed them to kill, loot, and burn at will.[4]

The Revolution was finally put down. It cost France dearly in money and prestige. In life, her losses were not heavy. Seneghalese troops, and, in a lesser degree, levies recruited from the minorities who lived within Syria, fought her colonial battles against the forces of freedom.

To the Syrians, the revolution meant a severe loss in life and property, but it restored their self-confidence and gave them a feeling of solidarity. It saw acts of heroism which have become a cherished memory.

Its lesson was not wholly lost on the French. Shaken by their losses and the publicity which the revolution received in the world press, they made an attempt to change their technique in dealing with the Syrians. They called elections for a Constituent Assembly, which met in Damascus in June 1928 and drafted a constitution for the state. Disagreements with the French High Commissioner over certain articles of the Constitution resulted in the dissolution of the Assembly in May 1930.

The people continued to press for elections. Two years later, disturbances and unrest forced the authorities to hold elections, but these were carried out under illegitimate pressure from the mandatory. A majority of moderates was returned, and the French,

3. Royal Institute of International Affairs, *Survey of International Relations, The Islamic World,* 1925, p. 426.

4. *Ibid.,* pp. 428–439.

thinking they had sufficient support within the Chamber, presented it with a draft treaty. The terms of the treaty roused a storm of protest, whereupon this Assembly was dismissed like its predecessor.

The deadlock continued. The increasing tension broke out in disturbances in January 1936, following the arrest and deportation of nationalist leaders without trial. Further arrests and punitive measures hardened the people's will, and they embarked upon a road of civil disobedience, expressed by a general strike in the principal towns which lasted for fifty days and was remarkable for discipline and organization.

The French decided to come to an understanding with the nationalists. Negotiations were opened, and a treaty of alliance on the model of the Anglo-Iraqi treaty was concluded. Elections were held and the new Parliament ratified the treaty amidst great popular rejoicing. But the French were unregenerate in their hearts. When the treaty came before the French Parliament it was defeated in spite of the French Government's publicly declared assurances of its immediate ratification. There was bitterness in Syria and great indignation against the power which could not keep her word nor learn by her experiences. The Syrian Government resigned, and a tense situation followed upon the suspension of the constitution and the dismissal of the Chamber. The High Commissioner clearly described the mood of the French authorities when he declared that there should be no doubt concerning the permanence of French rule in Syria.[5]

In 1939, the French gave away to the Turks a large and fair province of Syria, the Sanjak of Alexandretta. It was an unsavory affair, concluded with the blessings of England and the League of Nations as a helpless onlooker. It was a flagrant infringement of the terms of the mandate which stated: "The mandatory shall be responsible for seeing that no part of the territory of Syria and Lebanon is ceded or leased or in any way placed under the control of a foreign power."[6] A European conflict was looming on the horizon, and France, anxious for her safety in the Eastern Mediterranean, handed the Sanjak to Turkey as the price of her friendship.

When the second World War broke out, the French mandate had run a turbulent course of twenty years during which it had thoroughly alienated the Syrians from France. The entire period

5. Julien: "France and Islam," in *Foreign Affairs*, 1940, pp. 696–697.
6. Mandate for Syria and Lebanon, Article 4.

was one of unrelieved tension and continued conflict both civil
and armed. The armed risings, though sporadic and unorganized,
were not isolated incidents but an expression of the national struggle for independence. They were accompanied by a civil struggle
in the form of strikes, persistent demands for constitutional government and a representative assembly, and strong opposition
within the national parliament to the dictates of the Mandatory
Power.

Such was the situation in Syria when World War II broke out.
After the collapse of France, the Vichy regime was in control, until
it was overthrown by the British in collaboration with the Fighting
French in the summer of 1941, when a joint Anglo-French occupation took its place. On June 8th, the Representative of France,
General Catroux, in the name of Free France and her chief, General de Gaulle, proclaimed the termination of the mandate and the
independence of Syria and Lebanon. The proclamation was endorsed by British authorities in the Middle East. Shortly after, Mr.
Oliver Lyttleton, British Minister of State for the Middle East, and
General de Gaulle signed an agreement in which Great Britain
recognized the preeminent position of France in Syria and Lebanon. In September Catroux announced the establishment of the
independent Republic of Syria.

During the two years that followed, Syria was ruled in an anomalous way. The British were in military control, the administration was in the hands of the French, and the so-called independent
local government had very limited authority.

When the United States entered the war, the British and French
authorities approached her to recognize the independence of the
two Levant states. The United States refused her recognition on
the grounds that the independence of Syria and Lebanon was delimited, and that the local governments were neither representative nor in actual control.

Elections for Parliament were held in the summer of 1943. The
National Bloc, the force around which resistance to the mandate
had crystallized in the 1930's, was elected. The Parliament met in
August.

Although a representative government supported by a freely
elected parliament was formed, the French were reluctant to hand
over to the national authorities actual control and the functions
which made sovereignty a reality. Up to 1944 the French were in
control of education, the customs—an important source of revenue

—the telegraph, telephone, and postal services, tribal affairs, public security, and the armed forces. By the end of that year these services, with the exception of the armed forces, were transferred to the national government, now entitled to appoint and receive diplomatic representatives.

In the summer of 1944, the U.S.S.R. recognized the unconditional independence of Syria and Lebanon, and refused recognition of a privileged position in either of the two countries to any outside power. The United States and China followed suit and gave their full recognition without reservation.

In the spring of 1945, the transfer of the armed forces from French to national control was at issue. The French insisted on getting a treaty before giving up the army. The Syrians were unwilling to enter into treaty relations with France, but they were persuaded by Great Britain and some Arab states to open negotiations. The French proposals were unacceptable inasmuch as France demanded control over education, economic predominance, and military bases for naval, land, and air forces, for an indefinite period. As a threat and a measure of intimidation, French troops landed in Beirut at the time the terms were presented to the Syrian Government.

At this point violence broke out. The French tried to terrorize the Syrians into acceptance of their terms by bombing the chief cities. Damascus received the heaviest share of machine-gunning and bombardment. For the third time in twenty years, the French bombed this beautiful city, the heart and symbol of Arab nationalism. As the city was unprotected and undefended on each occasion, the bombing resulted in the wanton destruction of life and property. The Parliament House was singled out for attack and partially destroyed. It is characteristic of French antagonism to the institution which represented the people of Syria that every time a conflict broke out between the people and the French authorities, the Parliament was the target of reprisal.

The French action nearly precipitated a crisis between Great Britain and France. On May 31, 1945 Prime Minister Churchill informed General de Gaulle that in the interest of Middle East security, a region of communication with Japan, he had ordered the Chief Commander of the Middle East to interfere in the violent conflict and prevent the future shedding of blood. To avoid collision between British and French troops, de Gaulle was requested to order the French troops at once to cease fire and retire to their barracks. Churchill concluded that when fire had ceased and order was restored the British Government would be ready to begin tripartite talks in London.

The British ultimatum infuriated General de Gaulle. In his press conference, held on June 2, he accused Great Britain of interfering in Syria and Lebanon thereby rendering the task of France more difficult in a region assigned to French control by mutual agreement. His observations on Syria are astonishing for their complete failure to grasp the situation. Syria, according to General de Gaulle, was not a geographical and political unity like Egypt and Iraq, but a collection of regions differing widely from one another, inhabited by equally different populations who adhere to a variety of religions. In answer to Churchill's invitation to a tripartite conference in London, de Gaulle retorted that not only the Levant but the whole Arab question was involved, and since all the Great Powers had an interest in it he called for a Five Power Conference to consider the affair in the light of international cooperation.

Churchill, speaking in the House of Commons on June 5, declared that the British Government recognized the special position of France in the Levant but did not undertake to maintain it. The principal task of Great Britain in the Middle East, he said, was to see that communications were not interrupted. Churchill further explained that when he had met the President of the Syrian Republic in Cairo, in February 1945, he had insisted energetically on the necessity of a peaceful settlement with France. The Levant States, he went on, were persuaded by strong British pressure to agree to open negotiations with the French. The British Government had warned the French authorities against the landing of troops, but without success.

The Five Power Conference did not materialize. But Great Britain and France, in two conferences held in December 1945 in London and Beirut respectively, reached an agreement on the regroupment of their troops in the Levant. Syria and Lebanon protested strongly against any arrangement concluded without their consent. They demanded the complete removal of all foreign troops from their countries, and refused recognition of a privileged position to any foreign power. The United States and the Soviet Union expressed their disapproval of the Franco-British bilateral agreement. When the United Nations held its first session in London in January 1946 Syria and Lebanon forcefully defended their case. In March of the same year a conference, in which the two

Levant States participated with Great Britain and France, met in Paris. It was decided that all French and British troops would evacuate Syria by the end of April and Lebanon by the end of December 1946. In both countries the evacuation was completed as scheduled.

The National Government considered education of prime importance. Its first step was to free education from the all-pervading French control expressed in the exclusively French intellectual and cultural orientation of the country's youth and the dominance of the French language even over Arabic, the native tongue. The whole system of education was a replica of the French school system. Young Syrians wishing to continue their studies abroad were sent to France. Only French diplomas and certificates were given due recognition. The teaching profession was a monopoly in the hands of French officials and French-educated Syrians. In all appointments to public office, priority was given to candidates with French training.

The French were fully aware of the hold over the country which this educational monopoly gave them. When they lost their political power, they clung with even greater tenacity to the maintenance of their control over education. They conceived the plan of a cultural treaty with Syria, and to this effect they presented detailed proposals to the Syrian Government. The proposed treaty provided, among other things, for the confirmation of the paramount position of the French language which was to continue as a required course of study in all the primary, intermediate, secondary, and vocational schools, and which was to be assigned in the public examinations one fourth of the total grades given to all the subjects offered. Students who wished to take the public examinations in French would be allowed to do so. Special privileges were to be granted to French institutions controlled and supervised exclusively by a French Inspector General. This meant the setting up of a French school system on a level with the government system and independent of its supervision. At the same time the public system of education was to come under French control, for the treaty proposed that the Ministry of Education should consult with French representatives on all legislation for education, and asked for French officials the right to sit on the Government educational councils and committees and to participate in all public examinations. In brief, the French demands amounted to the establishment of a French cultural protectorate. They were, of course, refused.

It is characteristic of the national movement that it has always regarded education as a cornerstone in the struggle for liberation and the building of an independent state. In 1936, when the Syrians thought they were on the threshold of independence and a national government was in power, a vigorous program of education was launched. The tempo slowed down when the French went back on the treaty promising the termination of the mandate, and reassumed authority and control. The next attempt, made in 1944 was more thoroughgoing and lasting. The law passed in December of that year abolished all laws and regulations concerning education issued under the mandate and provided a new basis of departure.

The reorganization of the public system of education was entrusted to Sati'-al-Hosri, the man with whom the growth of education in Iraq is closely associated. The system as reorganized was free of foreign control; no priority was recognized for any foreign language or culture; all were treated on a footing of equality. A close integration was effected with the public systems of Egypt and Iraq. The democratic principle was established by the unification of the elementary and primary schools, providing the same type of school for all classes of the population. On the primary level education was made free; and aid was extended to a large portion of the pupils attending the secondary schools. School facilities were expanded considerably. Teacher training, which had been badly neglected under the French, was given serious attention. Here as in Iraq and Egypt, students preparing for the teaching profession receive their education, board and lodging at the expense of the State. Private schools, foreign and native, came under the supervision of the Ministry of Education. The Arabic language, Arab history, and the geography of the Arab countries became required courses to be taught in conformity with the program of the Ministry of Education. No schools were exempted from the public examinations.

The French viewed these educational developments with profound aversion. In the Franco-Syrian conflict of 1945, the cultural emancipation of the Syrians was one of the chief factors which inflamed the French and drove them to the bombing and shelling of Damascus and other Syrian towns. In the fall of that year the French schools, having refused to conform to the regulations which required all private schools, national as well as foreign, to register with the Ministry of Education, remained closed. Consequently, the government was faced with the serious problem of providing school facilities for the nearly 20,000 pupils who had attended the French schools in the previous year. The government and the private schools responded enthusiastically and effectively. A special budget annex was passed, many new elementary and secondary schools were opened throughout the country, old schools were expanded and new classes added to them. Financial aid was advanced to private schools for expansion and the establishment of new institutions. Thus the emergency was adequately met.

A comparison between the number of students attending public schools under the Mandate and under the national regime shows the expansion of the public school system during the past few years. In 1942–43, last year of French control in Syria, there was about 75,000 students in all state schools. Within seven years, in 1949–50, the number rose to over 200,000. In that year the students registered in all schools, public and private, were 265,700. The Syrian University was reorganized and expanded considerably in this period. Students increased from 450 in 1942–43 to 2205 in 1949–50. Four new colleges—the Colleges of Sciences, Literature, Engineering, and the Higher Teachers Training Institute— were added. Prior to the establishment of these colleges, the University had consisted of a College of Law, and a Faculty of Medicine comprising Medicine, Pharmacy, Dentistry, and Nursing. The education budget for 1949–50 was L.S. 24,697,000, over 17% of the total budget.

There is at present an enthusiastic drive to bring education within everybody's reach. The aim of the Ministry of Education is to found a primary school in every village, no matter how small and remote. Classes to combat illiteracy and disseminate knowledge have been organized all over the country, and all educated citizens are called upon to participate in teaching these classes. Syria is mobilizing her population in the campaign against ignorance.

Apart from the reconstruction of the system of education, the government's achievements in internal reforms were inadequate. Some measures for economic development were attempted. Legislation was put through Parliament providing for capital outlays for an Extraordinary Program of Agricultural Development. An American Agricultural mission, sent by the State and Agriculture Departments at the request of the Syrian Government, commented favorably on the Syrian agricultural program, and made recommendations and suggestions for further development. A British firm of engineers, Gibb, was charged with the task of making an extensive study of the economic resources and potentialities of the country. Several minor irrigation and reclamation schemes, some of them begun under the mandate, were carried through. Public works included the building of roads, numerous schools, some hospitals, clinics, and government buildings. Some of the public buildings are designed in a modernized Arab style, simple and dignified, and in keeping with the architectural tradition of the country. An automatic telephone system was planned by Egyptian engineers and installed under their supervision.

The regime which had to its credit the achievement of independence was nevertheless overthrown within six years of its establishment. Failure in Palestine was the basic cause for the resentment felt by army officers and by the people who supported the army coup. The army had been sent to Palestine unprepared and unequipped. Allowing for the lack of time—the army had been under national control for only three years at the time of the Palestine war—and the many problems pressing upon the government, it remains true that the army was neglected. In size it did not exceed the militia; its equipment consisted of light arms. It was intended for internal security, no thought being given to its preparation for the inevitable conflict over Palestine.

The coup d'etat struck on March 30, 1949 by Husni Za'im, the army chief of staff, was accomplished without bloodshed. The overthrow of the Kuwatli regime caused little surprise or regret. Frustration over the Palestine disaster, fear and anxiety for the future made the people welcome a change of regime, especially if it meant the strengthening of the army for the defense of the homeland.

The overthrown President, Shukri al-Kuwatli, has a distinquished career of struggle for national liberation first under the Turks and later against the French. His probity and patriotism are above suspicion. But he had come to look upon himself as the indispensable leader and head of the state, and was surrounded by a clique which did not command general confidence. The ruling group as a whole thought of themselves as the architects of independence, and therefore entitled to reap the fruits and glories of rule. The popular discontent at the monopoly of power in the hands of a few people, and at the general inefficiency in the administration, was aggravated when Kuwatli had himself elected for another term of office. The Constitution, to avoid the danger of an occupant entrenching himself in the presidency, had specifically stipulated that the president could not succeed himself and that a lapse of at least five years should separate his tenure of office from his reelection. The amendment of the Constitution to allow for the immediate reelection of Kuwatli was yet another evidence of the extent to which the Syrian republic was dominated by the President and the ruling oligarchy.

The Za'im coup had the double purpose of strengthening the army and setting up a progressive and efficient administration. In the first days of the new regime a number of progressive reforms were inaugurated, among them the promulgation of a new civil code and the granting of suffrage to women. But power turned the head of Husni Za'im, and he went back on the aims and spirit which had inspired the coup. He got himself elected head of the state and became preoccupied with his own aggrandizement and safety.

In its conception and execution, the coup had been entirely free of any foreign influence and orientation. But once it was accomplished, Great Britain, France, and the United States tried to use it each for its own particular plans. The United States was eager to put through the conclusion of peace between Syria and Israel. Britain pulled strings for the Union of Syria and Iraq—The Fertile Crescent Scheme—under the Hashimite crown, a project opposed by Shukri al-Kuwatli who had insisted on the maintenance of the republican regime. France, towards whom Za'im leaned, thought the time propitious for the restoration of her lost position in Syria. In his foreign policy as in his relations with the other Arab States Za'im was unbalanced and unstable. He inaugurated his rule by a rapprochement with Iraq and Transjordan, a policy which encouraged the sponsors of the Fertile Crescent Scheme. Suddenly he left the Hashimite camp and veered towards Egypt and Saudi Arabia. His headiness and lack of balance, added to his arbitrary and repressive rule, alienated from Husni Za'im his own army comrades and the people who so recently had welcomed his advent·with great hope. He was killed in the second army coup led by Colonel Hinnawi in August of the same year. Elections for a Constituent Assembly were held in November. The Assembly convened in December and was ready to vote union with Iraq, when the third coup raised by Colonel Shishakli intervened and arrested the plan.

The third coup professed to aim at restoring the ideals and purposes which had inspired the first army rising against the politicians' regime. Those responsible for it declared their intention of preserving the independence of Syria, maintaining the republican form of government, and ensuring the country's development along a progressive course.

The Constitution drafted by the Constituent Assembly and promulgated in September, 1950 was in line with the progressive trend current since the overthrow of the Kuwatli regime. The Constitution affirms the principle of government of the people, by the people, and for the people. It stresses the importance of the individual by providing for his full development and by emphasizing individual responsibility for the preservation of constitutional rights, the maintenance of the republic, and the defense of the fatherland. It is a socialist constitution envisaging the creation of a society free of fear, poverty, disease, and ignorance, where social justice prevails and all the citizens partake in the country's bounties. That the national wealth may be equitably distributed and fully utilized, principles are laid down for the ownership and use of property. The extent of property holding shall be determined by law, and ownership rights are forfeited if the land is not put to use during a period set by law. Small and medium holdings are to be encouraged and promoted. State domain is to be distributed in viable lots among landless peasants in return for small sums paid in instalments. The peasant shall be protected by law, his standard of living raised through the diffusion of education, the expansion of the cooperative movement, the provision of hygienic housing, and the construction of model villages. Labor is likewise protected by the State. Work is the right of every citizen, and an honorable duty. The State, through the development and planning of the national economy, shall make work available and secure for every citizen. Unionization is free within the law. The State may nationalize any establishment connected with public welfare in return for a fair indemnity. Taxes are to be levied on a progressive basis. The provision of social security is the responsibility of the State towards the citizen. A system of social insurance shall be set up and funds for it provided with the participation of the State, the individual, and business establishments. The State shall protect the health of its citizens by the provision of adequate medical care and treatment. Education is the right of every citizen. Primary education is compulsory; primary, secondary, and vocational education are free of charge in the government schools. In planning the educational budget, priority shall be given to expenditures on primary, secondary, and vocational education with the aim of achieving equality among the Syrians by universalizing the first stages of education.

While the constitution was being drafted, there was disagreement on the inclusion of a statement about the religion of the State. A compromise was reached by re-introducing the clause—present in the 1930 constitution—on Islam being the religion of the President of the Republic; and by inserting a statement about adherence to the ideals of Islam the religion of the majority of the people, about building the new state on a firm moral basis in accordance with the principles of Islam and the other revealed religions, and about combating atheism and moral disintegration.

The Syrian Constitution was the first Arab Constitution drafted and promulgated under a fully independent regime. It expressed the new trend in Arab nationalism: emphasis upon social and economic reforms.

After the promulgation of the Constitution, the Assembly was transformed into a Parliament where the *Sh'ab*—People's Party—had a majority. For a time, a semblance of cooperation between the *Sh'ab* and the army was maintained. The army continued to wield the real authority behind a façade of constitutional government, as it had done since March 1949. But mutual suspicion led the military leaders to assume the form as well as the substance of rule. The break came in December 1951. President Atassi resigned and General Silo became head of the state. Parliament was dissolved and the constitution suspended.

The evils inherent in military rule are mitigated by the fact that the army leaders are progressive men, eager for the realization of social reforms, and devoted to the cause of making the army an adequate instrument for the defense of the country. They are, on the whole, an honest group. Probity in the conduct of public affairs, efficiency, and a sense of public duty have characterized the Syrian administration since the coming of the army into control.

Although the military authorities suspended the constitution, they are trying to put into effect some of its more important provisions, such as the distribution of the extensive state domain among landless peasants. According to the legislative decree of October 1952, any Syrian who has attained the age of 18 may register in his name a maximum area of 50 hectares of uncultivated land which cannot be irrigated from rivers and canals by flow, or ten hectares where it can be so irrigated. The applicant must pledge to work the land himself. He cannot sell or otherwise dispose of the land within fifteen years after its acquisition except mortgage it to the Agricultural Bank.

A fiscal reform is being effected through the increase in tax rates and the introduction of new direct taxes; the income tax rates have been raised and a progressive inheritance tax has been introduced, thus making taxes more in conformity with the principle of taxation according to ability.

Another expression of the socialist trend is the nationalization of public utilities, such as the water and electricity companies. Since public utilities involve social obligations, it is believed that nationalization, and not private enterprise, in which the profit making motive dominates, can best secure the public interest.

An important legislative decree, issued March 30, 1953, established a modern monetary system and a Central Bank to regulate credit and act as the financial agent of the government, and to help provide needed capital for agriculture and industry and for developmental projects. The Central Bank will replace the Banque de Syrie et du Liban, a French institution which had been a dominant power in Syria's economy. The establishment of the Central Bank will free Syria from the French economic control and the consequent political influence represented by the Banque de Syrie whose policy was governed by its interests and those of France. The new measure, which has established Syria's economic independence, was hailed by the government and the public as an event equal in importance to the withdrawal of foreign troops in 1946 which marked the political independence of the country.

The military regime is committed to a vigorous program of economic development. Priority is given to the expansion of agriculture, the backbone of the country's economy. About 70% of the population of Syria depend upon agriculture for a living.

The agricultural potential of Syria is great. Unlike Egypt where land hunger is the problem, Syria has not enough labor to work the land. Only recently has machinery been introduced into farming. The fact that most agricultural work is done by man and beast explains the low productivity per farmer and per unit farmed. Another cause of low productivity is the system of land tenure under which about half the land is cultivated by share-tenants, and owned in absenteeship by landlords who live in towns and have little knowledge of or interest in agriculture.

Most of the arable land is under extensive farming. Cereal, mainly wheat, absorbs 75% of the cultivated land and makes Syria an important wheat producing area. What Syria needs is not so much the expansion of the arable land as increase in agricultural productivity by the extension of irrigation to land under dry farming. The water resources are capable of considerable development. At present only the smaller courses of water are adequately harnessed. Barada, which waters the Damascus Ghuta, has had a network of canals for hundreds of years. The Orontes is partly developed; the Euphrates awaits development.

The Syrian Government has applied to the International Bank for a loan to finance its development projects which include the drainage of the Ghab, an extensive swampy depression formed by the Orontes; control of the Khabur, a tributary of the Euphrates, for irrigation; the construction of a barrage on the Euphrates for the generation of electric power; irrigation works and a power station on the Yarmuk in southern Syria; and the enlargement of the Latakia port. A mission of the Bank has visited Syria and examined the projects which it is asked to help finance.

The agricultural possibilities of the Jazira in northeast Syria, through which the Euphrates flows, are only beginning to be tapped. The Jazira is a vast region of rolling plains with deep, fertile soil. The construction of major irrigation projects could put 300,000 to 400,000 hectares of virgin land under intensive cultivation.

Government participation in the development of the Jazira is still in the project stage. Pending construction of large scale irrigation schemes, agricultural development in the Jazira is proceeding by individual effort. Pumps have been installed to draw subterranean and river water for irrigation. Tractors work the soil. Cotton is beginning to supplant wheat as the principal export crop. Cotton is not new to Syrian agriculture. It was widely cultivated during the Middle Ages and exported to Europe from the principal Syrian ports. The finest quality grew in the plantations which covered the environs of Aleppo and Hama.[7] The present world demand for cotton has made its cultivation a profitable venture. There has been a veritable rush to the Jazira where people—some of them not even remotely interested or experienced in agriculture—are trying their hand in developing the land and laying it to cotton in the hope of getting rich quickly.

This inexperienced, unorganized adventure into cotton raising

7. Heyd, W., *op. cit.*, II, 612–613.

has caused havoc. To avoid recurrence of the loss recently incurred because of lack of control and planning, the Government has established a Cotton Bureau to direct the production of cotton by making select seed available, assuring the means of combating insects and disease, and growing the varieties in demand on the world market.

Rice is another of the expanding crops and is cultivated mainly in the Jazira. Groundnuts culture is a promising possibility because of the wide demand on the world market for groundnuts oil. Olives are the principal source of oil in Syria, where the cultivation of olive trees is one of the major agricultural activities of the population. Tobacco is another important crop and is grown on the Latakia slopes. Fruit growing now largely centered in the Damascus area could be expanded with the extension of irrigation. There is need for the improvement of the quality of the fruit especially with regard to canning and preserving.

Stockbreeding, an activity closely related to agriculture, is maintained largely by nomads, non-sedentary and semi-sedentary. The nomads, about 300,000, are being naturally and gradually absorbed as a result of the development of the Jazira, a welcome process in view of the shortage of labor in that region. Livestock breeding, an important source of agricultural wealth, has not yet received due care. In seasons of drought and severe cold a million head perish annually. Provision of adequate fodder, water, shelter, and veterinary facilities are urgently needed. The marginal lands, at present uneconomically used for cereals, could with advantage be converted into grazing grounds by being sowed with hardy grasses and shrubs.[8]

Industry has not yet been established on a stable basis. It received an impetus during the war when imports were reduced to a minimum. Capital, accumulated during the war, was invested in the construction and equipment of a number of industrial plants. A huge glass factory outside Damascus has a production potential sufficient to supply the whole Middle East. Lack of markets forces the factory to work at partial capacity. A large sugar and glucose plant has been set up in Homs. Fuller experimentation on the possibility of sugar-beet culture should have preceded the establishment of the factory which at present has to rely on imported raw

8. For a full account of the economic potentialities of Syria, see Sir Alexander Gibb: *The Economic Development of Syria.* See also: *Report of the United States— Syria Agricultural Mission,* Washington, 1947.

sugar. The tanning industry has a larger potential output than the market can absorb. It is a weakness of Syrian industry that large and elaborate plants were built before a full study of marketing facilities had been made. Another weakness is the venture of the inexperienced, encouraged by the ease of moneymaking during the war, into the industrial field, thus creating an unsound competition destructive to nascent industries. The textile industry is the most important, and is firmly established. It is centered in Aleppo and Damascus. Fruit and vegetable canning supplies the home market and produces a surplus for export. Production of vegetable oils, soap, cigarettes, and cement is sufficient for local needs. Cotton ginning and processing is expanding.

While it is the Government's policy, under planned economy, to extend aid to industry through protective measures, it is at the same time watchful that industry discharges its obligations to the consumer and the state by maintaining an acceptable standard of quality and price.

Handicrafts, for which Syria has been famed through the ages, still form an important part of industrial production. Hama is the center of the handloom industry which accounts for a high proportion of the total output of cloth. This cloth is of a better quality than machine made cloth, but also more expensive. A number of fine industries have survived in Damascus; wood and metal carving and inlay, and the weaving of beautiful silks and brocades. Syria has a large class of artisans and craftsmen who have inherited the skill of generations.

The high cost of power is a handicap to industry. Syria has no coal, wood, or oil. But oil pipelines from Iraq and Saudi Arabia pass through Syria on their way to the Mediterranean. In order to ensure an adequate supply of oil at reasonable prices, the pipeline agreement with Aramco provides for the yearly sale, if Syria calls for it, of 200,000 tons of crude oil at world prices. Two projects are under consideration for the generation of hydro-electric power. The Yusuf Pasha dam on the Euphrates will supply power to Aleppo and the towns in the Euphrates area. The Yarmuk dam will provide the Damascus region with light and power.

A labor movement was slow in forming, and the enactment of labor legislation was long delayed. It was not until 1946 that a comprehensive labor law was put into effect. Existing legislation provides for the fundamental needs of labor. The employment of women and children is regulated by law, hours of work are fixed, sick leave with pay and security against accidents and occupational diseases are provided. Committees have been formed for arbitration and conciliation and for the determination of minimum wages. Unionization is recognized in law. A General Federation includes almost all the unions and has a membership of over 60,000. The fact that the majority of workers are in small craft workshops, which employ few wage earners—sometimes only one—and where the relations between employer and employe are often determined by personal or family ties, has hindered the expansion of labor organization.

A sound economy for Syria depends upon maximum agricultural productivity and the development of agricultural industries. The present policy of planned economy and the serious pre-occupation with full utilization of the country's resources has already borne fruit in the greatly increased national income and in the fact that for the first time Syria has a favorable balance of trade.

*   *   *

In Lebanon, the Mandate had a less agitated course than in Syria.

Lebanon in its present boundaries is a creation of the French Mandate. Until the post-World War I settlement, the area covered by the Republic of Lebanon belonged to three administrative units. One was the Wilayet (Province) of Beirut which comprised Beirut City, Tripoli, Sidon, and Tyre. It extended southwards to Nablus and included Akka and Haifa, and northwards to Alexandria. The second, the Wilayet of Syria, covered of Lebanese territory the Beka', Baalbek, and Riyak. The third unit was the district of Mount Lebanon, ruled since 1860 by a special regime set up by agreement between the Ottoman Government and the Great Powers, under which the Mountain enjoyed a large measure of autonomy.

The regime of the Mandate, although it was not challenged with the persistent opposition it encountered in Syria, was nevertheless widely resented and vigorously criticized in the Lebanese Press. Following the Syrian Revolution of 1925, Lebanon was granted a constitution and declared a republic with a President and a Parliament. Simultaneously with the negotiation of the Franco-Syrian treaty of 1936, a treaty terminating the Mandate was concluded between France and Lebanon. Both treaties met the same fate of rejection by the French Parliament. Lebanese independence was proclaimed by General Catroux in June 1941 as the British and Free French forces were preparing to cross the southern frontier of Lebanon to drive the Vichy regime out, and again in November when a new Lebanese government was formed.

The first free elections which Lebanon had under the French were held in the fall of 1943. The electorate turned away from the pro-French candidates and returned a majority who stood for independence and cooperation with the other Arab countries. The first act of the new Parliament was to amend the Constitution to be more in conformity with the independent status of Lebanon. The French authorities took strong exception to the fundamental constitutional changes about to be enacted by Parliament. As they were unable to prevail upon Parliament to forego the constitutional amendments, they arrested the President of the Republic, the Prime Minister, and other members of the Cabinet. This high-handed action antagonized all sections of the Lebanese population and roused public opinion throughout the Arab countries. Great Britain, the power responsible for wartime security in the area, took a firm stand against the French and was supported by the United States. France backed down. The President and the Ministers were released and Lebanon was launched on its independent course.

Since the achievement of independence the Arab aspect of Lebanon has been emphasized. The Mandate had assiduously propagated the French language and culture as a means to win the loyalty of the Lebanese to France. French was recognized as an official language along with Arabic. It was used in the law courts by judges and lawyers even though the litigants may not have understood a word of French. Even deputies in Parliament at times debated in French. Since the termination of the Mandate, Arabic has been established as the only official language and all public transactions are conducted in the language of the country. Lebanon has carried its share of cooperation with the other Arab countries through the medium of the Arab League and has pressed for closer economic cooperation among the Arab states. In the field of international relations, Lebanon has rendered distinguished service in the compilation of the Charter of Human Rights, and Lebanon's representative, Dr. Charles Malik, has presided over the United Nations Economic and Social Council and the Human Rights Commission.

Some progress has been recorded in education. Under the Man-

date, the public system of education was deplorably neglected.
In 1918–1919, the first year after the French occupation, there
were 21,000 students in the public schools. The number dwindled
steadily until in 1925–26 it fell to 6733. During the last year of
French control, 1942–43, there were no more than 23,166, an increase of about 2000 students during twenty-four years of French
rule. The neglect of public education was not accidental. In the
absence of public schools, foreign schools—of which over 80 per
cent were French—undertook to educate the youth of the country
and consequently mold and orient its mind and spirit.

Since 1943 the number of students in the public schools has
increased steadily. In 1947–48,[9] there were 54,663 students in the
government primary schools. In the same year 82,792 students attended private primary schools where fees are paid.

About 75% of the Lebanese are literate. In this respect, Lebanon
by far leads the other Arab countries. Yet Lebanon depends to a
great extent upon private, mostly foreign schools for the education of its youth. Public instruction does not go beyond the primary stage except for a few technical schools, two secondary
schools—one of them incomplete—and one teachers' training college. Secondary education is carried by private schools, national
and foreign. French influence already strong even in primary education is preponderant in the secondary schools. The defects of
this educational setup are obvious. Since the bulk of education is
carried by private institutions only those who can pay the fees are
able to go to school. The system, besides being undemocratic,
tends to promote divided loyalties and to accentuate communal
differences because of the preponderance of foreign and denominational schools. The public system of education needs to be greatly
developed and expanded before national solidarity through education can be achieved. Higher education is entirely foreign except
for the Lebanese Academy of Fine Arts, a private institution under
government sponsorship. The Higher Teachers Training College,
offering courses in liberal arts and sciences, is expected to be the
nucleus of a state university.

The American and French universities have for over eighty years
provided the opportunities of higher education to Lebanon and to
students from all over the Middle East. The French university—
Université Saint Joseph, a Jesuit foundation—has a Faculty of
Medicine which comprises medicine, pharmacy, dentistry, mid-

9. The last year for which statistics are available.

wifery, nursing, and a hospital; Faculties of Engineering and Law; the Institute of Oriental Literature, and the Institute of Philosophy and Theology. The university has a famous press and a rich oriental library. The American University of Beirut consists of the College of Arts and Sciences, the schools of Engineering, Agriculture, Medicine, Pharmacy, Nursing and Midwifery, and a hospital. Both universities have preparatory schools attached to them. The American College for Women, a junior college since 1926, has recently raised its status to the full arts' course. A characteristic of all three higher institutions is their interest in social welfare work. The Fathers of the Jesuit University work among the Catholic youth, guiding and orienting them towards social responsibility. The University conducts a school for visiting nurses and social workers. The American University and the Women's College do social and educational work among underprivileged groups in the city and maintain camps for work among the rural population.

The economic development of the country is proceeding slowly. A number of development schemes have been approved by Parliament. They include irrigation, electrification, drainage, town planning, and public health projects. The Litani river project, which is being studied under Point Four of the Truman Program, will provide electric power and water for irrigation and for household use over a large area of southern Lebanon.

Foreign experts have been invited by the Government to study and report on the economic development of Lebanon. According to the Gibb Report, the rapidly increasing population of Lebanon is expected to double in less than 25 years.[10]

Since two thirds of the population live on agriculture, the future prosperity of Lebanon depends to a great extent on the development of the land. As the arable lands are very limited and the possibilities of extending them not great, further development lies along the lines of increasing the area under irrigation, the intensification of agriculture, and the cultivation of more valuable crops.

A wide range of crops are grown. Olives are the most important fruit-bearing trees. On the road between Beirut and Sidon, olive trees are massed in one of the largest groves in the world. Fruit culture has extended considerably in recent years and many new varieties have been introduced. Apples and citrus fruit are the main agricultural exports. Sericulture, once a principal activity, decayed when rayon entered the world market, and mulberry

10. Sir Alexander Gibb: *The Economic Development of Lebanon*, p. 4.

groves along the coast and on the mountain slopes were cut down and replaced by fruit orchards. The revival of sericulture is a possibility since the competition of artificial silk is more apparent than real, the two commodities catering to different markets.[11]

The problem of land tenure is not as serious in Lebanon as in some other Arab countries. In the plains, tenant farming is the rule, with the insecurity of tenure it entails; but small and medium holdings prevail over the Lebanon mountains. The mountain slopes are cultivated with care and devotion by thrifty and hardy peasants. But as their means are small they are unable to introduce important improvements. Cooperative societies for credit, collective marketing, and community ownership of farm machinery and transport have not yet developed in Lebanon.

Lebanese agriculture does not as yet aim at standards of excellence, which is important in a country where land is scarce. These standards, with proper guidance, are not difficult to attain in a peasant community like the Lebanese, where energy, ambition, and intelligence characterize the peasant.

Industry is still in its infancy. Spinning and weaving, cement manufacture, tanning, the manufacture of soap and oil, cigarettes and matches, and certain food products cover the range of chief industries. Industrial development is essential to supplement agriculture and raise the standard of living. Light industries, in which the cost of the imported raw materials is small in comparison to the price of the finished products, could with advantage be introduced into the Lebanon.

A labor movement is forming. The Labor Code of 1946 regulates the relationship between employers and employes, provides for employers' associations, labor unions, and arbitration. It restricts the employment of women and children, establishes the 48-hour week, makes provisions for sick leave, paid vacations, and the payment of a compensation upon dismissal. The unions, of which there are about forty organized into four confederations, suffer from the apathy of the worker, the employer's lack of sympathy, and the restrictions imposed by the government which must approve their constitutions and by-laws and may dismiss the union's executive committee.

Lebanon's swift water courses are suitable for the production of hydro-electric power. But because of the low flow of the rivers

11. Keen: *op. cit.*, p. 83.

during the dry season, water power stations need to be supplemented by thermal installations. Two pipelines terminate on the coast of Lebanon. The IPC line ends in Tripoli where a refinery has been installed. Zahrani, a few miles south of Sidon, is the terminal of Tapline which carries the oil from the Persian Gulf coast of Arabia to the Mediterranean. The Mediterranean Refining Company is to set up a refinery for fuel oil at this terminal.

Lebanon is a trade center. This trade, however, consists of very large imports, almost wholly consumption goods, and very little export. Hence an adverse balance is a consistent feature of Lebanese trade. Invisible exports in the form of services normally make up for the deficit. Emigrant remittances and expenditure by tourists and foreign residents are an important source of revenue. The possibilities of Lebanon for tourism, and as a summer resort of the surrounding Arab countries, are only beginning to be developed.

The economies of both Syria and Lebanon have been seriously affected by the dissolution of the customs union between them. Under the Mandate, Syria and Lebanon formed something like a federal state with the High Commissioner a sort of federal governor. Decrees (arrêtés) issued by the High Commissioner had the validity of law and were applicable to both states. Even the laws which were peculiar to each of the two countries were nevertheless similar because of the common source from which they emanated. The services common to both states and known as the Common Interests included the army, the customs, public health legislation, control of the Banque de Syrie et du Liban and other concessionary companies, the main connecting highways, economic, social, and archaeological studies, the topographical maps and cadastral survey services. The Common Services were under the control of the High Commissioner.

In the fall of 1943 the two states, having set up independent governments, concluded an agreement which maintained as common interests the customs union, the control of concessionary companies, and the currency which was one for the two countries.

The agreement was a hasty arrangement, concluded without adequate study. It therefore lacked many of the requisites essential for the maintenance of the customs union. Both parties were dissatisfied with the working of the agreement, but failed to replace it by one based on serious and extensive economic study. In the meantime Lebanon concluded a separate financial agreement with

France while negotiations between France and Syria were in progress; the monetary unity of the two countries was broken, and henceforth the two currencies were no longer exchangeable.

The dissolution of the economic union came in March 1950. The Lebanese Government assumed that the economy of Lebanon was basically different from Syria's. It claimed that Lebanon was a trading center and an entrepôt, and consequently its interest demanded free trade. Syria, on the other hand, considered it vital for her prosperity and the establishment of her international solvency to protect her agricultural and industrial production.

There were minor irritations over relative shares of the customs receipts, and dissatisfaction with the management of the customs department. The disadvantages of the customs union were emphasized while its benefits to both countries were largely ignored. Misconceptions could have been dissipated if the light of thorough studies had been available. But the two partners, instead of taking a constructive stand, allowed matters to drift until the break came.

The dissolution was harmful to both. Syria lost in Lebanon the natural market for her products. Lebanon's loss was even greater, for Syria supplied it with wheat and other essential products and was the market for the profitable re-export trade of Lebanon.

Since the dissolution of the customs union, Lebanese economy has deteriorated rapidly. Agriculture suffered, especially citrus which was formerly exported to Syria. Industrial plants reduced their output considerably, some of them closed down altogether. Unemployment increased. Even merchants and commission agents who had clamored for the open door policy felt the pinch now that much of the trade was diverted from Beirut.

The undue emphasis placed on trade by the Lebanese Government has hindered the development of agriculture and industry. A country like Lebanon, where two thirds of the population live on agriculture, cannot be considered and treated primarily as a trade center. The full development of agricultural possibilities is vital not only for the much needed increase in individual and national income, but for an even more important consideration, that of stimulating greater love for the land and inducing attachment to the soil, an attachment which would hold the people on the farms and keep them from drifting into the towns and out of the country altogether. The development of industry also, promoting technological and scientific studies and encouraging the aptitudes and skills related to industrial enterprise and management—apart from its contribution to national wealth—is essential for the proper functioning of a modern state. Finally the prosperity of Lebanese trade itself depends in a large measure on the expansion of agricultural and industrial productivity within the country.

Syria took advantage of the break to organize her economy on a planned and constructive basis. She expanded her agriculture and speeded her industrial production. Syrian merchants who had previously imported their merchandise through Lebanese agents and commissioners now communicated directly with the sources from which the goods come. They also exported Syrian products directly without the services of Lebanese middlemen. The foreign agencies held by Lebanese and centered in Beirut opened branches in Syria where they transferred part of their capital.

In foreign trade, the aim has been the achievement of equilibrium in the balance of trade for which purpose exports have been pushed ahead through increased productivity, and imports concentrated on capital goods and machinery; the import of luxury and other consumptive goods is being restricted.

The construction of a new port at Latakia is an expression of the planned and constructive Syrian economy. Latakia is the natural port for northern Syria, an area which furnishes by far the major part of the agricultural and industrial products of the country. Even if the break with Lebanon had not come about, the development of the Latakia port would still be essential for disposing of the rapidly expanding agricultural produce of the Jazira and the Northern Orontes region, and for the growing imports of agricultural and industrial machinery. Latakia could become an important port for the transit trade across Syria to and from Iraq, especially when the projected railroad from Latakia to Aleppo— the latter being connected by railway with Baghdad through Deir ez-Zor—is completed.

Since the break, several attempts have been made to negotiate a new agreement. An agreement concluded in March 1951 provided for free trade in rural agricultural produce and certain industrial products, while tariffs on other industrial products were reduced. This agreement, revised to include more products on the free list and new products subject to reduced tariff rates, has been extended for another six months. Meanwhile Syria has offered a tentative plan for what it called an economic union to provide for common legislation in matters that affect a full fledged customs union, including uniformity in taxation and the unification of currency. If this plan is accepted by the Lebanese Government, Syria would be willing to allow the free movement of all trade, whether in articles locally produced or imported, and the free movement of persons and capital. The Lebanese Government has accepted the plan as a basis for study.

A customs union, accompanied by the requisites essential for its proper functioning, is the only sound basis of the relationship between Syria and Lebanon. The economies of the two countries are not divergent but interdependent. Union would allow for regional specialization with consequent economy in the expenditure of capital and effort, the expansion of production, and improvement in the quality of the goods produced or the services rendered. Lebanon, endowed by nature with superb climate and scenery, would become the summer resort of both countries. Lebanese ports would remain the principal harbors, and Beirut the main commercial and financial center for both Syria and Lebanon. Fruit growing, especially the citrus of the coast, would find a ready market in the interior. Syria would supply both countries with their wheat, dairy produce, and meat, and with the products of her better developed industries: textiles, glass, and canned foods.

In the unstable conditions of the world, Lebanon, a country which depends on imports for most of the necessities of life, is in danger because the essentials of its livelihood may be cut off in case of war. Hence the necessity of economic union with Syria which in time of war would be the only supplier of Lebanon. Moreover, the importance of trade for Lebanon, even in peace time, can have meaning only if the break with Syria is healed. For trade presupposes a market and Syria is the only adequate market for Lebanese trade, as it is the medium for communication between Lebanon on the one hand and Iraq and Jordan on the other.

In the opinion of international trade authorities, customs unions are indispensable for small countries. In negotiating for commercial treaties small countries are at a disadvantage because their markets are of little value to world trade. Customs unions give them bargaining power in negotiating treaties with other countries.

In Syria, apart from a few groups who have profited by the break, opinion is strongly in favor of economic union, and such union has the support of the Syrian Government. In Lebanon, the Chambers of Agriculture, Commerce, and Industry, organized groups—among them the National Socialist Block—and individual producers and industrialists have come out overwhelmingly for union. But a fully developed customs union is feared by some groups in Lebanon as a step leading to full economic fusion and finally to political union.

It is unfortunate that at times the economic relations with Syria are viewed from the angle of religious particularism. The elements among the Lebanese Christians who oppose economic union with Syria and its political implications, do so because they are not willing to be merged in a predominantly Moslem state although they are ready to accept Arab cooperation through the League. On the other hand, those areas—inhabited mostly by Moslems—which had formerly been part of Syria and were annexed to Lebanon after the first World War, remained unreconciled to their status until the termination of the Mandate; since then, irredentism among their inhabitants has subsided considerably. But since the economic break with Syria has hit these regions severely, irredentism may again be stirred up, especially as the insistence of Tripoli and Sidon on economic union seems to carry a threat.

Communal differences are the most serious problem in Lebanon. The population is about equally divided between Christians and Moslems, and the adherents of each religion are again subdivided into numerous sects and denominations. The Mandate had accentuated religious and sectarian differences. The independent regime was established on the basis of a compromise—the National Pact of 1943—between the religious communities and their different tendencies and leanings. A system of proportional representation for all religious groups was instituted. Religious affiliations are taken into consideration in all appointments to public office.

The danger to the State inherent in a regime based on religious groupings is widely recognized. Sectarianism, which plagues the public life and is at the root of much of the evil in the administration, is under persistent attack by the press and all the liberal elements in the country, who warn of the shaky structure of a state built upon a conglomeration of religious blocs.

The conduct of government, which under the Mandate left much to be desired as regards honesty and efficiency, did not improve with independence. The government machinery, heavily burdened, inefficient, and ridden with nepotism and corruption, steadily deteriorated since 1943. The President of the Republic, Sheikh Bishara al-Khoury—an able and talented man, who had started with great promise and a wonderful opportunity—came in the course of his nine year administration to be regarded as the head of a political machine with the sole purpose of enriching and aggrandizing his large and grasping family and their associates. In the public mind, the state had become the private estate of the President and his crowd.

This was all the more dangerous since the President who wielded the decisive power in government and public life was not accountable to Parliament for his conduct. He appointed and dismissed governments to suit his plans. Parliamentary government was a mere façade for autocratic rule. Parliament, elected in 1947 under flagrant irregularities on behalf of official nominees, amended the Constitution to make possible the re-election of the President, who was actually re-elected eighteen months before his term of office expired.

Though Parliament was docile, opposition was maintained by the press and a few organized groups. A hopeful development was the founding in May, 1949 of the Progressive Socialist Party by Kamal Jumblatt, a sensitive and thoughtful young idealist who has been waging an unrelenting fight against all elements of evil in the state. In Parliament he maintained a steady, persistent opposition, though most of the time he was alone. His hand was strengthened after the elections of 1951 which returned to Parliament a small group—eight deputies, among them Camille Shamoun, present President of the Republic—committed to a socialist program. This group, called the National Socialist Bloc, aimed at cleaning up the administration, enforcing the law with vigilance and equal justice, and providing the state with progressive socialist legislation.

As the authority sank deeper in the abuse of the public trust, the opposition grew in intensity and reached ever widening circles. The economic crisis—aggravated after the disruption of relations with Syria; the high cost of living; the large numbers of unemployed; these made opposition to the regime not a political question, nor even a national issue, but a matter of daily bread. And so the masses were caught up in it.

The success of the army coup in Egypt encouraged the opposition to which the leaders of Beirut and Tripoli rallied, and all were backed by a three-day general strike in Beirut. The President, unable to find a candidate willing to form a government, resigned on September 18, 1952.

The new regime has not ushered a new age, but it has introduced a few important reforms. Changes in the electoral law have granted suffrage to women and replaced the large electoral districts by the one-or-two deputy districts where the candidate is accountable to electors who know him personally. This measure has broken the power of political feudalism. Some degree of decentralization has been effected, giving greater authority to local councils and district administrators. Improvements have been made in the civil service system, corruption has been arrested, and a law enacted for the prosecution of those who used their government position or political influence for illicit gain. Certain restrictions on the freedom of the press have been removed.

But these reforms are a long way from meeting the fundamental needs of the country; nor have they restored the people's confidence in the government and the rulers. The hopes are set on the coming parliamentary elections. If enough progressive elements are returned, Lebanon may experience radical reforms through constitutional government without the need of a military coup.

CHAPTER XI

Iraq

IRAQ, immured behind the vast Syrian Desert, remained a backwater to the liberation movements which stirred Egypt, and to a lesser extent Syria, during the nineteenth century and the early years of the twentieth. But Iraq was not altogether isolated from the forces which were then shaping Arab nationalism. The leading poets of the time, Ma'ruf al-Rasafi and Jamil al-Zahawi, denounced the evils of Turkish rule and censured a society which submitted to despotic government and to the tyranny of worn-out and injurious beliefs and practices. Their poetry stimulated people's minds and spirits and stirred their will for constitutional government and social reform. The schools of Najaf, the great religious and intellectual Shi'a center, revived the Arab cultural heritage and infused national feeling into their students. Iraqi officers in the Turkish army joined the secret society Al-'Ahd, founded in Constantinople to work for the independence of the Arab provinces. Al-'Ahd had branches in the three principal cities of Iraq, Baghdad, Basra, and Mosul. And Iraqi officers were prominent in the Arab Revolt.

At the outbreak of the war the British occupied Basra, important for the security of their position in the Persian Gulf and the safety of their communications with India. In the course of the war, lower Iraq up to Baghdad was conquered. Offers of Iraqi leaders to participate in the war against the Turks were rejected, since the British authorities realized that Arab help in driving the Turks out would entail commitments for Arab freedom similar to those undertaken by the British Government in sponsoring the Arab Revolt. Towards the Revolt, the British in Iraq assumed a hostile attitude and kept its news from reaching the public.

The British Civil Administration in Iraq had little sympathy for or understanding of the Arab national movement. The first Acting Civil Commissioner, Sir Arnold Wilson, was imbued with a pas-

sionate feeling and belief—these are his words—that the welfare
of the indigenous people depended upon the good government
which Britain could give.[1] Even the application of the mandatory
principle to the Arab countries, according to Wilson, was not in
the interests of the inhabitants. He spoke of self-determination as
"the popular heresy," denounced the Anglo-French Declaration
of November 8, 1918 as a "disastrous error," and assured his su-
periors that the Arabs were content with the British occupation.[2]
Wilson wrote: "The average Arab, as opposed to the handful of
amateur politicians of Baghdad, sees the future as one of fair dealing and material and moral progress under the aegis of Great
Britain."[3] While the Civil Commissioner was broadcasting these
smug views a volcano of resentment and unrest was smoldering
under his feet.

Iraq, Wilson went on, with its strategic position and its oil was
a key position in the British imperial structure. From Iraq, Great
Britain could dominate the whole Middle East and keep an eye on
the rest of the Moslem World. To assure this domination Iraq was
to be put under strong British government.

An extensive British administration was set up. The Civil administration and the British army in Iraq were based on India. Iraq
was intended to become an appendage of Britain's Indian Empire.
The London *Times*, organ of official opinion, wrote of settling three
million Indians in Iraq.

While the British authorities were proceeding in their policy of
Indianizing Iraq, an Arab government was in control in Syria. Between Syria and Iraq there was close communication, and the Arab
regime of Damascus declared on several occasions its support of
Iraq's independence and union between the two countries. A number of Iraqi leaders remained with Faisal in Syria, others returned
to Iraq to direct the resistance against British rule. The Iraqi public followed with keen interest the progress of events in Syria. In
the absence of a nationalist press in Iraq, the people read with
avidity the Syrian and Egyptian newspapers. News of the Egyptian revolution fired them with patriotic ardor. Sa'd Zaghlul, the
leader of Egyptian resistance, became an Arab national hero. The
simultaneous proclamation in Damascus of the independence of

1. Sir Arnold T. Wilson: *Mesopotamia 1917–1920, A Clash of Loyalties*, London,
1931, p. x.

2. *Ibid.*, pp. xi, 103, 104, 134.

3. *Ibid.*, p. 104.

Syria and Iraq was hailed with widespread joy and enthusiasm in both countries.

When at the conclusion of the San Remo Conference Iraq was placed under British Mandate, revolution broke out. The announcement of the Mandate was the spark that set off the explosion. The Arabs in Iraq as elsewhere had taken seriously the principles enunciated by President Wilson, and believed the promises and pledges made by the Allies. Instead of the promised self-determination and free institutions they found themselves in the grip of an all-embracing British rule. And it was a wholly alien rule, for the British were foreign in language, religion, and social customs. Various restrictions alienated the people still further. Freedom of expression was suppressed and political parties and gatherings were banned. The press was under strict control. Only three official papers—one in each of the principal cities—were allowed. There was fear for the future of the country because of a widespread rumor that Iraq was to be annexed to India.

The revolution broke out simultaneously in north and south Iraq. The tribes did the fighting. The cities, unarmed and under the eye of the authorities, stayed out of the fight. The tribesmen carried arms, however odd and ill-assorted. They were used to independence under the Turks, and now with the British in control, they recognized only the authority of their chiefs.

The revolution swept the country. Government authority broke down and provisional governments were set up in the areas conquered by the revolutionaries. For a time there was fear that Baghdad itself might fall.[4] It took several months of fighting, the dispatch of 70,000 British troops to Iraq, and the expenditure of a vast sum of money, to put the revolution down.

The Iraqi revolution, like the Syrian resistance to the French Mandate, was a continuation of the Arab Revolt. Although the offshoots, like the parent revolt, did not succeed in attaining immediately their objectives of independence and Arab unity—the latter still remains to be attained—they nevertheless forced the powers in control to loosen their hold, give a fuller measure of self-government than they were willing to give, and recognize rights which without resistance and revolution would have gone altogether unheeded. For Iraq, the revolution put a definite end to the Indianization policy and laid the basis for an Arab government.

In the meantime, the Arab regime of Syria had fallen; Faisal was

4. Wilson, *op. cit.*, p. 283.

in Europe. The British statesmen who knew Faisal respected and
trusted him. They admired his leadership of the Arab Revolt and
his reasonableness at the Peace Conference in Paris, where he had
been willing to come to an understanding with the Allies, especially Great Britain. In British official circles there was an awareness of the latent force and possibilities of the Arab movement
and a desire to make amends for letting Faisal and Syria down. It
was decided therefore to direct Faisal towards Iraq. At the Cairo
Conference—held in the spring of 1921 under the chairmanship of
Mr. Churchill, then Colonial Secretary, to dispose of the Arab question and the wartime commitments—the plan was agreed upon for
the establishment of an Arab government in Iraq under Faisal. In
August, Faisal was proclaimed King of Iraq.

The British continued to hold the reins of government. The
High Commissioner was the real head of the administration, notwithstanding the accession of a king and the formation of an Iraqi
Council of Ministers. This situation exasperated the Iraqis. The
sense of frustration and disillusion was not confined to the political
circles of Baghdad but was shared by all sections of the population. The tribes were again restless. On the first anniversary of
Faisal's coronation, an anti-British demonstration took place in the
courtyard of the palace, and a speech denouncing British policy
was delivered in the presence of the High Commissioner. The next
morning, as Faisal was getting ready for a surgical operation, with
doctors and nurses around him, the High Commissioner, Sir Percy
Cox, entered and presented to him for his signature a paper ordering the arrest and deportation of seven nationalist leaders. When
one of the doctors protested that this was not the time, Sir Percy
replied that the matter was urgent, for the country was in danger.
Faisal quietly told Sir Percy that in a few minutes he would be
under an operation which he might not survive. Should his last
action in this world be the exile of people from their own country?
This could never be. The High Commissioner left without saying
a word. He arrested and exiled the leaders himself and dissolved
the two nationalist parties which had just been formed.

Iraqi hostility to the mandate was evident from the outset. The
country demanded independence without a transitional period of
tutelage and supervision. The British, aware of this widespread
hostility, offered the mandate in the guise of a treaty of alliance.
But the treaty hardly differed from the text of the mandate. Signed
in October 1922 by the British-appointed Iraqi government, it was

widely criticized by the nationalist leaders and the public. Under popular pressure an annex added to the treaty in April 1923 reduced its duration from twenty to four years from the conclusion of peace with Turkey.

The Constituent Assembly, elected in August 1923, met in March of the following year. It was convened for the purpose of deciding on the treaty, laying down the Organic Law of the State, and drafting an electoral law. In the Assembly the treaty with its subsidiary agreements was denounced strongly. The British threatened that if the treaty was not ratified by June 10th, they would withdraw it and restore direct British rule. About this time the Mosul question began to loom up, and the Assembly, realizing that they would need British help in the boundary dispute with Turkey, ratified the treaty after a stormy session which lasted till midnight of the date set by the British ultimatum.

The Mosul dispute came before the League of Nations. The boundary commission appointed by the League recommended the retention of the Mosul area by Iraq, provided a new treaty was concluded guaranteeing the continuation of the British mandate for 25 years unless in the meantime Iraq were admitted to the League of Nations. The Council of the League endorsed the report of the boundary commission. Faced with the alternative of losing Mosul by refusing to conclude the new treaty, or keeping this strategic area and its important oil fields, the Iraqi government signed in January 1926 and parliament ratified the treaty in the same month.

In spite of the danger to Mosul, public opinion was not won over to the treaty. Attempts to modify it ended in the abortive treaty of December 1927. Tension continued and a hostile attitude towards Great Britain was evident throughout the country. A government crisis left the country without a ministry for over three months, from January till April 1929.

In the fall of 1929, the High Commissioner announced his government's readiness to establish a new basis of relationship with Iraq. After some delay, a treaty of alliance was concluded in June 1930, and is still in force to the present day. The treaty recognized Iraq a sovereign state and safeguarded the interests of Great Britain. The safety of imperial communications was assured. In time of war or threat of war Iraq would offer the use of all facilities, railways, rivers, ports, and airports. The British would retain two air bases—one near Basra, the other west of the Euphrates, where British forces would be stationed.[5] At the time the treaty was signed a new judicial agreement was initiated abolishing the judicial privileges of foreigners. The consent of the foreign states concerned was obtained and the agreement went into force in March 1931.

Once her strategic interests were secured Great Britain was anxious to end the mandate. She recommended Iraq warmly for membership in the League of Nations. The Report submitted by the British Government to the League described in detail the progress made since 1920. There was stability in the administration, public security was efficiently maintained, the judiciary was qualified to safeguard the interests of foreigners, the rights of the minorities were guaranteed by the Constitution. Economic and financial conditions were sound. Progress in education had been real. The report spoke of the continued nationalist pressure. It stressed the strength of the national movement and the difficulties of administration under the mandate in the face of the "marked impatience of mandatory control and a fervent desire for independence" expressed by responsible Iraqis who were willing and eager to accept the burden and responsibilities of self-government.[6]

Iraq was admitted to the League of Nations in October 1932. The term of the treaty is 25 years from the date of Iraq's entry into the League.

Notwithstanding the persistent strain between Britain and Iraq under the mandate, the British did much towards the building of the modern state of Iraq. They sent some of their ablest civil servants who, first as part of the staff of the High Commissioner and later as servants of the Iraqi state, helped to lay down the foundations of a stable administration. Once they were convinced that their interests were best served by promoting the independence of Iraq, the British gave their support to the political development of the country and hastened the termination of the mandate. British help was especially fruitful in guiding Iraq to establish friendly relations with her neighbors. Through a series of conferences prepared and sponsored by Britain's representatives in Iraq, boundary and tribal disputes with Saudi Arabia were settled. British influence saved Mosul for Iraq. It is true that the British wanted the oil of Mosul, but their interest coincided with the interest of Iraq

5. Royal Institute of International Affairs, *Documents on International Affairs*, 1930, pp. 131–136.

6. Special Report to the Council of the League of Nations on the Progress of Iraq during the Period 1920–1931, Colonial No. 58, 1931.

and with the facts of geography, ethnology, culture, and historical association according to which the province of Mosul is an integral part of Iraq. By a treaty concluded with Great Britain and Iraq, Turkey accepted the boundary fixed by the Council of the League.

Great Britain supported Iraq's admission to the League of Nations with enthusiasm and faith in Iraq's ability to discharge her international obligations. When the Permanent Mandates Commission expressed hesitancy and doubt, the British representative assured the members that the British Government would assume moral responsibility for Iraq's fulfillment of the trust placed in her.

Under the Mandate there was always a strong and informed opposition in parliament. But opposition and government worked together, united in the common purpose of freeing Iraq from the Mandatory power. In negotiating a treaty the government would make use of the opposition to get all it could from the British, while the opposition supported the government position by denouncing the treaty and insisting on more favorable terms. In spite of the frequent changes of ministry the tacit stand of the successive governments was that of opposition. No sooner was a treaty concluded than the ground was prepared for the resumption of opposition and the renewal of demands.

Iraq was particularly fortunate in having Faisal's leadership at a time when the new state was in the process of formation. Faisal was eminently fitted for his role. He had been the guiding spirit of the Arab Revolt and was at the heart of the emancipation movement. His two-year rule in Syria, with its tumult and tragedy, prepared him further for his new task. During the war and in the first years of peace he had dealt with the Western Powers, especially Great Britain, and had learned much that stood him in good stead in later dealings with them. He had a remarkable gift for handling people and an ability to reach a compromise without compromising his principles. His wisdom and sincerity won him the confidence and respect of both Iraqis and British, although the two were at odds with each other during most of his reign. By his balanced judgment, infinite patience, and tact he smoothed away obstacles and avoided deadlocks between Great Britain and Iraq. Faisal was always constructive and positive in his approach. He did not turn his back on a plan which fell short of his demands, but took what was available and from that position moved to one of greater vantage. His motto in dealing with the British was to take and strive for more. Occupied as he was with the many problems of Iraq, Faisal never lost sight of the Arab movement as a whole and its goal of freedom and unity, of which he had caught glimpses in the days when the Arab Revolt was on its victorious path. Under Faisal and his successors, Iraq became the center of Arab nationalism and the haven of patriots and exiles from the countries still under foreign rule.

Faisal's sudden and premature death in 1933 was an irreparable loss to Iraq and the rest of the Arab world. The years immediately following were, with respect to internal affairs, troubled and restless. The opposition to the British having somewhat subsided since the termination of the mandate, partisan politics came into prominence. Faisal's steadying hand was no longer at the helm to guide and restrain the conflicting tendencies. Inefficiency in the administration and the manipulation of public office caused widespread discontent.

In external relations the Iraqi leaders pursued the good neighbor policy initiated under Faisal. There was general agreement among them with regard to developing closer ties with the other independent Arab states. A treaty of alliance was concluded between Iraq and Saudi Arabia in 1936. A year later, Yaman joined the alliance.

Relations with Iran were especially constructive in view of the estrangement and strain prevalent during the twenties. Iran, which Great Britain and Russia had partitioned into spheres of influence in 1907, feared the presence of the British across the border. The Iranian government resented the exclusion of Iranian citizens from the privileges enjoyed by all foreign residents in Iraq under the judicial agreement of 1924 imposed upon Iraq as an annex to the 1922 treaty. In return, Iranian agents fomented trouble among the Shi'a of Iraq and instigated them to seek Iranian citizenship. There were also boundary incidents and disputes between the two countries. The friction abated when the judicial privileges of foreigners were abolished and all residents in Iraq, foreign and national, submitted to equal treatment under a unified system of justice. The frontier dispute, after having been taken before the League, was withdrawn from the agenda upon the request of the two parties concerned who proceeded to compose the difference between them without outside aid, and succeeded in reaching a settlement acceptable to both. The rapprochement between Iraq and Iran was further strengthened by the conclusion of the Sa'dabad Pact which included Turkey and Afghanistan. The

Sa'dabad or Middle East Pact, signed in Teheran on July 8, 1937, was a non-aggression pact aimed at the establishment of regional stability and the elimination of the interference of outside powers in the affairs of the Middle East.[7]

When the second World War broke out, Iraq severed diplomatic relations with Germany and stood by its treaty obligations to Great Britain. The treaty gave Great Britain all communication facilities and allowed the passage of British troops across Iraq, but it did not permit the stationing of such troops on Iraqi soil. When a British force was disembarked at Basra the Iraqi government asked the British authorities not to land any more troops until those already there should have left the country. Difference on this matter precipitated the armed conflict between the British and the government of Rashid Ali Kailani. The so-called Kailani revolt was publicized in the British and American press as a Nazi inspired and engineered plot against the democracies. Axis propaganda was active in Iraq as elsewhere in the Arab countries. That it found willing listeners among the Arabs was due not to Arab leaning towards Nazi ideology, as the counter-propaganda tried to show, but to a sense of frustration prevalent in the Arab world as a result of the policy followed by the democracies with regard to the Arabs. Iraq was not only dissatisfied with its own relations with Great Britain, but was strongly sympathetic and responsive to the unrest caused by foreign domination in the other Arab countries. Palestine was the paramount issue. Official and public opinion in Iraq was united and strongly articulate with regard to the injustice inflicted upon Palestine as a result of the British Mandate. More than any other issue, and even more than all the wrongs together perpetrated by imperialist powers in the Arab world, the fate of Palestine shook Arab faith in the Western democracies and alienated the Arabs from wholehearted cooperation with the West.

Since the end of the war, public opinion has pressed for the revision of the 1930 treaty which had become antiquated and was incongruous with present conditions and requirements. Great Britain welcomed the idea of revision in the light of new conditions, and a new agreement was reached between the two governments and signed at Portsmouth in January 1948. It was enthusiastically launched by the British government and hailed by the press as a model for a system of alliances with the other countries of the Middle East. But British optimism was premature,

7. R.I.I.A., *Documents on International Affairs*, 1937, pp. 530–531.

for the agreement proved wholly inacceptable to the Iraqi people.

The new treaty showed no essential change in British policy. Its provisions followed closely the terms of the treaty which it was to supersede; only the formality of equality between the two parties was more carefully observed than in 1930.[8] Its terms, as soon as they were made known, provoked violent protests and demonstrations. Popular disapproval forced the government to resign and the prime minister to leave the country. This intense public reaction left the British stunned. In the other Arab countries, the rejection of the treaty was widely approved and the fate of the Iraqi government which had signed it pointed out as a warning to other Arab governments should they consider entering into hampering and regressive agreements.

So much for the political progress. On the non-political level the most tangible results have been achieved in the field of education.

The Department of Education was the first government department to be freed of British control. In Iraq, more than in any of the Arab provinces placed under the Mandate, the national authorities had to start from nothing. At the beginning of the first World War there were 7,028 students in the state primary schools, and 349 in the secondary schools. During the war, many of the schools closed down and the pupils dispersed. The British opened a number of schools but they were chary in their expenditure on education and the other branches of the administration which directly benefited the public. The stringency was not due to the lack of funds because the appropriations devoted to Headquarters Administration increased by 220% between 1918–19 and 1919–20. "Indeed, the explanation for the failure to create adequate social services must be found, not in the lack of funds or of suitable personnel, but rather in the will to create them."[9] As a result, when the British withdrew their control over education in 1920–21 there were no more than 7,452 pupils enrolled in the public elementary schools, while the number of students in the secondary schools had fallen from the prewar level to 110. Yet the British, in the words of the head of the administration, thought that in matters educational they went too fast.[10]

When control over education was transferred to Iraqi authori-

8. *American Perspective*, published by the Foundation for Foreign Affairs, Washington, February 1948, pp. 558–566.

9. Ireland: *Iraq*, pp. 142–143.

10. Wilson: *op. cit.*, p. 175.

ties, they set themselves the double task of spreading education and creating a public system which would weld the various elements of the population into a national unity. In Iraq as in Egypt, the British had established two types of schools in the first stage of public instruction, the primary school for the rich and the elementary school for the poor. They had supported the denominational schools with public funds, without extending public supervision over the way the funds were spent and the schools were run. The first act of the national authorities was to create a democratic system of education proceeding from a unified first stage, with one type of school for rich and poor alike. The denominational schools were given the choice of coming under public control or losing public support. They chose the former.

In Iraq, where foreign schools are very few and private national schools not numerous, the burden of education has, from the outset, been carried by the state. The educational authorities entered upon their work with enthusiasm and faith. All the responsible leaders, from the King down, felt that education was the cornerstone of the new state which they were building. Faisal visited the schools and spoke to the teachers and students. He publicly expressed his readiness to teach in a secondary school for a few hours each week. The Department of Education was fortunate in having as its first Director Sati' al-Hosri, an educator of broad experience, a distinguished scholar, and an ardent patriot. Al-Hosri combined knowledge of modern pedagogical trends with a profound understanding of Iraq's educational needs. To Sati' al-Hosri more than to any other man goes the credit for what is best in the educational system of Iraq.

From the beginning, education on the primary level was offered free, and where facilities permitted attendance at school was compulsory. Recently fees have been abolished also for the secondary schools. The expansion of education during the last thirty years is worth noting. In 1920–21 there were 88 public primary schools, with 7,452 pupils taught by 486 teachers. Ten years later, in 1930–31, the number of schools had risen to 316, of students to 34,513, and of teachers to 1,325. In 1948–49, there were 1051 primary schools, 151,000 students, and 5,851 teachers, a twentyfold increase in students and a twelvefold increase in schools and teachers during twenty-eight years. Secondary education was practically non-existent in 1920–21. By 1930–31, 19 secondary and intermediate schools had been established, with 129 teachers, and 2,082 students. During 1948–49, 16,721 students attended 93 public secondary schools, and were taught by 800 teachers.

In Iraq as in Egypt, strong emphasis has been placed on the training of teachers. The number of students registered in teacher training increased from 90 in 1920–21 to 410 in 1930–31 and to 2,000 in 1948–49. There are eight teacher training institutions. Six of them prepare teachers for the primary schools, two for the secondary schools. In all the teacher training institutions, tuition, board, and lodging are free.

Higher education is given in seven colleges which have not yet been incorporated in a university. They are the colleges of Medicine—which comprises Pharmacy, Nursing and Midwifery, and a hospital—Law, Engineering, Commerce and Economy, The Higher Teachers College, the Institute of Queen Alia, and the College of Moslem Law (Sharia').

Vocational training, given in eight vocational schools, may begin at the end of the primary or of the intermediate stage of instruction. The state pays all the expenses of the students in the vocational schools. Art education is provided by the Institute of Fine Arts which has four branches, music, painting, sculpture, and drama.

During 1949–50, the total number of students enrolled in all the schools of Iraq was 243,372. Of these, 36,742 were in private national schools and 1,800 in private foreign schools. In the same year, appropriations for education were 2,438,000 Iraqi dinars,[11] and amounted to 9.7% of the national budget.

The development of education has been accompanied by the expansion of medical facilities for the mass of the population. Over five and one half million patients were treated in the public health institutions, according to the census of 1948. Successive Iraqi governments have aimed to establish a school and a clinic in every village of Iraq. Although the aim has not been reached, yet the simple square building in the center of the village, housing the school in one part and the clinic in another, symbolizes modern Iraq and is the most notable landmark throughout the country.

Iraq, like the other Arab countries, has a predominantly agricultural economy. Agriculture depends largely upon irrigation. Only in the northern section is the rainfall adequate for the growth of crops. In the alluvial plain, which covers about two thirds of the country, irrigation is by flow. The Tigris and the Euphrates are to

11. An Iraqi dinar is a little less than $3 U.S. currency.

lower Iraq what the Nile is to Egypt. But unlike the Nile, the flood time of the two rivers comes at an unsuitable season, in the spring when the crops are partly grown, so that the fields cannot be inundated as in Egypt.

Because of the topography of the land, the Tigris and Euphrates require great effort and organization for their management and control. Mesopotamia, south of Baghdad, is a low platform of alluvium built up by the coalescence of a number of river deltas. The lower valley emerged from the sea only recently.[12] Hence the swampy aspect of the area, which after the spring floods is a continuous marshland.

Both the Tigris and Euphrates are fast-flowing rivers. The Tigris has a swifter current, a steeper gradient, and receives tributaries, some very large, all along its course from Asia Minor to the Persian Gulf. These features make the Tigris subject to sudden and devastating floods which pierce the embankments, sweep away channels, and inundate hundreds of square miles. Ultimately the river carves a new course. In fact, the channels of both the Tigris and Euphrates have altered considerably within historic times.[13]

From remote antiquity, the peoples who have inhabited the valley have tried to control the two rivers. The system of irrigation reached its highest development in the Middle Ages, under the Abbasid Caliphate, when a splendid network of canals, watering the arid areas and draining the waterlogged zones, was efficiently maintained. The construction and maintenance of important irrigation projects is possible only under a strong and stable administration. Hence it was that during times of trouble and chaos the rivers ran wild and wrought havoc in the land.

Since the establishment of the modern state of Iraq, a few important control projects have been constructed or enlarged. The largest is the Kut Dam on the Tigris, completed in 1943. The Kut Dam, the Hindiyyeh Dam on the Euphrates, and other dams on the Euphrates and the Diyala, a tributary of the Tigris, have by raising the water level brought extensive areas under cultivation.

The flatlands of Lower Iraq do not lend themselves conveniently to raising the water level by dams. This circumstance, coupled with the abundance of fuel oil, has favored the raising of water by means of pumps. The government, to encourage the installation of pumps, passed a law in 1926 exempting land irrigated by pumps from taxa-

12. Fischer: *op. cit.*, pp. 343–347.
13. *Ibid.*, pp. 340–342.

tion for a limited period. The area under irrigation has increased by 4 million acres since 1918.

The central problem of agriculture in Iraq is irrigation and flood control. To overcome the danger of inundation and extend the water to the arid lands, two great projects, one on the Euphrates, the other on the Tigris, have been studied and are on the way to being carried out. The Habbaniyeh project is a flood control and storage scheme based on the utilization of Lake Habbaniyeh to the west of Baghdad. The plan provides for the digging of three canals. One would convey the flood waters of the Euphrates to the lake. In times of great floods, a second canal connecting the lake with a depression further south would drain the surplus water and deposit it in the depression. A third canal would carry the water back, in the season of low flow, from the lake to the river. The area to be irrigated by this scheme is estimated at 1.5 million acres.[14] The Wadi Tharthar project is designed to divert the Tigris floods to the Wadi Tharthar depression by means of a diversion dam on the Tigris and canals leading into and out of the Wadi. For further control of the Tigris, storage dams are planned on the upper course of the river and its tributaries.

The agricultural potentialities of Iraq are very great. The soil, constantly renewed by the deposition of great quantities of sediment carried by the two rivers, is of proverbial fertility. With the installation of an adequate system of flood control and the full utilization of the water resources, the cultivable land could be increased manyfold.

Land tenure is a serious problem. In northern Iraq, small proprietors own some of the land, but over the rest of the country share-tenancy is the most prevalent form of tenure.

The big landowners, a comparatively recent creation,[15] are of two types, tribal chiefs and influential pump-owning townsmen. Before the British Mandate, land was the communal property of the tribe. The Shaikh, in the true tribal tradition, was the first among equals. The Mandatory power, to win the support of the Shaikhs, allowed them to secure legal title to the land which by custom and tradition was the property of the tribe. The national authorities followed the example of the Mandatory and handed over large estates to their supporters. The diversion of large areas

14. Feliks Bochenski and William Diamond: TVA's in the Middle East, *The Middle East Journal*, January 1950, pp. 77–82.

15. Warriner, *op. cit.*, p. 107.

of land to a small group of holders has been a major cause of unrest in Iraq as it has been denounced by all the liberal elements, whose program of reform includes the limitation of the extent of landownership and the distribution of state lands among the peasants.

A step in the direction of land reform was taken in 1945 with the passage of the Dujaylah Law which provided for the transfer of state domain to landless peasants in the area south of Baghdad. Under this law, the tenant receives 62.5 acres to cultivate rent free for ten years, after which he is granted full legal title to the land, but cannot sell or alienate it until the lapse of another ten years. In 1950 the law was extended to a few more areas, and in 1951 the Government was empowered to settle state domain lands on the model of the Dujaylah settlement.

Extensive farming and shifting cultivation are characteristic of agriculture in Iraq. In the absence of proper drainage, salinity appears and the soil quickly deteriorates. Since there is no population pressure on the land the farmer moves from one plot to another, leaving the damaged plot to recover. Under such conditions, and given the tenancy form of farming, one can hardly expect the peasant to have an interest in the land, or to be able and willing to introduce long term improvements into farming.

The agricultural products vary with the topography of the country. The rolling elevated plains and the mountain valleys of the north grow the various fruits and trees of the temperate zone. Tobacco is one of the important products of this area. In the south barley and wheat are grown extensively. Rice is the most important of the summer crops. The soil and climate of Iraq are suitable for cotton growing. The possibilities of cotton cultivation are hampered by the present system of land tenure based as it is largely on share cropping. Tenants have no faith in cash crops; they prefer to grow the crops which they can consume. Furthermore, cotton growing requires heavy irrigation which tends to ruin the soil by inducing salinity unless an adequate system of drainage is provided. When the necessary requirements for the cultivation of cotton are met, cotton could become an important export crop as it is rapidly becoming in Syria. Dates are the principal export. Iraq provides 80% of the world trade in dates. The date palm is characteristic of the landscape from Baghdad to the Persian Gulf. The palm tree has many uses other than producing the date. Palm wood is used in building and furniture, and palm branches are woven into baskets, mats, and cords. Livestock breeding occupies a large section of the population. Sheep and cattle are exported to neighboring countries; hides, wool, and hair are exported to Europe and the United States.

The Government efforts for agricultural improvement, though limited, have had some effect. Several farms and nurseries are owned and operated by the government for experimentation and for the purpose of supplying the farmer with aid and guidance. In the experimental stations, various well-organized trials of cereals, linseed, and cotton are in progress. The development of fruit and nut growing is proceeding under the impetus of the Horticultural Station at Zafaraniyeh. The nurseries are doing successful work in making available new and improved varieties of plants and trees. The date crop is being improved by experiments on strains, and the date trade is promoted through publicity on the world markets and better methods of packing and marketing. Veterinary service and pest control are well developed. The Rural Education Department of the Ministry of Education is making commendable efforts towards developing a type of rural education with an agricultural emphasis.[16]

The development schemes have been financed largely from the oil revenues. The oil fields of Iraq, leased to the Iraq Petroleum Company, have been producing since 1934. The opening of the Zubair field west of Basra early in 1952 has expanded production, and royalties have increased as a result of the agreement which, beginning with January 1951, gave Iraq 50% of the profits. International loans are available provided the projects justify the investments. The International Bank of Reconstruction and Development has granted Iraq a $12,800,000 loan for the Wadi Tharthar project. At the request of the Iraqi Government, a mission of the International Bank visited Iraq in the spring of 1951 to study the country's economic potentialities and make recommendations designed to assist the government in formulating a long-term program of development.

Iraq has great potentialities: extensive lands, a vast supply of water, and adequate capital made available by the expanding oil industry. The immediate and full development and utilization of these resources for the welfare of the people is urgent.

All is not quiet in Iraq, although the opposition—both the constructive kind and the subversive—is temporarily held in check

16. Keen: *op. cit.*, pp. 65, 86–87.

by martial law and repressive measures. The disturbances of November 1952 were a symptom of the seething resentment against the existing order.

The opposition parties—the National Democratic Party, the National Socialist Party, the Independence Party, and the United Popular Front—are in agreement on fundamental reforms, which include the amendment of the Constitution to limit the power of the Crown; establishment of ministerial responsibility to parliament elected by direct primary; assurance of individual and public freedoms; the formation of a Council of State; and the purification and reorganization of the administration system. To spread social justice, these parties, especially the National Democratic Party, advocate the limitation of land holdings, the distribution of state domain among peasants, introduction of graduated income taxes, and social insurance, as well as the launching of large scale development projects. The abrogation of the Anglo-Iraqi treaty is part of their program.

Only one of these reforms has been put through so far: the substitution of direct for indirect elections. But the effect of this reform was vitiated by the fact that the parliamentary elections of January 1953—the first held under the new law—were conducted while martial law was in force, with the opposition parties dissolved and their leaders detained in prison until a few days before elections.

With the increasing pressure from public opinion, the growth of political parties with social aims, the radical changes in some of the other Arab countries—notably Egypt—no government in Iraq may safely ignore any longer the urgent need for fundamental and thoroughgoing reform.

CHAPTER XII

The Arab Island

THE most significant development in the recent history of Arabia is the rise of Ibn Saud, and the consolidation of the greater part of the Arab Island in the Kingdom of Saudi Arabia.

At the close of the first World War, Ibn Saud was in a relatively obscure position, far outshone by Sharif Husain, the King of Hijaz. Husain had led the Arab Revolt, and around him had gathered the liberal and national forces in the various Arab countries. His descent from the Prophet and his position as guardian of the holy cities of Mecca and Medina enhanced his moral prestige and gave him a unique position among Arab rulers.

But Husain dissipated the hopes which were focused in him. His autocratic behavior alienated the liberal elements. The maladministration of Hijaz under his rule spread chaos and insecurity which affected not only the inhabitants but the multitudes of pilgrims who annually came to Hijaz from all over the Moslem world. His megalomania led him first to proclaim himself king of the Arabs, and later to assume the title of Caliph when the Caliphate was abolished by the Kemalist regime in Turkey. This presumptuousness antagonized the other Arab rulers, particularly Ibn Saud. His incursions into Saudi territory led to battles with the Wahhabis and the conquest of Hijaz by the Wahhabi ruler.

With the British, Husain had a tragic relationship. He trusted implicitly in the Husain-McMahon agreement, a copy of which he carried in his pocket as a guarantee that all was well. The agreement, apart from its original ambiguity, was by later counter-pledges and commitments practically reduced to nothing. Yet Husain refused to compromise. He insisted on Britain's fulfilment of her promises to him. He was especially adamant with regard to

Palestine which he rightly understood to be included within the future independent Arab state delineated in the agreement with Great Britain.

Hijaz, as one of the Allied and Associated Powers, was eligible to become an original member of the League of Nations. Its membership never became effective because Husain refused to ratify the Covenant of the League which endorsed the British and French mandates in the Arab countries and the Jewish National Home in Palestine. In the summer of 1921, the British sent Lawrence to King Husain in Jedda with a treaty which sought Husain's recognition of British plans for the Arab world, especially the acceptance of the Zionist scheme in Palestine. Husain staunchly refused his approval although rejection of the proposed treaty meant the loss of British support and backing. "Neither bribes nor threats had any power to move the old man, who was thoroughly disgruntled with our attitude towards the whole problem."[1]

Much as Husain's steadfastness in refusing to barter Arab rights was admirable, his stand was nevertheless futile, not only because of the exigencies of British policy but also because of his own weak position in relation to the British negotiator. Had he been a successful ruler and leader, liberal in his dealings with his people and solicitous of their welfare, wise in his relations with the other Arab rulers and enjoying their confidence and friendship, the popular support behind him would have given him strength in his stand against the British. As it was, the British found Husain stubborn and lacking in judgment in his relations with them, and unpopular among his own people. They went ahead with their plans and gave little thought to his objections. When a few years later conflict broke out between Husain and Ibn Saud, the British, convinced of Husain's ineptitude, withdrew their support from him. Leaving Hijaz, he was taken by the British to Cyprus where he remained an exile till shortly before his death.

Ibn Saud, Lord of Arabia and one of the most remarkable figures of modern Arab history, began his life as a homeless refugee. The house of Saud, in alliance with the religious reformation of the Wahhabis, had in the latter part of the 18th century acquired hegemony over a large part of Arabia. In the course of the 19th century, the family lost ground first to the Egyptians under Mohammad Ali and later to the rival house of Ibn Rashid which, before the end of the century, expelled the Sauds from Najd, their

1. Philby: *Arabian Days*, p. 228.

native land. The exiles settled in Kuweit on the Persian Gulf. Abd-al-Aziz Ibn Saud, son of the exiled ruler, entered upon the stage of history at the age of twenty-one when, in 1901, he rushed Riyadh, the capital of Najd, with a group of forty companions and took it by surprise. He then regained the family patrimony and began extending his dominion. His most dangerous enemy was Ibn Rashid. He besieged Ibn Rashid in his capital Hail in 1921, and brought about the fall of the rival house. With the conquest in 1925 of Hijaz, the Holy land of Islam, Ibn Saud became a figure of importance to all Moslems, and his Wahhabis entered into a wider world than they had hitherto known.

In 1926, Ibn Saud convened a Moslem Congress in Mecca. The proceedings of this assembly are of great interest as revealing the modernizing trends already at work in the mind of the Wahhabi ruler. The agenda before the delegates included reforms in the administration, health regulations, plans for the construction of roads, and other measures for the general improvement of conditions in Hijaz.

Ibn Saud's rule is outstanding for the good neighbor policy which he initiated. He negotiated a series of treaties effecting conciliation with former enemies, replacing the older rivalries by friendly relations, and promoting cooperation and peace in the interest of the parties concerned. Through a number of conferences with Iraqi authorities, boundary and tribal matters were regulated. In the spring of 1936, a Treaty of Alliance was concluded between Saudi Arabia and Iraq. While negotiations were in progress in Baghdad, a dispute arose over a certain article of the treaty. The Iraqi representative, Yasin al-Hashimi, suggested that the Saudi delegate communicate with Ibn Saud and ask his opinion on the point in question. Ibn Saud's answer came promptly, instructing his representative to "do as Hashimi says" with regard to every article of the proposed treaty.

In 1933 a treaty of Friendship and Good Neighborliness was concluded with Transjordan, notwithstanding the dispute over Akaba which was annexed by Transjordan although it formed a part of Hijaz when the province was conquered by Ibn Saud.

In the summer of 1929 two more treaties of friendship were concluded, one with Turkey, the other with Persia. The agreement of the Wahhabi ruler with Shiite Persia is a measure of remarkable statesmanship, substituting understanding and cordial relations for the traditional religious antipathies between the Wahhabis and the Shia. A treaty signed in May 1936 settled a long standing dispute with Egypt.[2]

Of especial significance is the Treaty of Taif which terminated the hostilities between Saudi Arabia and Yaman. The dispute between the two states arose over their respective boundaries in Asia. Ibn Saud sent a delegation to Sana, capital of Yaman, in the hope of reaching an understanding with regard to the frontier, and pending the conclusion of an agreement he withdrew his troops from the disputed territory. The Imam of Yaman marched into the area vacated by his rival's troops and held his delegates as hostages. This provoked the conflict in which the Saudi forces won a sweeping victory. Ibn Saud proved himself a statesmanlike victor. Yaman lay open before his forces, but he ordered the suspension of hostilities and recalled his troops. The peace conference met in May 1934 at Taif in the hills of Hijaz. The treaty which issued from the conference brought neither punishment to the vanquished nor spoils to the victor. It was rather "designed to promote the unity of the Arab nation" by close collaboration between the signatories, to establish neighborly relations and bonds of friendship, and to re-enforce the structure of peace and tranquility between their two governments and peoples.[3]

After the conquest of Hijaz, Great Britain hastened to recognize Ibn Saud as an independent ruler. Her recognition was confirmed in the Treaty of Jedda of May 1927. It is interesting to note the difference between this treaty, and the draft treaties offered to King Husain in which the British Government made recognition of Husain's independence in Hijaz conditional upon his acceptance of a clause relating to Great Britain's "special position" in the territories under her mandate, and the application of the Balfour Declaration in Palestine. Husain preferred to lose his kingdom rather than sign away Arab rights to British and Zionist interests. His Majesty's Government did not repeat the experiment with Ibn Saud.

Ibn Saud is a born leader of men. His qualities of leadership were often put to the test during his eventful and steadily rising career. In a society where written laws are few and book knowledge counts for little, the first requisite of a leader is a knowledge of people and the environment in which they live. Ibn Saud has

2. Royal Institute of International Affairs: *Survey of International Affairs*, 1930, pp. 172–173; *Documents on International Affairs*, 1937, p. 517.

3. *Documents*, 1934, pp. 454–458.

this knowledge in full measure. He has complete mastery of his environment because he is the product of that environment at its best. He embodies the qualities of the traditional chief in a patriarchal society: wisdom in assessing men and situations, patience in dealing with people, availability to all even the humblest of the tribesmen, quick and impartial justice, courage, and generosity. As a result of Ibn Saud's vigilant justice, tribal raiding has disappeared and Arabia enjoys a security which surpasses the safety prevailing in some of the larger cities of the Western world. His generosity is proverbial; he gives to everybody and gives always. And his bounty is not the result of his new wealth accruing from oil; it is ingrained in his nature and was there when he was a penniless refugee: he gave the garment on his body when there was nothing else he could give. Those who have known him through the years say he is more bountiful than the clouds. The monument to his courage is the kingdom which he won with the strength of his arm, and on his body he bears the scars of the many battles which consolidated his state. To a man of lesser stature, the obstacles encountered at the earlier stages of his career might have seemed insurmountable. But Ibn Saud would not acknowledge defeat even in the darkest hour. His courage never faltered, neither did his determination fail. Nothing could deflect his course nor divert his firm steps from the goal to which he looked with confidence and hope. His courage has been steadfast alike in battle and in making decisions at times no less crucial than the outcome of battles. In true tribal tradition he consults with the leaders of the community, but once he is determined upon a course there is no hesitancy or wavering about his action.

Ibn Saud's tact and wisdom were especially evident in his dealings with the Ikhwan, a difficult community to manage. The Ikhwan, backbone of the Saudi kingdom, are fanatical in their religious zeal and stubborn in their determination. Their outlook is confined within the limits of their narrow experience. Ibn Saud prevails upon them by persuasion. When he was consolidating his state, the Ikhwan, impatient of any obstacle to their advance, pressed for action, as when they urged attack upon Kuweit and Akaba. But Ibn Saud, aware of the larger implications of the situation and of possible international complications, advised caution and restraint. Later on, when he was trying to introduce modern means of communication and other improvements into the country, the Ikhwan objected lest the innovations be contrary to

religious laws and precepts. Ibn Saud patiently strove to convince
and win them over to his plans. At all times he kept their loyalty
and support.

Ibn Saud rules as a patriarch. Like the responsible head of a
family he attends personally to all manner of complaints, and fol-
lows up his instructions to see that they are promptly carried out.
He is not a democratic ruler in the sense current in the Western
world, because the structure of his society is unlike Western society where democratic institutions are in force. In fact there is
no basis for comparison between Ibn Saud and the head of a modern democratic state. But Ibn Saud is not a despot and cannot be
in the type of society which he rules. Effective curbs to despotism
are provided by the Sharia—the Sacred Law—and the tradition of
freedom ingrained in the sons of the desert.

Considering the nature of Arab society in the desert, the changes
introduced in Ibn Saud's lifetime and under his direction have
been far-reaching. The earliest and one of the most significant developments was the settlement of the nomads, begun in 1912, in
colonies called Hijar. Ibn Saud fully realized that he could not
build a stable society on the shifting sands of nomadism. Neither
could he consolidate his kingdom as long as tribal loyalties were
paramount and tribal feuds rent the population. The Hijar[4] were
communities based on loyalties which transcended the tribe. The
Ikhwan—brothers, as the settlers were called—were held together
by allegiance to the Wahhabi faith and attachment to fixed homes
and cultivated soil. The agricultural activity of the settlements,
digging wells, tilling the soil, sowing and planting, converted the
desert into farmland. The Hijar were also centers for the propagation of the faith, sending out the Ikhwan to teach and preach to the
tribes and lead them to the settled life. The Ikhwan, preachers
and farmers, were also fighters for the faith. They formed the military strength of the state.

Until the discovery of oil, Saudi Arabia was a very poor country. The principal source of revenue were the pilgrims to Hijaz.
The exploitation of a gold mine in northern Hijaz brought an additional small income. Oil, found in great quantities, has transformed
Saudi Arabia from a poor to a potentially rich country. The development of the oil industry is bound to cause fundamental changes

4. From the root meaning "to emigrate"; in this case emigration from nomadism
and its habits to the ways of settled life.

in the structure of society in the Arab Island. Oil royalties to the amount of $200 million annually represent considerable wealth. To what extent the country and the people shall benefit from this wealth will depend on how it is spent, whether it is consumed in the purchase of unproductive goods or invested in projects designed to expand the country's own productivity.

A few development schemes have been launched, among them projects for agricultural expansion. An experiment conducted at Kharj, an oasis 50 miles southeast of Riyadh, in collaboration between the Saudi Government and Aramco engineers, consists of the installation of large pumps and the construction of a canal to irrigate 3000 acres of land where a variety of crops—some of them recently introduced after previous tests—are grown. Projects similar to the Kharj are planned for other additional demonstration stations.

The agricultural potentialities of Saudi Arabia are greater than is generally assumed. Even in the arid Hijaz there is evidence of lively agricultural activity in earlier periods. Literary sources describe the agricultural prosperity of Hijaz under the Omayyads. Northern Hijaz in particular was covered with prosperous towns and agricultural settlements. The ruins of numerous dams testify to the care and effort expended on irrigation. One of the dams located near Taif and built in 680 A.D. under Muawiya, the first Omayyad Caliph, is today in excellent condition, a tribute of nearly thirteen centuries to the engineering skill of its builder, Abdullah Ibrahim.[5] With full utilization of subterranean and rain water, substantial increase in the productive land is possible. The construction of dams and rainfall catchments in the mountains of Hijaz, Asir, and Central Najd is under consideration.

Communications within Saudi Arabia and with other countries have greatly expanded and improved. Highways and paved roads have been built. A railroad connecting Riyadh with Dammam on the Persian Gulf has been in operation since the end of 1951. A deep water harbor at Dammam has been constructed, and the port of Jedda deepened and enlarged. The air base at Dhahran was built during the war by the United States army and turned over to Saudi Arabia in 1949. The airport at Jedda maintains regular service with Cairo. Within Saudi Arabia, air service is available between Jedda, Riyadh, and Dhahran. Projects for the electrifica-

5. K. S. Twitchell: *Saudi Arabia,* Princeton University Press, 1947, p. 38.

tion of major cities and the construction of city water systems are under way. Jedda has been supplied with fresh water brought from Wadi Fatima, thirty miles away.

A beginning has been made with medical and educational services. A modern system of education has become an imperative necessity to train the personnel needed in running the affairs of the country and conducting its ever expanding relations with the outside world. A department of education has been established, but its work needs to be greatly expanded before it can begin to meet the country's need. The system of education is based on the Egyptian, and the schools are to a large extent staffed with Egyptian teachers. Technical instruction and vocational training are provided in the schools set up by Aramco. Student missions abroad, principally to Egypt, are increasing steadily.

The Saudi Kingdom is the leading state in Arabia. The second, Yaman, has been much more isolated than its neighbor, Saudi Arabia. This isolation was due primarily to the character of its late ruler, the Imam Yahya, who was suspicious of all outside influence. He was especially suspicious of the British, his neighbors in Aden and the Protectorates, and feared their designs on Yaman. Aware of the rivalry between Great Britain and Italy—the latter had at the time dreams of an empire on the Red Sea—the Imam invited the Italians to establish a medical mission at his capital, San'a, and gave Italian enterprise preferential treatment in the country. The presence of the Italians in Yaman helped bring the British to give formal recognition to the Imam and to conclude a treaty with him composing their differences. During his long reign the Imam succeeded in keeping Yaman from falling under any form of foreign control. In doing so he also succeeded in keeping away any form of modern civilization from the country.

Yaman has been so isolated even from the rest of the Arab countries that when the Imam was killed in January 1948, and a new ruler and government were proclaimed, most people were at a loss to explain this unexpected event. Few realized how unbearable the overthrown regime had become to those Yamanites who had some knowledge of the outside world, and how crushing upon the mass of the people. Few were aware of the existence of a reform movement in the country. Yamanite liberals who had settled in Aden formed a society and founded a paper—*The Voice of Yaman* —through which their ideas of reform were communicated to the people of Yaman and to those Yamanites living abroad. One of the sons of the Imam led the movement. It was clear from the various publications of the Yamanite Society and from the articles carried in its paper that violence was not contemplated. Reform was to be achieved not through revolution but by the gradual introduction of modernized institutions. The Society drew up a program which envisaged the establishment of a democratic regime based on the principles of Western democracy adapted to the traditions and usages of Yaman. The Imamate would be preserved but the individual, arbitrary rule of the Imam would be checked by a legislative assembly to be composed of appointed notables and educated youth; the elective principle was not considered practicable in the conditions prevailing in Yaman. The government was to be formed of ministers responsible to the legislative assembly, and the administration staffed with personnel selected on the basis of merit. The program enumerates the steps necessary for the reform of the judiciary, and of the financial and fiscal systems. It calls for the economic development of the country through the construction of irrigation projects and the expansion and improvement of agriculture, exploitation of mineral resources, the establishment of industries dependent on local raw materials, the development of a system of internal communications, and the enlargement of ports. Quick action is urged to combat illiteracy and spread education by founding all types of schools, sending student missions abroad, and bringing teachers from the other Arab countries. The need for public health services is not overlooked. Finally, relations with the outside world are to be expanded through the maintenance of consular and diplomatic services. At the same time the country's independence should be safeguarded by strengthening and modernizing the army.

It is interesting to note that the liberal elements were joined in their demands for reform by the religious leaders of Yaman, who submitted to the Imam petitions describing the wretched state of the people, urging reform as the only guarantee of stability, and warning that if remedy was not soon forthcoming the state was doomed to destruction. Speaking of the Yamanite Society, one of the most venerated religious leaders told the Imam that people flocked from every corner to join the Society and to give it moral and material support, so real were their grievances and so convinced were they of the justice of their cause.

The attempt to change the regime by force failed partly because the assassination of the aged Imam shocked Arab opinion

in Yaman and outside it, and partly because those who were responsible for the conduct of affairs mishandled the situation. It
would be rash, however, to suppose that the restored regime could
safely persist in isolationism or ignore the people's growing awareness of grievances and frustrations which might once again burst
into violence.

The rest of Arabia is encircled by a ring of treaties binding the
local chiefs to Great Britain in varying degrees of dependence.

Britain's hold is strongest in the southwest corner of Arabia—
the Aden Colony and the Protectorates. In 1937, the eastern Protectorate was virtually annexed, in the teeth of long-standing treaties with the chiefs of Hadramout. Since then it has been ruled
along colonial lines.

In the Persian Gulf states, some measure of internal freedom is
allowed. Great Britain controls their foreign policy and has reserved for herself the right to decisions with regard to the exploitation of their oil resources and pearl fisheries.

Oman is less closely tied to Great Britain. It has maintained
enough independence to have a British consul in its capital instead
of a political agent, as is the case with the Persian Gulf states.
During the 19th century, Oman had entered into treaty relations
with a number of Western powers, among them the United States
with whom a treaty of amity and commerce was concluded as
early as 1833. The United States regards this treaty as still in force.

In the Persian Gulf, a few miles away from the Saudi Arabian
coast and Qatar, are the islands of Bahrein with a population of
110,000. Oil royalties, trade—local and transit—and the pearl industry are the principal resources of the islands. A large number
of the inhabitants earn a living by fishing, and some are engaged
in ship-building. The presence of fresh subterranean water has
made possible the cultivation of the date palm and a few varieties
of fruit trees and garden vegetables. Fresh water springs are also
found under the Gulf not far from the shore. The Government is
run by the British Advisor to the Amir. Good work is being done
in education. A fairly adequate system of primary education for
boys and girls has been established. Vocational training is given
in an intermediate industrial school, and secondary education for
boys is available in a fine new high school. There is an active,
though small, literary group in Bahrein keenly interested in and
awake to developments in the other Arab countries. Their organ
is a monthly periodical: *Sawt Al-Bahrein.*

Kuwait has recently come into the limelight as the repository of vast reserves of oil, and has consequently assumed a position of economic and strategic significance. Prior to the discovery of oil, the Kuwaitis, like the other peoples of the Arab shore of the Persian Gulf, lived on trade, pearling, fishing, and ship-building.

Since the conclusion, in 1951, of the agreement between the Shaikh of Kuwait and the Kuwait Oil Company which established Kuwait's share in the oil profits on a 50% basis, Kuwait has been receiving £50 million annually. This is enormous wealth for a country whose population does not exceed 150,000. And this amount may soon double with the increased output. A new field was opened in 1952, and more recently production began in the Kuwait neutral zone.

Kuwait is expanding fast. New constructions, private and public, are changing the face of the city. Workers—masons, bricklayers, carpenters, blacksmiths, plumbers, electricians, and other artisans and unskilled laborers—are flocking to Kuwait by the thousands from a number of Arab countries, especially Iraq and Lebanon. Hundreds of professional men—teachers, doctors, engineers, accountants, and others—from Egypt, Palestine, Lebanon, Syria, and Iraq are working in the various government departments.

A health program has been launched. There are a state hospital, a tuberculosis sanatorium, and several clinics. A tuberculosis hospital—planned to be the best equipped in the Middle East—is nearing completion, and plans are ready for a new 750-bed general hospital. All medical services are free.

The most important developments are evident in education. Until 1936 there was no trace of public education in Kuwait. Instruction consisted of attendance at Koranic schools and at two schools, Mubarakiyah and Ahmadyah, where some modern instruction was introduced. These schools, the one founded in 1912 and the other soon after the first war, were supported by private funds.[6] The Department of Education began on a budget of ½% of the 5% customs duty levied on imported goods. This duty formed at the time almost the entire revenue of the Kuwait Government. Since the production of oil in commercial quantities began in 1946, and especially after the 1951 agreement with the KOC, funds have been available in abundance. The education budget for 1951–52 was 27 million rupees.[7]

6. The Ahmadyah received an annual gift from the ruling Amir.
7. There are 13 rupees and a fraction to the pound sterling.

There were 32 schools in Kuwait city and the villages in 1951–52, attended by over 8,000 students, of whom 2500 were girls. Secondary education for boys has been available for some time, but for girls it was introduced only recently. A boys' secondary school, designed to accommodate 600 boarding students and composed of a main building for classes, lectures, and laboratories, a mosque, library, gymnasium, residence halls for students and houses for the Staff, has been established on a wide beach a few miles west of the Kuwait city wall. Extensive playgrounds are an integral part of the unit. This establishment, expected to be ready for the school year 1953–54, surpasses with regard to equipment, educational and recreational facilities, and housing accommodations anything of its kind not only in the Arab Island but in any other Arab land.

All educational services are free and the system is thoroughly democratic, in keeping with the democratic tradition of the desert Arabs. A number of young men are studying abroad, mainly in Egypt, a few in the American University in Beirut, and others in England, as government bursaries.

Kuwait, one of the largest oil producers in the world, has practically no fresh water. Unlike Bahrein, whose subterranean springs make up somewhat for the lack of rain, the quantity of fresh water so far found under the sands of Kuwait has been negligible. Drinking water has had to be imported by boat from Basra. A large plant for the distillation of sea water was put into operation early in 1953. The plant has an initial capacity of one million gallons per day and a possibility of expansion to 5 million.

An oil town, Ahmadi, about thirty miles southeast of Kuwait city, has sprung up within the last four or five years. Nothing could present a greater contrast to life in the desert than this modern town with its airconditioned houses, the offices of a great company which handles business on an international scale, its refinery representing industrial machinery on a highly developed and intricate level, its harbor crowded with tankers served from the large loading jetty, and its labor quarters teeming with activity.

Saudi Arabia also has its oil towns: Dhahran, Abqaiq, Ras Tanura; and Bahrein has its Al-Awali. Arabia no longer lives in isolation. An industrial civilization has suddenly been transplanted to an environment as remote from industrialization as any society could be. The impact is tremendous and presents a great challenge to the inherited values of the Arabs in the Island.

CHAPTER XIII

Palestine

THE outcome of the establishment of a Jewish State in Palestine has been the displacement of the Arab population of the country. Close to a million Arabs have been torn away from home and hearth. They have been supplanted in their native land by an alien people. The refugees left everything behind them, and are living for the most part in desperate conditions. Many of them live in tents which collapse under a strong wind and are hardly a shelter from the inclemencies of the weather—snow and bitter cold in the winter, burning heat in the summer. Some have found shelter in buildings, often crowded and sometimes dilapidated. A few took refuge in caves after having for some time lived under the shelter of trees.

The events which have taken place since the United Nations decided to partition Palestine have in no way changed the nature of the moral principle involved, the principle that self-preservation and self-determination are the elemental and inalienable rights of any people. In Palestine these rights were denied to the Arabs. Under international sanction—represented first by the League of Nations and later by the United Nations—the indigenous population of Palestine was deprived of security in its native land; and under the same international authority, of which a great democratic power, Great Britain, was the instrument, the Arabs of Palestine were denied democratic, representative institutions, the only safe guarantee against tyranny from within and from without. Because these principles were ignored or distorted in making the fateful decision, because the issues involved are still largely unknown even to the enlightened public, and because their consequences continue to be of grave significance, the necessity of stating them is compelling.

It is essential to emphasize at the outset and keep in mind throughout that the tragedy of the Holy Land was created by forces and circumstances wholly external to the country itself, over which the indigenous population had no control, and for which, therefore, they cannot be held responsible. The Balfour Declaration, the British Mandate in Palestine, the persecution of the Jews in Europe, the interference of outside powers, especially the United States, under Zionist pressure, have brought about the conditions which have rent the Holy Land and wrought hatred and strife in the land which above all others should be dedicated to peace on earth and good will among men.

Rarely has there been an issue so ridden with emotion and beclouded with prejudice as the Palestine issue; rarely has so much confused thinking beset a problem; and hardly ever has there been such fear and recoil from facing the facts as they are and providing a solution based upon their inescapable and inexorable logic.

It is well to remember the size of Palestine. Its length is a hundred and sixty miles, its greatest width not more than seventy. From the top of its hills it may be seen in its entire breadth from the Mediterranean to the Dead Sea. Its ten thousand square miles are largely desert and rocky hills; a small part only is fertile land, suitable for intensive cultivation. Clearly there was no room in this diminutive country for the introduction of a new people upon the people already established there.

The history of Palestine is also instructive and bears directly upon the issue in question. To the average Christian—especially the Protestant—brought up on the Old Testament, Palestine is the land of the Jews; its history closes with the coming of Christ. The two thousand years that followed are a vacuum. Hence the widespread notion of an empty country waiting to receive its long dispersed people. Hence also the popular saying: give the country without a people to the people without a country. A brief acquaintance with the facts of history is enough to dispel this error.

The Hebrew tribes entered Palestine in separate groups and at different times. The earliest migration came from Mesopotamia and is associated with Abraham. A later migration, in the 14th century B.C., is connected with the Aramaean invasion of Syria. By that time Palestine had been inhabited for about 2000 years by a settled population with an advanced culture, the Canaanites after whom the country was named Canaan. Compared to these, the Hebrew invaders were crude and backward. Their civilized opponents called them Habiru, an old Babylonian term meaning nomad, bandit, mercenary, from which the word Hebrew is derived.[1]

1. A. T. Olmstead: *History of Palestine and Syria*, New York, 1931, p. 196.

Slowly the Hebrews conquered the hills and open country. The plains with their lines of fortified cities remained in the hands of the old inhabitants, the Canaanites. At no point did the Hebrews reach the sea or even the fertile coastal plain.[2]

Shortly after the Hebrews arrived in Canaan and were making their way into the hills, another people of a different origin were settling on the coast. These were the Philistines. Pushed out of their islands in the Aegean by the influx of the Greeks, they wandered along the Mediterranean shores and finally settled on the Canaanite coast to which they gave their name, Palestine.

The Hebrew kingdom was established about 1000 B.C. Jerusalem was conquered from the Jebusites by David. At the end of Solomon's reign it ceased to be the capital of a united Israel. After his death the kingdom broke in two, Judah in the Judaean hills and Israel in Samaria. The Philistines remained in possession of the plain and held a good part of the Shephelah, the lowhill country. The Negeb was lost to the nomads under Solomon's son.[3]

In 722 B.C., Sargon the Assyrian conquered Samaria, the northern kingdom. A large scale transfer of population followed. Israelites were deported to Babylonia and in their place were settled captives deported from other conquered lands. The Kingdom of Judah fell to the Chaldaean king Nebuchadnezzar, who destroyed Jerusalem and the Temple in 586 B.C. The higher classes of the population were carried into captivity; the peasants were left on the land.[4]

When half a century later the Persians, who had conquered the Chaldaeans and extended their empire to the Mediterranean, allowed such of the Jews as wished to do so to return and rebuild the Temple, few responded to the offer. The majority were already at home in Babylonia where they formed a prosperous community. Those who returned did not meet with a cordial welcome, for the land from which their ancestors were sent to exile was not a vacuum. Successive Assyrian kings had settled captives on the vacated land at various times. Southern Palestine up to Hebron was occupied by the Edomites. The Philistines continued to hold the Shephelah and the plain. Even the native Hebrews themselves were not sympathetic to the returning exiles.[5] The Temple was not

2. *Ibid.*, p. 270.
3. *Ibid.*, p. 352.
4. *Ibid.*, pp. 460, 527.
5. *Ibid.*, pp. 557–559.

rebuilt until another group of exiles returned in the reign of Darius I. In the reorganized empire of Darius, Palestine with Syria and Cyprus formed the fifth satrapy.[6]

Towards the end of the 4th century B.C., Alexander the Great defeated the Persians and inherited their empire. After his death Palestine came under the Seleucids, a Hellenistic dynasty, who succeeded to the Asiatic part of Alexander's empire. One of their kings pursued vigorously the policy of Hellenizing the Jews. Then as now the Jews were divided among themselves with regard to integration in the world around them. Some favored Hellenization or assimilation, others reacted violently against the spread of Greek culture. The Maccabaean revolt, inspired by religious and nationalist feelings, broke out during the 2nd century B.C., and a Jewish state was set up as a reaction against Hellenism. Such was the zeal of the Maccabaeans for Judaism that toward the peoples whom they conquered they practiced a policy of conversion or destruction. To the inhabitants of Galilee—Iturians of Arab stock and Aramaic tongue—they offered the choice between expulsion and circumcision.[7]

When the Seleucids were succeeded by the Romans, Palestine with the rest of Syria passed under Roman rule. It was constituted a subject kingdom under Herod, an Idumaean Jew. In this as in earlier periods, the Jews were only a part of the population; Samaritans and pagans shared the country with them. A revolt of the Jews against the Romans resulted in the destruction of Jerusalem and the Temple. This was the year 70 A.D., and it marked the end of the Jewish state. Another rebellion broke out in 132–4 and was suppressed. After that, Jewish nationalism ceased until it was revived by the modern Zionists.

Although at times the Jews were deported and expelled from Palestine, their exodus from the Promised Land was largely voluntary. The Jewish dispersion was part of the general Syrian emigration during the first centuries of the Christian era, when large Syrian communities were settled in numerous cities of Italy, France, and Spain. The Jews, like other emigrants, left Palestine to seek their fortune in countries that offered greater opportunities than the arid hills of Judaea. Even in the time of Christ, Jewish communities flourished in Persia, Babylonia, Asia Minor, Egypt, Rome, and the other countries of the Mediterranean.

6. *Ibid.*, pp. 560–562, 577.
7. Hitti: *History of Syria*, p. 246.

When Palestine became an Arab country in the 7th century A.D. it had long ceased to be Jewish. Not only had the Jewish state been relegated to history since the first century, but the Jewish religion itself had few adherents among the inhabitants who were predominantly Christian in religion and, since before the time of Christ, Aramaic in language and culture. Racially they were descended from the people who had lived in Palestine throughout its long history, Canaanites, Philistines, Edomites, and a host of other less known groups, and of Jewish converts to Christianity. The Arabs intermarried with this native population, and Palestine became Arab not merely by conquest but by assimilation.

Under the Arabs, as under the Romans and the powers which had preceded them, Palestine was not a separate state but part of a regional unit. During the Arab period Palestine experienced many political changes and vicissitudes, among them the Crusades which lasted over two centuries. But the basic character of the country was not changed. When Palestine along with the rest of Syria and the other Arab provinces, passed under the domination of the Ottoman Turks early in the 16th century, the life of the people continued to function undisturbed within the inherited pattern. The Arabic language and culture were preserved intact, and unity with the surrounding Arab countries was maintained. Turkish authority was more or less effective in the larger towns; in the countryside it was shadowy and nebulous.

At the time of the first World War Palestine, though a province of the Ottoman Empire, was not a colony. It had a larger measure of self-government than it received under the subsequent British Mandate, and its people elected representatives to the Imperial Parliament in Constantinople. During the war the Arabs rebelled against the Turks not so much because of the oppressiveness of Turkish rule as out of a strong and natural desire for independence and the opportunity to recreate their culture unhampered and unobstructed.

As for the Jews, a few scattered communities continued to live in Palestine after the country had become Arab. Their principal center was Galilee where for a time they maintained Rabbinical schools. The religious center of Judaism, however, had been transferred to Mesopotamia several centuries before Islam. There it remained when that country—known to the Arabs as Iraq—became part of the Arab-Moslem Empire; later in the Middle Ages it was transferred to Spain, another country under Arab rule in those days. In modern times, eastern Europe, which until the end of the 19th century had the largest concentration of Jews, was the Jewish religious center.

In Palestine, the Jews were accorded the tolerance and protection which their religion enjoined the Moslems to show to the People of the Book. During the interval of the Crusades the Jewish community suffered; in Jerusalem itself it was practically extinct. When the Jews were expelled from Spain at the end of the 15th century, a few of them found their way to Palestine. Many settled in the other Arab countries, North Africa, Egypt, and Yaman. Some went to Europe, especially Holland and Germany. A large number found refuge in Salonica, then a part of the Ottoman Empire. In the first half of the 19th century, about 8,000 Jews lived in Palestine—according to Montefiore, a wealthy English Jew who visited the country to study the possibility of acquiring land and settling some of his co-religionists from Europe in agricultural colonies.[8] Their number increased during the latter part of the century when several agricultural colonies were established by Russian Jews who fled from the persecution which followed the assassination of Tzar Alexander II. While Palestine received a few thousand Jews from Eastern Europe, nearly three million of them emigrated to the New World.

It was in this period that Jewish nationalism began to be formulated. Its chief exponent was Theodor Herzl. Though an emancipated Austrian Jew himself, Herzl became a nationalist when he attended the Dreyfus trial as correspondent of a Viennese liberal paper, and witnessed the anti-Semitism that accompanied it. In his book *"Der Judenstaat"* he developed the theory that a Jewish state would reduce anti-Semitism by absorbing immigrants from the countries which had a large number of Jews. Herzl, who at first attached no importance to the locality of the state and was willing to accept the British offer of a territory in East Africa, later looked to Palestine because of its sentimental and religious appeal to the Jews. He founded the Zionist Congress to represent the Jews of all nations. The Congress became the tribunal of Jewish nationalism.

Herzl made contacts with monarchs and statesmen in the hope of procuring Palestine for the Jews. He approached Abdul Hamid, the Sultan of Turkey and suzerain of Palestine, to whom he offered Jewish wealth to pay off Turkish debts and restore the finances of

8. Nevill Barbour: *Nisi Dominus,* London, 1946, p. 32.

the Empire in return for Palestine being ceded to the Jews. To this offer Abdul Hamid replied: "Let the Jews keep their millions. If my Empire is dismembered they will perhaps receive Palestine gratis. But it must be our corpse which they cut up; I cannot agree to vivisection."[9]

Herzl nevertheless kept on negotiating and offering inducements to the Sultan. In the negotiations he represented the Jews as the natural allies of the Moslems against the Christians. He foresaw a bright future for the Ottoman Empire re-invigorated by Jewish finance, and promised that the Jews would use their influence to quiet down the anti-Turkish feeling and agitation in Europe which the Armenian massacres had aroused. To these offers and inducements came the unrewarding answer that Jews would be allowed, if they became Turkish subjects, to settle in a dispersed manner in all the Asiatic provinces of the Empire except Palestine.

Meanwhile Herzl sounded the Kaiser on the subject of large-scale Jewish immigration to Palestine. To the German ruler he said that a Jewish Palestine would be an outpost of German culture. The Jews would also help to carry out the chief project of German expansion in the East, the Berlin-Baghdad railway.[10] Herzl advised the Kaiser that he would do well to get rid of some elements among the population, such as usurers who could be transferred to Palestine. He also warned that if the Palestine project miscarried, "hundreds of thousands of our supporters will at a single bound join the revolutionary parties."[11] But no encouragement came from the Kaiser who at that time was cultivating the friendship of the Sultan and the Moslem world. Similar allurements were offered to the Tzar from whom they elicited no response. Finally, Herzl turned to England and from the Colonial Secretary received the offer to colonize a tract of land in British East Africa, corresponding to what is known today as Kenya. The place had a healthy climate, it was good agricultural land, and was about the size of Palestine. Herzl was delighted with the offer but the Zionist Congress would not accept it as a substitute for Palestine.

During the first World War, the Zionists again tried to enlist the support of Turks and Germans. To the Turks they renewed their financial offers, and promised to recruit an army of Polish Jews who would fight with Turkey if she gave assurances about Jewish

9. Quoted in Barbour, *op. cit.*, p. 45.
10. *Ibid.*, pp. 47–48.
11. Elmer Berger: *The Jewish Dilemma*, pp. 90–91.

colonization of Palestine. For the first time Arab nationalism was brought into the picture. The Zionists reminded the Turks of Arab restlessness and pointed out that the Jews in Palestine would be a counter-weight to Arab demands for autonomy.[12]

In approaching the Germans, the identity of Jewish and German interests was stressed. The culture of the Jews was German. They wished "to establish, on the eastern shore of the Mediterranean, a modern cultural and commercial center which will be both directly and indirectly a prop of Germanism."[13] The enterprise was not only cultural; it had economic and political significance as well. "Palestine by Jewish immigration . . . could become a politico-commercial base, a Turkish-German Gibraltar, on the frontiers of the Anglo-Arab ocean."[14]

The only negotiations which bore fruit, however, were those conducted with the British Government. They resulted in the Balfour Declaration of November 2, 1917, which reads: "His Majesty's Government view with favour the establishment in Palestine of a national home for the Jewish people, and will use their best endeavours to facilitate the achievement of that object, it being clearly understood that nothing shall be done which may prejudice the civil and religious rights of existing non-Jewish communities in Palestine or the rights and political status enjoyed by Jews in any other country."

The Balfour Declaration gave the Zionists what they had strenuously sought since political Zionism was formulated—"a publicly recognized home land under legal guarantee."[15] That the word home instead of state was used was designed to win a wider support for the idea among the Jews, many of whom feared that the establishment of a Jewish State would endanger their status in the various countries of which they were nationals. But the intention of the Zionists to set up a Jewish state was there at the beginning of the movement, as is amply illustrated in the statements of Herzl, founder of political Zionism, and of the leaders who came after him. Not a refuge or cultural home but Jewish sovereignty was the aim.

The Balfour Declaration is a masterpiece of evasiveness and

12. Barbour, *op. cit.*, pp. 54–55.
13. Quoted in Barbour, p. 54.
14. Quoted in Barbour, p. 55; see also Berger, *op. cit.*, pp. 77–96.
15. Herzl at the First Zionist Congress, quoted in Jeffries: *Palestine the Reality*, p. 39.

ambiguous phrasing. In fact, it was given different interpretations by British Governments and statesmen themselves. While it promised the Jews nothing definite it could be interpreted to mean anything from a cultural home in Palestine to the turning of the country into a Jewish state. As for the Arabs, who in 1917 were 93% of the population, the Declaration does not even mention them by name. They are referred to as the "existing non-Jewish communities," a reference that was bound to create the impression, whether intended or not, of a nondescript conglomeration of inhabitants without entity or identity, towards whom therefore no political responsibility exists.

The Balfour Declaration opened the tragedy of Palestine. As the plot unfolded, the problem grew in intensity and bitterness to dimensions far out of proportion to the size of this small country.

Various explanations have been given for Britain's support of Zionist plans in Palestine, among them Britain's need, at a critical time in the war, of rallying the support of world Jewry to the Allied cause, the gratitude of British statesmen to Dr. Weizmann for scientific services connected with ammunitions, the religious bent of some of these statesmen, and the romantic appeal of the idea of the Jewish Return. One explanation, however, seems to dominate all others. It is Britain's concept of imperial strategy in the eastern Mediterranean. A large Jewish population, planted in Palestine under British auspices and protection, owing allegiance to Great Britain, and eventually incorporated in the British Commonwealth as one of the dominions, would be a safeguard for British imperial interests in the region. To this effect Weizmann spoke when he told C. P. Scott, the editor of the *Manchester Guardian* that the Jews would "form a very effective guard for the Suez Canal,"[16] and when he wrote, on October 3rd, 1917, to the Foreign Office for transmission to the War Cabinet: "We must respectfully point out that in submitting our resolution *we entrusted our national and Zionist destiny to the Foreign Office and the Imperial War Cabinet* in the hope that the problem would be considered in the light of imperial interests and the principles for which the Entente stands."[17]

The British, with Arab help, conquered Palestine from the Turks. They were not free to dispose of the country. For besides

16. Chaim Weizmann: *Trial and Error*, Hamish Hamilton, London, 1949, p. 191.

17. *Ibid.*, p. 258.

the pledges which committed Great Britain to Arab independence, a new system came into being after the war replacing the old methods of annexation and colonization. This was the mandate system, offspring of Wilsonian idealism, under which conquered territories were placed by the League of Nations in the hands of the Allied Powers to be administered temporarily as a trust. The welfare and development of the inhabitants was the primary concern and purpose of the mandate. Before the mandates were assigned, the Powers had renounced their rights as conquerors.

Great Britain received the Mandate over Palestine. The obligations which Britain undertook towards the Jews were contradictory to the spirit and purpose of the mandate institution, and violated the Covenant of the League of Nations from which the Mandate derived its legal basis. The text of the Palestine Mandate was based upon drafts prepared by the Zionists. Its terms gave the small Jewish minority a privileged position over the 93% of Arab inhabitants who are nowhere mentioned by name but referred to as "other sections of the population" and "existing non-Jewish communities." The Mandate adopted the Balfour Declaration, opened wide the doors of Palestine to Jewish immigration, and provided for a Jewish Agency to advise and cooperate with the administration in all matters that affected "the establishment of the Jewish national home and the interests of the Jewish population in Palestine." Recognition of the Jewish Agency by the Government made possible the penetration of Zionist influence and control into the various government departments, and opened the way to Zionist interference in all the affairs of the country. The Hebrew language, which even the small Jewish community did not then speak, was made an official language and placed on a level with Arabic, the language of almost the entire population.

Armed with the Balfour Declaration and the Mandate, the Zionists began to plan and work for the eventual setting up of a Jewish state. The British created the necessary conditions to bring about its coming. In view of the subsequent denunciation of Great Britain by the Zionists it is necessary to remember that it was British backing and armed support which transformed Zionism from a dream into a political reality. Under Britain's wing, Jewish national institutions were developed and the Jewish Agency became a state within the state, performing with respect to the Jewish community all the functions of government. The Jewish Agency had its own political institutions, directed the economic life of the community, maintained hospitals, schools, and other social services, and controlled the para-military organization, Haganah. The Agency had, moreover, "its own intelligence service with virtually all Jewish Government officials as voluntary informers."[18] Under the aegis of Great Britain, over 600,000[19] Jews came into Palestine, and a privileged Jewish community was set up in the country. During the first twenty years of the mandate, the British continuously suppressed the Arabs, at times with extreme severity, to make way for the Jews.

The Arabs have never accepted the Balfour Declaration nor the Mandate which was designed to give it effect. Great Britain did not own Palestine when she made the Declaration nor has she owned it at any time since. Having promised what was not within her right to give, her promise was null and void. At the time the Balfour Declaration was issued, Palestine was politically a province of Turkey, but it was not Turkish. It was an Arab country; it belonged to its Arab inhabitants and to the larger Arab nation which was then fighting as an ally of Britain against a common enemy, the Turks. The Balfour Declaration was issued without the knowledge of the Arabs; whatever was promised in it was done behind their backs and over their heads. That Britain had qualms about it is evident from the secrecy with which the Declaration was kept from the Arabs. When news of it transpired, a messenger was rushed to King Hussain in Hijaz with the reassuring statement that the return of the Jews to Palestine would be allowed "insofar as is compatible with the freedom of the existing population, both economic and political."[20]

At the outset, the Arabs made known their opposition to the Zionist scheme. The Zionists claim that Faisal, in an agreement drawn up between him and Weizmann in January 1919, endorsed the Zionist policy of large scale Jewish immigration and settlement in Palestine. The agreement, however, was subject to the reservation which stated Faisal would be bound to its terms only if an independent united Arab state were established. Since Faisal's condition was not met, the Agreement had no validity. Arab pub-

18. Arthur Koestler: *Promise and Fulfillment*, p. 12.
19. It is interesting to note that the number of Jews brought to Palestine as a consequence of the British mandate was equivalent to the population of the Jewish Kingdom under David. Olmstead, *op. cit.*, p. 330.
20. *Cmd*, 5964, 1939.
22. Antonius: *op. cit.*, Appendix H, pp. 449–450.

lic opinion knew nothing about this document which was not published till 1936 when Dr. Weizmann made it known in a letter to the London *Times*. That he should have waited seventeen years—eventful and turbulent years in Palestine—to disclose the contents of the agreement indicates that Weizmann himself could not have attached much importance to it. One aspect of the agreement is worth noting: The Arabs were not hostile to the immigration of Jews as Jews. Faisal was willing to accept Jewish immigration provided Palestine had a representative local government and was part of a larger independent Arab state. King Husain himself, who refused to sign the Covenant of the League of Nations because it endorsed the Jewish National Home, welcomed the Jews not only to Palestine but to the other Arab countries as "lodgers in the Arab house." But for Zionism and its threat to the very existence of the Arabs, the Jews could have found refuge in many of the Arab countries and would have lived as equal citizens in a society wholly free of racial prejudice.

The Syrian Congress, which met in Damascus in July 1919 and was attended by representatives from Palestine as from the other parts of Syria, passed the unanimous resolution: "We reject the claims of the Zionists for the establishment of a Jewish commonwealth in that part of southern Syria which is known as Palestine, and we are opposed to Jewish immigration into any part of the country. We do not acknowledge that they have a title, and we regard their claims as a grave menace to our national, political and economic life. Our Jewish fellow-citizens shall continue to enjoy the rights and to bear the responsibilities which are ours in common."[21]

The King-Crane Commission sent by President Wilson was in Syria at this time. On the basis of its findings which fully substantiated the Congress resolution, it recommended "serious modification of the extreme Zionist programme for Palestine of unlimited immigration of Jews, looking finally to making Palestine distinctly a Jewish state." Quoting from President Wilson's address of July 4th, 1918—that one of the great ends for which the war was being fought was "The settlement of every question whether of territory, of sovereignty, of economic arrangement, or of political relationship upon the basis of the free acceptance of that settlement by the people immediately concerned, and not upon the basis of the material interest or advantage of any other nation or people

21. Antonius, *op. cit.*, Appendix C, p. 441.

which may desire a different settlement for the sake of its own exterior influence or mastery"—the Commissioners say:

"If that principle is to rule, and so the wishes of Palestine's population are to be decisive as to what is to be done with Palestine, then it is to be remembered that the non-Jewish population of Palestine—nearly nine-tenths of the whole—are emphatically against the entire Zionist programme . . . there was no one thing upon which the population of Palestine was more agreed than upon this. To subject a people so-minded to unlimited Jewish immigration and to steady financial and social pressure to surrender the land would be a gross violation of the principle just quoted, and of the people's rights, though it kept within the forms of law.

"It is to be noted also that the feeling against the Zionist Programme is not confined to Palestine, but shared very generally by the people throughout Syria. . . .

"The Peace Conference should not shut its eyes to the fact that the anti-Zionist feeling in Palestine and Syria is intense and not lightly to be flouted. No British officer consulted by the Commissioners believed that the Zionist programme could be carried out except by force of arms. . . . That of itself is evidence of a strong sense of the injustice of the Zionist programme on the part of the non-Jewish populations of Palestine and Syria. Decisions requiring armies to carry out are sometimes necessary, but they are surely not gratuitously to be taken in the interests of a serious injustice. For the initial claim, often submitted by Zionist representations, that thay have a 'right' to Palestine, can hardly be seriously considered. . . .

"In view of all these considerations, and with a deep sense of sympathy for the Jewish cause, the Commissioners feel bound to recommend that only a greatly reduced Zionist Programme be attempted by the Peace Conference, and even that be only very gradually initiated. This would have to mean that Jewish immigration should be definitely limited, and that the project for making Palestine distinctly a Jewish Commonwealth should be given up."[22]

The warnings of the Commission went unheeded, and the British Mandate which denied Arab rights in their own country and threatened Arab national existence was forced upon the Arabs. The subsequent development of the Palestine Mandate substantiated Arab fears, for it proved to be the instrument of Zionist aggression and the medium through which Great Britain and the League of Nations, in the name of "Sacred trust," prepared the way for the uprooting of a whole population and the destruction of a culture associated with Palestine for over thirteen hundred years.

The Mandate was for the Arabs a period of tension, fear, and insecurity punctuated at intervals by violent outbreaks. After each outbreak, a Royal Commission of Investigation was sent to Palestine. Beginning in 1920 and ending with the Peel Commission of 1936, their investigations revealed the same underlying causes for every outbreak and revolt, namely "the desire of the Arabs for national independence" and "their hatred and fear of the establishment of the Jewish National Home." These two causes, according to the Peel Report, "were and always have been inextricably linked together. The Balfour Declaration and the Mandate under which it was to be implemented involved the denial of national independence at the outset. The subsequent growth of the National Home created a practical obstacle, and the only serious one, to the concession later of national independence."[23]

The Arabs foresaw, even when the Jews were yet few in numbers, that the ultimate goal of Zionism was to dominate and supplant them. No amount of assuring statements by the British Government could allay their anxiety about their future. They insisted that their only safeguard lay in the immediate establishment of representative government, which would check the wave of alien immigrants that was intended to submerge them and control the sale of land which was daily alienating from them more and more of the soil of their country.

Besides this fundamental and overriding objection to Zionism as a threat to their national existence, the Arabs had other grievances against the Zionists and the pro-Zionist policy of the government. Because of the widely propagated claim that the presence of the Jews in Palestine benefited all sections of the population, it is necessary to correct the allegation by pointing to the hardships which the National Home has inflicted upon the Arabs.

The sponsoring of the National Home was an expensive undertaking for the government and a heavy burden upon the taxpayer. Special services had to be established to put the policy into effect, among them a large immigration department. The imposition of Hebrew as one of the official languages meant the duplication of

23. *Cmd.* 5479, pp. 110–111.

official transactions and consequently the employment of a double staff. The Jews did not attend the public schools, so the government paid them an annual grant in aid for their educational system. In times when unemployment was widespread among the Arabs, thousands of Jews were admitted for whom the government artificially created work, and the Jewish laborer was paid double the rate which the Arab received for the same work.[24] The heaviest of the financial burdens was the security services which absorbed by far the largest item of public expenditure. The Mandate, having brought to Palestine an alien element whose aims were detrimental to the national rights and legitimate aspirations of the native population, fell back upon the maintenance of a large force to repress the Arabs whenever they rose to defend their existence.

The Mandate gave the Jewish community a preponderant hold upon the economic life of the country. Two monopoly concessions, one for the generation and distribution of electric power from the whole Jordan system, the other for the exploiting of the mineral deposits of the Dead Sea, virtually placed the development of the country in the hands of the Zionists. Thus the trustee, instead of developing the country's resources for the benefit of all its inhabitants, bestowed its potential wealth upon a minority whose aims and interests were inimical to the native population.

Jewish industry in Palestine was maintained by discrimination at the expense of the Arabs. The government imposed heavy artificial tariffs to protect the various industries which otherwise could not compete with foreign goods. "Large industry in Palestine," says the Peel Report, "appears to depend upon manipulation of the tariff. The rest of the population is taxed in order that the proprietors of these industrial concerns may be in a position to pay the wages of their labourers and to make a profit for themselves."

Jewish economic enterprise in Palestine, industrial and agricultural, did not rest on a normal economic basis, because the aim in view was not economic but political. The acquisition of land, the development of agricultural settlements, the setting up of various industries were primarily designed to secure and extend the Zionist hold on the country and provide work for Jewish immigrants, large scale immigration being the cornerstone of Zionist policy in Palestine. Since the Jewish National Home was heavily subsidized by

24. Barbour: *op. cit.*, p. 110, n. 1, and p. 134.

outside sources, economic considerations could be waived, and agriculture and industry could be maintained under a perpetual deficit.

The land problem has been among the most serious grievances of the Arabs against the Mandate and the Zionist scheme which it sponsored. It is true that the Arabs were not forced to sell land to the Jews. It is necessary, however, to explain the circumstances which led to the sales. The bulk of the land sold to the Jews was owned by non-Palestinian, absentee landlords who succumbed to the inflated prices offered by the Zionists. The temptation was all the more enticing because of the separation of Palestine from the rest of Syria and the erection of political and economic barriers between the newly created countries. Another group who sold land were the poorer peasants, who were weighed down with debts and a heavy taxation made necessary by the imposition of the National Home and amounting to twice or more what the peasant paid in Syria, Lebanon, or Iraq. The land was bought largely by the Keren Kayemeth—the Jewish National Fund—and became the inalienable property of the Jewish community. The Arab tenants were evicted by force. The government, instead of laying down laws to secure the peasants on the land and guard the country against this invasion through money, took part in the forceful eviction by sending troops in armored cars to tear the peasants away from their homes. The Arab villages were then demolished and Zionist settlements took their place. The process of obliterating the Arab village, initiated under the Mandate, was a preliminary to the obliteration of Arab Palestine when the Jewish National Home had come of age and no longer needed the mandatory's protection.

The inadequacy of the public system of education was considered by the Arabs a further indication of the government's intention to keep them down. The neglect is all the more unpardonable since the necessary funds were available. The Simpson Report of 1930 stressed the need for considerably increased expenditure on education. How little the government heeded the advice may be seen from the financial provisions made for education. In 1931, the education budget amounted to 6.19% of the total expenditure, by 1936 it was down to 3.99%, although at the end of that year there was a surplus of £P6,627,810.[25] The Peel Commission deplored the

25. *Cmd.* 5479, p. 339; £P, the Palestinian pound, was on a par with sterling then equivalent to about $5.

inadequacy of the school system and expressed the belief that "if the claims of education had been rated as high as they deserve, more money might somehow have been found for it, at the expense, for instance, of such material needs as public works of a not vitally urgent kind."[26] The appropriation for education never exceeded 7% of the general budget; the average was 5%. This stringency on the part of the government was in strange contrast to the thirst for education among the Palestinian Arabs and their wholehearted readiness to contribute towards the extension of educational opportunities. They pushed the government to open schools for them by providing the land for the school and the funds to put up the building. The villagers felt a strong attachment to and a pride in the school which they built. During the Arab revolution of 1936–39, when government authority broke down over large areas of the countryside, the village schools continued to function under the protection of the revolutionaries who would come down from the mountains to pay their dues to the school, and return to the hills to resume the fight against the government which ran those schools.[27] In 1942 the Assistant Director of Education estimated that in order to provide for compulsory education to Arab children between the ages of 7 and 12 there would need to be an annual increase in expenditure, according to pre-war prices, of £P250,000, with an additional cost of £P450,000 for school buildings. He further estimated that all children 5 to 15 years old could be put in school at an annual increase of £P750,000. The cost of the necessary additional buildings would be £P1,300,000.[28] This sum was not beyond the means of the government had the will been there.

As the Jewish National Home grew and expanded under the protection of the Mandatory Power, Arab resistance increased steadily; it was consolidated in the thirties, when it became a force to be reckoned with. The danger which the Arabs had sensed in the twenties stood before them as a horrible reality in the decade that followed. Waves of immigrants flooded their country. The year 1933 brought 30,000 Jews, in 1934 the figure rose to 42,000, and in 1935, 61,000 entered Palestine, a country about the area of the state of Vermont. The danger was further aggravated because

26. *Cmd.* 5479, pp. 337–339.

27. Jibrail Katul: "Education in Palestine from 1920–1948," *Al-Abhath*, Quarterly Journal of the American University of Beirut, June 1950, pp. 177–187.

28. Jibrail Katul: *Education in Palestine.*

of the power wielded by world Jewry on behalf of the Jews in Palestine.

Two examples may be cited here to illustrate the degree of Jewish influence in the British Government and Parliament. In 1929, riots broke out in the Holy Land; a Royal Commission of Enquiry was dispatched to investigate the causes. Upon receiving the Commission's Report, the government sent an expert, Sir John Hope Simpson, to make a purely technical report on the questions of "immigration, land settlement, and development." The Labor Government, and particularly its Colonial Secretary, Lord Passfield—better known as Sidney Webb, the celebrated socialist investigator and writer—were sufficiently impressed by the findings of the Shaw Commission and by the Simpson Report to issue the White Paper of 1930 which interpreted the principle of the "economic absorptive capacity of the country"—a principle established by the Churchill White Paper of 1922 as the only criterion to be considered in admitting Jewish immigrants to Palestine—to mean the safeguarding of Arab economic interests. The 1930 White Paper stated that "in estimating the absorptive capacity of Palestine at any time account should be taken of Arab as well as of Jewish unemployment in determining the rate at which Jewish immigration should be permitted." Although the Paper paid attention neither to the observations of the Shaw Commission regarding the political conditions of the country which were at the basis of the unrest, nor to the national grievances of the Arabs detailed in its Report, yet because it made this concession to Arab security the Zionists received it with an outburst of denunciations and exerted pressure so intense that the Government was forced to revoke its position. In a letter from Prime Minister MacDonald to Dr. Weizmann, the White Paper was explained away in a manner which amounted to its abrogation.

The other example is furnished by the High Commissioner's offer of a Legislative Council and its subsequent withdrawal under Zionist pressure. A Legislative Council, proposed in 1922, had been rejected by the Arabs for two reasons: one, that it gave a majority to official and Jewish members; two, that because the Council had no power, Arab participation in it could not safeguard Arab rights but would mean acceptance of the Zionist-committed Mandate and only serve to legalize the Government's Zionist policy which otherwise had to be carried out by force. In 1935, when the Arabs were seething with unrest as a result of the heavy im-

migration that threatened to make their complete subordination
a not too distant possibility, the British Government as a reassuring measure renewed the offer of a Legislative Council, this time
in a more acceptable form. The Council was to be composed of
28 members, 5 of whom would be officials, 7 Jews, and the rest
Arabs. The President was to be "an impartial person unconnected
with Palestine." While the Council's powers were very limited—it
had no right to question the validity of the Mandate—it could discuss such important matters as immigration. Control of immigration, however, remained with the High Commissioner. The Council
did not establish self-government in Palestine, but made allusions
to it, however faint. It was therefore promptly crushed by the Zionists and their sympathizers. Its fate, in the words of the Peel Royal
Commission, was determined outside Palestine. When it came up
for debate in the British Parliament, the Jewish viewpoint found
elequent support in both Houses. The Arab case went by default,
the Arabs not being members of Parliament, nor voters in Parliamentary elections.

The years 1936 saw the Arabs in a state of despair of ever attaining justice from the Mandatory Power. Once again, armed resistance broke out, but this time on a much larger scale than had
occurred before. It was accompanied by a widespread strike which
affected the cities and the country districts. The strike developed
into civil disobedience and caused a standstill in the life of the
whole country outside Jewish settlements.

The British Government responded with the usual remedy, the
dispatch of a Royal Commission of Investigation. The Arabs of
Palestine received appeals from Arab rulers to call off the strike
and the revolt pending the results of the Commission's enquiry.
After several months' investigations the Commission gave the verdict that the Mandate was unworkable. It therefore proposed the
partition of Palestine into Arab and Jewish states, with an en-
clave to remain permanently under the British Mandate. To this
proposal the Arabs reacted by resuming the revolt with renewed
determination. The revolution, which now swept the country, detached a large part of it from government control, and lasted from
1937 to 1939, was a revolt of peasants against the forces which
sought to deprive them of their land and dispossess them of their
soil and the culture so inextricably woven into the soil.

Among the stock allegations of the Zionists is the claim that
Arab opposition to the Jews was artificially created and inflamed

by a few self-seeking leaders, while the mass of the population welcomed the establishment of the Jews in the country. For a time the British authorities themselves assumed and expected that Jewish money and alleged benefits would buy Arab acquiescence and smooth the way for Jewish domination. But there were well informed and responsible British observers who from the very beginning dissented with this view. The Haycraft Royal Commissioners, sent to investigate the disturbances of 1920, reported that they could not share the view which brushed aside the disturbances as the result of an artificial agitation fomented by disreputable leaders. On the contrary, they discerned an apprehension of the Zionist aims that was "well-nigh universal" among the Arabs and "not confined to any particular class." The leaders, the educated youth who "are sons of the soil," and the mass of the people were united on this issue "because they feel that their political and their material interests are identical."[29] Another Royal Commission of Enquiry, the Shaw Commission, sent after the outbreak of 1929, expressed similar views when it stated that the experience of the Commissioners in Palestine did not support the contention which represented the demands for a national government as artificially promoted while the mass of the population were generally apathetic about the future of their country. "Villagers and peasants alike," the Report said, "are taking a very real and personal interest both in the effect of the policy of establishing a National Home and in the question of the development of self-governing institutions in Palestine. No less than fourteen Arabic newspapers are published in Palestine, and in almost every village there is someone who reads from the papers to gatherings of those villagers who are illiterate. . . . The Arab fellaheen and villagers are therefore probably more politically minded than many of the people of Europe."[30] Dr. Weizmann himself, who at convenient times spoke of cooperation between Arabs and Jews, wrote in his autobiography that as early as 1920 "by the time a civil administration under Sir Herbert Samuel took over, the gulf between the two peoples was already difficult to bridge."[31]

The revolt of 1937 was carried on with increased intensity after the leaders had been dispersed and exiled. Arab opposition was spontaneous, widespread, and deep-rooted. Nor were the Arabs

29. Quoted in Jeffries, *op. cit.*, p. 425.
30. *Cmd.* 3530, p. 129.
31. Chaim Weizmann: *Trial and Error*, p. 281.

of Palestine alone in the struggle. In the neighboring countries committees for the defense of Palestine were set up, and volunteers joined the rebel forces. Inter-Arab conferences held in Syria and Egypt expressed the solidarity of the Arab world with Palestine. With the large-scale revolt in Palestine itself and the general support of the Arabs to their threatened brothers in the Holy Land, it became evident to the British Government that further expansion of the National Home would involve the armed suppression of the Arab population in Palestine, and intensify the bitterness and enmity which their pro-Zionist policy had earned for England throughout the Arab world.

The British Government, fearing a conflict in Europe in which the Middle East was bound to be an important stake, made an attempt early in 1939 to reach a settlement for Palestine by calling a conference of Arabs and Jews to which the governments of the independent Arab countries were invited. Following the conference, a White Paper setting out the Government's policy was issued. It stated: "His Majesty's Government therefore now declare unequivocally that it is not part of their policy that Palestine should become a Jewish state. They would indeed regard it as contrary to their obligations to the Arabs under the Mandate, as well as to assurances which have been given to the Arab people in the past, that the Arab population of Palestine should be made the subjects of a Jewish state against their will."[32]

The White Paper dealt with the three fundamental issues of the Palestine problem, immigration, the sale of land, and self-government. With regard to immigration the British Government believed that its continued expansion against the strongly expressed will of the Arab people meant rule by force. This policy was contrary to the spirit of Article 22 of the Covenant of the League of Nations and to the specific obligations towards the Arabs in the Palestine Mandate. Continued immigration would perpetuate the enmity between Arabs and Jews. The situation in Palestine could become a permanent source of friction amongst all peoples in the Near and Middle East. Common sense and justice required that these circumstances should not be ignored in framing an immigration policy. In view of these considerations, the statement declared that during the next five years 75,000 Jews would be admitted, after which Arab consent would be necessary for further immigration.

32. *Cmd.*, 6019, 1946, p. 4.

On the subject of land sales the Paper stated that until then no restriction on the transfer of land from Arabs to Jews had been imposed. But since the Reports of several expert Commissions had indicated that in some areas there was no longer room for further transfers of land, while in other areas such transfers must be restricted to avoid creating a considerable landless Arab population, further transfers of land, therefore, would be regulated or prohibited at the discretion of the High Commissioner. With regard to self-government the White Paper envisaged, subject to a number of conditions, independence at the end of ten years. The conditions were so restrictive, however, that independence seemed unattainable within their framework.

The proposals of the White Paper were vague, contained too many loopholes, and were circumscribed by numerous precautions and reservations. For these reasons, the Arabs felt constrained not to accept them. They were hopeful, however, that since the British Government had at last recognized Arab rights in their own land and had formulated the Statement of Policy, however inadequately, upon these principles, there would be in the future a working basis and a possibility of cooperation leading to a satisfactory solution.

The White Paper of 1939 met the fate of earlier attempts made by the British Government to recognize, however partially, the rights of the Palestinian Arabs. It was bitterly attacked by the Zionists, and was consequently withdrawn.

When the war was declared, the Arabs called off the revolution which had been going on since 1936. In the summer of 1940, the British Government sent an emissary, Colonel Newcombe, to Baghdad where many of the Palestinian leaders were then living, with instructions to come to an understanding with the Arabs on the basis of the White Paper of 1939. An agreement was reached and signed. The negotiations were conducted and the agreement signed with the knowledge and approval of representatives of the Iraqi and Saudi Governments. Because the basis of a settlement of the Palestine question acceptable to the Palestinian Arabs had been reached, the Iraqi government declared its readiness to enter the war and place the Iraqi army at the disposal of the Chief Commander of the Middle East. It was at Great Britain's darkest moment of the war that the Arabs declared their readiness to join her cause. But the British did not implement the Baghdad agreement, and the Palestine question remained throughout the war the burning issue of the Arab world, alienating Arab sympathies from Great Britain and her allies, and providing a real and fundamental wrong which Axis propaganda eagerly exploited.

The Zionists benefited by the war to strengthen their position in Palestine through military training and the acquisition of arms. After the battle of Alamein, when the immediate menace of Hitler had receded, "service of Jews in the British Army or the European underground resistance movements was effectively considered as preparatory training for service in Haganah or one of the terrorist organizations after the war."[33] "Haganah (an illegal military force controlled by the Jewish Agency) organized the theft of arms and ammunition from the British forces in the Middle East."[34] A campaign of terror was let loose. From 1942 "until the end of the war, Jewish extremists carried out a number of political murders, robberies and acts of sabotage."[35] The Jewish Agency claimed to have no authority over the terrorists. It insisted on its rights under the Mandate, as it interpreted those rights, but refused to cooperate with the authorities to repress the terrorists. While Agency spokesmen condemned terrorism, the Agency worked in close collaboration with the terrorist groups.[36]

During the war, the Zionists transferred the center of their political activity and pressure from Great Britain to the United States. Until then they had looked to America mainly for financial support while Great Britain enforced and protected the Zionist scheme in Palestine. But as the war progressed it became evident that Great Britain would emerge from it greatly weakened. A weakened Britain would not be so free to formulate her own policy but would have to obey the United States, the stronger power whose help Britain needed. The Zionists therefore shifted to the stronger party.

The demand for a Jewish state was openly declared for the first time by American Zionists in 1942 in a statement known as the Biltmore Program. This proclamation was followed by the passage of Zionist-inspired resolutions in a large number of state legislatures, favoring the setting up of a Jewish Commonwealth in Palestine. Since the resolutions entailed no commitments, they met no

33. Royal Institute of International Affairs, *The Middle East, A Political and Economic Survey*, p. 292.

34. Text of the British Statement on Palestine on the Termination of the Mandate, *New York Times*, May 14, 1948.

35. *Ibid.*

36. Text of the British Paper Linking Jewish Agency to Zionist Terrorism in Palestine, *New York Times*, July 25, 1946.

opposition and were passed as a matter of routine. In the winter of 1944, a resolution was introduced into both houses of Congress, calling for unlimited Jewish immigration to Palestine and the establishment of a Jewish State. It was withdrawn, however, upon the recommendation of the War and State Departments which feared its repercussions in the Middle East at a time when the war was still in full swing. Almost immediately after the cessation of hostilities the resolution, in a slightly modified form, was passed by the U. S. Senate and House of Representatives.

In the meantime, Zionists maintained an intense and systematic drive to influence American public opinion. The press and the radio were widely used; to a lesser extent, but very effectively, stage and screen propagated the Zionist views. Resolutions and petitions supporting Zionism were circulated among labor organizations, church groups, and numerous other organized bodies to endorse and sign. They were then piled upon the desks of Congressmen and of the Chief Executive, in the endeavor to create the impression of a widespread support of Zionism among the electorate.

At this stage, the White House took the initiative in making statements and commitments favoring Zionism, often against the advice of the State and War Departments. This policy begun under President Roosevelt was furthered with intensity by President Truman.

Under Zionist pressure, official circles in the United States put pressure upon the British Government to hasten the implementation of the Zionist program. The British, irked by too much advice and rebuke and too little willingness on the part of the Americans to assume responsibility, invited the American Government to participate in a commission of inquiry. The Anglo-American Committee composed of six British and six American members—two of the American members, Bartley Crum, and James McDonald, were ardent Zionist propagandists before their appointment to a supposedly impartial commission of investigation, as was the British member Crossman—journeyed to Palestine early in 1946. Its Report, submitted in the spring of that year, advised that Palestine should be neither an Arab nor a Jewish state. It recommended the immediate entry of a hundred thousand Jews into Palestine, and left the door wide open for future immigration, thus virtually assuring the establishment of a Jewish state by making Jewish numerical preponderance attainable through the continual influx of

JORDAN: King Husain.

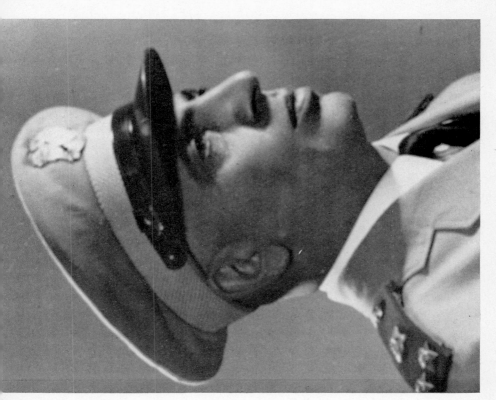

SYRIA: Colonel Adib Shishakli.

IRAQ: The late King Faisal I.

SAUDI ARABIA: King Abd-el-Aziz Ibn Saud.

SAUDI ARABIA: Street scene in Riyadh, capital city of Saudi Arabia.

PALESTINE: Jerusalem with the Dome of the Rock.

Left. LEBANON: Kamal Jumblatt, leader of the Progressive Socialist Party.

Below. JORDAN: A desert patrol.

Ewing Galloway

MOROCCO: Fortress gate in Rabat.

TUNISIA. The Mosque of the Swords at Kairouan

immigrants. The 100,000 figure was originally set by President Truman in his communications with the British Government and in public statements, on occasions connected with the elections when the Jewish vote was eagerly sought. This particular recommendation, therefore, seemed to indicate that the Committee was following a set policy rather than trying to formulate an independent opinion based on the result of its investigations on the spot. Upon the publication of the Report, President Truman urged the immediate admission of the 100,000 Jews. The British Government answered that the Report should be implemented as a whole and stated that the disarmament of the Jewish illegal forces, and the assurance of American financial and military support, were essential preliminaries to its implementation.

A committee of British and American officials working on the Anglo-American Report formulated federal proposals known as the Morrison-Grady plan, according to which Palestine would be divided into four areas, an Arab and a Jewish province under Arab and Jewish provincial governments respectively, the Negeb under British authorities, and Jerusalem and Bethlehem under the British Central Government which would handle security, foreign affairs, and customs for the whole country.

In the fall of 1946, the British Government invited the Arab Governments to a Palestine Conference in London. The Arabs submitted proposals for a unitary, independent state in Palestine, with democratic institutions and safeguards for minorities. Although the Conference went on through the winter of 1946–47, no agreement was reached. Great Britain thereupon decided to take the Palestine question to the United Nations.

A special session of the United Nations Assembly was convened in April 1947. The Arabs were hopeful. Their views would have a chance to be widely heard and their case, judged by the principles of the United Nations Charter, was bound to be vindicated. Their hopes were soon shattered when the debates, under Zionist pressure and with United States backing, took a Zionist color. In the terms of reference of the United Nations Special Committee on Palestine (UNSCOP) the bias in favor of Zionist ambitions was evident. No reference to the country's independence which the Arab delegations had supported was included among the terms; on the other hand the linking of the problem of the Jews in the displaced persons camps in Europe with Palestine, one of the main objectives of the Zionists, was implied in the Committee's instructions.

UNSCOP submitted its findings to the United Nations on September 1, 1947. They consisted of a majority report which recommended the partition of Palestine, and a minority report favoring a federal state. Since the partition plan was accepted by the United Nations General Assembly, it is necessary to analyze it in some detail.

The Committee begins by stating that the total area of Palestine is about 10,000 square miles, "but about half of this area is uninhabitable desert." Then it proceeds to divide this country into an Arab state, a Jewish state, and a permanent international trusteeship consisting of the city of Jerusalem and its environs. The two states are not and could not be well-defined and consolidated units. Since Arabs and Jews lived together in many parts of Palestine, the country was gerrymandered in order to include practically the whole Jewish population, outside Jerusalem, within the proposed Jewish state. The result was a patchwork of three Arab and three Jewish fragments sprawled and sprinkled here and there, with utter disregard for the realities of geography and the problems of communication, to say nothing of the human beings involved.

In one part of the Report, the Committee declares that the viability of the two states is essential to a partition scheme. In another part it admits that the Arab state would have to begin its life as a pauper and continue to subsist on charity.

In divising the partition scheme, the Committee claims to have been impelled by the desire to satisfy the conflicting national aspirations of Arabs and Jews. For the realization of Jewish national aspirations, the Committee performed a *coup de force* by juggling boundaries so that only 8,000 Jews remained within the Arab state. Was the same solicitude shown to Arab aspirations? The figures give the answer. In the proposed Jewish state itself, the Arabs were a majority, 506,000 Arabs, including 90,000 Bedouins, against 500,000 Jews. Can anyone help asking why the Jews, a minority in Palestine, and for the most part recent immigrants, should not be expected to live with the rest of the inhabitants, while an Arab majority who have lived in the country since time immemorial should be subjected to the rule of recently imported aliens?

Other figures tell the same story of arbitrariness and injustice. The Committee reports that the Arabs own 85% of the land in Palestine; they are also two-thirds of its population. Yet the state assigned to them under partition would occupy 40% of the total area of the country. The Jews who formed one-third of the population and owned 15% of the land were given 60% of the country for their state.

More disparate still is the relative apportionment of the fertile lands to the two states. It will be remembered that the fertile parts of Palestine are a small fraction of its total area; the rest is desert and rocks. Under the partition scheme the Arabs got the rocky hills; the Jewish state received 84% of the irrigated and intensively cultivable areas. Practically the whole land under citrus, chief agricultural export of Palestine, is within the Jewish state, although half the citrus groves are owned by Arabs.

Having dissected and splintered the country, the Committee, fully aware that the broken parts could not survive, hastened to provide for economic unity to run parallel with the political amputation. The relevant recommendation, unanimously adopted, reads: "It shall be accepted as a cardinal principle that the preservation of the economic unity of Palestine as a whole is indispensable to the life and development of the country and its peoples." Since the Committee decided that Arabs and Jews could not work together politically, on what basis is it assumed that they could do so economically? And if cooperation is possible in one field why not in the other as well? Is it unreasonable, therefore, to conclude that economic union, coupled as it was with political division, was meant to give the Jews a more complete control over the economic life of the whole country?

Finally, the Committee recommended that the Jerusalem area be placed under international trusteeship because of its religious significance to Christians, Moslems, and Jews throughout the world. But no new laws and regulations were proposed for the holy places. The international trusteeship would maintain the status quo. "The sacred character of the holy places shall be preserved and access to the holy places for purposes of worship and pilgrimage shall be insured in accordance with existing rights." This is affirmed in another part of the report: "Existing rights in respect of holy places and religious buildings or sites shall not be denied or impaired."

It should be noted that these "existing rights" have been in effect for hundreds of years, during which they were properly and successfully upheld and maintained by the Arabs. Since the Committee upholds the "existing rights," and since for so many centuries before mandates and trusteeships were invented the Arabs protected and preserved these rights, why are they now deemed incapable of carrying on a tradition which through the ages they have upheld to the satisfaction of countless generations of worshippers and pilgrims?

To Arabs, Christian and Moslem alike, Palestine is holy. To the Christian Arabs it is their holy land and their home, in which they have lived and worshipped since the days when Christ walked on earth. To the Moslems it is holy as the land where God revealed Himself to man through the Hebrew and Christian Scriptures, both of which they revere. It is for this reason that the Prophet of Islam commanded his followers to turn to Jerusalem in prayer before Mecca was cleansed of its heathen associations. And in Jerusalem, the Arabs raised the earliest standing monument of Moslem art, the Dome of the Rock, a marvel of loveliness and reverence-inspiring beauty. Through thirteen hundred years of occupation, the Arabs have preserved the sanctity of the Holy Land to the three monotheistic religions; for Islam, youngest of the three, venerates the Scriptures, prophets, and holy places of the two older religions. This veneration, accompanied by the freedom of Moslem society from racial prejudice, has made of the Moslems ideal guardians of the Holy Land. "In the exercise of their rule over the Holy Places in Palestine, the Arabs showed a generous tolerance, in the spirit of the original Islam of Arabia, a tolerance of which there can scarcely be many other examples in the Middle Ages or even in modern times."[37]

The partition plan, a scheme full of inconsistencies which defies the laws of geography, history, economics, and human nature, and which is untrue to the principles of the United Nations Charter, was adopted by the United Nations on November 29, 1947.

The adoption of partition, and the pressures and maneuvers attendant upon the debates and proceedings which led to it, are a sad and pitiful episode in the young life of the United Nations.

In voting for partition, the United Nations Assembly acted under the impact of persistent and intense pressure. The United States delegation, acting on instructions from the White House where Zionist influence was supreme, led the Zionist camp with a mind and spirit closed to the merits of the case and its implications. This partisan attitude of the United States influenced the stand taken by a number of smaller nations who generally follow her lead. In this atmosphere the debates were warped, the issues were

37. Kohn: *Western Civilization in the Near East*, p. 55.

confused, and the case was hopelessly misrepresented and tangled. For if the case is approached with a free spirit and an open mind, it is not a problem at all. Extraneous issues were dragged in to make a problem of it. Shorn of these it is simple and clear as the day. Palestine is an Arab country; it belongs to the Arabs by the same laws under which any country belongs to its people, namely, long occupation of the land. The Arabs, the only people with prescriptive, indisputable rights in Palestine, are subjected to an invasion by an alien people who seek to establish themselves in the country by force. All other considerations are extraneous and irrelevant. The function and duty of the United Nations in this case was to stop the invasion and preserve the country for its rightful owners.

Serious doubts were expressed about the authority of the United Nations to partition any country against the wishes of its people. A resolution was introduced into the proceedings of the Ad Hoc Committee on Palestine to refer several legal questions concerning Palestine to the International Court of Justice. The most important section of this resolution questioned:

"Whether the United Nations, or any of its Member States, is competent to enforce or recommend the enforcement of any proposal concerning the constitution and future Government of Palestine, in particular, any plan of partition which is contrary to the wishes, or adopted without the consent of, the inhabitants of Palestine."

This section of the resolution was voted on separately by the Ad Hoc Committee (representing all 57 members of the United Nations) and was defeated by only *one* vote: 20 in favor; 21 opposed; 13 abstained.

By refusing to consult the International Court before making its decision on a very questionable scheme, the United Nations laid itself open to the accusation that it was more interested in political considerations than in a solution based upon justice.

To illustrate the confusion and lack of candor which accompanied the United Nations discussions and the final voting which resulted from them, the treatment of the Jewish refugee problem furnishes an enlightening example.

The refugee problem has been the most persistent one of the extraneous issues in the Palestine tangle. No other consideration has been urged with so much insistence by the Zionists in their attempt to present Zionism to the world as an essentially humanitarian movement, and no other has made a wider appeal upon the world outside Zionist circles.

UNSCOP, of which a majority recommended partition, unanimously made the following recommendation with regard to the refugees: "The General Assembly undertake immediately the initiation and execution of an international arrangement whereby the problem of the distressed European Jews, of whom approximately 250,000 are in assembly centers, will be dealt with as a matter of extreme urgency for the alleviation of their plight and of the Palestine problem." What was the fate of this unanimous recommendation? Many fair words were spoken and fine feelings expressed, but when it came to pinning down the states with the lofty sentiments to allocate quotas among themselves, the response was a shameful shirking of responsibility.

Another proposal on the subject of Jewish refugees was presented by the Arabs to the Palestine Committee of the United Nations General Assembly. It reads: "The General Assembly, having regard to the unanimous recommendations of the United Nations Special Committee on Palestine, that the General Assembly undertake immediately the initiation and execution of an international arrangement whereby the problem of the distressed European Jews will be dealt with as a matter of extreme urgency for the alleviation of their plight and of the Palestine problem,

"Bearing in mind that genuine refugees and displaced persons constitute a problem which is international in scope and character,

"Being further of the opinion that where repatriation proves impossible, solution should be sought by way of resettlement in the territories of the members of the United Nations which are willing and in a position to absorb these refugees and displaced persons,

"Having adopted a resolution on 15 December 1946 calling for the creation of an international refugee organization with a view to the solution of the refugee problem through the combined efforts of the United Nations; and

"Taking note of the assumption on 1 July 1947 by the preparatory commission of the International Refugee Organization of operational responsibility for displaced persons and refugees;

"Recommends:

"(1) That countries of origin should be requested to take Jewish refugees and displaced persons belonging to them, and to render them all possible assistance to resettle in life;

"(2) That those Jewish refugees and displaced persons who cannot be repatriated should be absorbed in the territories of members of the United Nations in proportion to their area, economic resources, per capita income, population and other relevant factors."

A vote taken on this proposal showed 16 in favor and 16 opposed, with 28 abstentions and 2 absentees. That is as far as the United Nations went in alleviating an urgent humanitarian problem.

As for the final vote on partition, it was obtained in this manner. The voting was set for Wednesday, November 26, 1947. As the delegates gave their views in the course of the day, it was obvious that the two-thirds majority necessary to carry the vote was not going to be secured. The partisans of partition sponsored a resolution to adjourn the Assembly till after the Thanksgiving recess. Over the holiday, the necessary pressure was applied and dissidents were brought into line. American and foreign observers remarked that the vote for partition was forced through the United Nations by the United States Government. Throughout the session the attitude of the United States carried the impression that the overriding consideration was the creation of a Jewish State. To many observers the strength of the Jewish influence in Washington was a revelation.[38]

To the Arabs, the United Nations decision on partition meant that the spirit of the Charter was destroyed. Among other delegations, doubts and misgivings were expressed over an action that was morally questionable and legally unenforceable. Some comments in the press reflected similar anxiety about the moral foundation of the United Nations, and its ability to hold people's hope and faith. An extract from the *Christian Century*, December 17, illustrates this view:

"We are gambling with the future of the United Nations. We are gambling with its hope to gain moral authority in international affairs, for the imposition of partition against the opposition of two-thirds of the inhabitants of Palestine makes the announced devotion of the United Nations to the democratic principles of self-determination and majority rule look like unblushing hypocrisy."

The general tone of the press, however, was one of relief that the United Nations, with a record of frustrations and deadlocks,

38. *New York Times*, Dec. 1, 1947; Millar Burrows: *Palestine Is Our Business*, Philadelphia, 1949, p. 71.

had at last achieved a success. There was enthusiasm even that the two giant antagonists, the United States and the U.S.S.R., found themselves in the same camp on this important issue. But optimism was premature and short-lived. No sooner was partition endorsed than its disastrous implications began to loom up, assuming more hideous shapes every day.

Before proceeding to relate the subsequent developments in Palestine, it may be well at this point to summarize the claims which the Zionists have put forth as giving them title to the Holy Land.

According to the Zionists, the historical and religious connection of the Jews with Palestine entitle them to rebuild a Jewish State in the country. It is only in Palestine, they say, that the Jews were a nation, and because of their association with Palestine the Jews have made their distinctive contribution to the spiritual heritage of mankind. The Balfour Declaration, issued by a Great Power and endorsed by an international body, the League of Nations, adds legal title to the historical association. The achievements of the Jews in Palestine demonstrate that the Jews are better fitted to develop the country than its inhabitants, the Arabs. And finally, the Jews need Palestine to rehabilitate Jewish refugees and to remedy the feeling of homelessness which has haunted the Jews throughout the long centuries of the diaspora.

These claims, widely and persistently propagated, have impressed public opinion in the Western world. It was seldom asked to what extent they were valid or whether they conflicted with the rights of another people already established in the country. When given more careful thought, the Jewish claims lose much of their plausibility.

The contention that the Jews should have Palestine because of their historical association with the country passes over three fundamental historical facts connected with the Jewish occupation of Palestine. That occupation was short in duration both in relation to the history of the country and of the Jews themselves; it was limited in extent, at times to a small fraction of the country; and it ceased nearly 2000 years ago when the last vestige of a Jewish state was destroyed in the first century A.D. Since then the country has been uninterruptedly inhabited by the people whose descendants the Zionist scheme sought to dispossess and supplant. Had Palestine been an empty country, the Jews could reclaim it as their ancient homeland. But Palestine has not only been an

Arab country for many hundreds of years, it is an integral part of the larger Arab world from which it cannot be separated without grave damage to Palestine itself and to the larger unit of which it is a segment.

As for the religious attachment of the Jews to Palestine, is the re-creation of Jewish nationalism essential to strengthening the religious ties to the Holy Land? The evidence points to the contrary. The nationalist Zionists have little interest in religion. Their symbol is not Jerusalem but Tel Aviv. To the religious Jews, Jerusalem and not Palestine is the symbol of their faith. When they remember Zion in their prayer they are not impelled by any nationalist consciousness. It is a Zion of the spirit which they seek and towards which they turn. These Jews did not contemplate a return to Zion by force—the way of the nationalists—nor even by any human effort. The return would come in God's good time with the appearance of the Messiah. Jewish nationalism, based as it is on force, and with its anti-religious bias, is destructive of the Jewish heritage. It may also be remembered that religious attachment to Palestine is not confined to the Jews; neither has Judaism alone made Palestine holy.

As for the promise made in the Balfour Declaration, it has been shown that Great Britain acted beyond her rights when she issued the Declaration. Moreover, Britain was bound to the Arabs by pledges which preceded the Balfour Declaration and which were reinforced by more pledges and assurances issued at various intervals after the Declaration. The Mandate for Palestine itself comes under the same category of invalid undertakings insofar as it violated the Covenant of the League of Nations by creating a situation bound to lead to the alienation of an elemental and inalienable right, the right of an indigenous population to its native land. The Mandate could not undertake to establish a national home for an alien people against the will of the native inhabitants and still conform to the principle of a trust. The right of self-determination was a basic principle of the League. The Covenant of the League recognized the provisional independence of the Arabs subject to the rendering of administrative advice and assistance by a Mandatory power. Contrary to these principles and provisions, the Palestine Mandate reduced the Arabs to colonial status by denying them any form of self-government, and threatened their security in their native land by forcing upon them a permanent invasion by an alien people. That the League of Nations endorsed the mandate does not alter the moral wrong inherent in it nor does it make it any more acceptable to the people upon whose rights and vital interests it so seriously infringed. The League of Nations, an association of States, was as a body subject to the same motivations which impelled its individual members, and often succumbed to their errors. On the Palestine question, both the League and its successor the United Nations acted not in the light of the principles espoused in the Covenant and the Charter respectively, but their action was diverted under pressure into a course diametrically opposed to the principles which they professed.

The claim to Palestine which rests on Jewish superior abilities is strongly reminiscent of Hitler's theory of the master race, and is hardly becoming the Jewish people who have been the victims of this utterly false and morally repugnant theory. The Jewish immigrants to Palestine, mostly Europeans, had the benefits of western science and technology which gave them in these fields a temporary advantage over the Arabs. This does not mean that the Jews have inherently superior abilities. But apart from its fallacy the argument is morally objectionable inasmuch as it seeks to justify aggression under the cloak of improving a country. In the name of cultural and racial superiority, colonial powers propagated the fiction of the "White man's burden" whereby they sought to justify their predatory incursions into Asia and Africa during the 19th century. More recently, the Germans have acted on this theory in their relations with other European peoples to whom they considered themselves superior because they were more efficient. And Japan has used her efficiency and competence as justification of her aggression against fellow Asiatic peoples. In this connection it may be illuminating to describe the Japanese achievements in Korea.

"In fairness to the Japanese it must be conceded that in a material sense they have done a magnificent job in Korea. When they took it over the country was filthy, unhealthy, and woefully poverty-stricken. The mountains had been denuded of their forests, the valleys were subject to recurrent floods, decent roads were nonexistent, illiteracy was prevalent, and typhoid, small-pox, cholera, dysentery, and the plague were epidemic annually. Today the mountains are reafforested; railway, telephone and telegraph systems are excellent; the public health service is efficient, good highways abound; flood-control and irrigation works have vastly increased the food production, and fine harbors have been devel-

oped and are well managed. The country has become so prosperous and healthy that the 1905 population of 11,000,000 had risen
to 24,000,000 and the average scale of living is today almost im-
measurably higher than it was at the turn of the century."[39] And
yet the Japanese were not allowed to keep Korea although they
had not sought—like the Jews in Palestine—to submerge and supplant the native inhabitants, but had merely extended their political domination over them.

Jewish achievements in Palestine, if viewed by themselves, are
admirable. But when placed against the background of the injustice done to the Arabs, the whole Zionist scheme—of which the
economic and social achievements are one phase—emerges as one
of the most shockingly aggressive plans ever conceived and perpetrated.

The need for Palestine as a refuge for displaced and persecuted
Jews has made the widest appeal of any of the Zionist claims, and
has elicited the sympathy and response generally accorded to humanitarian movements. The Zionist attitude to the refugees was
not as humanitarian as it was represented. Political and not humanitarian considerations were paramount in the Zionist insistence
upon settling the displaced Jews in Palestine, because in Palestine
alone was immigration designed to swell the Jewish population
for the purpose of hastening the establishment of a Jewish State.
Both the Anglo-American Committee and UNSCOP found that
Palestine could not meet the problem of Jewish refugees. They
placed the responsibility of settling this problem upon the whole
world. This aspect of the two Reports evoked no response or cooperation from the Zionists because their primary purpose was
political rather than relief and rescue. The Zionists even evaded
possibilities and offers of settling refugees in countries where opportunities for immigration were available.[40] Had the Zionists directed a fraction of the influence and means at their command
from political aims towards truly humanitarian considerations, and
had Zionist sympathizers been more enlightened in their humanitarianism, it is likely that the Palestine tragedy could have been
avoided. As it was, the political intention behind the humanitarian
cry for a home for Jewish refugees resulted in turning a million
Arabs into homeless refugees.

39. Hallett Abend: *Pacific Charter*, 1943, quoted in Jawaharlal Nehru: *The Discovery of India*, pp. 426–427, footnote *.
40. Berger: *op. cit.*, pp. 19 f.

It is difficult for the Arabs not to feel bitter about the professed humanitarianism of the Zionists and their supporters.

While there is no doubt that the plight of the European Jews hit a sensitive chord in the heart of thousands of people it is also true that these people did not do all they could to provide a refuge for the Jews in their own large and prosperous countries. Zionism has found its strongest support in the Anglo-Saxon countries—the United States and the British Commonwealth. What have these countries done for the displaced Jews? Great Britain alone took a fair share of displaced persons, Jews and non-Jews. Canada, Australia, and New Zealand supported the partition of Palestine with its avowed purpose of crowding immigrants into this small country, and its inevitable consequence of displacing the native population, but not one of them offered to take a fair share of the refugees, although all three countries are dangerously under-populated, and the first two have vast resources. What has been the record of the United States? Bills readily passed through Congress for opening the doors of Palestine to unlimited Jewish immigration—endless petitions endorsed by big names and large groups pressing for the unrestricted admission of Jews to Palestine. When President Truman asked the British Government to admit 100,000 displaced Jews to Palestine, senators hailed his request as a "magnificent gesture." But how did the majority of senators and representatives—many of them ardent and vociferous supporters of Zionism—respond to the President's repeated messages urging Congress to pass suitable legislation for admitting into the United States a fair share of the displaced persons? After delays consuming eighteen months, Congress passed a bill denounced by the President as "flagrantly discriminatory." Under a maze of technicalities, the bill excluded the Jews from entry into the United States. Is it unreasonable for the Arabs to consider much of the talk about the humanitarian appeal of Zionism as hypocrisy?

Finally, to the Zionists' claim that in Zionism alone lies the remedy to Jewish homelessness, maladjustment, and fear of being turned upon at any time by a hostile world, that only a Jewish state can provide the security which the Jews lack and relieve the tension between them and the rest of mankind.

It is best to hear the objections to this view from some responsible Jews themselves.

To establish a state on the theory of Jewish homelessness, they say, is to stamp the Jews as strangers wherever they live. It is a reversal of the whole historic process of emancipation and integration. The Zionist approach, by treating the Jews as a group apart and insisting on their difference and separateness, is akin to anti-Semitism. Zionism with its insistence upon a political state sharpens the cleavage between Jews and non-Jews. A Jewish state is bound to create the problem of conflicting loyalties; it will prejudice the position of Jews outside that state and provide an excuse for anti-Semitism. The Jews are not a race. Peoples representing a variety of racial types were converted to Judaism in the course of centuries. From them the modern Jews are descended; only a small group come from the Semitic race which lived in Palestine long ago. These on the whole have continued to live in the Near East. Neither can the Jews be considered a nation. Their national affiliations and loyalties belong to the countries of which they are citizens. The Jews are a religious community; the bond between them is not racial nor national, it is religious. Judaism shed its nationalistic implications long ago; modern Jewish nationalism is a misrepresentation *of the spirit* of the Jewish faith. Not by the creation of a political state but by the integration of Jews into their environment can normalization be achieved.[41]

It is doubtful whether the Zionist scheme would have succeeded had public opinion been more adequately and impartially informed of the issues involved. Even if governments had erred and individual statesmen and politicians had succumbed to Zionist pressure, a properly informed public opinion would have provided the necessary corrective. But for thirty years public opinion in the Western world has seen the Palestine question through Zionist spectacles. Not only are the Jews represented in the governments and parliaments of the various countries of which they are nationals and therefore have access to official circles on a high level, their influence draws even greater strength from the amenability of the press —especially in the English speaking countries—and the various other channels of disseminating news and molding public opinion. By contrast, these various opportunities are denied to the Arabs. The Arabic press which often carried pertinent information on the Arab case was inaccessible to the Western public. The voice of the few Western observers who tried to present the Arab side of the Palestine question was drowned in the vast output of a highly organized and all-pervading Zionist propaganda. The injustice and

41. *Zionism versus Judaism:* A Collection of Editorials from the Information Bulletin of the American Council for Judaism, 1944.

wrong inherent in the Zionist scheme was submerged in a flood of propaganda which represented Zionism as a force for progress, liberation, and prosperity in a benighted Arab world.

As long as they could, the Zionists ignored the Arabs altogether. It will be remembered that neither the Balfour Declaration nor the text of the Mandate mentioned the Arabs by name. When the Arabs, goaded to rebellion by what the pro-Zionist Mandate was doing to them, drew some attention from the world press, the Zionists promptly described their struggle for self-preservation and self-determination as rioting inspired by fanaticism and led by reactionary leaders who sought to keep Zionist progress out so they could keep the Arab masses down. Opposition to Zionism was represented as opposition to progress. Arab society was a medieval society, dominated by feudal lords in alliance with imperialist Britain. The Arab masses were either downtrodden peasants, or nomads and roaming bedouins. Sometimes the Arabs were likened to the Red Indians, a comparison especially realistic to the American imagination, while the Jews were the counterpart of the white man charged with the mission of civilization. The upshot was this, that the Arabs of Palestine had no culture, no national loyalties, no way of life worth defending and preserving. Consequently the Arabs had nothing to lose, they had much to gain by the improvements which the Jews were bringing to Palestine.

Much has been said about Arab backwardness and Jewish progress. But backwardness is a relative concept and depends upon one's point of departure. Arab technology is backward and Arab society, based primarily upon agriculture, has lacked the means which an industrial civilization provides for educating the masses and raising their standard of living. Yet in this the Arabs are not alone. It is a status which they share with the overwhelming majority of mankind. Furthermore, technological proficiency, a dominant characteristic of modern civilization, is not the whole of civilization. With regard to the human aspects of civilization, the Arabs may have something to teach those peoples who are technologically more proficient than themselves.

But to return to the United Nations partition resolution and its aftermath. Partition was decreed as a compromise solution on the assumption that Arabs and Jews had equal but irreconcilable rights in Palestine.

The Jews have the same rights in Palestine to which they are entitled in every country where they live, namely full equality

with their fellow citizens. But they have no more right to a state
or separate national existence in Palestine than they have in any
other country. Their rightful status is a life in accordance with the
existing laws and institutions of the country. The nation long established in Palestine is the Arab nation. Partition is no compromise. If the country belongs to its indigenous population, then, as
a matter of principle, the alienation of a part of it is as morally unjustifiable as the alienation of the whole. That the Jews who asked
for the whole of Palestine were willing to accept a part does not
make a compromise. In foregoing a part and accepting another
the Jews were foregoing and accepting what belongs to another
people.

The proposals submitted by the Arab delegations to the United
Nations Assembly in 1947 were conceived in a genuine spirit of
compromise, and as an effort to satisfy Jewish cultural aspirations
while maintaining the territorial integrity of the country and the
right of the indigenous majority to determine their future government. Although the majority of the Jews in Palestine were recent
immigrants who entered the country against the will of the native
population, and although their presence created numerous political, economic, and cultural difficulties, yet the Arabs were willing
to accept them as equal citizens in a common state. A democratic constitution would guarantee individual liberty and personal
equality to all the citizens. Local autonomy, similar to the Swiss
plan of Cantonization, would give the different communities wide
powers and responsibilities with regard to education, health, and
other social and cultural services. In the sections where the Jews
were a majority, Hebrew would be recognized as an official language.

The Arabs, having despaired of receiving justice at the hands
of the United Nations, decided to oppose the United Nations resolution on partition. In doing so they were not challenging the spirit
and purpose of the United Nations but were resisting a measure
which itself was opposed to the principles of the United Nations
Charter. They were challenging the fiction that Palestine was a
special case to which generally recognized principles did not apply, with the consequence that irregularities which everywhere
else were censured and condemned were here justified and upheld
by international sanction. The concept of self-determination which
was a basic principle of the League of Nations; the Atlantic Charter which bans "territorial changes that do not accord with the

freely expressed wishes of the peoples concerned," professes to "respect the right of all peoples to choose the form of government under which they will live," and aims to establish "a peace which will afford to all nations the means of dwelling in safety within their own boundaries"; and "the principle of equal rights and self-determination of peoples" of the United Nations Charter—if these are universally valid, by what reason or justice can Palestine be exempted from their universal applicability and treated as a singular, lone case outside the pale of international law and justice?

For it is precisely this assumption that universal principles do not apply in Palestine which is responsible for its tragedy. Upon it was constructed the text of the Palestine Mandate which violated the principles of the Mandate system, and subjected to mortal danger the existence of the people for whose protection and well-being it was devised. From it have flowed the inevitable consequences which follow the substitution of irregularities for law and equity. From this assumption proceeded international bodies, first the Anglo-American Committee, then the United Nations Special Committee on Palestine, instead of striking a new, clear path—with the result that their labors added to earlier errors and increased the existing confusion. Finally, upon this assumption, the United Nations recommended partition in violation of the spirit of the Charter from which it derives its being. For let it be repeated that no power or combination of powers, and no international body whatever its authority, can legally deprive a people of their primordial right to self-determination and the preservation of their native land.

The Arab opposition to partition was natural. It sprang from an outraged sense of decency and justice of the Arab masses. Their resistance was for a time effective enough to induce the United Nations and the Government of the United States to question the efficacy of partition. An influential weekly wrote of partition as "evil" and "unworkable."[42] A special session of the United Nations General Assembly was called in April 1948 to reconsider the Palestine problem in the light of new developments. A plan for trusteeship was under consideration as a substitute for partition when the Zionists proclaimed their state. American recognition, accorded within minutes of the announcement of the Jewish State—the U.S. delegate at Lake Success was caught talking about trusteeship

42. *Life*, March 29, 1948.

when the President recognized Israel—coming when the United Nations was trying to reach a more equitable solution, capped a series of blunders and was a blow to the cause of peace in Palestine. It was bruited that the President took this precipitous step without consulting his State Department or notifying his delegation at the United Nations, in order to placate the Zionists and win the Jewish vote in the approaching elections.

A series of outrageous reprisals committed by the Palestinian Jews—in the massacre of Deir Yasin about 200 Arabs, many of them women and children, were murdered and some of them mutilated —had the effect intended and openly admitted by Zionist spokesmen, to terrorize the Arabs into leaving the country. On May 15, when the Jewish State was proclaimed, most of the Arabs in the section of Palestine allotted to the Jews had become refugees. The Palestine Arabs called upon the Arab States to help them defend their country. The entry of the Arab armies into Palestine was denounced as aggression and defiance of the United Nations. Had moral principles and universally valid criteria prevailed in settling the Palestine issue, not the Arabs who were defending an integral part of their territory, but the aliens to the country who were supplanting a nation on its native soil would appropriately have been called invaders and aggressors.

It is worth keeping in mind that the states which did not endorse partition represented the majority of the peoples of mankind. It is significant that these states were Asiatic, and that Zionism—supported by Europe and America—represented to the peoples of Asia a new form of Western aggression upon the soil of Asia. The Arab delegations to the United Nations had repeatedly warned that their governments would not be bound to a recommendation which was not only unjust to them but wholly detrimental to the spirit of the United Nations Charter.

The Arabs failed completely in Palestine. The Palestinian Arabs suffered from divided leadership, lack of organization, and deficiency of arms. Elsewhere, the Arab masses were only emotionally aware of the danger to Palestine but they were powerless. Arab rulers and leaders held divided counsels. Neither the political set-up in the Arab countries—with their divisions and the concentration of power in the hands of a few people—nor their economic structure was suited for the successful conduct of a modern war. Rivalries and misunderstandings among the Arab governments, and the fact that there were seven states instead of one, militated against united leadership and concerted action. The Arab armies were poorly equipped and trained, and totally unprepared for the war. Two of the states, Syria and Lebanon, had only recently achieved their independence and assumed control of their armies. Egypt and Iraq were bound by treaty to depend upon Great Britain for their supply of arms. As a result, Egyptian and Iraqi armies were inadequately armed. Only the Arab Legion of Transjordan had reasonably adequate arms and mechanized equipment. But the Arab Legion, for which the British treasury paid, was under British command as in fact the state of Transjordan itself was under firm British control. The Legion, therefore, was an instrument of British policy.

Much has been said about Britain fighting the Arab war. Glubb Pasha—the British Commander of the Arab Legion—was represented as a Crusader in Islam's holy war. Nothing could be farther from the truth. Britain was not only unwilling to risk United Nations disapproval by allowing the British sponsored Arab Legion to fight seriously in Palestine, but the Legion, by withdrawing suddenly under orders from its British commander, allowed the Israeli to occupy a number of important cities and areas in Palestine. The unpredictable stand of the Legion was one of the major causes of the military breakdown. It must be said, however, that the Arabs have only themselves to blame for thinking they could count upon an army financed and commanded by the British.

The Israeli, on the other hand, had mobilized all their forces, planned their economy, regulated every detail of their life, and subordinated all other considerations to the realization of their State. Their determined effort, coupled with the ruthless violence perpetrated on the Arabs of Palestine and with their persistent disregard of the United Nations authority, succeded in eliminating the Arab population and placing over three fourths of the country within the Jewish state.

The record of Israel since its proclamation has been one of continuous agression. The assassination of Count Bernadotte, the United Nations mediator, was one of a series of acts where physical force triumphed over the United Nations. The Israeli readily submitted to the first cease-fire order issued by the Security Council in June 1948, because they were in a difficult position. The first truce gave them a respite during which they managed to smuggle large quantities of arms by air and by sea. By the time the second truce came into effect they felt strong enough to acknowledge or repudiate the truce at will.

Since then, Israel has followed a deliberate policy of provocation and aggression. Security Council orders went unheeded, and United Nations observers were not admitted to the scene of the fighting. Israel has refused to comply with the United Nations resolutions to withdraw within the boundaries defined in the partition scheme and to repatriate the refugees and compensate those who did not wish to return. It has challenged the United Nations resolution of December 1949 for the administration of Jerusalem through the Trusteeship Council. Government departments have been transferred to Jerusalem which has been declared by official spokesmen to be the capital of Israel.

Israel, committed as it is to unlimited immigration, is bound to expand. It can expand only at the expense of the neighboring Arab territory. As the Arabs of Palestine had opposed large-scale Jewish immigration under the Mandate, because they rightly foresaw their own submersion under waves of alien immigrants, so Israel's policy of unlimited immigration is a legitimate and serious concern of the surrounding states. This view was shared by the late Count Bernadotte who, in a letter to the Israeli Foreign Secretary, expressed the opinion that immigration concerned not only the Jews of the Jewish state but also the surrounding Arab world.

The resources of Israel are extremely limited. Land surveys conducted under the Mandate estimated the cultivable area of Palestine at about 2 million acres, of which less than half is located in the fertile plains; the rest is either in the hills where the soil is poor, or in the arid Beersheba region. The Zionists contend that the cultivable area can be greatly expanded, especially in the semi-desert of Beersheba, if sufficient quantities of water are available. All indications so far prove that the water in this area is scarce and brackish.

A widely advertised Zionist scheme, the Jordan Valley Authority, proposes to divert the waters of the Jordan to irrigate the Plain of Esdraelon, the coastal plain, and other areas of Palestine outside the Jordan valley. To compensate for the loss of the Jordan supply, water would be brought in tunnels from the Mediterranean to the Dead Sea to maintain its level. The waterfalls would be used for the generation of electric power. If the plan is feasible from an engineering point of view, its economic value is negligible in relation to the enormous cost. Furthermore, the Jordan is not the exclusive property of Israel. It is a major source of water for Arab Palestine and Transjordan. The diversion of the river would mean the conversion into desert of the lands watered by it, and the despoliation of the people who live on those lands.

Neither are the prospects of making Israel a highly industrialized state very promising. The country is poor in all the basic materials needed for industry. Commenting on the scarcity of raw materials in Palestine, UNSCOP reports: "In the physical resources which are typically the basis of modern industrial development, Palestine is exceedingly poor, having neither coal nor iron nor any other important mineral deposit." The industries which have taken root in Palestine, according to the same Report, "are either consumption goods, industries based to a great extent on the local market, industries whose location is not determined by the presence of raw materials but which depend on local skill as in the case of the diamond industry, or in some few cases, as for example the potash industry and some good processing industries, those which depend on local raw materials. It must be remembered that almost all of these industries are small-scale enterprises."

What is more, most of these industries were made possible by abnormal conditions which are not likely to last or recur. Cheap capital, provided through gifts and invested with a primarily political aim—economic returns were a secondary consideration—and high protective tariffs have been largely responsible for the growth of Israel's industry. During the war these industries expanded because of the absence of competition and the presence of the British army who bought up large quantities of goods. It is doubtful whether Jewish industries can be maintained, let alone expand, in the face of competitive goods from Europe and America, the growing industrialization of the Arab countries, and Arab boycott of Zionist goods made necessary by Zionist aggression in Palestine.

Considering the dubious natural resources of Israel, the policy of unlimited immigration has been possible only by heavy subsidization from outside the country. As the Jewish community in Palestine under the Mandate depended for its maintenance and expansion largely upon the hundreds of millions of dollars collected in the United States, so the Jewish state, unable to live on its own resources, will depend for its existence upon outside financial help. A three-year plan—1951–53—designed to bring 600,000 immigrants is estimated to cost $1,500 million. The Israeli government has agreed to provide $500 million. American Jewish leaders

and representatives of various Zionist organizations have pledged
that the Jews in the United States would provide $1 billion towards
Israel's three-year immigration and development plan.[43]

This enormous financial burden is not likely to be carried in-
definitely by American Jews. Even if it were, it could not cope
with the needs of the millions of Jews whom Israeli leaders hope
to bring into the country. The only alternative to a curb on immigration is the inevitable expansion into more Arab territory.

This is not a far-off prospect, as past events have amply demonstrated. The record of the Zionists before and after the establishment of the Jewish State indicates that they accepted partition as
a step towards expansion. Those Zionist elements who expressed
their dissatisfaction with the boundaries of the proposed Jewish
State, and declared their intention of annexing the rest of Palestine and Transjordan, were at the time called dissidents and extremists, and therefore not representative of the Jewish community
and its aims. Nothing could be more erroneous than to think that
the expansionist elements are a small and unrepresentative minority. It is necessary to remember that Zionism has always been
amicably split into two wings, professing at times different aims
and following different tactics and externally in disagreement and
strife, but in reality working together for a common purpose. It
was advantageous for the Zionist movement that its excesses and
outrages should be blamed on groups of so-called dissidents whom
official spokesmen of Zionism could denounce and disown while
actually dissidents and respectable Zionists were in collusion. Thus
under the Mandate, the Jewish Agency, trying to maintain the
appearance of keeping within the law, made the Revisionists, the
Irgun, and other terrorist groups the scapegoat for the terrorism
and the murder which shocked world opinion. All the time the
Jewish Agency sheltered the lawless elements which it pretended
to condemn. Irgun was again made the scapegoat for the massacre
of Arabs in the conflict which followed upon partition. During the
first truce, Israeli authorities, in utter disregard of the truce conditions, conducted an uninterrupted large scale traffic in smuggled

43. It is interesting to note the steady and fabulous increase in the demands made
first by the Jewish National Home and later by the Jewish State upon the Jews of
the United States. At the Zionist Annual Conference in London in 1920 the European
group set a budget at about £2 million a year to which they admitted they could
contribute very little. The American delegation, headed by Brandeis, was shocked
by this astronomical figure and said they could not guarantee more than £100 thousand a year. Weizmann: *op. cit.*, p. 327.

arms, and when United Nations observers happened to detect a smuggler after she had unloaded her consignment of arms, Irgun was held up as the truce breaker.

The expansionist aim of Zionism is not a recent development. It is inherent in the Zionist movement and was there at its inception. In the Articles of Association of the Keren Kayemeth it is stated that shekels were to be collected from the Jews of the world with the objective of purchasing land to be registered in trust in the name of the Jewish people of the world; such land was to be bought and thus registered not only in Palestine, but in Egypt, Transjordan, Lebanon, Syria, and Iraq.

Dr. Weizmann is held up as a model of Zionist moderation. In the spring of 1918, Weizmann journeyed to Faisal's camp near Akaba carrying the assurance that the Jews had no intention of working for the establishment of a Jewish Government in Palestine. All they wished to do was to help in the development of the country without damaging the legitimate interests of the Arabs.[44] Shortly thereafter, at the Peace Conference, Weizmann himself explained that the Jewish National Home meant "Palestine shall be as Jewish as America is American and England is English." At the Zionist Congress of 1921, Dr. Weizmann, answering an interpellation about the inclusion of Transjordan within the Palestine Mandate and the applicability of the provisions of the National Home to the eastern bank of the Jordan said: "The question will be still better answered when Cisjordania is so full of Jews that a way is forced into Transjordania."[45] In 1946, the Jewish Agency officially expressed the view held by the Revisionists[46] with regard to Transjordan. Shortly before the announcement of the Treaty terminating the British Mandate over Transjordan, the Jewish Agency Executive objected to the Colonial Office that "the Jewish people had a contingent interest in the retention of Transjordan within the scope of the mandate."

In the light of past events, Zionist talk about a Jewish state extending from the Euphrates to the Nile should not be lightly dismissed. To expand beyond their present state, the Israeli will use the same arguments and the same methods which they have successfully used in creating their state. Considering the tremendous

44. Antonius, *op. cit.*, p. 285.
45. Quoted in Barbour, *op. cit.*, p. 104, note 1.
46. The Revisionists received their name from their demand for the revision of the Palestine Mandate to bring Transjordan within the provisions of the National Home.

influence which world Jewry wields, the ruthlessness of the Zionists in Palestine, the utter impotence of the United Nations in its
dealings with the Jewish state which it created, and the inability,
or perhaps lack of determination, on the part of Great Britain and
especially the United States to check Jewish aggression, is it to be
wondered at that the Arabs have grave misgivings with regard to
Israel, and that all talk about stability in the Middle East is bound
to be futile as long as Israel is allowed to pursue its aggressive
course?

Israel is the most serious and pressing danger threatening the
security and peaceful development of the Arab countries. The
creation of Israel has aggravated the tension between Great Britain
and the Arabs, and created new tension between the Arabs and the
United States who had enjoyed a genuine good will of long standing throughout the Arab world until her championship of an alien
state in the heart of the Arab lands. Israel, a wedge thrust into a
most sensitive spot in the Arab world, has cut off the Arabs of Asia
from the Arabs of Africa; and this separation was inflicted at a time
when world trends are moving towards greater integration and
when Arab society, in keeping with modern trends and in harmony
with its heritage, is working for the recreation of its unity.

Israel has not solved the Jewish problem. On the contrary, it has
created a Jewish problem in a part of the world where that problem did not exist before. Israel, carved by force out of an Arab
country, has had the consequence of creating anti-Semitism among
the Arabs, a people until then wholly free of this peculiarly Western disease. As to the Jews living outside Israel, the establishment of a Jewish state is bound to aggravate and accentuate their
separateness from their fellow citizens in the countries of their
residence. A responsible Jewish leader, Lessing J. Rosenwald, President of the American Council for Judaism, has expressed the alarm
of a thoughtful group among the Jews when he said: "The creation
and recognition of a sovereign state of Israel has with alarming
speed tremendously intensified the Jewish nationalists' desire to
control our lives and to advance their claim that all Jews possess
a 'Jewish Nationality.' "[47] This claim of the nationalist Jews is likely
to lay all Jews open to the accusation of divided loyalty, and to be
used as an excuse for anti-Semitism.

The creation of Israel is a defeatist and backward step, backward in its concept of a society based on racial and religious af-

47. Quoted in Burrows, *op. cit.*, p. 133.

filiations, and defeatist because it is an expression and symbol of loss of faith in the endeavors of honest men to build a world where Jews and Gentiles and all the races of mankind can live together in dignity and peace.

In accepting the implications of Zionism, the Jews have themselves confirmed Hitler's view of their irremediable separateness and have furthered his purpose of making Europe a continent without Jews. In turning their back upon Europe, they have severed their connection with a heritage in which they shared for about 2000 years. And in forcing themselves upon the Arabs, they have alienated and consequently cut themselves off from the immediate world of the new order which they have created. The Jewish state, therefore, is neither of the East nor of the West, much less can it be a link between the two, the role often claimed for it by its supporters. It has turned its back upon the one and is not acceptable to the other.

Palestine cannot live in isolation from the rest of the Arab world of which it is an integral and inseparable part. The separation of mandated Palestine from the rest of Syria had no basis in history or geography. The creation of Israel is as artificial as it is unjust. Throughout its long history Palestine has been closely interlocked with its neighbors. Geographically it is a prolongation of Syria, economically it depends on the surrounding countries; culturally it lives by the same values which are the common heritage of all the Arabs from North Africa to Iraq. Politically—except for few intervals when Palestine was permitted to order her own affairs— authority over Palestine has resided in some center extraneous to it, one which controlled larger regional or inter-regional interests. "Has there been a change in the basic conditions to reverse this determined trend? Obviously not."[48] As in the past so in the future there can be no life for Palestine in isolation, and no peace in the region, unless the region is once again integrated into a whole.

48. Speiser: *The United States and the Middle East,* p. 197.

CHAPTER XIV

Al-Maghreb

AL-MAGHREB—the West—comprises Libya, recently proclaimed an independent state, and the three French dominated territories of Tunisia, Algeria, and Morocco.

Libya, poorest of the North African territories, is mostly desert, relieved only by a narrow coastal belt where the rainfall, although scanty, allows a certain amount of cultivation. The inland oases grow the date palm, typical of the North African landscape.

Formerly a province of the Ottoman Empire, Libya came under European domination when Italy invaded the country in 1911. Native resistance forced the Italians to confine their authority to a few points on the coast. With the advent of Fascism after the first World War, the Italians set out upon a systematic conquest of the country, in the course of which the indigenous population was subjected to campaigns of extermination. The infamous task was entrusted to Grazziani who was later to achieve notoriety for his cruelty in Abyssinia. The Fascists found that in a country where water was as scarce as in Libya, a sure way of exterminating the population was to seal their wells. The effect was devastating. People and flocks died in heaps around the water holes. Others dispersed in the desert out of Italian reach.

Resistance to the Italians centered around the Sanusis, a religious order founded about the middle of the 19th century. Like the Wahhabis of Central Arabia, from whom Sidi Muhammad Ibn Ali Al-Sanusi drew his inspiration for the founding of his order, the Sanusis preached the renovation and reinvigoration of Islam by a return to the faith in its original simplicity, purity, and vigor. Like the Wahhabis, they encouraged the settlement of the nomads and the cultivation of the land. The Sanusi settlement, called Zawia, was the nucleus from which the faith was propagated. The Zawias were likewise centers of education and religious training. At the same time they were self-sufficient economic units living on the produce of the soil ploughed and cultivated by members of the order. Like the Wahhabi Ikhwan, the Sanusis were preachers, teachers, and farmers, and at the call of *jihad*, they were fighters for the faith.

Sanusi influence spread far beyond the confines of the settlements. These were located on the caravan routes; and as they did provide hospitality and free accommodation at the hostel of the Zawia for the three day period set by Arab custom, they were meeting places for merchants and travelers coming from widely separated parts of Africa. Along these routes traveled the students who sought the schools of the Zawias and the preachers who set out to spread the faith. Thus the Sanusi teachings penetrated into the heart of the African continent. Along with preaching, the Sanusis were actively engaged in combating slavery, and indeed, through their influence, the extent of slavery diminished.

The Italians, realizing the power of the Sanusis as a force of resistance, struck at the order by closing down the Zawias and confiscating their property. The Ikhwan and the tribes gathered around them dispersed. With the dissolution of the Zawias, the backbone of the resistance broke.

Fascist rule in Libya was a regime of political repression and economic impoverishment. The Fascists fully realized the strategic importance of Libya, lying so close to Italy at the center of the South Mediterranean coast. To hold it firmly in their grip they vigorously pursued the policy of settling Italians in the country. State domain, property confiscated from the rebelling communities, and lands appropriated by one means or another, were given in perpetual grants to the Italian colonists. Colonization was an elaborate scheme financed largely by the state and carried on under its supervision. There were two categories of grants, private concessions and para-statal settlements. In the former category, extensive areas were granted to individual Italians who commanded large capital for development. On these estates colonists were employed under contract. The second category of settlements was developed through the joint efforts of government and private enterprise. The government gave the land, erected the central buildings, and provided funds for digging wells and constructing roads. The development of the land into colonies devolved upon two colonizing societies who cleared the land, laid out the farms, set up the houses and other farm buildings, provided the livestock and farm equipment, and developed the water supply. The land thus prepared was distributed in lots among the settlers who after the lapse of a set period acquired full ownership rights.

Italian agricultural enterprise in Libya resulted in some remarkable achievements. Both the private concessions and the para-statal settlements were the greatest economic asset of the territory. About 250,000 acres were developed or prepared for development. Thousands of acres were laid to olive and other fruit trees, especially citrus, almonds, and vines. Large areas were put under fodder, wheat, and barley. Where irrigation was possible, garden produce was grown. Sand dunes were anchored and afforested. Tamarisk windbreaks surrounded the irrigated fruit area.[1]

But the Libyans derived little or no benefit from these developments which were primarily intended to absorb Italian immigrants. In fact, Italian agriculture in Libya, however admirable in its achievements, resulted in hardship and privation for the Libyans who were indeed at times expropriated and dispossessed to make room for strangers.

During the last War, British forces conquered Libya from the Italians. The Libyans, oppressed and impoverished under Fascist rule, rallied to the cause of the Democracies in the hope of ridding themselves of their oppressors. Some joined the armies and fought in the Western Desert. Others sabotaged enemy activity, while others yet acted as guides and informants, or gave shelter to members of the Allied forces, and in numerous ways rendered them aid and service.

Having occupied Libya, the British set up a military administration over the greater part of the country with the exception of Fezzan which passed under French control. The Italian Peace Treaty required Italy to renounce her right to her former African possessions, Libya, Eritrea, and Somaliland. The final disposal of the territories, to be made "in the light of the wishes and welfare of the inhabitants and the interests of peace and security," was left to the Four Powers—France, Great Britain, the United States, and the U.S.S.R. The Treaty further provided that, should the said Powers fail to reach an agreement, the matter would be referred to the United Nations General Assembly whose decision in this case was to be binding.

In the fall of 1947, a Four Power Commission of Investigation visited Libya, supposedly to inquire and report upon the wishes of the people with regard to their future status. But the Commis-

1. Keen: *op. cit.*, pp. 30–35.

sion's findings were contradictory, for they represented not so much a detached analysis of actual conditions in the country as the views and interests of the several governments represented on the Commission.

Since the Four Powers failed to determine jointly the disposal of the former Italian territories in Africa, they took the matter to the United Nations. The decision of the General Assembly, given in November 1949, stated that Libya—comprising Cyrenaica, Tripolitania, and Fezzan—was to be constituted an independent and sovereign state, independence to become effective not later than January 1, 1952. A United Nations Commissioner was appointed to assist the people of Libya in the formulation of their constitution and the establishment of independent government. A Council to aid and advise the Commissioner was formed of ten members, six representing Egypt, France, Italy, Pakistan, the United Kingdom, and the United States and nominated by their respective governments, and four appointed by the Commissioner, one for the minorities living in Libya, the others to represent the people of each of the three sections of the territory, Cyrenaica, Tripolitania, and Fezzan.

The implementation of the United Nations resolution met with numerous difficulties and obstacles. Not the least of the difficulties sprang from the internal conditions of Libya itself. The country is poor and underdeveloped and is consequently unable, if left to its resources, to maintain the machinery of an independent government. The paucity of the resources was matched by the dearth in leadership and the scarcity of trained personnel. The situation was further aggravated by the presence of self-seeking elements who, to promote their petty interests, were willing to be the tools of the Occupying Power.

The Occupying Power, Great Britain, and her junior partner, France, were more concerned with securing their own interests in Libya than with the achievement of Libyan unity and independence. It was indicative of the British policy to divide and rule, presently to be applied in Libya—a policy persistently followed elsewhere in the Arab World since the first World War—that the Secretary of State for Foreign Affairs, speaking before the House of Commons on June 8, 1942, singled out one section of Libya—Cyrenaica—for a promise of liberation from Italian rule in recognition of the aid rendered by the people of Libya to the British forces. The Foreign Secretary's statement, that under no circumstances would His Majesty's Government allow the return of Cyrenaica to Italian rule, envisaged the separation of Cyrenaica from the rest of Libya and viewed the future of the Sanusis apart from that of their countrymen.

The policy inaugurated in the Foreign Secretary's statement was diligently pursued by His Majesty's Government. The Foreign Office worked out the Bevin-Sforza plan, presented by Great Britain to the United Nations. Under this plan, Libya was to be divided into three sections, Cyrenaica and Fezzan to be handed over to Great Britain and France respectively for a ten year trusteeship, while Tripolitania would be placed under Italian trusteeship for eight years. At the United Nations, the British delegation championed the cause of a divided Libya.

In Libya itself, the British, seconded by the French, had gone a long way towards the establishment of division in the territory before the United Nations pronounced its decision on the future status of Libya. The British set up separate military administrations in Tripolitania and Cyrenaica, and the French were established in the Fezzan. Thus in a territory whose inhabitants numbered slightly over a million, there were three separate administrations, with customs barriers between the artificially separated parts, three different currencies in circulation, and numerous restrictions on the movement of persons and goods, all newly imposed since liberation from Italy.

The British emphasized still further the separation between Cyrenaica and Tripolitania by creating a special position for Cyrenaica and its leader the Sanusi Amir, Sidi Mohammad Ibn Idris, whom they encouraged to proclaim himself the ruler of an independent Cyrenaica.

When the Amir announced, June 1, 1949, the desire of Cyrenaica to achieve independence he was recognized on the same day by the British Government as ruler of Cyrenaica with power to set up a government in charge of internal affairs. What this Cyrenaican independence meant was stated in the Transitional Powers Proclamation issued on September 16, 1949 by the British Chief Administrator. The Proclamation empowered the Amir to enact a constitution by edict, and defined the powers which that constitution should confer. At the same time it listed the matters reserved for the British Resident in Cyrenaica. The reserved powers included control over foreign affairs, defense, air navigation and external communications, currency and trade, immigration and the issue of passports and visas. The alienation of mineral deposits was subject to agreement between the Amir and the British Resident who retained the right to decide upon the validity of any legislation under the Transitional Powers Proclamation, and to comment upon all financial matters with the ultimate power of decision. The Constitution could not be amended or suspended without the approval of the British Resident.

Upon the enactment of the Constitution, a regional government was set up. This was followed by a £1,000,000 grant in aid from the British Treasury to Cyrenaica.

The separation promoted by Great Britain prior to the United Nations decision on the future of Libya was not relinquished with the passage of the resolution on the independence of a united Libyan state. It only took a slightly modified form. The British, having failed to put through the United Nations their plan for a divided Libya under three separate trusteeships, now worked to keep the implementation of the United Nations resolution in line with the policy and set-up they had conceived for Libya. Hence their insistence upon a federalized instead of a unitary state. Federalization was to replace division, and to maintain the special status created for Cyrenaica as well as the preponderant position of Great Britain in that section of the federated state.

The separatism promoted by the British authorities was not approved by the United Nations Commissioner, Mr. Adrian Pelt. When these authorities expressed the desire to transfer to the Amir the powers reserved to the British Resident, the United Nations Commissioner observed that the transfer would invest so much authority in the ruler of one portion of the country as to cause prejudice to the unity and sovereignty of the whole. Again Mr. Pelt intervened to prevent the conclusion of a treaty between the British and the Amir saying that an independent, all Libyan government could conclude a treaty with any power, while a treaty with one part of Libya would wreck the United Nations resolution.

But Mr. Pelt was not successful in checking the progress of regionalization. In Cyrenaica, where a local indigenous government had been set up, an Assembly of Representatives was elected in June 1950 under an especial Electoral Law for Cyrenaica which provided for Cyrenaican rather than Libyan nationality. In Tripolitania, an Administrative Council was created in May 1950, and it prepared an electoral law for Tripolitania. In March 1951, a government was formed in Tripolitania on the model of the Cyrenaican government. Over and above the fact that this process was detrimental to the country's unity, these local institutions were mere shadow governments with little or no real authority, and therefore totally inadequate to prepare the Libyans for self-government.

This was the view expressed by the United Nations Commissioner who considered the steps taken by the British authorities as obstacles to the implementation of the United Nations resolution. In his opinion, the establishment of regional governments in the territories of Libya, especially if done without preliminary consultation with the inhabitants, would place a *de facto* limitation upon the freedom of choice of the Libyan National Assembly which was to decide upon the constitution of Libya, including the form of government. Mr. Pelt further stressed the need for associating the Libyans as soon as possible in the affairs for which they would soon be responsible.

In the Fezzan the French authorities created a replica of the British model in Cyrenaica, with local government and assembly, both equally ineffective.

The development along these divisive lines was not only harmful to the real interests of the country but had no basis in the wishes of the majority of the population. The United Nations Commissioner observed that the concept of Libyan unity was not confined to the more intellectual section of the population, or to the younger generation in general, but was widespread throughout the country, even the hinterland.[2]

Mr. Pelt reported that the administering powers were not ready to grasp the fact that the General Assembly intended the creation of a single Libyan Government rather than three separate governments. While they put forward a number of suggestions for the development of constitutional machinery in each of the three territories, they offered no proposals for promoting the unity and independence of Libya as a whole for which the General Assembly resolution held them responsible severally and together.[3]

The Commissioner's Advisory Council was sharply though unevenly divided on the form of government for Libya. On one side stood the representatives of Egypt, Pakistan, and Tripolitania. They held to the establishment of a single government in a unitary state.

2. Report of the United Nations Commissioner in Libya to the Secretary-General A/AC. 32/1, 4 Sept., 1950, p. 112.
3. *Ibid.*, pp. 109–110.

On the side of federalization were ranged the British, French, and American members, followed by the compliant councilors from Cyrenaica and the Fezzan. The representatives of Italy and of the minorities living in Libya maintained a neutral position.

Mr. Pelt, as his report to the United Nations showed, was fully aware of the dangers inherent in the policy of the administering powers, yet he was unable to check its development. The constitutional measures, intended to prepare the Libyans for independence under the auspices of the United Nations, were cast in the mold of regionalization and continued to develop within the framework constructed for a federalized state. Thus the Preparatory Committee, formed in July of 1950 as a step towards the preparation of the Constitution by a National Constituent Assembly, was composed of 21 members, seven from each of the three sections of Libya, placing Tripolitania with a population of 800,000 on a par with Cyrenaica with 300,000 inhabitants, and even with the Fezzan and its 60,000 inhabitants. The introduction of the principle of numerical equality for Tripolitanian, Cyrenaican, and Fezzani representation on the Preparatory Committee emphasized sectionalism and led, as it was bound to do, to further steps along the same path.

The Committee, whose Cyrenaican and Fezzani members were nominees of the British and French authorities respectively, decided that the National Assembly should be composed of 60 representatives on the basis of equal representation for the three territories. This decision not only established division but held other dangerous implications. For it is a fact that the middle class of the towns of Tripolitania is more politically aware and articulate than the predominantly tribal communities of Cyrenaica and the Fezzan. The principle of equal representation on the National Assembly gave a preponderance to the illiterate over the enlightened elements, as it was likely to pack the Assembly with yes-men from Cyrenaica and the Fezzan ready to do the bidding of the powers in control of their respective territories. The Assembly thus constituted passed a resolution in December 1950, establishing Libya as a federal state with the Sanusi Amir as king designate.

Mr. Pelt admitted before the United Nations that the National Assembly, as it was composed, had neither the political backing nor the moral support which entitled it to lay down a constitution for the State. Yet the Assembly remained because it was supported by the representatives of Great Britain, the United States, and France, who maintained that since it was legally constituted its decisions were binding. The National Assembly was therefore allowed to become a Constituent Assembly with the exclusive right to draw up the Constitution. In line with its federal tendencies the Assembly promulgated, in October 1951, the Constitution for a federalized state. The Constitution gave wide powers to the Sanusi ruler who became king of the United States of Libya.

On December of 1951, Libya was proclaimed an independent state. A difficult course lies ahead. On the one hand, relations with the three Powers—Great Britain, the United States, and France who look upon Libya primarily as a Mediterranean base of great strategic importance—may cause strain and friction in Libya itself and have disturbing repercussions in other parts of the Arab World. On the other hand there are fundamental internal problems to be coped with. Two needs are especially urgent, the training of personnel to run a modern state—civil servants, teachers, doctors, agricultural specialists, and other technical experts—, and the investment of capital to develop and put to the best use the limited resources of the country. Great Britain has offered financial help to Libya. But a gift from a single power is fraught with danger, since it is bound to tie the beneficiary to the donor. Economic and technical aid can best be supplied by the United Nations, itself the sponsor of Libyan independence.

While Libya, under the auspices of the United Nations, has achieved independence, however limited, the other North African territories, with far greater potentialities, remain in the grip of an oppressive French rule, wholly out of tune with the contemporary world.

Algeria, oldest of the French possessions in North Africa, was invaded in 1830. The Algerians put up a stubborn resistance. Led by Abd-al-Kadir al-Jazairi, a pious and learned man fired with patriotism and courage, the Algerians fought the French persistently and with valor, defeating time and again the superior French forces. The country was not subdued until 1847 after it had been ravaged by seventeen years of warfare and the people reduced to misery. But Algeria was not pacified; violent outbreaks occurred throughout the 19th century with great losses in life to the French and Algerians alike. The brutality with which the French retaliated upon the population continues to be characteristic of their rule in North Africa to the present day.

For over a century the French have ruled Algeria under a regime of unrelieved oppression, political, economic, and cultural.

Algeria is considered part of France. It is under the jurisdiction of the Ministry of the Interior. Its laws are made by the French Parliament. The political set-up is designed to perpetuate French rule and ensure for the European community—predominantly French settlers—a privileged status and an effective monopoly of the economic resources of the country.

Until 1940, Algerian participation in the government of their country was limited to representation in the Assembly of Financial Delegations, an elected body with authority to vote on the budget, but not permitted to discuss political issues. This participation was in reality totally ineffective, not only because of the restricted competence of the Assembly but also due to its composition, for it was made up of three delegations, two of which represented the interests of the French colonists, agricultural settlers and business communities—about 800,000—while only one was reserved for the native population of nearly eight million. More pernicious still, this native delegation was subdivided into Berber and Arab membership.

There was a law—the Crémieux Law of 1870—which allowed the Algerians to become French citizens if they gave up their personal status and accepted the French civil law. To the Moslems this was close to apostasy, since it meant departure from Moslem law and customs and renunciation of religious status. Hence extremely few Moslems responded to the offer. The Crémieux Law had the one effect of turning, at the stroke of a pen, 140,000 Jews, natives of Algeria, into French citizens and consequently a privileged class, swelling the numbers of the foreign community which under the protection of foreign laws and a foreign citizenship lived off the good earth of Algeria and at the expense of its indigenous population.

An attempt to make the Crémieux Law acceptable to the Moslems was made in 1944 when an electoral law was passed by the French Parliament granting the westernized section of the Algerian Moslems full citizenship rights without incurring loss of their Moslem status. But this law touched only a small fraction of the population, and it came too late, for even the westernized elements were no longer satisfied with the right to be represented in the French Parliament.

The Algerians are depressed by impoverishment. The resources of the country are dominated by the French settlers as the laws are made for their benefit. The European community, which forms 10 per cent of the population, controls about 70 percent of the country's economic resources.

Algeria is an agricultural country where the population lives almost wholly on the produce of the land. But about 40% of the land has passed out of native hands into the possession of the colonists; and this area includes the major portion of the fertile lands. The land acquired by the French authorities under a variety of circumstances for which appropriate laws were passed—acquisition of the state domain, appropriation on property set apart in perpetual trust for religious foundations and other institutions of a public character, expropriation following upon a local rebellion, appropriation of forest and tribal lands—this vast accumulation of land, which the natives were deprived of, was largely bestowed upon the colonists. The inevitable consequence was the creation of an immense landless native proletariat. Some of the dispossessed population drifted from the fertile coast to the desert and wastelands of the interior.

A European feudalism, protected by the State, has sprung up in Algeria. Thousands of the European proprietors own more than a hundred hectares each. Their individual holdings average 235 hectares, while many estates are beyond 1,000 hectares[4] in extent. This in the presence of a land proletariat of 4 million living on the verge of starvation in normal years, and decimated during the bad years by famine and epidemics. The European feudality furthermore is almost the only group to benefit from the public works and projects for agricultural development.

It is the opinion of an informed French observer that agriculture and livestock breeding are no longer adequate to provide the minimum level of existence. No more arable land is to be found and livestock figures have been stationary for forty years, while the population increases by 150,000 per annum.[5] Some relief for this depressing poverty could be found in the industrialization of the country. But although Algeria has mineral resources of industrial value, among them coal and iron, industrialization is not encour-

4. A hectare is equivalent to 2.471 acres.

5. Robert Montagne, "Evolution in Algeria," *International Affairs*, 1947, pp. 42–51.

aged because the French wish to retain Algeria as a market for the goods manufactured in France. They also foresee that industrialization would draw large sections of labor away from the land by offering another means of livelihood, thus depriving the French settlers of a cheap and abundant labor supply. But an even more important consideration for a colonial power is the fact that a community kept at the stage of pastoralism and primitive agriculture on the level of mere subsistence is easier to hold down than a society teeming with the ideas, problems, and potentialities which industrialization creates.

Algeria's proximity to Europe, and the early maturing of crops in its warm climate, offer favorable conditions for the development of trade. Yet Algeria's trade remains small in volume because of the widespread poverty, the control of agriculture by the colonists, their monopolistic hold over the mineral resources, and the absence of industry. Whatever the extent of trade it is in French hands. High duties on all goods other than French exclude the possibility of competition and force the Algerians to buy French products at a higher cost than world prices.

The worst aspect of French rule in Algeria has been the persistent effort to undermine the Arab-Moslem culture in an attempt to uproot the people morally and spiritually, and consequently sap their inner sources of resistance. The Moslem religion has been placed under the strict supervision of the French authorities who have appropriated the wakf or habous—the property of the religious foundations. Before the days of the French the wakf had provided for the social and educational services which had devolved upon the Moslem religion as a social institution. Schools, public works, and charity were maintained from the wakf revenues. When these trusts were appropriated, privation followed. A fraction of the appropriated trusts was reserved for the upkeep of the Moslem institutions. The mosques are under the direct control of the colonial administration. All Moslem preachers and judges are appointed and paid by the State, and are consequently its servants. The sermons of the Imams are censored, and only the official clergy—those in the pay of the administration—are allowed to preach.

Arabic, the native language, is not officially recognized. French is the language of all government transactions and of public instruction. The public system of education serves primarily the colonists. The French program of instruction is followed, and the Arabic language is either excluded altogether or taught in the colloquial form. In 1950, the number of Algerian children of primary school age was estimated at one million. Only 20% were in school. By contrast facilities were provided for all the school age population of the settlers on all levels of instruction. Of the students attending secondary schools, 10% were Algerians, and 90% French, in inverse proportion to the size of the two communities. In 1948–1949 there were 7,640 students in the university of Algiers. Of these 282 were Algerians. There are two types of Arab private schools. Those which receive a government subsidy are required to devote one third of the total hours of instruction to the French language. The second type is run by the Society of Algerian Ulama; it depends on private donations and is given wholly to the teaching of Arabic and Moslem learning. The Society maintains 125 primary schools and one secondary school—the Institute of Ibn Badis which prepares students for the Zaitouna Theological Academy in Tunis.

The Society of Algerian Ulama is a religious-political organization founded in 1929. It stresses religious and social reforms as the basis of political freedom and as providing immunity and resistance to the French policy of assimilation. It carries its message through its schools, numerous clubs, and the weekly magazine *Al-Basa'ir*. Politically, the Society works for the independence of Algeria, its union with the other North African countries, and entry into the Arab League. The Ulama have kept alive the Arab-Moslem culture in Algeria and have maintained a close touch with the two centers of this culture in North Africa; the Karawiyyin University Mosque in Morocco and Jami' al-Zaitouna in Tunisia.

A secularist party—the Fédération des Élus Musulmans d'Algérie—drew its members from among the French educated groups. It aimed at the achievement of equality between the Moslem and French citizens and representation in the French Parliament. This party was, by its nature, remote from the mass of the people and remained confined to the small circle of westernized elements. Its membership decreased still further when separatist tendencies appeared among those who had previously looked to France.

The leader of the separatists, Farhat Abbas, a forceful Berber of the Kabyle, founded the Party of the Algerian Manifesto, so named after the Manifesto or program launched by Abbas in February

1943 in which he asked for the constitution of Algeria into an autonomous republic within the French Union, with a government formed along Western lines, and a parliament providing equitable representation for the Europeans settled in Algeria. The Manifesto rejected the policy of assimilation and demanded recognition of Arabic as an official language. But this party itself is no longer satisfied with the dominion status which was the object of the Manifesto of 1943. It has recently tended towards the more radical and popular party of Massali al-Haj. Even the name of the Party's paper, *Égalité*, has been changed to *La République Algérienne*. This change of title is indicative of the change in the Party's trend and objective.

The most important of Algeria's political parties, because it has the widest popular support, is the party led by Massali al-Haj. As early as 1924, Massali al-Haj, one of the many Algerian workers in France, organized his fellow workers and countrymen into a party, the North African Star, for mutual aid among the workers. This organization later evolved into a political party working for the independence of Algeria. Dissolved in 1937 for its political activities, it was immediately replaced by the Party of the Algerian People, also founded by Massali al-Haj and, like its predecessor, rooted in the people from whom it drew its membership and its strength. In 1947, the Movement for the Triumph of Democratic Liberties under the leadership of Massali al-Haj succeeded the Party of the Algerian People. The M.T.L.D. continues the work begun with the formation of the North African Star and aims, like its forerunners, at the achievement of independence as the only guarantee for a decent life for the mass of the people. It therefore vigorously rejects the inclusion of Algeria within the French Union, declares all reforms ineffective within the present set-up, and calls upon the Algerian people to persist in the struggle until independence is achieved. In 1951 the M.T.L.D. of Massali al-Haj joined with Abbas Farhat's party, now called the Democratic Union of Algerian Moslems, the Society of Algerian Ulama, communists and independent nationalists in forming the Algerian Front for the Defence of Liberty.

The French are still a long way from meeting the national aspirations of the Algerians. After much deliberation, the Statute for Algeria was promulgated in September 1947. But it brought no basic change. In the local Assembly, set up under the Statute to replace the Financial Delegations, the representation of the French settlers remains disproportionately large. This Assembly furthermore has little authority. It may deliberate on the budget but must pass it. It may legislate on minor matters, but all important legislation continues to be the sole prerogative of the French Parliament. Executive power is vested in the Governor-General who is responsible directly to Paris.

The Status of Algeria under the Statute is far removed not only from the independence to which the people aspire but even from an acceptable basis of internal autonomy. Under the Statute, effective control remains as before with the Governor-General and the central legislative and executive organs in Paris. The Algerian Assembly, for which the Statute provides, is only very remotely akin to the kind of Assembly which national opinion asked for a sovereign assembly elected on the basis of universal suffrage, free of racial and religious distinctions, with authority to give Algeria a constitution and power to secure and safeguard national rights. Nevertheless, the nationalist parties led by Massali al-Haj and Farhat Abbas were willing to participate in the elections for the Algerian Assembly held in April 1948, their participation being a sign of their good will and their readiness to give this trial of democracy, however limited, a fair chance. But they were rudely deceived, for the elections, conducted with police search and military intimidation, were a brutal farce. Voters were kept away from the polls by violence, candidates were arrested, votes were bought, and the voting manipulated. The abuse of all democratic principles was so flagrant that liberal opinion in France itself censured the conduct of the French authorities and warned that French rule in Algeria could henceforth rest only upon force.

The violence and fraud attendant upon the elections of 1948 are an expression of the French reaction towards any attempt on the part of the Algerians to loosen the grip of the colonial power. This reaction is in line with the policy of repression which, enforced throughout a century, culminated in the massacre of May 1945 when about 20,000 Algerians (a conservative estimate) were indiscriminately killed, and villages destroyed, in retaliation for the loss of some two hundred French lives in a clash between the police and a procession celebrating V Day. Such conduct parades weakness and failure, and carries its own doom.

Meanwhile Algeria, after a century of direct foreign rule, and of subjection to a persistent policy of assimilation, has kept its culture alive and its national identity unimpaired, and has maintained its determination to reconquer a life of freedom and dignity.

Established in Algeria, France was bound to expand to the neighboring North African territories. One immediate excuse for the annexation of Tunisia was found in the incursions of Tunisian tribes along the Algerian border; another took the form of offering protection to the Bey against his restless subjects.

The story of foreign penetration into Tunisia, which led to the loss of its independence, is similar to contemporary developments in Egypt. In both countries, foreign loans introduced foreign financial control which entailed political domination. Burdensome taxes were imposed to pay off the foreign debt. Crushed by taxation and impoverished, the people rebelled. Rebellion and chaos gave France the opportunity to proclaim Tunisia a French protectorate.

Prior to French intervention, Tunisia had been an autonomous province of the Ottoman Empire bound by nominal allegiance to the Porte. The middle of the 19th century witnessed in Tunisia, as in other parts of the Empire, some signs of reform. The guiding spirit and mind of the reform movement was Khair-ed-Din Pasha, a wise and liberal statesman. Khair-ed-Din, who had traveled in Europe and the Moslem countries, recorded his observations in a book intended to awaken the Moslems to their degraded status as contrasted with the power, progress, and prosperity of the kingdoms of Europe, and to point the way toward building a strong and enlightened Moslem society. Knowledge, Khair-ed-Din wrote, was the foundation of all progress. But the expansion of knowledge was possible only in a society where justice and freedom reigned. And there was no guarantee for the permanence of the rule of justice and freedom except in representative institutions. Therefore, Khair-ed-Din urged the establishment of the representative system of government as the cornerstone in the program of reform for the Moslem countries.

Khair-ed-Din's book is all the more significant because the author was in a position to put into practical application the ideas propounded in the book. He was behind the movement for the establishment of a State Council as a first step towards representative government. He dealt successfully with the problem of the economic ruin of the country, and with the plight of the people deserting their farms and fleeing before the tax collector. Khair-ed-Din attended personally to the grievances of the common people. He placed a box in the public square of Tunis where the oppressed could deposit their complaints, secure in the knowledge that their wrongs would be righted; for Khair-ed-Din, who himself carried the key to the box, was careful to examine every complaint and deal justice to the plaintiff. His vigilance restored respect to the government and security to the people. In line with his concept of the importance of knowledge, he helped to found a college where Moslem learning was taught along with modern science and European languages. He introduced reforms into the Zaitouna University Mosque which he endowed with a large library brought together from various mosques, and added to the collection his own donation of over 2000 manuscripts.

But Khair-ed-Din was not allowed to remain at his post directing the policy of the state. Reactionary elements of various origins united against him. The French in particular were not pleased to see liberal and progressive ideas take root across their Algerian border. It is reported that when Napoleon III was presented with a copy of the organic law of the Tunisian State Council he remarked: "If the Arabs get used to liberty and justice we shall have no peace with them in Algeria." In view of the designs of France and Italy on Tunisia, Khair-ed-Din had sought to strengthen his country's ties with the Porte as a means to counterbalance the influence of the European powers. This policy roused the Bey's suspicion of his minister, and Khair-ed-Din was removed from office. He left Tunisia and settled in Constantinople where he became Grand Vizier, the highest official in the Empire.

The French occupied Tunisia in 1881 and concluded a treaty in which they professed that the occupation was temporary and would terminate when the local administration was in a position to preserve order and security. The occupation is still in force to the present day.

In Tunisia, the French left a semblance of native rule. The Bey is the nominal head of the state. But the actual ruler is the French Resident-General who controls the administration and promulgates the laws. Frenchmen head all government departments in the capital and the provinces.

The economic situation is similar to that of Algeria. Economic life is dominated by the European settlers of whom there are about 240,000 among a Tunisian population of nearly three million. Here as in Algeria, the colonists are settled on the best lands. In developing the land they are given privileges from which the native population is debarred. Land is given to them in return for payment over a long period of years, credits are advanced at reduced rates, and loans are redeemable at long terms. Contrasted with their prosperity, the poverty of the Tunisian peasant becomes all the more striking.

Here also, assimilation was attempted by the suppression of the Arabic language and the establishment of a system of education which severed the youth from its cultural background. Resistance to cultural assimilation has found a bulwark in the Zaitouna University Mosque which, like the Azhar in Egypt, has been for centuries the custodian of the Arab-Moslem heritage.

The nationalist movement in Tunisia took on an organized form after the first World War, having received an impetus from the independence movements in Egypt and the other Arab countries of the East, and from the proclamation of Wilson's principles of self-determination.

Resistance has been organized by the Dustur (Constitution) Party and its successor the Neo-Dustur. The Dustur Party, formed in 1920, presented to the French government in Paris a program of reform with proposals for constitutional government, freedom of association and the press, free education, and economic opportunities for Tunisians. The program fell on deaf ears. Instead the Tunisians were offered French nationality which they, like the Algerians, rejected.

Early in the 1930's, the fighting wing of the Dustur, led by Bourguiba, broke away from the old party and formed the Neo-Dustur. The Neo-Dustur has had wide popular support, since its membership is drawn largely from among the working classes. It is also an efficiently organized party with local branches all over the country; the branches are held together through regional organizations, and all are directed from a central office which formulates the party's policy. Members of the central committee travel constantly and extensively over the country sounding public opinion and directing it. Meetings are held at frequent intervals in towns and villages and in the open spaces of the desert. By means of these meetings, as well as through the party's paper, the national issues are kept before the public.

The Neo-Dustur Party was dissolved in September 1934 and its leaders arrested. A regime of repression reigned for two years.

Upon the release of its leaders the party resumed its activity. The following year, repression returned, accompanied by arrests on a large scale. Giant demonstrations held in protest all over Tunisia testified to the excellent organization of the Neo-Dustur Party and the consolidation of the people behind it. The French responded by declaring martial law, and by imposing long-term penal servitude upon the arrested leaders. A reign of terror ensued. Even the sanctity of homes was violated, with soldiers breaking in and dealing violence to the occupants.

Repression did not uproot the movement. It merely drove it underground. Secret cells carried on the work of the party branches, and clandestine publications took the place of the suppressed papers and the banned gatherings in keeping the people informed and their spirit alive.

The collapse of France early in the war armed the nationalists with the logically sound argument that since France herself was occupied by the enemy she was in no position to discharge her responsibilities in Tunisia under the terms of the Protectorate. They therefore demanded the immediate termination of the Protectorate and the proclamation of Tunisia's independence. This step was met with the usual French response. But the detention of leaders did not arrest the movement, for here as in Egypt and India, new committees were formed and came forward to lead the movement as soon as one group of leaders was arrested.

The accession of Monsef Bey in June, 1942 gave fresh vigor and hope to the national movement. For many years, since he was a youth, Monsef Bey had been a member of the Dustur Party and had given his support to national aspirations. But Monsef Bey was soon deposed and exiled to France. He was exiled to France on the grounds of alleged cooperation with the Axis. It was customary during the war for the powers in control to brand the resistance movement in any Arab country and its leaders with the fascist label. In fact, while French officials on a high level in Tunisia and elsewhere in North Africa cooperated with the Axis, Monsef Bey maintained an attitude of strict neutrality. His fault lay in the support he gave to his people's aspirations for freedom.

The growth of the national movement in Tunisia has been accompanied by the awakening and consolidation of the working class. The workers have been the backbone of the resistance. The first leader and organizer of the workers was appropriately a self-made man, Mohammad Ali al-Kabisi, who died in 1927, still a young man. Al-Kabisi began his life as a worker. He took part in the Libyan war against Italy in 1911, and accompanied the Turkish general Anwar Pasha to Constantinople whence he found his way to Germany as a student. Having received a degree in political economy he returned to Tunisia in 1924, to take up the cause of the working class.

Upon his return he found that the political struggle was consuming itself in agitation and emotional outpourings with little thought and energy being directed to solid, constructive work. He remarked that as long as social solidarity was lacking and economic life primitive and unorganized, the enthusiasm of youth and its sincerity, which found expression in the press and in public gatherings, were like vapor in the air. The task of leadership, therefore, was not to agitate and arouse hostility against the ruling power while the people were still weak and defenseless—that was bound to expose them to reprisals by their rulers. Rather, the duty of the leaders was to summon and direct all the forces of the nation to the purpose of remedying the social ills, and striking at the root of the misery and sorrow in which the people were steeped. The first step towards liberation was a critical self-examination without which there can only be self-deception.

Al-Kabisi practised what he preached. He kept close to the people and fully shared their life with all its privations. He was of an ascetic nature himself. The barest necessities satisfied his needs. Often his food consisted only of bread and olives eaten on the road as he tramped across the country to meet and organize the workers. He communed with people wherever he found them, in the workshops or in the fields, in the coffee-house and the public square, and on the stones at the curb of the road. Wherever the workers were gathered he was there to organize, direct, and inspire them. Yet even these workingmen's meetings—held for the purpose of finding a way to lift the laborer out of utter poverty, exploitation, and insecurity, and directed by a man who by nature, training, and purpose was anything but an agitator—these meetings were fired at and dispersed by French police, as subversive of the public order.

Premature death removed this man of the people as he had just begun his work of awakening the masses with whom he had so fully identified himself. Yet in the brief period of a mere three years, between his return from Berlin and his death, he founded unions for the Tunisian workers independent of the French labor unions in which the Tunisian laborers were discriminated against, and launched the project of cooperatives, thus giving the political struggle the support of social and economic organization, and rooting the national movement in the life of the common man.

The labor movement has been an essential and integral part of the people's struggle for freedom. Labor organizations have been the victims of official reprisal every time suppressive measures were enforced against the elements of resistance. During the last war the labor movement expanded. The French authorities, realizing that labor was the basis of the war effort, allowed the workers greater freedom of activity. Numerous unions were founded for workers in the mines, in ports and on railroads, and in other public utility works. A significant event for labor as for the national movement was the formation in January, 1946 of the General Federation of Tunisian Workers (Union Générale des Travailleurs Tunisiens). In 1949, agricultural workers were unionized. The General Federation of Tunisian Agriculture (U.G.A.T.) combats apathy and ignorance among the Tunisian peasants and their exploitation by French interests. This organization, like the U.G.T.T., is nationalist, and so are the Association of Chambers of Commerce and the Feminist Movement. In 1951 the U.G.T.T. entered the International Confederation of Free Trade Unions, and has been recognized by this anti-communist organization as its official Tunisian representative. Delegates of the Tunisian Federation have participated in international labor conferences and defended forcefully the case of Tunisia and the cause of freedom before these forums of world opinion. The head of the U.G.T.T., Farhat Hashshad, a liberal and enlightened leader known and respected in international labor circles, was murdered by French terrorists in the winter of 1953.

Since 1950, Tunisian leaders have been trying to come to an understanding with France whereby the Tunisians would assume the responsibility of governing themselves while the economic and strategic interests of France in the country would be secured. The inconsequential reforms offered by the French Government in February 1951 were accepted as a start, negotiation to proceed on the next stage of reform which, the Tunisians insisted, should be based on the establishment of an all-Tunisian Representative Assembly, to replace the Grand Conseil. This Grand Conseil is a consultative body in two sections, one French, the other Tunisian, with no authority over political matters, its competence being re-

stricted to economic and social questions. The French Government
was reluctant to go beyond the February reforms, and even these
were only partially implemented. In the fall of 1951, the Tunisian
Prime Minister, Chanik, presented to the Government in Paris proposals for a settlement which called for a Tunisian Cabinet and
Legislature. Once representative institutions had been established,
Tunisia would enter into agreements with France to assure French
cultural, economic, and strategic interests. The civil rights of the
French settlers and the security of their property would be guaranteed. It was the first time that the Tunisian Government had
officially sponsored the national cause which had hitherto been
upheld and presented by leaders of political parties with no official
capacity.

The answer of the French Government to these proposals was
a glorification of French achievements in Tunisia and insistence
on the right of the French settlers—upon whom the civilizing work
of France rested to a large extent—to participate in the political
life of the country. This the Tunisians rejected because the recognition of political rights in their country to the citizens of a foreign
country meant acquiescence in the principle of co-sovereignty and
consequently the permanence of French domination. The French
achievements in Tunisia, Chanik said, had the sole purpose of promoting the aims and interests of France and the French settlers,
and did in no way justify the continued subjection of the Tunisian
people. The financial aid advanced by France was charged as a
debt against Tunisia, while its benefit accrued to the French companies who held a virtual monopoly over the country's resources,
means of communication, and public utilities. Finally, the French
Government had made no mention of Tunisia's aid during two
world wars, when Tunisian troops had fought to defend a France
herself occupied by the enemy.

The French Government arrested Chanik and the members of
his cabinet. It is worth noting that Chanik had been a collaborator
with the French, having stayed out of the nationalist movement.

Tunisia tried to bring its case before the United Nations in the
fall of 1951, but was refused a hearing. The United States explained
that it had voted against bringing the Tunisian conflict before the
United Nations in order to avoid aggravating the situation, and to
give France a chance to settle the controversy through the continuation of direct negotiations. But the situation grew worse,
because France showed no sign of willingness to accede to any

significant change. When the Tunisian question came before the
U.N. in 1952, the French delegate boycotted the sessions. During
the winter of 1953, the French authorities in collaboration with
the colonists unleashed a reign of terror over Tunisia. Yet it is generally recognized by neutral foreign observers that the Tunisian
nationalist movement is moderate and restrained, and does not
aim to achieve independence at one stroke, or to throw the French
out of the country. If the "civilizing mission" of France in Tunisia
continues to be what it has been so far—oppression and exploitation—it is not unreasonable to expect that the moderate elements
will not long remain in control of the nationalist movement.

Morocco was the last of the North African countries to pass under foreign rule. Unlike Algeria, Tunisia, and Libya, which owed
allegiance to the Ottoman Sultan, however nominal, Morocco was
until 1912 an independent state in full possession of the attributes
of sovereignty, among them the right to conclude treaties and exchange diplomatic missions.

In 1912, Morocco was proclaimed a French Protectorate. But
the Moroccans, sturdy mountaineers attached to their independent ways, were subdued only with great difficulty. Not until 1934
was the conquest complete and the country pacified. The Riffian
revolt of 1925, most spectacular of the Moroccan uprisings, was
characteristic of the people's love of freedom, their indomitable
courage, and their readiness to plunge into a fight even against
overwhelming odds.[6] The Riffians fought the Spanish and French
at the same time, and inflicted serious defeats upon both. Their
victories brought hope and exhilaration to North Africa. In France
they caused much perturbance. So serious and menacing did the
French government consider the revolt that it dispatched large
forces under Marshal Pétain to fight the Riffians.

In Morocco, the suppression of native institutions has been less
drastic than in Algeria and Tunisia. This was partly due to the
fact that the first Representative of France in Morocco, General
Lyautey, was a wiser colonial administrator than the French Colonial Office is wont to turn out. It was also due to the more recent
introduction of French rule into Morocco which allowed for only
a short interval between the imposition of the Protectorate and the
national awakening. The country had hardly been subdued when

6. Vincent Sheean: *An American Among the Riffi,* and *Personal History.*

political parties began to be formed with the aim to effect internal reforms and work for the restoration of the country's independence.

The French have left the native government—Makhzan, with the Sultan at its head—practically intact. They divested it, however, of real authority. Parallel to the Makhzan, they set up a French administration which discharges all the important functions and responsibilities of government.

The French are proud of their achievements in Morocco. They consider Lyautey, Resident-General from 1912 to 1925, the architect of Moroccan unity. In their view the country was at the beginning of the century a conglomeration of independent fiefs and dissident mountain regions whose pacification and unification Lyautey undertook in the name of the Sultan. Government control has been established over local chiefs and outlying provinces, and the construction of roads has linked the distant parts of the country. The economic resources have been developed largely through French initiative and capital. Agricultural colonization by the French settlers was, under Lyautey's plan, to be limited in scale and to serve as an example to the Moroccan farmers.

Lyautey's successors did not have his breadth of vision. They established direct rule, sponsored large scale immigration and land acquisition by French settlers, and geared the machinery of the State to the benefit of the colonists.

In Morocco as in Algeria and Tunisia, the colonists have settled on the best lands. In acquiring and developing the land they have the aid of the Colonization Fund into which an appreciable portion of the State budget is diverted. The benefits of the Fund are denied to native landowners and farmers. The extent of the land acquired by the settlers is far out of proportion to their number: 300,000 Europeans, among eight million Moroccans, own 30% of the sown area. In some regions native farmers were compelled to sell their land to the colonists. As the holdings were small the forced sales affected a large number of peasants.[7] The colonists, on the other hand, are forbidden by law to sell land to the natives.

The mineral wealth of the country—coal, oil, phosphates—is in the hands of the Europeans who also control the railroads, airways, and mercantile navigation. The budget is almost wholly absorbed by a heavily loaded bureaucracy, and by the policing of a restless, discontented people. Even the small amount allotted to public health and education goes largely to institutions serving the Euro-

7. *Survey of International Affairs;* 1937, p. 493, and note 4.

pean population. A mere trickle reaches the people of the country.

The Moroccans resent more than any other aspect of French rule the "Berber policy" which, by accentuating the differences and creating cleavages between Arabs and Berbers, aims at keeping the population permanently divided and under control. How strong the antagonism to this policy is may be gauged by the fact that it was the promulgation of the Berber Dahir (decree) in 1930 which started the nationalist movement off. This decree gave validity to Berber customary law in preference to the Islamic Canon Law. The idea behind it was that once the Moslem personal status had been abrogated, the Berber law could be assimilated to the French law and the Berbers would become French citizens. In brief, the law aimed at the de-Islamization of the Berbers. The proclamation of the Berber Dahir thoroughly infuriated the Moroccans and caused a widespread upheaval, rallying Moslem opinion throughout the Islam world.[8]

Political parties began to form in the early thirties, and have had a turbulent existence ever since. No sooner do they appear than they are suppressed, their leaders arrested and imprisoned or deported to the Sahara.

Before the war, the nationalist movement aimed at securing internal reforms. Developments during the war have made independence the goal. The Independence Party, led by Allal al-Fasi, has the largest following. In January, 1944, the Party issued the Proclamation of Independence which demanded the termination of the Protectorate on the grounds that France had deviated from its terms and transformed it into direct rule and economic exploitation, and because world conditions had changed radically since its imposition in 1912. The Proclamation pointed to the weakened position of France, a defeated and occupied country, and to the substantial aid in men and resources rendered by Morocco to the cause of freedom through her participation on the side of the Democracies in two world wars. Such participation entitled Morocco to join the nations signatory to the Atlantic Charter as an independent country. The Proclamation stressed internal reforms based upon representative institutions as the pillar of independence. The establishment of a democratic regime was to be entrusted to the Sultan, Sidi Muhammad. The legitimate interests of foreigners living in Morocco would be safeguarded.

8. Robert Montagne: "Morocco Between East and West," *Foreign Affairs*, January, 1948, pp. 360–372.

The French authorities responded to this declaration by arresting the leaders. When demonstrations occurred in Rabat, Fez, and Casablanca, French tanks and guns mowed down the demonstrators.

One of the most hopeful and constructive aspects of the national movement is the concern of its leaders with education. The paucity of funds supplied by the state left the task of providing and financing schools to individuals and private organizations. Schools have been established by the various political parties, and rich men and women have donated funds and founded schools. Teaching, in some of these schools, is done partly by volunteers, men who are otherwise occupied but eager to participate in the work of educating their people. Among the prominent political leaders some have worked in education. Allal al-Fasi taught night classes at the Karawiyyin University Mosque where his lectures drew large crowds. The Secretary-General of the Independence Party, Ahmad Bilafreij, is the director of his own modern school in Rabat, one of the oldest and most influential of the national schools.

Two types of schools have been established by the nationalist groups. One evolved from the Kuttab—Koranic school—into primary schools. Here an Arabic program is taught, preparing the students for entrance to the section of secondary education at the Karawiyyin Mosque in Fas, an institution similar to Al-Azhar. The second type are the modern primary schools which prepare students for the secondary schools of the government. A number of girls' schools have been founded. One of them, a model school at Casablanca, has been established through a gift of fifty million francs from three women, daughters of a rich merchant. Princess Aisha, the Sultan's daughter, has given her encouragement and support to the education of girls.

Education has received moral and material support from the Sultan who has sponsored the movement. He has given generously of his own means as he has authorized the use of wakf property and funds for the construction and maintenance of schools. His presence at the ceremonies celebrating the founding and opening of schools makes the occasions noteworthy.

The French have not been sympathetic to this educational development. They have placed obstacles in its path, such as the imposition of taxes upon school buildings. Another obstacle is the difficulty of obtaining a permit to open schools. Even the Sultan and his family have been "requested" not to attend the school ceremonies because their presence evoked nationalist celebrations.

Since the close of the war, the Sultan has come out as the central figure in the national struggle. He had asserted his independence during the war when he refused to associate himself with General Noguès, the French Resident-General, in opposing the Allied landing, in November 1942. When Noguès ordered Vichy troops to fight the Allies, the Sultan made it known to him that if he intended to obstruct the landing he should go out into the open sea and fight. At the Casablanca Conference in January, 1943, the Sultan met President Roosevelt who expressed concern for the independence of Morocco and the development of its resources. Roosevelt is said to have spoken of French rule as the worst that could be inflicted on a people. The Sultan's prominence was emphasized after his visit to Tangier in the spring of 1947. The visit, which included the Spanish Zone of Morocco as well as the international city of Tangier, was meant to assert Moroccan unity and nationhood. In both sections of the country, the Sultan was met with enthusiasm as the symbol of the struggle for independence and unity. At the principal mosque in Tangier, he made a forceful speech which received world-wide publicity, and in which he spoke out for independence. The speech emphasized the Arab essence of Morocco and the ties which linked it to the Arab East. These ties were to be strengthened, on the political level through Morocco's entry into the Arab League, and culturally by the establishment of educational institutions on the model of the higher institutions in the Arab countries of the East. Finally, the Sultan declared the people's right to representative government and expressed his intention to give effect to democratic institutions. The Sultan's son and daughter also made public speeches in which they affirmed Morocco's unity and stressed the identity of her culture and of her interests and aspirations with those of the eastern Arabs. On this memorable trip, the Sultan took time to lay the foundation stone of a school for which funds had been provided by diverting the gifts traditionally carried to the descendants of a venerated local saint. That simple people were beginning to value education more than saint-worship is indicative of the trend of the national movement.

The French Government recalled the Resident-General who had given the Sultan this chance to become a national leader and to make public statements on Moroccan freedom and Arab unity. In his place, they appointed General Juin, a soldier bred in the colonial tradition who had spent most of his career in Algeria where he was born. The high handed policy of Juin exasperated Moroccan feeling, and strained still further the already tense relations with France. French liberal opinion criticized the appointment of Juin as dictated by big business—banks, trading firms, and agricultural companies operating in Morocco—under whose pressure the government made the choice.

A crisis arose after the Sultan's official visit to Paris in the fall of 1950, where he was invited to discuss Franco-Moroccan relations with the French Government. The views presented by the two parties clashed. The French offered insubstantial reforms. The Sultan pointed out that the relations based upon the Protectorate, and the regime that issued from it, were no longer acceptable. He urged that a new form of relationship be worked out in the light of world trends and in conformity with the wishes and aspirations of the Moroccan people.

Upon his return, the Sultan announced the failure of the Paris talks and made known the views which he had presented to the French Government. These views included the reconsideration of the status of Morocco in relation to France, and the full development and utilization of the country's wealth for the welfare of the people. The Sultan upheld democracy as the best form of government and gave his support to the people's right to democratic institutions. He further expressed his concern for the workers, and his determination to respect the right of labor to unionize.

An indictment of French rule came from another source. In the State Council, a body formed of appointed and elected members to advise the administration on economic matters, an attack was launched by the nationalist members against the economic policy of the government which resulted in the exploitation of the country and the impoverishment of the people. The documented attack, for which facts and statistics were drawn from official publications, so infuriated Juin that he expelled the two outspoken members. Their sympathizers withdrew in protest.

French hostility towards the Sultan increased in proportion as his prestige among his people grew. Earlier, when the French had branded the national movement as the work of irresponsible agitators who had little popular support, they had held up the Sultan as the highest authority in the state and the only leader who represented the people. But since the national movement has crystallized around the Sultan, he has become, in French eyes, a despot whose regime should be democratized. Democratization, as Juin conceived it for the Moroccans, was to consist of the transfer of what authority the Sultan still had to his ministers. In the absence of a representative assembly or any form of public control over the government, it could not be expected that this measure would bring the people any nearer to democratic government. It was merely intended to isolate the Sultan and counterbalance his prestige by placing the authority still left to him with officials who were expected to be more tractable than the Sultan had recently been.

In February, 1951 matters came to a head between the Sultan and the Resident-General when the latter demanded that the Sultan dismiss his cabinet and disavow the Istiqlal—the Independence Party. The demand was presented in the form of an ultimatum accompanied by the movement of Berber cavalry, the followers of Gellawi, a feudal chief who had always supported the French and had become their protégé. These men encamped at the entrance to the principal cities. At the same time, rumors were circulated of the descent of mountain tribes upon the towns.

Under these circumstances, the Sultan took the course designed to relieve the tension and save the country from civil strife. He dissolved his cabinet and denounced the methods of extremists.

The Moroccan events received wide publicity in the Arab press which severely censured French action. In an interview with a well known reporter, the Sultan declared in a written and signed statement that he had been subjected to threats, and that in the face of the gathering of tribes who knew not why they had been gathered, he complied with the French demands in order to avoid the dangers inherent in such a situation. Resident-General Juin, interviewed by the same reporter, admitted that he had asked the Sultan to disavow the Independence Party, and that, when the Sultan had refused, he had insisted that the Makhzen should issue a declaration condemning the methods of a "certain party" without naming it. Juin further said that he had urged the Sultan to sign a number of decrees, and warned him of the possibility of his deposition.[9]

In 1952, the Sultan again tried to reach an agreement with France, but encountered the usual French immobility. The recent repression, in Tunisia, has had its counterpart in Morocco where the political parties have been dissolved, hundreds have been killed, and thousands thrown in prison—among them many women.

9. *Al-Ahram,* Cairo, March 27, 1951.

The position and the policy of France in North Africa are no longer tenable, neither in relation to the spirit of the time as expressed in the United Nations Charter, nor in their effect upon stability and security in the area. The liberation movements in Algeria, Tunisia, and Morocco cannot be dismissed as local rioting staged by self-seeking leaders or instigated by subversive agents. The nationalist leaders are not "enemies of the worst kind, racial and religious fanatics that are threatening the south flank of Europe," as General Guillaume, Resident-General of Morocco, recently described them.[10] Nor is it true, as an otherwise informed Frenchman says, that the Moslems are at heart full of goodwill towards the French if no one turns their heads, as amply proved by their loyalty during the war.[11] Nor may the French go on denying a national spirit to the North African peoples as the same authority did when, speaking of the 90,000 mountaineers who fought in Tunisia, Italy, and France, he asserted that "no national spirit filled the hearts of these fighters."[12]

The people of North Africa want to be free. Their national struggle is essentially and inherently an expression of their attachment to their own way of life, and of their determination to preserve their culture and retain their identity. Resistance to French domination is not confined to any one section of the population, but has a wide base in the ranks of labor and among the masses.

With the growing sense of Arab solidarity, events in North Africa have vast repercussions throughout the Arab countries. And not only among the Arabs, but among the other peoples of Asia and Africa the struggle for freedom of the North African countries finds sympathy and support. A significant development was the association of the Asiatic and African diplomatic representatives with the Arab States, who met in a North African Conference in Cairo, December, 1952. There they issued a joint statement, expressing their deep sympathy for the peoples of North Africa in their struggle for freedom, and concern about the events in Tunisia and Morocco which resulted in great losses in life and property; calling upon France to settle the North African conflict in accordance with the principles of the United Nations Charter; and warning that should the present state of disturbances continue, future

10. *The Middle East Journal*, Winter 1952, p. 79.

11. Robert Montagne: *International Affairs*, July, 1949, pp. 286–294.

12. Robert Montagne: "Morocco between East and West," *Foreign Affairs*, January, 1948, pp. 360–372.

cooperation between the Asiatic and African states and France may prove impossible. At the United Nations, the delegations of these states, especially India and Pakistan, have forcefully supported the cause of freedom in North Africa.

France relies upon Great Britain and the United States to support her position in North Africa as part of the plan for Mediterranean security and defense against communist expansion. But French misrule in the area creates precisely the conditions in which communism thrives. To the extent to which the United States and Great Britain back up French action in North Africa, they range themselves on the side of imperialism against the liberal forces in Africa and Asia, and contribute to discrediting further the cause of the West in the East. The two great democracies of the West may yet convince the peoples of Asia and Africa that they mean the democracy which they profess. North Africa is a testing ground.

CHAPTER XV

The Arab Woman

THE changes which Arab society is undergoing are reflected in the status of woman whose emancipation has progressed apace and in direct relation to the national liberation and the general social reconstruction.

Western people associate seclusion and the veil with the Arab and Moslem woman. It is seldom realized that side by side with this institution there was a long and well-established tradition of liberty.

This tradition goes back to the Arabian desert before the rise of Islam. In the desert, woman participated fully in the whole structure of society. There were no occupations to which she was limited and none from which she was excluded. She shared the hardships of desert life with her mate and like him developed the qualities of survival in its rugged environment. If she was deprived of the life of ease enjoyed by women in fertile lands and among prosperous communities, she was also spared the penalties of such a life. Here there was no room for the idle; consequently society did not look upon woman as an ornament or an object of luxury and pleasure. With the hardships that she bore she carried the rewards and satisfactions of freedom and personal dignity and worth.

In the open life of the desert a comradeship developed between man and woman unknown in the congested, hemmed-in existence of town life. Man respected woman and protected her even though she was not his kin. Chivalry is a child of the desert. Man went to war with a woman's name on his lips. He strove to earn her favor through brave and noble deeds. She presided at his tournaments and poetical festivals, where her judgments and decisions were duly obeyed.

Poetry, as we have seen, reflected faithfully the desert life. It was the principal form of artistic expression and represented the sum of the community's wisdom and lore as well. Women poets were numerous, and some of them achieved distinction and fame. They participated in the contests at the annual fairs and shared with the poets the festival honors and the admiration of the poetry loving crowds.

Many are the wise women whose advice and counsel men sought and acted upon. There were priestesses also who, in the discharge of their religious functions, enjoyed the reputation of superior knowledge and foresight.

In war, women occasionally took part as fighters; but they were always on the battle fields to give moral support and minister to the wounded. Women gave refuge to the enemy who sought their protection; and such was the chivalry of the desert that the whole tribe extended its protection to the enemy who sought asylum under a woman's tent.

It was not uncommon for the pre-Islamic Arabs to be ruled by queens. The Queen of Sheba has achieved legendary fame for her splendor, and for her love of wisdom which impelled her to make the long journey to Solomon the wise king. Even more celebrated is Zenobia, queen of Palmyra, the caravan city of the Syrian desert. Zenobia made a profound impression on her contemporaries, and later generations surrounded her name with a halo of romance and wonder. For Zenobia was richly endowed with the qualities that evoke admiration and delight. She was of striking beauty with large, black eyes, and teeth as white as pearls. Her intellectual endowments were equally remarkable. She spoke several languages, studied history and philosophy, and wrote a short history of the East and Egypt. With the knowledge of a scholar she combined the qualities of a great general. She rode at the head of her armies in battle and walked for miles with her foot-soldiers. This dazzling queen built a kingdom in the eastern part of the Roman Empire which extended from Egypt to Asia Minor, and for a time challenged and defied the power of Rome herself. Successive Roman armies sent against her were defeated until Aurelian finally defeated her. Zenobia spent her last days in honored captivity in Rome.[1]

With the coming of Islam and the development of a universal civilization, the heritage of the Arab woman was enriched and her horizons expanded on every side.

From the inception of Islam, woman took an active part in upholding and propagating the new faith. The first convert was a

1. Macurdy: *Vassal-Queens*, pp. 111–121.

woman, Khadijah the Prophet's wife. A woman of intelligence,
wealth, and noble birth, she offered her hand to Mohammad when
he was yet an unknown youth. Her wisdom was a constant support to him, and her wealth, which relieved him of the cares of
earning a livelihood, freed him for his vigils and meditations in
preparation for the mission upon which he was presently to be
called. But it was her unfailing devotion which above everything
else gave him the strength and courage to face and triumph over
the approaching spiritual crisis. When doubts assailed him whether
he was really the chosen instrument of God, and his soul and mind
suffered the torments of uncertainty, he took refuge in Khadijah's
steadying devotion; and as she poured her tenderness and sympathy over him, a balm to his spiritual wounds, he was healed, and
reassured he went abroad to proclaim the message of his Lord.
The ninth-century biographer of the Prophet speaks of her: "So
Khadijah believed and attested the truth of that which came to
him from God. Thus was the Lord minded to lighten the burden
of His Prophet; for he heard nothing that grieved him touching
his rejection by the people but he had recourse unto her, and she
comforted, re-assured and supported him."[2]

Women gave Islam their unsparing support. They contributed
their wealth. They defended the faith with their lives when its
followers were subjected to persecution and torture. As the first
convert was a woman, so the first martyr of Islam was a woman
also. Women bore willingly the hardships of exile for their religion.
And, at times, they were the means through whom their menfolk
came to see the light and embrace the faith. Thus Omar, the second caliph and generally considered the second founder of Islam,
was brought to the faith by his sister Fatima.

Islam recognized woman as an independent being and not merely as an appendage to the male. The Moslem law gave her full
legal personality and assured her economic independence; she had
complete power over what she possessed and could dispose of it
freely without the intermediary of a male guardian. She was herself a guardian over minors.

Woman had the freedom to choose her religion. A pagan husband could not keep his wife from embracing the Moslem religion
and joining the community of the faithful if she chose to do so.
Neither could a Moslem husband force Islam upon his wife if she
wished to cling to her paganism.

2. Quoted in Arnold: *The Preaching of Islam,* p. 9.

The Koran speaks of the relationship between man and woman as one of mutual confidence, affection, and compassion.[3] The Prophet enjoined upon the faithful the loving care and kindly treatment of their women. The most perfect among the believers, according to the Hadith, the sayings of the Prophet, are the kindest to their womenfolk.

In the early days of Islam, the status of woman and man's attitude towards her were regulated by the tradition of the desert, the teachings of the Koran, and the Sunna or precedent of the Prophet. In those days women were not secluded or veiled but appeared at public functions in the company of men. Contemporary sources describe a society in which woman moved about freely and fully held her own. The restrictions upon her freedom came in a later age under social and economic influences which were foreign to Arab and early Moslem society. The poetry of the first Moslem century treats woman with romantic respect. Every poet had his beloved to whom he sang in lines of exquisite beauty a chaste and tender love. This romantic love, sung by the early poets of Arabia, in which the beloved was conceived as an unattainable object, found wide acceptance among the Arabs of Spain where it inspired literary products of great refinement and charm. From the Iberian Peninsula, this idealized concept of woman and the form of poetry which expressed it found its way to medieval Europe.

The first century of Islam was the age of Arab expansion, and it evoked acts of individual and group heroism. Numerous accounts are given of women who fought bravely by the side of men.

But the conquests which brought wealth, power, and a world state to the Arabs, also brought evils in their wake. Not least were those which affected woman's life and status. As society grew wealthy and prosperous, men and women became more segregated. Wealth precluded woman from a life of usefulness. In the homes of the rich she was more of an object of ornament than a person of worth. The veil and seclusion were introduced to differentiate the free woman from the slave girl who was exposed in the market to the public gaze. Men thought they were honoring the free woman by confining her to the home while the slave moved in and out among the men. This classification of women into free and slave harmed the free woman no less than the slave, for thereby the relationship between man and woman suffered and

3. *Koran,* 30:21.

in time seclusion degenerated into a form of enslavement of the
free woman herself. Fortunately the classes which could afford to
keep idle women and slaves were small, and generally restricted
to the city dwellers. The majority of women in the country, among
the peasants and the bedouin tribes, went about their work un-
veiled and free.

The Moslem religion gave an incentive to learning, and Moslem
society provided ample opportunities for study. Learning was not
confined to men. A saying attributed to the Prophet makes the
acquisition of knowledge a duty required of every Moslem, man
and woman. A large number of women distinguished themselves
as scholars, especially in religious studies. In the science of Hadith,
women's knowledge was highly thought of, and women were considered important links in the chains of authorities transmitting
the sayings of the Prophet. One of the prominent traditionists is
Aisha, the Prophet's wife whose knowledge and talents were widely recognized and held in high esteem. She was often sought out
by learned men who consulted her on questions of theology and
law.

Women lectured in the university-mosques where famous men
attended their lectures and received from them certificates or li-
censes to teach the courses which they had attended.

One of the most celebrated women was Shuhda, surnamed the
"Glory of Women," and the "Woman Scribe," for her extensive
reputation of learning, and for the beautiful hand she wrote. She
lived in Baghdad during the 12th century and was ranked among
the foremost scholars of the age. Her teachers were the leading
authorities of the time, and in turn she instructed large numbers
of students.[4]

A contemporary of Shuhda, Zainab of Naisapur, received certificates to teach from a number of eminent men. Among her students was her biographer, Ibn Khallikan, author of the celebrated
biographical dictionary in Arabic literature which is "one of the
most important works of its kind in world literature."[5]

The traveler Ibn Batuta, passing through Syria in 1326, attended
the lectures of two women in Damascus and received from them
permission to teach. One of them was known as the "goal of everyone's journey," presumably for her great learning and wide fame.[6]

4. Ibn Khallikan, translation, vol. I, pp. 625–6.
5. *Ibid.*, p. 551; Sarton: *Introduction to the History of Science*, II, 1120.
6. Ibn Batuta, ed. Defremery, I, 253–4.

In the spiritual life, women rose to the highest ranks. Moslem hagiography is full of the names of women saints. Women achieved complete equality with men as "friends of God." Men saints often sat at the feet of saintly women and accepted them humbly as guides in the religious life.

Foremost among the women saints is Rabi'a Al-Adawiyeh who lived in Basra in the 8th century. Her life was one of complete renunciation of the world, and of consecration to God. Yet it was not a withdrawal from the world, for she had many disciples and companions who gathered to seek her guidance and hear her preach. An important part of her life was teaching others what she had learned along the Way which leads to divine knowledge and fellowship with God. Rabi'a is ranked among the greatest Sufis (Moslem mystics). Sufi writers hold her in reverence and quote her sayings as highest authority on the spiritual life.[7]

Among the Sufis, men and women were united in a spiritual comradeship. To the Sufi, the wife was a companion in God, and his love for her was part of his love for God. In the poetry and legends of the Sufis, the beloved was idealized as the symbol of Divine Wisdom, through whom God inspired the lover with all that was noble and good.[8]

Since Islam is a religion of good works, Moslems fulfilled the requirements of their faith in the measure that they helped their fellowmen. Pious women gave generously of their means to charitable foundations and to establishments of public welfare. The outstanding example of munificence is Zubaida, wife of the Caliph Harun al-Rashid, who undertook an extensive project of waterworks for Mecca and built wells and cisterns along the nine-hundred-mile pilgrim road from Iraq to Hijaz. Zubaida's good works for the pilgrims of Islam and the dwellers in its holy city have assured her an honored place in the Moslem hall of fame, and have earned for her the loving gratitude of the multitudes of pilgrims who call upon God to bless Zubaida every time they refresh themselves at her springs.[9]

Women rulers are almost unknown in Moslem history, but not infrequently women wielded considerable power behind the throne. Histories abound in accounts of women of strong character and

7. Margaret Smith: *Rabi'a the Mystic and Her Fellow-Saints in Islam*, pp. 19, 47.

8. Asin, *op. cit.*, p. 273.

9. Nabia Abbott: *Two Queens of Baghdad*, pp. 240 ff.

intelligence who influenced the lives and actions of their men folk, and through them the course of public affairs.

The status of the Arab woman has generally reflected the conditions of her society. When Arab society was productive, creative woman participated in its activities and shared in the general strength and well-being. When vitality ebbed away and deterioration set in, woman suffered along with her community. With the stirrings of new life in the Arab world she regained a consciousness of her heritage and came to realize the needs and demands of the modern world. Today she is participating in the building of a modern Arab society.

The need for educating woman and preparing her to assume her responsibilities in the community was recognized by the leaders of the reform movement in the 19th century. Afghani, the dynamic spirit of the reform, believed that woman was endowed with the same intellectual constitution as man but was handicapped by her upbringing. While he recognized the equality of her natural endowments with man's, Afghani did not think it desirable or sound to seek equality between man and woman in every way. For, he said, woman's mission as a homemaker to whom the upbringing of a new generation is entrusted is far superior to many of the occupations pursued by man. Mohammad Abdu, Afghani's disciple and an able and indefatigable reformer, was mindful of the necessity of educating woman and improving her condition as an essential requirement in a scheme of social regeneration.

A distinguished disciple of Mohammad Abdu, Kasim Amin, took up the cause of woman with courage and devotion. In two books, *The Emancipation of Woman* and *The New Woman,* published in Cairo at the end of the 19th century, he described the status of woman, analyzed the causes of her condition, and prescribed the remedy which, by curing the particular ills from which woman suffered, would relieve at the same time the ailments which afflicted society as a whole.

Kasim Amin was a social reformer of rare courage and sincerity. His love for his country found expression in a life dedicated to eliminating the sorrows and waste that grow from injustice and ignorance. Like two other social reformers of his time—Abd-al-Rahman al-Kawakibi and Wali-ed-Din Yagan, both sensitive and outspoken critics of their society—Kasim Amin traced the social ills to tyranny in all its forms. When tyranny strikes a nation, he said, it proceeds from the ruler downwards, infecting all classes and poisoning all relations. The stronger becomes a tyrant to the weaker. Man is a tyrant to woman, and his tyranny is responsible for her degraded state. In his arrogance and egotism, man crushed woman's personality and left her ignorant and weak. As a result he had no respect for her, neither had woman confidence in man. Both suffered from this wretched relationship, man's loss being no less real and tragic than woman's. For, says Kasim Amin: "Is there any happiness for a man who has not by his side a woman to whom he can give his life, who by her own excellence holds up before his eyes perfection as a goal, so that he admires her, desires her approval, seeks her favor by noble actions, and approaches her with the attributes of a fine character?"

Kasim Amin strongly advocated woman's education. He even believed that the education of girls should take precedence over that of the boys because the education of the whole nation depended upon woman. He proposed the then novel idea that woman should be educated for herself, so that she may complete her personality, and enter society as a fully developed and independent individual. Marriage, he wrote, was a comradeship and friendship made strong and perfect through intellectual equality and spiritual harmony between man and woman. He advocated the gradual elimination of the veil and the training of women to earn their living instead of being dependent upon their male relatives.

Kasim Amin's defense of woman at first brought a storm of anger upon his head. Such were the cobwebs that had accumulated through the centuries that the reforms which he advocated were considered ungodly innovations. Notwithstanding the protest which they roused, his ideas met with a warm reception among the more thoughtful and sensitive spirits. Foremost among Kasim Amin's supporters and sympathizers was his friend, the national leader Sa'd Zaghlul, to whom he dedicated *The New Woman*. Another friend, the well-known author and educator Lutfi al-Sayyid, opened the columns of his paper *Al-Jarida* to him, to publish what he wished on the question of woman and other social problems. With supporters and opponents arguing vehemently over Kasim Amin's books, the cause of woman received wide publicity and the movement for her emancipation was set afoot.

Kasim Amin's books on the emancipation of woman have been widely read in the Arab countries, and are known in the West through translation. In 1912, Kratchkowsky translated *The New Woman* into Russian, and in 1928 a German translation of *The Emancipation of Woman* was published.

Some of the reforms which Kasim Amin espoused with eagerness and hope have been outgrown; but his books will always live in the simple beauty of their style and their intense sensitivity to injustice.

The liberation of woman found forceful champions in Iraq. Iraq was removed from the influence of western ideas and did not experience the political, intellectual, and social reform movement which stirred Egypt during the 19th and the early years of the 20th century, and of which the trend towards the emancipation of woman was a phase; yet the writers and social critics of Iraq were even more outspoken than their Egyptian contemporaries in denouncing the evils which enveloped woman's existence, and the bonds which kept her down.

The two outstanding poets of Iraq, Rasafi and Zahawi, vigorously attacked oppression and injustice in every form, including the restrictions imposed upon women. Both urged the need for woman's education. Rasafi attributed the subjection of the peoples of the East to their upbringing by downtrodden women. Zahawi, in an incisive poem on the veil, called for a social revolution expressed by woman discarding and burning her veil, which has ever been but a false protection and is a social malady and disgrace.

It was natural that men took the lead in calling for the emancipation of woman, since women were on the whole too ignorant and subdued to initiate such a movement. Towards the end of the 19th century, however, a few women's magazines appeared and a number of women began to write on social problems and matters related to women. In the early part of this century, the two outstanding women writers were Malak Hifni Nasif who wrote under the pen-name of Bahithat-al-Badia, and Marie Ziadeh known by the pen-name May.

Bahithat-al-Badia, an intelligent and keen observer of society, communicated her observations in a persuasive and graceful style. A sharp critic of contemporary Egyptian life, she dedicated poetry and prose to social reform. Fired with enthusiasm and righteous indignation, she spares neither man nor woman. Her heart broke, so she wrote, at the sight of this corrupt society. Woman was ignorant and idle. Her life was given to superficiality and extravagance. Having no confidence in herself she had none in her husband, relations with whom were tormented by jealousy, selfishness, and anger. Man for his part had little respect for woman; his treatment of her was an expression of his egotism and tyranny. Men should begin by reforming themselves if they wished to see their women, their homes, and their nation regenerated. For, she asks, how can men continue in their despotic ways and hope at the same time to raise children imbued with the love of freedom and liberty? To Bahithat-al-Badia, as to all other reformers, education was a cornerstone in any plan for social reformation. She believed that elementary education should be made compulsory for all classes of the population, and that girls should have the freedom to follow an academic course. Priority in the opportunities for education should be given to woman because she is more ignorant than man. Only if woman is free can her children be brought up in freedom.

Bahithat-al-Badia exempts from her general denunciation life among the peasants and bedouin tribes where woman is man's companion in toil and rest. She admires the pride of the peasant woman, her strength of character and seriousness, and contrasts her vitality and usefulness with the pampered existence of women among the idle class of city-dwellers. Hence, she concludes, the peasant stock, healthy, independent, and hard-working, has given Egypt its greatest men.

May was a talented writer and linguist. Besides Arabic, of which she was the master, she knew several European languages and was at home in their literatures. Her extensive reading influenced her style, which is smooth, elegant, and cultured. In all her writings she strove for renewal, both literary and social. Her concern for women's problems is reflected in her active participation in the women's movement as well as in her writings. Among her works are studies of other women writers: Warda al-Yazigi, a poetess of the famous Lebanese family of poets who in the 19th century rendered outstanding service to the revival of the Arabic language and culture; Aisha al-Taimuriya, a member of the celebrated Taimur family of scholars, poets, and playwrights, herself a distinguished poetess of the second half of the 19th century whose poetry compares favorably with the products of contemporary poets; and Bahithat-al-Badia for whom May had a great admiration.

An organized women's movement came into being soon after the first World War. The struggle for national freedom gave women the opportunity to emerge from their homes and take part in public affairs. In the Egyptian revolution of 1919, women appeared for the first time in large processions on the streets. There was nothing timid or shy about this first appearance. Women demonstrated carrying flags, denouncing the Protectorate, and acclaiming the nation's independence. Women helped in building barricades, joined with the men in destroying communications, and picketed government buildings to keep officials away. They held a mass meeting in the Coptic Cathedral in protest against Milner's Commission of Investigation (the choice of a church as the place of meeting is indicative of the union of Christians and Moslems in the common cause). When the resistance entered the stage of non-cooperation and boycott of British goods, the organizers of the campaign announced that its success depended in large measure upon the participation of women. The wife of the national leader Sa'd Zaghlul was a worthy companion of her great husband. She stood staunchly by him, giving him great moral support. When at the beginning of the struggle with the British, Sa'd came to his wife, Safia, saying: "I have placed my head on my hand," she readily said: "Then place mine on your other hand." During Sa'd's exile, messages reached her of his failing health and friends urged her to beg him to come back. To their pleadings she answered: "If Sa'd's exile benefits the cause, then it is my desire that he should remain in exile." Safia, known as the "Mother of the Egyptians," became a highly revered national figure herself. During her husband's absence in exile she kept her home open to delegations and meetings which she addressed with striking dignity and forcefulness. Even after her husband's death she remained a central figure in the political life of Egypt. Political leaders of various party affiliations held her in esteem and respected her counsels.

In the Arab countries, the customs and conditions relating to women did not undergo sudden changes as they did in Turkey and Persia. The change has been gradual but none the less real. Although no authority has ordered women to discard the veil on a certain date, women are dropping their veils fast as they hurry on their way to schools and colleges, clinics, offices, and public meetings.

The progress in women's education has been one of the most constructive developments within Arab society during the past thirty years. In all of the independent Arab countries—with the exception of Saudi Arabia and Yaman—the education of girls has steadily expanded. The steps already taken are best described by giving a few statistics.

In Egypt, there were 24,316 girls in the government schools in 1921–22. The bulk of these were in the elementary schools. Only 43 girls attended secondary schools, and 653 received teachers training. Higher education was then unavailable to women.

Within less than thirty years—in 1949–50—the number of girls registered in government and state subsidized private schools reached 527,008, an increase of over twentyfold. And they were no longer confined to the elementary stage of education but attended every variety of educational institution, from the kindergarten through the post-university institutes. The secondary schools enrolled 19,511, the vocational schools 9,940, while 3,751 were in teachers training. In line with the policy of diversifying education on the secondary level, a number of technical and vocational schools for girls were established. There are Social Service Schools, an Institute of Domestic Science, Agricultural Schools where rural girls are trained in dairying and agricultural industry, Schools for Commerce, and schools where needlework, embroidery and dressmaking are taught preparing girls to set up their own independent business and workshops.

Art education is provided in a well-staffed and well-equipped Institute of Women Teachers of the Arts, and in the coeducational Higher School of Fine Arts. The School of Dramatic Art is coeducational also.

Health and physical education receive due emphasis in all the girls schools. The Girl Guide Movement has a membership of over 15,000. The girls are trained in sports and outdoor life, set up camps in various parts of Egypt, and go on long tramping tours through the country.

Higher education which was not open to women until 1927 has since then been given to thousands of women. In 1949–50, there were 2,460 women in universities, post-university institutes, and other institutions of higher learning. All the Egyptian universities are open to women with the exception of Al-Azhar. But since women attended Al-Azhar hundreds of years ago, it is not likely that the modern Arab woman will continue to be debarred from a privilege which she enjoyed in the Middle Ages.

In Iraq, women's education started from nothing after the first World War. In 1922, there was only one elementary school for girls, attended by 160 pupils. Until 1924–25 there was no trace of secondary education for girls. But girls' education was launched with so much enthusiasm, and met with such eager response, that when the Monroe Educational Commission visited Iraq in 1931 it could report: "No feature of the educational situation offered more surprise to the members of the Commission than the very genuine interest that everywhere appeared in the education of girls and women."[10] Further on, the Commission reports that the increasing interest in the education of girls and women in Iraq is one of the prominent and most hopeful signs in the educational life of the country, as it is evidence of a progressive outlook.[11]

Today, thousands of Iraqi girls attend school and college. In 1949–50 there were 44,371 girls in government primary and secondary schools, and 466 were being trained to teach in schools below the secondary level. In the same year, 866 young women were receiving higher education. Of these, 667 attended the Higher Teachers Training College, a coeducational institution, and Queen Alia College, for women teachers, while the remaining two hundred were distributed among the Colleges of Law, Medicine, Dentistry, and Pharmacy, Arts and Sciences, Commerce and Economy, and Engineering. A striking illustration of the sudden change from one generation to the other is provided by the presence of an illiterate mother with a daughter who has gone through all the stages of education and come out with a university degree. Another example worth recording, rare in any country, is the case of five sisters, all of whom have completed an academic education and are now following professional careers in medicine, pharmacy, law, engineering, and teaching.

The trend towards organized group work and the growth of social consciousness evident in Arab society are reflected in the number and scope of women's organizations. Since state and municipal relief is either absent or, where it does exist in the Arab countries, is still in its initial stages, the bulk of relief and social work has been handled by private organizations. Women's societies, sometimes with government help, have been attending to the alleviation of poverty and other social problems. Women's branches of the Red Crescent and the Red Cross are organized along similar lines and serve the same purpose as their counterparts in Western society. Women finance and run clinics, dispen-

10. Paul Monroe: *Report of the Educational Inquiry Commission*, Baghdad, Government Press, 1932, p. 56.

11. *Ibid.*, p. 130.

saries, and milk centers for undernourished children, and nurseries and kindergartens for children who otherwise would be on the streets while their mothers are at work. Women's organizations cooperate with the governments in making labor laws and other social legislation, in prison reform and the improvement of prisoners' conditions, in fighting juvenile delinquency and saving youth from lapsing into crime, and in the establishment of orphanages, asylums, and free hospitals.

Many are the women's organizations which are doing good and much needed work. An example of an efficiently run Egyptian organization is the Women's Society for the Improvement of Health, managed by a group of capable women who are doing a serious and sound job with little publicity. The society works with consumptive patients and their families. Wherever it is possible, the patient is hospitalized; otherwise, he is given proper nourishment, medicine, and medical care. Upon recovery, the society helps to reestablish him in his previous work or find a suitable job for him. In the meantime his dependents are taken care of. The mother is given a paid job, often as seamstress, to help support the family during the father's illness. But the most hopeful and fruitful work is done with the children for whom a settlement has been established at the foot of the Pyramids, in cheerful surroundings with neat dormitories, a nursery for the infants, large playgrounds, and flower-beds ablaze with colors. The children's health is adequately taken care of with proper diet, training in cleanliness, and ample opportunity for outdoor games. Four hundred children are housed in the settlement; they attend the settlement's primary school, financed and staffed by the Ministry of Education. The school, besides offering the regular program of studies, gives due attention to handicrafts, carpentry, weaving, and needlework. Nor are the children left stranded when it is time for them to leave the settlement; they are guided and helped in finding employment which ensures them of an adequate livelihood.

Organized social work has necessitated social studies based upon field investigations. Some of the women's organizations conduct careful case work before they make the benefits of their institution available to applicants. Women have participated in an interesting study, the first of its kind, of social conditions among the inhabitants of Alexandria. The study is co-edited by a woman, and women were represented in equal number with the men on the staff of investigators.

Women have entered all the professions and are practising with success medicine, law, journalism. But education is their main field. Thousands of women teach in the expanding educational systems of the Arab countries. A number of successful private schools have been founded, and are managed, by women. And women, individually or through organizations, have joined the campaign for adult education.

Women have been interested in the preservation and revival of native arts and crafts. Beautiful specimens of needlework, tapestry, and other handcrafts are exhibited and sold in the "artisanat" established by a group of women in Beirut who employ scores of village women, providing them with a living and at the same time keeping alive the tradition of fine workmanship. In Egypt, the feminist leader Huda Sharawi included among her many interests and activities the establishment of a pottery factory. She sent young Egyptians to Europe at her expense, to study design and the potter's craft in order to revive the ancient Egyptian and Arab styles in the ceramic arts.

In the cinema industry, women have taken a pioneering part. One of the earliest Egyptian companies, Isis Film, was founded and financed by a woman who was at the same time both producer and leading actress in the firm. Likewise today, one of the largest and best known of the theater companies in the region belongs to an actress who has toured almost all the Arab countries with her troupe.

The franchise has been granted to women in Syria and Lebanon. In Syria the franchise was limited to women with at least a primary education. Syrian women went to the polls for the first time in the fall of 1949. With the enthusiasm for a newly acquired right, a higher percentage of women voted than men. Observers agreed that women conducted themselves with dignity and a sense of responsibility at their first experience of political liberty. In Lebanon, suffrage has been extended to all women without restriction.

What the Arab woman has been able to do in public life, although she was debarred from political suffrage, was demonstrated in the life of Sitt Nazira Jumblatt whose death in the spring of 1951 called forth a genuine and unanimous tribute to her greatness. Her funeral, attended by tens of thousands of people gathered from all over the Lebanon mountains and from the cities of the coast, was a spontaneous popular expression of the respect and affection in which she was held by all sections of the population.

Nazira Jumblatt, the Lady of al-Mukhtara, came from a prominent Druze family whose fortunes were closely associated with the recent history of Lebanon. Her husband's early death left her with two infants to bring up, a large estate to administer, and a family name and prestige to uphold. She rose nobly to the task.

She symbolized leadership at its best in a society where personal loyalties and relationships still count for much. She kept close to the people, all kinds of people, and all communities alike. All day and into the night she sat listening patiently to people's troubles and complaints and tactfully smoothed out their difficulties. The family residence, an impressive castle, became the refuge of the oppressed and an unofficial tribunal where conflicts and feuds were peacefully settled under the wise guidance of the Grand Lady, without recourse to the expensive, drawn-out proceedings of official litigation. Hospitality was there, always, in the best tradition of gentle-folk. Though she had no official capacity herself, her influence was always reckoned with in the determination of state policy. Her counsel was sought by prominent men, and her will obeyed by those in authority. Her tremendous influence, both among the people and in official circles, was wielded for the public good, the promotion of peaceful relations among people, and the strengthening of the bonds which united the various communities to each other and to their country.

The death of Sitt Nazira marks the end of an age, the age of benevolent feudalism. But the sense of social responsibility which characterized that era at its best has returned in a new form and with renewed vigor in Kamal Jumblatt, young heir of the distinguished house and son of the great lady. Kamal has founded and is leading the Progressive Socialist Party to combat the remnants of a decadent feudalism and break the ground for a new age of social justice, liberty, and security.

In most of the Arab countries secular laws regulate people's actions, excepting personal relations—inheritance, marriage, and divorce—which remain under the jurisdiction of the religious laws. The Moslem law, while it gave women rights and privileges unknown in Western society until very recent times, nevertheless gave men a higher status. With regard to inheritance woman receives half the share of man, although it is true that man is bound to support his family and dependents with his share. Marriage and divorce laws are more favorable to man than to woman. Even though anything may be written into the marriage contract to strengthen the woman's position and safeguard her rights—such as, for example, a clause preventing the man from marrying another woman, giving the wife the right to seek divorce, or securing for her adequate alimony in case of divorce—yet, on the whole, in marriage and divorce man has had the upper hand. So far, no attempts have been made to remove matters related to personal status from the domain of religious law and place them, along with other relationships, under the authority of the secular law. There is, however, increasing criticism of present conditions, and a growing demand for the full equality of woman. A Tunisian socialist, Tahir al-Haddad, has written an outspoken book, *Our Woman in the Religious Law and in Society,* in which he forcefully advocates the improvement of woman's condition and affirms that the spirit of the law and its ultimate end are more important than its particular prescriptions; therefore, the religious laws should not be taken as final and unalterable, but should evolve with the needs of the time.[12] Tunisia has the beginning of a feminist movement, nationalistically oriented.

Whatever her legal or political status, the Arab woman has been a greater force in her society than is generally recognized, and continues to exert a more powerful influence than is apparent to the casual observer.

Her power derives from the close integration of Arab society and the importance of the family in Arab life. The family is the basic social unit throughout all Arab countries and includes not only the members of the immediate family in the Western sense but a much wider group of relations. The individual is at all times part of this enlarged family circle; in it he finds security and self-fulfillment, and to it he brings his devotion and loyalty. Within the family, each member, according to his age and status, has a secure place and definite duties and obligations. Woman's responsibilities begin when as a girl she cares for the younger children and is generally useful around the house. As wife and mother she assumes the many cares in the management of the household, the upbringing of the children, and the integration of the family with the larger social background. As grandmother she is respected and valued for the experience and wisdom which are associated with, and generally accompany, age among the peoples of the East.

Integrated in the family where at all stages of her life she has

12. H. A. R. Gibb: *Modern Trends in Islam,* p. 93; Rudi Paret: *Zur Frauenfrage in der Arabisch-Islamischen Welt,* p. 18.

essential tasks, woman feels secure in her usefulness and derives power and importance from the broad responsibilities and fundamental functions she performs. Consequently, Arab women are, on the whole, at peace with their society and in harmony with their environment; drifting, uprooted, and neurotic women are practically unknown among them.

It is sometimes said that the Arab woman, always considered in relation to others, has little personality or individuality. The contrary is the truth. Living for others as she does, the Arab woman has achieved the strength and force of character which come from rising above self and projecting one's life into other lives. Such a concept of self-fulfillment through others has banished restlessness and frustration from her life and given her dignity, serenity, and poise.

The absence of a mechanized existence, her close fellowship with people, and her intimate association with nature, particularly among the peasant class who form the backbone of the population, have endowed her with wisdom and discernment and a great capacity for human understanding. Her own position in the family and the place of the family in the larger society have made her the custodian of the family tradition and the repository of the culture and wisdom of the group. She may be, and often is, illiterate, but the tradition of a civilization many thousand years old has given her the stamp of culture and good breeding.

And so it is that as new freedoms and opportunities come her way, the Arab woman takes them in her stride. The broad responsibilities of family and group life have trained her for the wider social activities which she is now called to undertake, and the heritage of a rich and mature civilization has prepared her for the increased power which comes with greater knowledge and learning.

The Arab world today is astir with great ideals and hopes, and women and men are working together for their realization.

CHAPTER XVI

Towards Arab Unity

I T IS NOT impertinent to ask how Arabs or anyone else can speak of Arab unity when the Palestine debacle, a miserable show of utter discord among the Arab states, is so fresh in people's minds. Even if one were to forget for a moment the Palestine tragedy—the apparent differences within Arab society, the dissensions in Arab political circles, and the rivalries of the rulers give the impression that Arab unity, if not wholly unreal, is still very far off.

And yet in the midst of dissension and discord the voice of Arab unity is clearly and forcefully heard, and the ideal of recreating a united Arab nation is one of the real forces which contend for the allegiance of the Arab peoples, an inspiration and a message of hope to a large section of the nation's youth and other representatives of articulate public opinion.

What, then, are the elements of reality in this idea which seems a dream so difficult to realize?

Unity is the basic underlying norm in the life of the Arab peoples; their division into separate entities is a transient phase of recent intrusion. The similarity of climatic conditions in the Arab countries with their long, dry summers, and the scarcity of water in the midst of the enveloping aridity, have made for similarities in the social structure, the structure of a peasant society practising dry farming, and irrigating the soil by flood in the favored regions near rivers and springs.

The continuity of civilization has also made for a unity of outlook. In a town like Jebeil, on the Lebanon coast, the history of man is represented in an unbroken line from the cave to the present day. In the tells—mounds—excavated all over Syria, Mesopotamia, and Egypt, the successive covers piled one on top of the other testify to the remote origin and continuity of human effort in this region. Beliefs and practices, which can be traced to pre-Islamic and even pre-Christian origins, are still current among the people, and form part of a folk culture shared alike by the various communities irrespective of their religious affiliations.

The unity of civilization is further expressed in the organization of the family which is essentially the same whatever the religious background of the community. Solidarity is the basic characteristic of the family in Arab society. The family in which the individual finds security and self-fulfillment has the first right upon his loyalty and devotion. The stability of family life and the strength of its bonds have been a stabilizing force in Arab society.

A great unifying force is supplied by Islam, which is not only a religion but a culture and a way of life as well. Strong as the religious bond is, the unifying power of Islam comes not only from adherence to a common faith, but perhaps even more from the common social structure and way of life which it enjoins. It should also be remembered that the Moslem religion and its Holy Book, the Koran, have saved the Arabic language from disintegrating into a variety of local dialects, and thus have preserved unity of thought and expression. In this sense Islam belongs not only to the Moslems but is the heritage of the Christian Arabs as well.

The Arabic language is one of the strongest bonds which hold the Arabs together. Arabic is the mother tongue of all the people[1] living in the countries from Morocco to Iraq. Though the local dialects vary, the classical form is one, and even the dialects are easily understood and spoken by the inhabitants of the various localities. A deep attachment to the Arabic language is characteristic of all Arabs, learned and simple. All have a love almost mystical for their language whose beauty and rhythm stir them deeply. The modern Arab renaissance began with the revival of classical Arabic. A newly Arabicized leader, Ibrahim Pasha, placed the confines of the Arab countries at the limits where the Arabic language was spoken. When during his campaign, which aimed at the detachment of the Arab provinces from the Ottoman Empire, Ibrahim Pasha was asked how far he intended to carry his conquests, he answered, "As far as the Arabic language is spoken and as I can communicate with the people in that tongue."

The culture of which Arabic is the medium of expression is the common heritage of all Arabs. The memories of the Caliphate with its power and splendor are real even though centuries of fragmentation have intervened. This cultural, historical consciousness is not confined to the intellectuals, though naturally their awareness

1. The few exceptions are noted below.

is more articulate. It is shared in a real sense by the simple peasant and the illiterate nomad who, despite their lack of formal learning, are aware of and attached to this heritage which finds expression in their folklore and heroic tales.

The loss of political unity early in Arab history did not affect the basic unity of Arab culture and society when the political life after the first Moslem century became remote and unreal. The states into which the Arab Empire broke up had no relationship to the people; they were the affairs of the ruling families. Successive dynasties of various origins came and went, leaving no trace on the life of the people who were generally unaware of their rise and fall except when these events led to war and chaos.

The political break-up which followed the Golden Age of the Abbasids was healed when the Ottoman Turks extended their hegemony over the Arab lands. For four hundred years, from 1516 to 1918, the Arab countries formed part of one political system, the Ottoman Empire.

An attempt to recreate the Arab nation as a political entity independent of the Turks was made by Mohammad Ali who during the first half of the 19th century undertook to liberate the Arab provinces from Turkish rule. The attempt failed, partly because the Arabs were not ready. Nationalism, a 19th century western product, had not yet permeated Arab society. While the Arabs felt themselves a nation apart from the Turks, they were not yet prepared to take concerted action against the Turks in the name of Arab nationalism. But they readily rose in sporadic and scattered revolts against the vexations of Turkish rule. These local uprisings were motivated by a desire to be left unmolested by outside controls. They sought freedom for a clan or a community within a circumscribed region. The urge for freedom did not embrace the nation as a whole. Moreover, the movement lacked genuine, native leadership. Muhammad Ali's plan to set up an independent Arab state was motivated primarily by personal ambition, the desire to carve for himself and his heirs a kingdom out of the Ottoman Empire. Although his son Ibrahim spoke of himself as an Arab, and was enthusiastic about the qualities of the Arab people and the glories of their civilization, yet both he and his father remained largely outside the main stream of Arab life. It should also be remembered that the obstruction of the Powers—especially England, who intervened to save the Ottoman Empire from dismemberment and to preserve the status quo in the eastern Mediterranean—was in large measure responsible for the failure. Nevertheless, the currents set in motion by Muhammad Ali and Ibrahim—the defeat of the Turks by Arab armies, the new ideas that accompanied the march of the soldiers, the independence of Egypt from Turkish rule, the renewal of intellectual life stimulated by political independence, and increasing cultural contacts with Europe—caused a stir in Arab society and provided a stimulus and foundation for future work.

The Arab Revolt, led by the Sharif of Mecca during the first World War, aimed at the creation of one independent state out of the Arab provinces in Asia. The leader had the prestige of his noble birth—descent from the Prophet—and of his position as guardian of the Holy Cities, but he lacked the vision and the qualities of leadership necessary to call forth a united and coherent movement.

The Revolt did not achieve its goal. As in the case of Muhammad Ali's attempt, the failure was due to internal conditions and to the pressure of forces from the outside. Internally, the movement suffered from two serious weaknesses. In the first place, the articulate and more enlightened classes were divided in counsel. Some highly respected leaders and thoughtful men, while they denounced the ills of Turkish rule, were yet unwilling to join a movement which sought to break away from the Ottoman Community—especially when they sensed the presence of elements who were motivated to join the Arab movement not so much by genuine Arab feelings and concern for the cause of Arab freedom as by foreign leanings and affiliations. They feared that once the Ottoman bond was broken the Arabs would pass under the domination of the West. Secondly, the people as a whole were unprepared and inarticulate. The movement had not yet penetrated into their consciousness but hovered on the fringes of their life.

Still, major blame for the unsuccessful outcome of the Arab Revolt, and the consequent retardation of the process of Arab unity must be laid at the door of Great Britain and France who parcelled out between them the Arab lands of the eastern Mediterranean, reduced Syria to a number of petty states, and sponsored the Zionist scheme in Palestine.

The post-World War I settlement did not only put obstacles in the path of political unity; it shattered the economic structure which was one for the entire region, by introducing large groups whose cultural background was foreign and whose presence tended to impair the cultural unity of the area.

National states, dependent in varying degrees upon the Mandatory Power, were set up under different forms of government. Their citizens were called Iraqis, Syrians, Lebanese, Palestinians; before the war they had all been known as Arabs. Then, they had moved freely throughout the Arab provinces of the Ottoman Empire, settled where fancy or interest took them, and felt equally at home in Baghdad, Jerusalem, Damascus, or Beirut. Now the citizens of one state were regarded as aliens in the other. The economic separation —except between Syria and Lebanon—was as complete as between entirely foreign countries, with customs, tariffs, and a variety of currencies. Before the war, goods and commodities had traveled as freely as people, and were paid for in one currency, a stable gold coin. The economic barriers created after the war, the difficulties of exchange, and currency fluctuation and depreciation especially of the French franc, resulted in the dislocation of trade and caused economic crises and impoverishment. From the point of view of Arab unity, political, economic, and cultural, the postwar settlement forced upon the Arabs by Great Britain and France was definitely a retrogression from the conditions in existence under the Turks.

The dependent states which emerged from the post-war settlement followed separate paths during the period between the two world wars, each preoccupied with its own local problems and with the struggle to free itself from the foreign power in control. In the process, local nationalisms were born and fostered that for a time seemed to supplant the larger Arab idea. But even in their separate existence, the various Arab states were bound to be drawn together by a number of forces working within their society or coming from the outside. The struggle for independence itself, though carried on locally, was a unifying force. The public systems of education established in this period strengthened the feeling of Arab solidarity by stressing the teaching of Arabic language, history, and civilization, and by disseminating education among the mass of the people, and developing a greater awareness of national issues and a deeper sense of public responsibility. Modern communications, physical and intellectual, drew the Arabs closer together. Distances contracted before the motorcar and airplane. The radio and the press reached remote villages and out of the way places, and informed increasingly large numbers of people. The gradual diffusion of a simplified classical Arabic, understood by the average man all the way from Morocco to Iraq, was another unifying element. Above all, the idea of a united Arab nation was far more inspiring and satisfying than any local nationalism could be, and was therefore embraced with greater enthusiasm especially by the younger generation.

During this period, a definite trend towards closer relationship and cooperation between the Arab states can be discerned. On the non-official level the trend took the form of cultural activities and the convening of a number of inter-Arab conferences. Some of these were meetings of professional groups. Others were convened for the purpose of dealing with the political situation in the Arab countries and especially the fate of Palestine. Even the first Arab Women's Congress ever held was given up wholly to the Palestine question.

On the official level, the trend expressed itself in the form of treaties of friendship and good neighborliness concluded between several Arab states. A series of agreements settling boundary disputes was reached between Saudi Arabia on the one hand and Iraq, Transjordan, and Yaman on the other. A Treaty of Arab Brotherhood and Alliance was signed in April 1936 between Iraq and Saudi Arabia. It expressed the need for cooperation and mutual understanding, arranged for the peaceful settlement of all differences, and provided for the exchange of cultural and military missions. Adherence to this Treaty, which Yaman joined in the following year, was open to any independent Arab state.[2] In May 1936, Ibn Saud and Egypt became parties to a treaty which settled their differences.

Another document of interest and significance is the Treaty of Taif, signed in May 1934, which ended the hostilities between Saudi Arabia and Yaman. It will be recalled that the war ended in a complete victory for the Saudi forces over the Yamanites. Yet nowhere in the treaty is there a touch of accusation or revenge or even triumph. On the contrary, the treaty is conceived in a generous, conciliatory spirit, as between two partners and equals. Extracts of its terms deserve to be quoted:

The two Parties "call upon God to witness their good intentions and their desire for harmony and agreement both openly and in secret, and call upon His Glorious and Holy Name to assist them, their heirs and successors, and their governments, to pursue this upright conduct, which enjoys the approval of the Creator and is endowed with the force of their two peoples and their religions."

2. *Documents on International Affairs,* 1937, pp. 522–526.

They undertake to refrain from resort to force, and endeavor to solve their differences by friendly consultation. They agree to proclaim full general amnesty for all offenses and hostile actions committed by the subjects of one party residing in the territory of the other. They proclaim their desire to do everything possible to facilitate communication, promote the exchange of goods, negotiate a customs agreement, and in every way increase the contacts between them. Where both maintain representatives, these shall consult and unify their policy in the interests of their two countries which are as a single nation. "The Two High Contracting Parties, bound by ties of Islamic brotherhood and of the Arab race, proclaim that their two nations are a single nation, that they desire ill to no one, that they will strive to further the affairs of their nations in peace and tranquility, and that they will make every effort in all circumstances to operate for the benefit of their two countries and their nations, at the same time entertaining no hostile intentions towards any other nation."[3]

Saudi Arabia and Yaman were not members of the League of Nations. They were as little affected by the influence of modern Western civilization as any two states could be. Yet they succeeded in concluding a peace the spirit of which, in the opinion of a western publication of distinction, teaches a lesson and sets an example to the Western world.[4]

In the decade following the first World War, with Arab society disrupted, and Arab lands fragmented and most of them under foreign rule, it looked as though Arab unity was a lost cause. During the next decade, the thirties, events moved toward bringing the Arabs, the states and the people, closer together, and a vague form of unity of purpose and direction began to take shape which gave promise and hope that the recreation of a fuller unity was not out of reach. Developments leading towards this aim were accelerated during the second World War.

The necessities of war compelled the powers to view the Middle East as a unit. A regional organization, the Middle East Supply Center, was established for the purpose of assuring the essentials of livelihood for the civilian population of the area within the framework of the requirements and exigencies of conducting a global war. Since it was imperative to save, as much as possible, shipping space, port capacity, and internal transportation for war

3. *Documents,* 1934, pp. 459–464.
4. *Survey of International Affairs,* 1934, p. 318.

supplies material, the shipment of civilian goods had to be drastically reduced. But as all the countries of the Middle East depended heavily upon foreign imports, this drastic reduction of imported supplies threatened the area with a serious shortage. It was necessary, therefore, on the one hand to develop as fully as possible the local resources and to arrange for their exchange between the various states, on the other hand to survey the essential needs which could not be locally supplied, to provide the required transport, and to assure equitable distribution. Thus the Middle East Supply Center, created by Great Britain in 1941 and coming under joint Anglo-American control in the following year, had to consider the Middle East as a single whole in ascertaining its needs and developing its potentialities. The Center arranged for regional conferences on economic problems in which the various governments participated. Apart from the experiences and knowledge pooled and exchanged at these meetings, the conferences showed the need, and the possibility, of organizing the Middle Eastern countries on a regional basis. From economic to political regionalism was a short step.

Under the pressure of war also, the British Government announced its support of Arab unity; in May 1941, British Secretary of State for Foreign Affairs Anthony Eden made the statement: "It seems to me both natural and right that the cultural and economic ties between the Arab countries and the political ties, too, should be strengthened. His Majesty's Government for their part will give their full support to any scheme that commands general approval." Two years later, in February 1943, he said in Parliament: "As they have already made plain, His Majesty's Government would view with sympathy any movement among Arabs to promote their economic, cultural, or political unity."

When these statements were made the war was not going too well for Great Britain. The Middle East was vital for the conduct and outcome of the war. Any disturbances in that area could seriously affect the war effort. The Arabs who occupied the greater part of the region were restless and frustrated as a result of the problems and tensions created by the settlement which issued from the first war. The British, aware that it was imperative to keep peace and tranquility in the Middle East, and recognizing the growing strength of the Arab movement, thought it best to swim with the tide rather than try to stem it. The statements of the Foreign Secretary in extending Great Britain's sympathy for the cause of Arab unity hoped to regain for Britain what her inter-war record had lost her in Arab friendship and confidence.

All the while the idea of unity had been maturing among Arab leaders who were anxious about the fate of the Arab countries and realized that their position in relation to the Western Powers would be greatly strengthened if they could meet them as a united front. In the summer of 1943, a series of consultations began between the Egyptian Premier on the one hand and successive delegations of the independent Arab countries on the other. The consultations extended into the winter of 1944. When they were finally concluded they revealed that the participating states were ready for a general conference on Arab unity.

While the consultations were in progress, the Franco-Lebanese crisis of November 1943 occurred. It was a test of the measure and extent of popular and official feeling towards Arab solidarity. The response of the Arab world was immediate and strong, and Lebanon itself proved that it could no longer be considered a foothold for a foreign power.

A preliminary conference met in Alexandria, from September 25 to October 7, 1944. It was attended by delegates from the seven Arab states, Egypt, Iraq, Syria, Lebanon, Transjordan, Saudi Arabia, and Yaman. A representative of the Palestinian Arabs, Musa Alami, participated in the Conference on a footing of equality with the delegates of the independent states.

At the Alexandria Conference, as during the preparatory talks which preceded it, three forms of Arab unity were proposed. The closest form of union under a central government was not considered possible or desirable. Another proposal was for a federal union with binding authority upon the component states, federal authority to be vested in an assembly, to which each state would send representatives in proportion to its population, and in an executive committee responsible to the assembly. But this form also was considered impracticable under present conditions. It was finally decided to establish, as a first step, a loose form of union whose authority would be binding only upon those states which accepted its decisions and resolutions.

The Preliminary Conference drew up a document known as the Alexandria Protocol which provided for the establishment of a League of independent Arab states for the purpose of strengthening the existing bonds and relations between them, consolidating their efforts, and promoting closer cooperation on the political, economic, and cultural levels, thus securing their well-being and protecting their independence.

The Conference and the Protocol that issued therefrom did not create Arab unity. Rather, as the Preamble to the Protocol states, the Conference met "in affirmation of the indissoluble bonds and numerous ties which bind all Arab countries, and in an earnest concern to strengthen and consolidate these ties and direct them towards the welfare of the whole Arab world, to improve its conditions, insure its future, and realize its hopes and aspirations." That the Conference was not merely the expression of official opinion or the outcome only of the deliberations of government circles but expressed a general feeling and a popular urge, is again made clear in the Preamble which affirms that it met "in response to Arab public opinion in all Arab countries." While recognizing the independence of the several participating states, the Protocol specified that in their relations with the outside world their policy would conform to a common pattern. "In no case will the adoption of a foreign policy which may be prejudicial to the policy of the League or an individual member state be allowed," the Protocol announced, forestalling the danger of the several states being drawn into the orbits of various big powers, and then forced to follow conflicting policies and courses of action. War is proscribed. "In no case will resort to force to settle a dispute between any two member states of the League be allowed." In case of dispute the Council of the League, in which all the states irrespective of their size are equally represented, will mediate to effect a reconciliation. Thus several months before the San Francisco Conference, from which issued the United Nations, the Arabs arranged for the establishment of a regional organization to keep the peace in an area where numerous conflicting and vital interests are involved.

But political considerations were not the only concern of the Alexandria Conference. The Protocol envisaged close cooperation between the states in economic, cultural, and social matters. A special resolution concerning Lebanon emphasized the respect of the other states for its independence and sovereignty, thereby allaying the fears of certain sections among the Lebanese population with regard to the purpose and spirit of the League. Another special resolution reaffirmed that Palestine was the responsibility of the whole Arab world, and that there could be no peace and stability in the Middle East until the natural rights of the Arabs of Palestine were safeguarded by the establishment of an independent state. Finally, the Protocol stressed the evolutionary aspect of the League and called it a first step which, it hoped, would in the future lead to further steps toward a closer union.

In March, 1945, a general conference was held in Cairo at the close of which the Pact creating the Arab League was promulgated. The Pact, although it followed the general principles laid down by the Protocol of Alexandria, was nevertheless a weaker document. The sovereign independence of the member states was reiterated and emphasized; the clause forbidding the pursuit of a foreign policy prejudicial to the League was dropped, as was the statement which looked forward to the strengthening of the ties with a view to closer unity. The special resolution with respect to Lebanon was omitted because sufficient stress had been laid in the Pact itself on guaranteeing the sovereignty of the member states. With regard to Palestine, an annex recognized its *de jure* independence and provided for its representation in the Council of the League. Another annex provided for the admission of the Arab countries still under foreign rule into the committees of the League, and enjoined upon the Council "that it should spare no effort to learn their needs and understand their aspirations and hopes; and that it should work thenceforth for their best interests and the safeguarding of their future with all the political means at its disposal."

Arab opinion regarded the establishment of the League as an auspicious step, although many felt that its Pact was not binding enough a document and fell far short of the people's aspirations for unity. It was a beginning in the right direction, however, and the general feeling was that under the impact of the popular will the League would grow to be a more effective organ for the achievement of greater coherence and solidarity among the Arabs.

But the League, as it has developed, has dissipated much of the hope that was placed on it. Instead of working towards a greater consolidation of Arab ties, the League has immobilized the relations between the Arab States at the stage where it found them. It has proved, during these eight years of its existence, to be not the first step leading to a more binding union but an instrument to consecrate the status quo.

The major responsibility for the League's failure rests with the member states over whom the League has no binding authority. These states, persisting in a course which gave precedence to local problems and considerations over more vital matters of general Arab concern, have lacked the vision and the willingness to develop an Arab policy directed towards the realization of the broad and ultimate interests of the entire Arab nation. During the 1930's, when the Arab states were struggling to loosen the control of the Mandatory Powers, the nationalists believed that with the achievement of independence, unity would be attained, since the major obstacle in its path, foreign control, would have been removed. But actual developments have not fulfilled this expectation. In each state a class was formed of rulers, politicians, office seekers, and those who moved in their orbit with vested interests in the maintenance of the existing order. Nor can the people of these states, especially the educated and articulate elements among them, be absolved of responsibility for the policy of their respective governments: they, the people, have failed to impress upon these governments their serious intention to make real the unity which they so often proclaimed as the will of the Arab nation. Articulate opinion has been vociferous rather than actively and constructively engaged in the positive, solid work without which no ideal, however noble and practicable, can actually be realized.

In making any estimate of the Arab League, it should also be kept in mind that since its inception it was confronted with problems of great magnitude and complexity over which the League and its member states had only partial control; these problems involved Arab relations with two imperialist powers, Great Britain and France, and with militant Zionism backed by world Jewry and the tremendous influence it exerted in the political circles of the western world.

In dealing with Palestine, the League failed deplorably. Its member states had neither the trained armies equipped with modern arms nor had they worked out a joint plan of defense backed by a common foreign policy.

But the League was successful in meeting the French provocative action in Syria in 1945, when the Arab states through the League rallied to Syria's aid, their united support, along with the determination of the Syrian people and the opportune intervention of the British, being instrumental in forcing the French to withdraw. The League has given more than lip service to the cause of freedom in North Africa. It has sponsored and supported the work of the Committee for the Liberation of Libya. The preliminary contacts between the League and the diplomatic representatives of a large number of states paved the way for the enlistment of a majority of United Nations members on the side of Libya's independence.

Caught in the whirlpool of political issues, the League has given inadequate thought to the economic and social aspects of Arab cooperation specifically provided for in its Pact. It is only in the cultural field that some tangible results have been achieved.

A Cultural Treaty, to which all the member states have adhered, aims at the integration of the education systems in the Arab countries, the dissemination and advancement of learning, and the development of a uniform culture based on the Arab heritage and enriched by the achievements of modern knowledge. The Cultural Section of the League's Secretariat has issued a number of publications on Arab affairs; the most important among them is the *Educational Annual,* published in 1950 and written by Sati' al-Hosri, the man who founded public education in Iraq and reorganized the educational system of Syria, and who in many ways is the most competent authority on education in the Arab World. Under the Cultural Section, the Manuscript Institute has been founded for the purpose of making the Arabic manuscripts in public and private collections more generally known and easily accessible to workers in the field, by compiling a general index based on the various manuscript indices, and by photographing and publishing important manuscripts. The Institute had photographed 5000 manuscripts by the end of 1949. The collection is available to scholars who may use it at the Institute, buy copies, or borrow them through academic institutions. The nucleus of an educational museum has been formed where documents, charts, statistics, and other material and publications related to education are kept and exhibited.

Two congresses have been held under the auspices of the Cultural Section of the League. The Archaeological Congress, meeting in Damascus in the summer of 1947, recommended to the League the formation of an archaeological committee to cooperate with the Arab states in excavations and other archaeological work. It approved a resolution for the completion and publication of an Art and Archaeological dictionary in Arabic. The Congress advised that the League obtain permission to excavate in Saudi Arabia and Yaman, because of the importance of these two countries for Arab civilization.

In this connection it may be noted that a decade earlier an Egyptian mission, composed of four scientists, had visited Yaman and made some studies in archaeology, anthropology, geology and geography, botany, and entomology. It was the largest scientific mission that had appeared in Yaman since the pioneer Danish expedition, led by Niebuhr, visited the country about the middle of the 18th century.

The Cultural Congress, meeting in Lebanon also in the summer of 1947, emphasized the study of the Arabic language, history, and geography as a means for the achievement of Arab unity. It stressed the social aim of education and the need of instilling the democratic way of life into the spirit of the young people.

Aspects of thought and training designed to promote Arab unity were given precedence in formulating the resolutions of the Congress. Emphasis was to be placed upon the geographical connection between the Arab countries of Asia and Africa, their close association through all the periods of their long history, and their unique cultural heritage and contributions to world civilization. The consolidation of all elements of the nation is the aim, as it is the mainstay, of the Arab national idea. This idea is not and has not been at any time the exclusive possession of a special group or a particular religious community, but is the common heritage of all Arabs, a heritage in the formation of which the various religious communities have participated both during the Middle Ages and the Renaissance of the modern period. The Arab League is to be understood as an expression of the evolution within Arab society towards unity, an evolution in line with world trends towards integration and unification. Independence is the natural right of every people, and imperialism is a form of enslavement. United action should be exerted for the liberation of all the Arab countries. And finally, the resolutions concluded, since democracy is of all systems the surest way to secure liberty, justice, and equality, every effort should be exerted to make the spirit of democracy a living faith in the lives of youth.

In appraising the work of the Arab League, it is often asked: Has the League justified its existence? Has it really brought the Arabs any closer together? Thoughtful Arabs contemplate with dismay the division of the League into rival camps. They sadly observe that certain divisive tendencies have been accentuated, and rivalries between states and ruling families sharpened, since the League has come into being. Although the Pact of the League provided for a closer union between any two or more members, yet such union has been hampered on the grounds—astounding enough—that it would upset the balance among the member states. While most observers realize that it would be unfair and unreasonable to attribute these unfortunate developments to the League, they nevertheless wonder whether it is in the interest of Arab unity that the League should continue in its present form or whether, if it cannot be made a more effective instrument, it should be replaced by bilateral unions, which though more restricted than the League are in effect more substantial and of greater value in advancing the cause of Arab unity.

Such a union, comprising the countries of the Fertile Crescent, was contemplated by Nuri Sa'id, Iraqi statesman, before the Arab League was founded. Another plan, the Greater Syria project, had in view the establishment of one state within the area known until the end of the first World War as Syria. The reintegration of the divisions of Syria created by the post-war settlement has been the aim and hope of all workers in the national field. But the Greater Syria scheme as it has been proposed during the last few years has met with opposition chiefly because of its sponsorship, being advocated by the late King Abdallah of Transjordan. A brief statement about Transjordan and its late ruler is here given as a background for the scheme.

Transjordan did not exist as a separate entity, nor was it even known by this name, before 1920. In the Turkish period it had been a district[5] of the province of Syria, and so it continued under the Arab Kingdom of Faisal when it was directly ruled from Damascus. No one could have thought, prior to 1920, that this barren district, with a population of about 200,000, largely nomadic, with no resources actual or potential, would at any time become a separate state. And yet, even though it had none of the requisites of statehood, it was made a state, even a kingdom.

Transjordan is the creature of Great Britain. It came into being upon an agreement with France when the latter was given a free hand in Syria in return for her acquiescence in Britain's mandate over Palestine and her annexation of the area beyond the Jordan. The British appreciated the possibilities of Transjordan as a military base, all the more so since for some time to come they did not need to fear any troublesome national movements in this undeveloped, sparsely populated area. Committed to the Balfour

5. Mutasarrifiyeh, an administrative unit under a mutasarrif or district commissioner.

Declaration in Palestine, and not willing to extend its applicability beyond the Jordan, they created the Amirate of Transjordan, with Amir Abdallah as its ruler. Transjordan came under the authority of the High Commissioner for Palestine who was represented by the British Resident in Amman. The pattern of ruling through treaty was introduced into Transjordan in 1928, when the British drew up a document defining their relationship to this state and its ruler. The Treaty, after having endowed the Amir with the rights and powers that reside in the people and are exercised through their elected representatives—the powers of legislation, granting concessions, exploiting the country's resources—tied the Amir hand and foot to Great Britain. For it is explicit in stating that the Amir would be guided in every act and decision by the British Resident in Amman.

That such a relationship was not acceptable to the more educated and articulate elements was expressed by the National Transjordanian Congress convened in Amman in the summer of 1928. The National Pact adopted by the Congress repudiated the mandate except in the form of technical assistance defined by a treaty concluded on the basis of equality. It declared Transjordan an independent constitutional state and called for elections on a truly representative basis.[6]

The 1928 Treaty was not revised until 1946, when the mandate was terminated and Transjordan made an independent state in name though not in fact. This nominal independence was calculated to give Great Britain a freer hand in Transjordan, since dependent areas were becoming more and more the object of international concern and were likely to come under international supervision exercised through the United Nations. Denounced in Transjordan and elsewhere in the Arab countries, the treaty was revised two years later, the revision making some concessions to national feelings. But Transjordan remains a British military base.

The history of Transjordan during the thirty years of its existence has revolved around King Abdallah, its late ruler, the British Resident—the real ruler—, and Glubb Pasha, Commander of the Arab Legion. Glubb has acquired Transjordanian citizenship and is presumably a servant of Transjordan, but through this role he is one of those pillars upon which the British Empire has rested.

6. *Survey of International Affairs*, 1928, pp. 326–327; *Documents on International Affairs*, 1928, pp. 213–219.

The Legion is financed by the British Treasury and is commanded by British officers. It was until very recently the best trained and equipped of the Arab armies, but such being its dependence upon the British, it has been an instrument of British policy in the Middle East.

King Abdallah, who owed his position to the British and continued to owe them the maintenance of his state which without British financial and political support could not exist, was Great Britain's chief supporter in the Arab States. His eager support and his garrulousness at times embarrassed his patrons who may have preferred a more discreet ally. In all important matters, Abdallah acted under British direction. His actions and public statements as often conflicted with the wishes and real interests of the Arab peoples as they clashed with the professed tendencies of other Arab rulers and government circles. On the question of Palestine, Abdallah was in agreement with the British. He accepted the first partition plan put forth by the Peel Commission in 1937, which had proposed the annexation of Arab Palestine to Transjordan. In the Palestine conflict, he kept in touch with Zionist leaders by correspondence and clandestine meetings. His Arab Legion participated in the fighting to the extent that Glubb Pasha allowed. After the cessation of hostilities, his government ceded to Israel part of the valuable area known as the Arab Triangle—around Nablus, Tullkarm, Janin—where no Jews lived, and where they did not own any land. Neither was the area involved in the fighting except in the battle of Janin where the Jews suffered heavy losses, the Iraqi troops in collaboration with the local inhabitants having won one of the few Arab victories of the Palestine conflict. On the subject of the internationalization of Jerusalem, Abdallah opposed the unaminous opinion of the Arab states and asked for the partition of the city between Arabs and Jews, his stand being in accord with Israel's demand, and with the view of Great Britain and the United States.

In his dealings with his subjects, Abdallah was autocratic. It is true that he kept some of the simple ways of his early upbringing in Hijaz, and that he was too poor to maintain an elaborate court. But he was willful and could not bear to be questioned or opposed. He neither understood nor had any use for the role of opposition in government.

Abdallah was full of his own importance, and he paraded it. He considered the Arab Revolt a Hashimi show, and he expected that Arab unity should come through his clan, the Hashimis. Some of his views, publicly expressed in his official speeches and in press interviews, or written down in his autobiography,[7] were irresponsible and disquieting.

After the loss of Hijaz to Ibn Saud, Abdallah considered himself a refugee. To him, Transjordan was a stepping stone from which to rise to the Kingdom of Greater Syria and thence with added strength and prestige proceed to the reconquest of Hijaz.

Such being the circumstances surrounding King Abdallah, it is no wonder that his Greater Syria scheme was not acceptable to the majority of the Syrian people, nor approved by the peoples and governments of the other Arab States.

When in the summer of 1943 the Egyptian Premier was sounding the opinion of the Arab governments with regard to Arab unity, the delegation of Transjordan proposed the unification of the four parts of Syria, suggesting that if it should prove impracticable to include Lebanon and Palestine, then the union should be confined to Syria and Transjordan. The Syrian delegation affirmed their country's attachment to the republican regime for which they did not wish to substitute a monarchy. The question was again raised by Transjordan's delegation to the League's meeting in the fall of 1946, when the Arab states were getting ready for the London Conference on Palestine. The Syrians countered with the suggestion that since Transjordan had always been a district of Syria, it was not in the natural order of things that Syria should come under Transjordan's regime, but rather that Transjordan, the off-shoot, should rejoin the mother country under its republican regime.

The Greater Syria scheme failed to command public support because it was involved in the personal ambitions of King Abdallah, an autocratic ruler and a tool in the hands of Great Britain. The extension of the Transjordan regime over the rest of Syria would have meant the abolition of the republic and the loss of Syria's independence; and Syria, more free from foreign controls than most Arab states, would have come within the order which made Transjordan a British satellite and military base. The Greater Syria scheme was opposed by Ibn Saud because of its connection with the intended conquest of Hijaz by Abdallah, and by Farouk's Egypt because it strengthened the Hashimis. Hence the insist-

7. *Memoirs of King Abdallah of Transjordan*, tr. by G. Khuri, New York, p. 195.

ence of successive Syrian governments upon the republican regime as an instrument for peace among the Arabs and the form of government which best suited the people.

King Abdallah's death, as later the removal of Farouk, has eliminated some of the causes of dissent among the Arab states. The annexation of Arab Palestine to Transjordan in October, 1948 more than tripled the country's population, adding new problems and introducing new elements to deal with the problems. The presence of Palestinians in the public life of the Kingdom of Jordan has made itself felt in a number of ways, notably in the promulgation of a new Constitution in January, 1952, which limited the King's authority and established ministerial responsibility to parliament.

The Fertile Crescent project, worked out by Nuri Sa'id in 1942, envisaged a united Syria joined to Iraq in a union to which other Arab states might later adhere. The plan was not favorably received. It was feared that in a unified Syria the Jews would have greater opportunities for expansion and might gain economic control over the whole area. The provision that the Christians of Lebanon could have an autonomous state in part of the country was a retrogressive step inasmuch as it recognized a cleavage among Arabs on the basis of religion. The idea that Syria and Iraq were more closely related to each other than the rest of the Arab countries was inacceptable, and considered a dangerous notion which might stand in the way of a wider Arab unity. The plan was dropped, and in its place the Arab League came into being.

The plan was revived under inauspicious circumstances. It was immediately after the Palestine collapse, when the Iraqi Government proposed union between Syria and Iraq as a means to safeguard Syria against the Israeli. The Iraqi army, withdrawn from Palestine, was stationed near the Syrian border for the purpose, they said, of coming to Syria's aid in case of Israeli attack. But the device was too obvious to be taken seriously. The Iraqi army had been sent to Palestine without adequate arms, and while in Palestine had not been allowed to fight. Popular feeling in Iraq was inflamed over the outcome of the Palestine conflict. The government feared that should the frustrated army be recalled to Iraq while the situation was so tense, a revolution might break out. To divert the people's anger, it was necessary to provide an emotional outlet for their pent-up feelings. The revival of the plan of union with Syria, a subject popular in Iraq, was to be such an outlet calculated to occupy people's mind, give relief to their feelings, and wear off their anger.

Moreover, the plan, as it was then presented, concealed an unfriendly attitude toward Egypt. There was a feeling that the plan intended to exclude Egypt from the Arab movement which was to be confined to the Fertile Crescent.

After the removal of President Shukri al-Kuwatli from office, the subject of union was again raised. Under the Hinnawi regime, established by the second military coup, the plan made considerable headway, being adopted by Hinnawi and a large group in Parliament. The third coup prevented its realization, denouncing it as a plot to destroy Syria's independence, weaken her army, and establish a monarchy which would be a further obstacle in the path of greater Arab unity.

There is no doubt that the idea of union between Syria and Iraq has wide appeal. In Iraq it is espoused by all the political parties and by a large section of articulate opinion. The desire for union is real in Syria where Arab feeling is strong. The Syrians also remember that on the day of March 8, 1920, when the independent Arab state of Syria was proclaimed under Faisal, the independence of Iraq and its union with Syria were announced amidst demonstations of public joy and enthusiasm. Why then has the union not been realized?

It is only a partial explanation to say that those in power in Syria, first al-Kuwatli and then the military authorities, opposed union for personal considerations. Although the personal motive was present, it was not the only nor perhaps the major obstacle to union. The attitude of the Syrian authorities was determined, to a great extent, by the belief that since political circles on the highest level in Iraq were under British influence, it was possible that Great Britain was behind the plan. Why had Iraq and Transjordan not united, people asked, when they were both ruled by the same dynasty, the Hashimis, and both bound by treaty to Great Britain? They feared that the Fertile Crescent scheme might result only in the creation of a throne for the Regent of Iraq, and in placing Syria within the British scheme of defense, without effecting a real union or bringing Syria and Iraq any closer together than the relationship between Iraq and Transjordan. The fact that the Constitution of Iraq gives undue powers to the Crown has been another deterrent to union. Negotiations were in progress between responsible circles in Syria and Iraq for the liberalization of the Iraqi Constitution as a preliminary step towards union when the third military coup took place.

Syria, which has so far demurred at projects of union under the ruling house of Iraq or Transjordan, has nevertheless expressed, through successive governments and regimes, an enthusiastic support for the cause of Arab unity. During the Preparatory Talks, in October 1943, the Syrian Premier, Sa'dallah al-Jabiri, announced his government's readiness to sign a blank paper and hand it over to the Egyptian Prime Minister to write upon it any conditions and arrangements for unity which he saw fit, and pledged the word of his government to put into effect such an arrangement. He added that Syria preferred the type of union with a binding effect.

At the Alexandria Conference, Jabiri expressed Syria's willingness to part with her sovereignty for the furtherance of Arab unity. Again he expressed his government's preference for the most binding form of union, one whose executive organ was a central government. Failing this, union by federation or confederation might be considered. Jabiri emphasized the need of developing a common foreign policy and joint defense.

The President of the Republic, Shukri al-Kuwatli, declared on important public occasions that Syria looked forward to the day when her sovereignty would be merged in an Arab union. The military regime which ousted Kuwatli has proclaimed its adherence to the ideal of Arab unity and its concept of the Syrian army as the servant of this cause.

The Syrian Constitution, promulgated in 1950, emphasizes Arab unity. The Preamble reads: "We the representatives of the Syrian Arab people . . . announce that our people, who are part of the Arab nation both in their past history as in their present and future, look forward to the day when our Arab nation shall be united in one state, and will exert their utmost endeavour to fulfill this sacred desire." Again, in article one, the Syrian people are spoken of as part of the Arab nation and Syria is described as a democratic Arab republic. In the oath sworn by the Representatives (Art. 46) as in the oath which invests the President of the Republic (Art. 75), both President and Representatives solemnly promise to work for the realization of the unity of the Arab countries.

The continuity of Syria's Arab policy through the many changes in its government during recent years was again brought out by

Nazim al-Kudsi, then Prime Minister, in his plan for Arab unity submitted to the League's Political Committee in the winter of 1951. The plan, which pointed to the ineffectiveness of the Arab League in its present form and to the people's impatience with its slow ways and insubstantial results, stressed the need for an effective union under one of three forms: a united Arab state, a federation, or a confederation. Whatever type was chosen, the union was to put into effect a common foreign and defense policy and a unified economy. But nothing came out of Kudsi's project, nor of another sound and carefully thought out plan for the unification of currency presented by the Syrian Statesman Khaled al-Azm in the spring of 1946.

Kudsi's proposals are reminiscent of the statements repeatedly made by Jabiri, although the two men were at the head of the government under two different regimes and both had been rival leaders in frequent disagreement over matters related to local politics. Both leaders repeated that Syria was prepared to go to any length, provided it met with general approval, in order to achieve Arab unity. The Arab Liberation Movement, launched by Shishakli, and intended to replace the dissolved political parties, avows its dedication to the cause of Arab unity.

In Iraq, the presence of a large non-Arab minority, the Kurds, made it necessary to stress Iraqi nationalism in order to unite Arabs and Kurds in loyalty to a state to which the two groups could feel they belonged. The relatively early achievement of Iraqi independence gave the people a sense of pride in Iraqi nationalism. These circumstances, however, were outweighed by other facts and conditions which have made Iraq strongly pan-Arab. Iraq is an inland country with no shore on the Mediterranean beyond which it could look to the West. Her horizon is defined by the desert and the Peninsula of Arabia; consequently, her outlook is Arab. The presence of a large tribal element among her population further accentuates her connection with the desert. The builder of modern Iraq, King Faisal, had been the leader and guiding spirit of the Arab Revolt. Although he concentrated on his immediate task of building Iraq and achieving her independence, he never lost sight of the greater object of freeing and uniting the Arab nation. In the thirties, Iraq became the haven of political refugees from Syria and Palestine. The presence of these leaders and of a large number of teachers from several Arab countries made Iraq the center of Arab nationalism. Iraq has always been responsive to the liberation movements in other Arab countries. It has championed a closer union between the Arab countries than the League provides for. Although Iraq, in deference to its ruling family, has at times overlooked the infractions of Transjordan, there is a strong feeling in the country that the separate existence of Transjordan should be eliminated and the state joined to Iraq.

It is sometimes believed that Lebanon lies outside the Arab fold. This was the French view, and as long as France held the Mandate, her representatives and agents worked to alienate Lebanon from the rest of the Arab world. They encouraged sectarianism, exaggerated local differences, and tried to discredit the Arab movement by representing it as Moslem and Bedouin by which they implied fanatical and backward.

In Lebanon a local product, Phoenicianism, sprouted. It was a counterpart of Egyptian Pharaonism. The Phoenicians, the earliest settlers on the Lebanon coast where they developed a flourishing civilization built largely upon a seaborne trade, disappeared with their language and culture before the Christian era. The Phoenician legend was created to counteract the trend towards Arab unity, but as it was an artificial concept it soon died out. It has been succeeded by the "Mediterranean movement" which seeks to identify Lebanon's culture with the civilization of the Mediterranean world in an attempt to draw Lebanon away from the Arab heritage which the movement considers Asiatic. But the culture of Lebanon is fundamentally Arab, and the strength of Arab culture lies in its synthesis of the Mediterranean with Asiatic civilizations.

It is worth remembering that Lebanon was in the vanguard of the Arab literary revival in the latter part of the 19th century, and that Arab nationalism found its earliest adherents among the Christian Arabs who were less attached to the Moslem Caliphate embodied in the Ottoman Empire and had been exposed earlier than the Moslems to western influences, among them the nationalist concept. Lebanese emigrants to the New World opened new horizons for modern Arabic literature and broke unfamiliar paths for Arab writers. Their own mind and spirit having been liberated and vitalized by the freedom and exhilarating life around them, they communicated their experiences in an unfettered Arabic style. The content and form of this emigrant literature influenced considerably Arab poets and writers in the early part of this century, especially in Egypt. Lebanese emigrants, both in North and South

America, have always responded with enthusiasm to the liberating movements in the Arab countries, and have supported morally and materially the struggle for independence in the homeland. Of the distinguished emigrant writers two may be mentioned for their strong attachment to the cause of Arab freedom. One is the poet Rashid al-Khouri, a resident of Sao Paolo, Brazil, whose poetry breathes a deep longing for his native land and a strong feeling for its sorrows and trials. He celebrates with pride the resistance and revolution against foreign rule, and radiates enthusiasm and devotion to the national cause. The other, Amin Rihani, was a widely read author, whose works express his pride in the Arab heritage and faith in the Arab movement. Rihani traveled extensively over the Arab countries. His books on Faisal and Iraq, on Ibn Saud and the Arab Island, form an important collection in the modern Arabic library of biography, history and travel.

Since the termination of the Mandate, Lebanon has drawn closer to the other Arab countries. Lebanese independence was strongly supported by all the Arab states who were relieved at the elimination of French political control from this Arab land. French cultural influence remains strong and will continue so until Lebanon has developed a more adequate system of public education. Once Lebanon's independence was assured, the attitude towards it of the other Arab states, especially Syria, became more positive and trusting. When the head of the first independent government, Riad Solh, declared that Lebanon shall not be a foothold for imperialism nor a gateway through which imperialism might pass to the other Arab countries, the Syrians were assured, and blessed Lebanon's independence. At the Conference of Alexandria and in the Pact of the League, the Arab States agreed to respect the present status of Lebanon, and Lebanon in its turn has cooperated in the Arab movement through the League. Lebanon has pressed for closer economic cooperation and has presented to the League a project for a free trade area among the member states, which project was inserted into the Inter-Arab Security Post.[8]

The largest by far, and the most influential state in the League, Egypt, is sometimes considered a newcomer into the Arab family. Those who hold this view stress Egypt's geographical connections

8. The visit of Amir Saud—Crown Prince of Saudi Arabia—to Lebanon in April 1953, was acclaimed with genuine joy by all sections of the Lebanese population. Church bells rang to greet the Wahhabi Prince.

with Africa and the Pharaonic aspect of her history. But since the beginning of recorded time Egypt's history has been interwoven with the countries of western Asia with which her relations, economic, cultural, and political, have been more close and constant than with the adjoining African regions.[9] Egypt was Arabicized within a century after the Arab conquest. The Egyptian historian Ibn Abd al-Hakam, writing in the 8th century A.D., describes a society thoroughly Arab in thought and outlook, in customs and everyday ways. Beliefs of an Arab-Moslem origin supplanted the traditions transmitted through the centuries of a long history. Even genealogies were manufactured to produce an Arab ancestry. Egypt has not only remained Arab, but since the Mongol Invasions in the middle of the 13th century has been the custodian of Arab culture and the principal center of Moslem learning. Throughout the Arab period, the pattern of life has been one and the same for Egypt and the other Arab countries, and her history has been inextricably involved with theirs.

Under the Omayyads and during the early part of Abbasid rule, Egypt formed part of a great empire governed from one center, first Damascus and then Baghdad. Later, during the age of political break-up, Egypt itself was the center of an extensive state which included part of North Africa, Syria, and the Hijaz. At a critical time in Arab history, when Mongol waves broke upon the Fertile Crescent with havoc and destruction, Egypt stemmed the tide in the decisive victory of Ain Jalut, near the Palestinian coast. The Crusaders, another outside danger, established for two centuries in the Levant, were finally expelled by Egyptian forces under the Mamelukes. The Mameluke Sultan, Kansuh al-Ghuri, trying to check the Ottoman invasion, fought the Turks not at the border of Egypt but a long distance away, at Marj Dabik, near Aleppo, close to the Turkish frontier.

It is only within the last century that Egypt's vision has been confined within her borders. This confinement was forced upon her by the Powers who intervened to prevent Mohammad Ali from founding an Arab state comprising Egypt and the Levant. But even then, developments in Egypt, both political and cultural, left their mark upon the other Arab countries, especially Syria which participated in the cultural renaissance of Egypt through the many distinguished writers of Syrian origin.

It is true that Egypt was outside the aspect of the Arab move-

9. Speiser, *op. cit.*, p. 8.

ment which expressed itself in the Arab Revolt.[10] While the national aspirations of the Arabs of western Asia took the form of a
revolt against Turkey, carried in alliance with Great Britain, in
Egypt—which a century earlier had freed herself of Turkish rule,
and had fallen under British control in 1882—the struggle for freedom was directed again at the British. In the interwar period, a
local nationalism was born and fostered. In the course of the national struggle, the two sections of the Egyptian population, Moslems and Copts, were united on the basis of a common origin and
history which went back to the pre-Islamic, hence pre-Arab, period. Consequently, Pharaonic origins, history, and civilization
were stressed, and Egyptian nationalism was draped in a Pharaonic
garb. Furthermore, many Egyptians believed that the realization
of the Nile Valley unity through the union of the Sudan with Egypt
was a more vital and pressing matter than Arab unity.

In recent years, Egypt has resumed her place in the Arab movement. She took the lead in preparing the ground for the Arab
League. The preparatory meetings with the various Arab states
were convened at the invitation of the Egyptian Government. The
Preliminary Conference which laid down the principle and out-
lines of the League was held in Alexandria, and the General Congress which established the League met in Cairo, where the
League's permanent headquarters have been set up. Egypt has
steadily supported the League, but under Farouk its Arab policy
tended to accentuate the divergences among the member states.
The Inter-Arab Security Pact, presented by Egypt to the League,
was intended to counterbalance Iraqi pressure for the achievement
of Fertile Crescent unity. The Pact, which has been ratified by
four parliaments—the Egyptian, Syrian, Iraqi and Lebanese, has
officially come into effect.

Arab solidarity was severely put to the test after the Palestine
war. Egypt felt that she had been let down by the other Arab
states who looked on while the Egyptian army fought the Israeli
in the Negeb. Voices were raised in Egypt calling for her withdrawal from the League. This reaction coincided with views held
in certain political circles in some Arab countries expressing a

10. It is worth noting that of the political organizations which prepared the way
for the Arab Revolt, the most influential—Al-'Ahd—was founded by the Egyptian,
Aziz Ali al-Misri, an irreproachable patriot, a valiant soldier, having rendered distinguished service during the Libyan war against Italy in 1911, and a thoroughly
cultured gentleman, equally at home with European thought and art as with his
troops on the battlefield.

trend to confine the Arab movement to the Fertile Crescent. But the Arab feeling recovered. Egypt is again upholding the cause of unity, as she is defending with determination the right to freedom of the Arab peoples still under foreign rule. With Mohammad Naguib's direct approach to whatever problem he tackles, it is reasonable to expect that the trend towards closer unity among the Arabs will acquire a more substantial form than was hitherto possible. Evidences of strengthening the Arab League are discernible in the attempts to reorganize the Secretariat of the League, the establishment of a Department for Palestine, the tightening of the economic boycott of Israel, and the founding of an Institute of Arab Studies. Libya, which had demurred at joining the League, has recently been welcomed as the eighth member state. The visit of Libya's king to Egypt was celebrated with enthusiastic pan-Arab demonstrations, and the visits of Shishakli and later President Shamoun were occasions for deliberations on a common Arab policy. At the Inter-Arab Press Conference held in Cairo, April 1953, Mohammad Naguib spoke of his desire to see the United Arab States a reality.

In evaluating Egypt's place in the Arab movement, it is necessary to remember the role of the Egyptian press which widely circulates throughout the Arab countries. Carrying profuse material in the form of news for articles—sometimes exaggerated but often well informed—on Arab affairs, it keeps before the public the issues of general Arab concern. It is also important to keep in mind that Egypt is the intellectual center of the Arab world, that thousands of Arab students from every Arab country are enrolled annually in Egyptian universities and other educational institutions, that hundreds of Egyptian teachers help in the work of education in a number of other Arab states, and that books published in Egypt are read all over the Arab countries and the Moslem world.

In estimating the difficulties in the path of Arab unity, outside observers claim that an obstinate barrier is the so-called heterogeneity of the Arab world. They point to the "human islands" which represent cultural and religious backgrounds from the vast Arab sea different in which they are anchored, as serious obstacles precluding the practical realization of Arab unity. As used to be done in the case of India, western imperialists have stressed these differences as a justification for their intervention under the pretext of protecting the minorities. In view of these concepts it is desirable to describe briefly the status and extent of minorities in the Arab world.

There are numerous religious and cultural groups in the Arab world—but there are no racial divisions since Arab society admits of no distinction on the basis of race. The religious communities are the Moslems who represent about 95% of the entire population, and the Christians and Jews who are the religious minorities. Among the cultural minorities, the largest and most important groups are the Kurds in Syria and in northeast Iraq, and the Berbers in northwest Africa, at the opposite extremes of the Arab world. Other, far less numerous cultural minorities are the Circassians in Syria and Transjordan and the Turkmans in Iraq. There are minorities who differ from the majority with respect to both culture and religion, such as the Assyrians in Iraq, and the Armenians in Syria and Lebanon. The Armenians fled from Turkey during and immediately after the first world war. They came as refugees with no plan of acquiring any special rights or a privileged status. A few have returned to their homeland, the Soviet Armenian Republic; the majority have remained and acquired Syrian and Lebanese citizenship. They are about 200,000, concentrated mostly in the larger cities, Aleppo, Damascus, and Beirut.

The Assyrians, a community of 25,000, also left Turkey during the first war, but unlike the Armenians they sought to establish a "national home" in Iraq, the country where they took refuge. Because of the publicity which the Assyrian disturbances of the early thirties received in the press of the Western world, and because of some misconceptions and misjudgments which that publicity carried, it is worth while to review the Assyrian case.

The original home of the Assyrians is the Hakkiyari mountain country in southeast Asia Minor. During the 1914–1918 war, the Assyrians, at that time subjects of Turkey, sided with Russia against the Turks. When the Tsarist regime collapsed and Russia made peace with the Central Powers, the Assyrians, left to face the Turks alone, fled to Iraq. Here they considered themselves the protégés of the British Government, and the fighting men among them enlisted in the British army and formed the Assyrian levies. In 1927, the Iraqi government in collaboration with the British authorities started to settle the Assyrians on suitable lands.

The work of settlement was under the direction of a British officer who had served with the levies and was responsible to the

British High Commissioner. By the end of 1929 all but 350 families
were settled. The settlers were granted exemption from taxation
for a number of years, and the men who had completed their service with the levies were allowed to keep their rifles and ammunition. Yet the Assyrians were not satisfied. They demanded to be
settled together in a land resembling their old Hakkiyari home
and under their own autonomous government. The Settlement Officer answered that there was no land belonging to the government
which fulfilled "the requirements demanded by the Assyrians—
namely, mountainous country with fertile valleys and running
water." He further stated that it was impossible to settle the Assyrians in homogeneous groups without the forcible ejection of
Arab and Kurdish peasants in a wide area.

As the time for the termination of the British Mandate drew
near, the Assyrians became more restless and their attitude towards the Iraqi authorities more provocative. They sent petitions
to the League of Nations stating that they could not live in Iraq
after the termination of the Mandate. In the summer of 1933 armed
bands of Assyrians crossed the Tigris to Syria. When they returned
under French pressure two weeks later, carrying their arms, they
found the Iraqi army facing them. The Assyrians have a tradition
of military prowess of which they are very proud. The strength
of the Iraqi army had not been tested yet. The Assyrians launched
two attacks and were repulsed, whereupon some of them returned
to Syria while others slipped to their villages in Iraq. It was then
that a tragic act occurred when some soldiers fell upon an Assyrian village and killed the inhabitants. This has been called the
Iraqi massacre of the Assyrians and is still being used in propaganda against the Arabs. Yet in a fair estimate of the events, the
principal responsibility for the troubles rests with the Assyrians
themselves, who by their intransigent attitude and inordinate demands alienated the people among whom they had taken refuge;
and with the British authorities, who by taking the Assyrians under their protection compromised their relations with the Arabs.
"Of the three parties to the tragedy of 1933, the Iraqui Arab Government were assuredly the least to blame."[11]

As for the cultural minorities, the Kurds and the Berbers, and
the other minor groups, though differing from the Arabs in language, share very largely a common heritage with them since they
are Moslems—and Islam is a social system and a culture as well as

11. *Survey of International Affairs*, 1934, pp. 136–211.

a religion. In Iraq, the Kurds form a large, compact community of about 600,000. The Iraqi government has followed a liberal policy towards the Kurds and other cultural minorities—the Turkomans of whom there are about 40,000, and the Assyrians—by making the language of each of these groups the language of the government and the primary schools in the area where the group is in a majority. All the officials of the Kurdish provinces are Kurds or Kurdish-speaking; Kurds are represented in Parliament in proportion to their numerical strength and have one or two seats in the cabinet. Nevertheless there are separatist tendencies among the Kurds. The separatists envisage a Kurdish state which would include the Kurds of Iraq, Iran, and Turkey. A Kurdish republic was proclaimed in Mahabad in January, 1946, following the secession of Azerbaijan from Iran, but it was a short-lived venture falling at the end of the same year. The attempt may be made again, especially as Russia favors and might aid such a scheme. But it should not be impossible to keep the Kurds satisfied within Iraq and, beyond Iraq, within the larger Arab world if a wise, constructive policy is pursued with regard to improvements in their territory, and they are made to feel that they have more to gain by participating in the building of a great Arab society than by withdrawing into their mountains and shutting themselves up in a small, closed community. For the Kurds have religious and cultural bonds with the Arabs and have been closely associated with them throughout their history. One of the greatest figures in Arab history was the Kurd Salaheddin, hero of the counter-Crusade. The Kurds may have other Salaheddins for whom the Arab world offers greater scope and opportunity than their own circumscribed mountain home. Besides the Kurds of Iraq, there are about 250,000 of them in Syria and Lebanon, mostly in Beirut, Damascus, and the province of Jazíra. Beirut and Damascus are the intellectual capitals of the Kurds and the centers of their political activities.

Like the Kurds, the Berbers are Sunni Moslems and indigenous to the country which they inhabit. They speak a different language from the Arabs, but their culture is not alien; it fits into the country and its Arab-Moslem civilization. In fact, the Arabs of North Africa are largely Arabicized Berbers, and the process of Arabization continues. The French policy of detaching the Berbers from the Arabs has failed. It broke against two rocks: the recalcitrance of the Berbers to assimilation by the French, and the determined opposition to foreign rule among Arabs and Berbers alike. The independence of the Arab countries in the East and the establishment of the Arab League have drawn the people of North Africa, Arabs and Berbers, to the eastern Arabs. Some of the foremost nationalist leaders in North Africa are Berbers, and they speak of Arab solidarity and work for membership in the Arab League.

One of the most important developments during the past thirty years has been the gradual breakdown of the barriers between the various religious communities. The majority religion, as has already been stated, is Islam, but Islam itself is divided into Sunni (Orthodox), the predominant rite, and a number of minorities of whom the largest is the Shi'a of Iraq. Until the end of the first World War relations between Sunni and Shi'a were characterized by hostility. In the days of the Ottoman Empire, the Turks favored the Sunni against the Shi'a who in turn looked to Persia, a Shi'a state, for protection and support. With the formation of the Iraqi state, their mutual antagonism gradually gave way to loyalty to a common state and to the larger Arab nation. In Syria and Lebanon there is a larger variety of Moslem sects; besides Sunni and Shi'a there are Druzes, Alouites, and Ismailis. Until recent times, there were few contacts between the Sunni who lived largely in the cities and plains, and the other sects who on the whole made their home in the mountains; even among these mountain communities themselves, contacts were limited. Modern methods of travel and transmission of ideas, and the growing national consciousness, have drawn together the previously distant groups. Another and still more striking example of the weakening of sectarian differences is the increasing cooperation between the Wahhabis of Arabia and their fellow Moslems and fellow Arabs. During the 18th and 19th centuries, the Wahhabis, imbued with the zeal of religious reformers, considered all other Moslems as deluded. Those who were thus branded did not have much love for their denouncers. This mutual antagonism has softened considerably in recent years.

As for the non-Moslem minorities, about 3,000,000 Christians and 500,000 Jews live in the Arab countries. Before the days of the nationalist state all the religious communities, Moslems, Christians, and Jews, regulated their life in accordance with the principles of their faith. The state was an external organization and barely touched the life of the individual whose personal relations and daily work were governed by religious law and local custom. There was no question of equality before the law since the law, which was a personal matter, differed from one community to the other and from one locality to the next. The religious minorities lived in autonomous communities under their own laws. This was known as the millet system. A council of clergy and laymen constituted the millet court and handled matter pertaining to religion, education, and personal status. The state enforced the decisions of the Council. The head of the millet occupied a high rank in the hierarchy of the state.

The Jews have been long settled in the Arab world. The Iraqi Jews are in part descendants of the Babylonian captivity. Jews have lived in Egypt since the pre-Christian and first Christian centuries. They reached North Africa in the early days of the Diaspora, and many centuries later they came from Spain from which they were expelled after its reconquest by the Christian kings. Among the Jews of North Africa are some of Berber origin who were converted to Judaism. The Jews in Yaman are partly converted Arabs, and partly descendants of immigrants who fled from the persecution of Byzantine rule in Syria and Palestine about the middle of the first millenium A.D.

The lot of the Jews in the Arab countries was on the whole a happy one. They prospered and rose to high positions in the state under the Caliphs of Baghdad, Cairo, and Cordova. In a number of ways they were integrated in Arab society. Their mother tongue was the Arabic language, and it was also the medium of their literary and intellectual products. The greatest Jewish philosopher, Ibn Maimun (Maimonedes), was an Arab by culture and wrote all his works except one in Arabic.[12] With the advent of the modern secular state the Jews were becoming more integrated—until Zionism became a serious threat to Palestine. Among the evils of Zionism is the strain it has placed upon the loyalty of the Jews in the Arab countries. Zionism has introduced anti-Jewish feeling into a part of the world which had so far been free from racial prejudice, and remarkably tolerant of religious differences.

The Christians live in the countries of the Fertile Crescent and in Egypt. They are an indigenous population, descended from the pre-Islamic inhabitants of these countries. A large variety of Christian sects is represented among the Arabs. There are the two orthodoxies of the East and West, the Greek Orthodox and the Roman Catholic Churches. The schisms of the 5th century survive in the Coptic Church of Egypt, and the Jacobite, Gregorian, and Nes-

12. Sarton, *op. cit.*, II, pt. I, p. 369.

torian Churches in Lebanon, Syria, and Iraq. There are the Uniat Churches which have been reconciled to Rome; they submit to the authority of the Pope but retain their own liturgy and rites.[13] These Christians are Arabs in language and culture. In the Middle Ages, they participated brilliantly in the building of the great Arab civilization. In modern times, they were among the first to sound the call for the renewal of the classical Arabic language and the revival of the intellectual heritage of the Arabs, and applied themselves whole-heartedly to this task. Today, Christian and Moslem Arabs are united in combating the external dangers and threats to their common heritage, and in sharing the common task of building a modern Arab society.

There are many difficulties in the path of Arab unity, but they are not of the nature to defy a determined and organized effort born of a faith in the fundamental validity and intrinsic goodness of the idea of unity, and illumined by a vision of the constructive and creative possibilities of a reunited Arab nation. Hampering as these difficulties are, and serious though some of them may be, none of them is inherent in the Arab situation. The great unity of civilization is the essential fact—a unity which embraces even the ethnic and religious dissidents.[14] The differences are by comparison superficial, and many of them are of recent introduction. The realization of Arab unity in political and economic terms awaits the effective machinery which the League has failed to be.

The failure of the Arab League does not signify the failure of the Arab movement. The League, as it has been already stated, is a League of Arab states; this is its official name, as its development has reflected the policies of the individual states. Thus the League is not identical with Arab unity. It is a phase of the movement and a step along the path. The general impatience expressed at the slowness and ineptitude of the League indicates the popular urge towards unity.

The Arab movement is not an innovation, a borrowed concept, or an alien ideology. On the contrary it is a recreation of a social order which the Arabs knew at a time when their society was creative, dynamic, and constructive. It aims at the realization of social solidarity and political stability, and the reestablishment, through moral rebirth, of the place and mission of the Arabs in the family of nations.

13. Hourani, *Minorities in the Arab World*.
14. Weulersse, *Les Paysans de la Syrie et du Proche Orient*, p. 68, and note 2.

Finally the Arab movement is not anti-foreign. It is opposed to foreign domination in any form, political, economic, and cultural. It aspires to build a strong Arab structure in order that the Arabs may resist more effectively the domination by outside forces, free themselves from being considered a pawn in international relations, and deal with other powers on a basis of equality.

CHAPTER XVII

The Powers in the Arab World

THE Arab lands, from Iraq on the Persian Gulf to Morocco on the Atlantic, occupy one of the most vital strategic regions on the face of the earth. North Africa, Egypt, and the Levant, flanking the Mediterranean on its southern and eastern shores, are the doorway to Asia and Africa and a bridgehead between these two continents and Europe. Iraq and Arabia hold fabulous deposits of oil, the prime motor of modern civilization in wartime as in peace. And all these countries form important links in world communications by land and sea and air, lying astride the land routes through Asia and Africa and extending along the Mediterranean and Red Sea, the maritime highway between Europe and the East. The area, enjoying as it does conditions favorable to flying all year round, has become a pivot for air communications across the world.

Lands that command such assets are naturally coveted by the Great Powers anxious to promote their economic and strategic interests.

The Powers directly involved in the Arab world today are France, Great Britain, and the United States. The U.S.S.R. is trying to get a foothold in the Arab countries. A brief historical account may throw light on present day relations between these Powers and the Arab world.

France was the earliest arrival on the scene, and for a time held a pre-eminent position. Her connection goes back to the Crusades, a European adventure in which Frenchmen took a major part, hence the Arabic word *frangi* (Frank) applied to all Europeans. Although the Crusades ended in the defeat of the West and its withdrawal from the East, the memory of that episode was not extinguished with the fall of the last Crusaders' fort on the Syrian shore. It lingered on in the chronicles of the times, in the epic poems, and in popular songs and ballads.

Later, under the Ottoman Sultans, France as the foremost European power was accorded a privileged position in the Ottoman Empire. Capitulations, which exempted foreign nationals from internal taxation and local jurisdiction, were a privilege granted by the Sultans first to France and later extended to other European nations. Nationals of other countries wishing to do business in the Ottoman Empire sought the protection of the French flag upon the sea and of French consuls on the land. The prestige of France was enhanced by her role as protector of the Catholics of the Near East. Her position was further strengthened by the despatch of French educational missions, the earliest of which arrived in Lebanon during the first quarter of the 17th century.

Then, at the end of the 18th century, came the Napoleonic invasion of Egypt. Napoleon's repulse set back French political ambitions in that area, but political failure by no means meant the end of French influence. On the contrary, throughout the 19th century French culture and economic interests were predominant in the Ottoman Empire, especially in Egypt which, in its attempts at westernization, looked primarily to France for inspiration and guidance.

Cultural influence and economic interests were presently overshadowed by the establishment of French political control in North Africa. France, partly to make up for her losses to Great Britain in India and Canada during the 18th century, and partly to recover her prestige after the disaster of the Franco-Prussian war of 1870, looked for expansion towards the Mediterranean where in the course of the 19th century she conquered and annexed Algeria and extended her protectorate over Tunisia. During the first decade of the 20th century—following a deal with Great Britain, the 1904 agreement—France secured a free hand in Morocco in return for her acquiescence in the British occupation of Egypt. The first World War gave France what she had coveted for centuries; a hold on the Levant. Established at both ends of the Mediterranean, her prestige reached its height immediately after the first war. Since then it has followed a steadily declining course.

The decline came partly as a result of the greatly weakened and reduced position of France in relation to other powers, and partly because she has persisted in an anachronistic and rigid colonial policy. Unlike Great Britain which toyed with the idea of Arab freedom and tried to direct and make use of it, France looked upon the Arab movement, as it expressed itself in the Arab Revolt and in the national struggle of the inter-war period, as her enemy.

French official circles were hostile to the Revolt from its inception to its end. With the purpose of minimizing its significance they denied it the name Arab and arbitrarily called it the Sharifian or Hijazi Revolt, as if it were a personal project of the Sharif of Mecca and confined to the outlying province of Hijaz. As the Revolt progressed and the Arab army marched into Syria at the side of the Allies, French hostility increased. The Arab kingdom set up in Syria and its head, Faisal, were the chief target of French antagonism. After France evicted Faisal from Syria and extended her control over the country, she used the Mandate as a cloak under which a colonial policy was pursued. She failed completely to understand the Syrian struggle for freedom and its place in the larger Arab movement. She discounted the national leaders and the popular support behind them and looked upon Syria not as an Arab unit but as a mosaic of religious and ethnic minorities, behind which concept she entrenched herself, and in that position felt secure. The world in which French policy was formulated and the world of Arab realities and aspirations were so remote from one another that they hardly ever met. Consequently, France lost her earlier influence on the Arab movement. For it is worth remembering that until the end of the first World War French prestige was paramount in those Arab countries which had relations with Europe. The pre-war liberation movement of the Arabs drew inspiration from the principles of the French Revolution and the ideals of French political democracy. More than any other European country France had a cultural hold upon educated Arabs who admired French literature and thought, and considered the French language as the primary medium of culture. This moral prestige was rudely shaken as a result of French political control over Syria and Lebanon.

France persisted in her unrealistic policy even after her collapse under the German attack which revealed the inner weakness of the nation. Following her surrender to the Germans, her position in the Levant was no longer tenable. That position had depended on the legal basis of the Mandate, on the ability of France to enforce the Mandate, and on the moral prestige of the Mandatory Power. The prestige which had accumulated in pre-Mandate days had been dissipated in the course of a quarter century of French rule. Still France had maintained a show of strength. Now that vanished also. And finally the last tie was cut when France withdrew from the League of Nations in the spring of 1941. All the while the Arab movement was growing in strength.

The French, nevertheless, clung rigidly to their old ways until they were compelled to leave Syria and Lebanon under the force of local resistance, backed by British intervention and later supported by the United Nations.

There remains for France cultural and economic links with Syria and even more with Lebanon. The French University in Beirut is a cultural center of merit and great potentiality. Established in the 1870's, half a century before the French Mandate, this university had shared in the Arab revival through its editing and publication of classical texts. Under the Mandate it became the mouthpiece of the French High Commissioner and an instrument of French cultural and political control. Now that the Mandate has been terminated, the university may again distinguish itself in intellectual and professional services. A French university free of political ties can be a wholesome influence in the Arab world. It could bring to the Arabs French culture at its best and serve as the interpreter of Arabic culture to the French and perhaps other European peoples.

The withdrawal of France from the Levant has had its repercussions on her North African Empire. It is precisely in anticipation of this reaction that France held on to Syria and Lebanon so tenaciously. But her methods were discreditable and resulted in utterly defeating their purpose. There is little evidence, however, that her Syrian adventure has taught France to deal more constructively with her remaining Arab dependencies.

North Africa presents a more difficult problem than the Levant. If Syria and Lebanon were important to France for sentimental connections and reasons of prestige, the importance of the North African territories stems from the more tangible forces of economy and security. The French hold over North Africa is much stronger than it ever was over the Levant. Here there is no Mandate and, therefore, not even the semblance of an international responsibility. France has a free hand in Tunisia, Algeria, and Morocco which Frenchmen consider an extension of France beyond the sea. To assure the permanence of French control, a French population exceeding a million colonists has been settled in these dependencies. The colonists who control the governments and resources of the North African territories have bitterly, and so far successfully, opposed any changes which might loosen their monopolistic hold.

The post-war years, eventful in North Africa as elsewhere in the world, have brought little change to French policy which continues to view the region from the angle of narrowly conceived French interests to which North Africa is an appendage: a reservoir of man-power in time of war—as indeed it has been during two world wars—and in peace time a field for economic exploitation. Rather than loosen her hold on North Africa as a result of her weakened world position, France holds on tenaciously to the region to counterbalance her weakness. As a result, restlessness and outbreaks have persistently marked the North African scene. The ruthlessness of the French authorities in meeting native resistance has inflamed the people of North Africa and antagonized the entire Arab world. Consequently the presence of France in North Africa, instead of contributing to Mediterranean security, is a major source of instability in the area.

France's more powerful and also more successful rival in the Arab world, Great Britain, became actively interested and involved in the area during the 19th century when the Mediterranean came to be regarded as the lifeline of the Empire. To guard this line, Great Britain established herself at its two gates, first Gibraltar and later Suez, and at strategic islands along the way, Malta and Cyprus. But the line of Empire did not end at the eastern gate of the Mediterranean. Beyond, it extended through the Red Sea and the Indian Ocean. Hence the importance of controlling both ends of the Red Sea—the Straits of Bab-al-Mandab at the southern exit as well as the Suez Canal in the north—and keeping a close watch on the Persian Gulf and the Arabian shores.

During the 19th century, Great Britain's Mediterranean policy ran against two rivals, France and Russia. France was pushed out of Egypt. As a recompense, the British connived at her expansion in North Africa. To thwart Russia's attempts at expansion towards the Mediterranean, Britain supported the Ottoman Empire by maintaining the principle of its territorial integrity.

The insistence of Britain on the maintenance of the status quo in the Ottoman Empire brought her for the first time into conflict with the national aspirations of the Arabs. The British Government, in its concern for the safety of the route to India and the general security of the Empire, believed that the moribund Ottoman Empire was a better guarantee than a budding Arab nation whose place in the imperial pattern could not be predicted. Hence the determined opposition to Mohammad Ali and his son Ibrahim in their attempts to free the Arabs from Turkish rule and establish an independent state in the Arab provinces of the Turkish Empire. From that time to the present day British policy has been one of the main obstacles in the path of Arab freedom and unity.

This, despite the fact that the Arab ideal has had an emotional appeal to individual Englishmen and women, a number of whom have responded dramatically to its attraction. More than any other people the British have contributed to the literature of travel, exploration, and adventure among the Arabs. Some of that literature has taken its place among the classics of the English language, such for example the *Arabia Deserta* of Doughty, and Lawrence's *Seven Pillars of Wisdom*. English men and women have championed the Arab cause. In the 19th century, Sir Wilfred Blunt and Lady Anne espoused Arab freedom with the ardour and conviction which Lord Byron had felt towards the cause of Hellenic freedom. Early in this century Lawrence and Gertrude Bell supported Arab liberty, but unlike the Blunts, their support was colored with the imperialist's view which looked upon the Arab movement as the handmaid of British imperial interests.

While individual Englishmen have been romantic about the Arabs, there has been little romance about British policy in the Arab world. The British dealt a heavy blow to Arab aspirations when after the first World War they dismembered Syria in agreement with France and created the most serious problem in the Arab world by sponsoring the Jewish National Home. In Iraq as elsewhere, new minorities were introduced and communal and ethnic differences stressed. "Divide and rule," seen at its worst in Syria, was practised in the Sudan where steps were taken, on the one hand to alienate the Sudan from Egypt, and on the other to divide the Sudan itself by separating the southern part from the north. Later, the same policy was applied in Libya where, after the defeat of the Italians, three different administrations were set up and separatist tendencies encouraged.

The policy which emerged from the first World War and was practised in the inter-war period rested upon the assumption that a series of weak, dependent states would fit better into the scheme of imperial interests than a strong and united Arab nation. In this scheme the Jewish National Home, as it was then conceived, had its place. Created by Britain, it would owe her gratitude and allegiance, and would further contribute to the weakening of the Arabs by thrusting an alien wedge into their midst.

Self-justification led the British to the delusion that they had done enough for the Arabs by liberating them from the Turks and setting up these semi-independent states under Arab kings and Amirs. Even Lawrence believed that Britain had acquitted herself of her wartime promises and commitments to the Arabs by the settlement which issued from the Cairo Conference of 1921 which placed Faisal on the throne of Iraq and created the Amirate of Transjordan under Abdallah. His satisfaction with the settlement is in strange contrast with his bitterness about the "Fraud."[1] This showed how little even informed Englishmen understood the Arab movement whose purpose was freedom from foreign rule of any kind, not only Turkish rule, and whose ideal and hope was the re-creation of a united Arab nation and not the provision of thrones for kings and princes.

Throughout the inter-war period, Great Britain made common cause with reactionary elements among the Arabs and in return relied upon them for support. She stood behind the kings she created. In Egypt, she balanced the king, however autocratic and corrupt, against the *Wafd* which, for all its faults and failings, did stand for the people. She supported King Abdallah for Transjordan, whom she considered her best friend among the Arabs, although he had forfeited the respect of his subjects, and of all patriotic Arabs outside his kingdom. Great Britain preferred monarchy to the republican regime for the Arabs, the former supposedly representing stability and continuity. Furthermore, monarchy with its court pomp and ceremony and the respect due to kings as symbols set apart was a sort of opium to the people. High society tried to imitate the ways of the court and were in turn imitated by those below, and so on down. This tended to divert the people's energy from serious preoccupations and to deflect the course of development away from the basic issues.

The natural conservatism of the British, coupled with what they conceived to be their interests, issued in a policy which favored the maintenance of the *status quo,* allowing only for such evolution as could be kept under control and confined within the limits and in the direction charted by British authorities. The general pattern of evolution rested on the creation of a shadowy independence,

1. *Seven Pillars of Wisdom,* 1935, p. 276, footnote; Antonius, *op. cit.,* p. 319.

with native governments and representative assemblies under constitutions giving undue power to the ruler who owed Britain his position and was bound to her by treaty. Such a set-up was then defended as representing the will of the people and therefore legal. Popular opposition to it was termed violence and chaos to be put down by force. The treaty assumed sanctity. Attempts to abrogate it were branded as international lawlessness. Such being Britain's course, she alienated the youth of the nation and its progressive elements who turned away from her after losing all faith and hope in what she had to offer.

In recent years there have been signs of a change in Britain's policy. The change is partly the outcome of Britain's emergence from the war greatly weakened—she no longer commanded the force and the resources necessary to make her will effective. Partly it is due to developments within Arab society itself. Britain's endorsement of the idea of Arab unity through the establishment of the Arab League, and her aid to Syria and Lebanon in their conflict with France, were tokens of this change. Further evidence was Britain's willingness to reconsider her treaty relations with the Arab countries with the view of making concessions to national sovereignty. British-Arab friendship found a forceful spokesman in the late Foreign Secretary Ernest Bevin, who expressed this trend when he declared in Parliament that Britain's policy of consolidating her position in the Arab world should rest on the only secure basis of friendship with the Arabs.[2]

But Britain's steps in the direction of a constructive Arab policy have been faltering, her actions hesitant and half-hearted. Though it supported the independence of the two Levant states, the British Government recognized the special position of France in the Levant as it continues to support the repressive French policy in North Africa. The revision of the Anglo-Iraqi treaty of 1930, which issued in the abortive Portsmouth treaty of January 1948, offered the old bonds in a gilded form. Its immediate and violent rejection by the people of Iraq revealed once again that the gulf between British policy and Arab aspirations remained wide. Nor have attempts at the revision of the Anglo-Egyptian treaty of 1936 fared any better. After protracted and fruitless negotiations the Egyptian Government announced its unilateral abrogation of the treaty. Excesses committed by British forces stationed in the Suez Canal Zone in meeting Egyptian resistance, and the invitation of

2. Bevin's speech in the House of Commons, May 24, 1946.

Prime Minister Churchill to the governments of the United States, France, and Turkey to send troops to Egypt, brought Anglo-Egyptian relations to the breaking point.

That the Arabs should still consider England as imperialist may shock certain sections of the British public who sincerely believe that imperialism is dead as far as England is concerned. They point to the relinquishment of India, capstone of the Empire, as proof of the validity of their belief. But for the Arabs the fact is that England remains in their countries against their will. She maintains troops in Egypt and holds two air bases in Iraq. Transjordan is a British stronghold. The Sudan has been ruled like a colony, and Libya's independence is delimited by Britain's predominant position in the country. The coasts of the Arab-Island—except for the sectors in Saudi Arabia—are under British control, and the Persian Gulf is a British lake.

But England is no longer able unaided to maintain her position in the area either in the face of internal resistance and impatience at any form of foreign control, or against potential danger from the outside. Another power, the United States, has come into the region as Britain's ally and also her rival.

Of the powers dealing with the Arab world, the United States alone was unhampered by a record of imperialism. No other country had among the Arabs such a reputation for disinterestedness, and none enjoyed in such measure their good will. The cultural institutions which Americans have maintained in several Arab countries during the past hundred years have rendered valuable educational services without trying to promote American political or economic interests. In fact, America had no political and few economic interests in the area before the outbreak of the second World War. When, after the first War, the Syrian National Congress expressed a willingness to seek technical and economic assistance from America in preference to any other power it did so "in the belief that the American nation is devoid of colonial ambitions and has no political designs" on Syria.[3] The principles and declarations of President Wilson made a deep impression upon the Arabs and gave them hope all the way from Iraq to North Africa. In the inter-war period, when the hand of France and England weighed heavily upon the Arab peoples, America continued quietly and constructively her educational work among them. To the Arabs, as to the other nations in the East, the United States was the cham-

3. Antonius, *op. cit.*, Appendix G, p. 441.

pion of freedom and the friend of peoples struggling to achieve their liberty and independence. Thus trusted and loved, the United States had an auspicious start which held promising opportunities of fruitful cooperation for the mutual benefit of Arabs and Americans. That happy situation has been seriously impaired by America's stand on Palestine.

The United States, which had played second fiddle to Britain on the Zionist question, came out during the last war and the years that followed as the arch-champion of Zionism. When Great Britain had become too weak to continue the imposition of her Zionist policy upon the Arabs by force, as she had done between 1920 and 1939, and was willing to give belated recognition to Arab rights by confining the Jewish National Home within the limits it had then reached, the United States threw her full weight on the Zionist side, utterly disregarding Arab rights in their own country and amazingly careless of the long range interests of America herself in this vital area. Pressure was exerted on Great Britain, not only through the press and other instruments of public opinion, but officially and on the highest level. President Truman was an ardent Zionist and used his power and influence to promote Zionist aims. Threats issued from senators and representatives to the effect that should England fail to comply with the wishes of the American Zionists, American financial aid to Britain through loans and the Marshall Plan would be withheld. Hundreds of millions of dollars were raised in the United States for the Zionists in Palestine. With these millions Jewish terrorism was financed, immigrants smuggled, and arms bought.

The Government of the United States, more than any other, is responsible for the partition of Palestine and the establishment of the Jewish state. It was United States pressure which forced partition through the United Nations Assembly where throughout the proceedings on Palestine the American delegation assiduously supported the Zionists, canvassing votes for partition. Its attitude amounted virtually to an anti-Arab offensive. These dealings produced throughout the Arab world a wave of resentment and bitter disillusion with American action as contrasted with what many Arabs had come to believe as American principles.

The United States continues to support Israel notwithstanding the repeated acts of aggression of this new state, its expansionist intentions, and its utter disregard of United Nations decisions. But for United States financial and moral support the new state would have collapsed, based as it is on a precarious economy. American pressure is believed to be behind the decision of the German government to indemnify Israel for the damage inflicted upon Jewish life and property under Hitler, an indemnity which rightly belongs to Jewish victims wherever they are and not to Israel the representative of militant Jewry.

The American public has come to see the Arabs through Zionist spectacles. Zionist propaganda, in its effort to win American support and hide the injury and injustice done to the Arabs, has presented a picture of Arab backwardness out of all proportion to reality. At times the denunciation by the Zionists and their friends of everything Arab descended to the level of vilification and abuse. The liberal press was particularly hostile. According to sections of this press, the Arabs are the last remnants of a feudal society and fight bitterly against any democratic or civilizing innovation.[4] A violent invective appeared under the name of a well-known writer who concluded his diatribe with the assertion that the Arabs had "no rights which the civilized world in the Twentieth Century should respect."[5]

Thus insult heaped upon injury left the Arabs stunned and antagonized by the abuse and harm so recklessly dealt them by a friendly people, the Americans. And as America has come to see the Arabs through a Zionist glass so have the Arabs seen America with a Zionist mask on her face.

The attempts to alienate the sympathy of the American public from the Arabs, and the anti-Arab policy of the United States Government with regard to Palestine, came at a time when the Arab world was beginning to assume new and great importance for America.

For the interests of the United States in this area are no longer confined to American educational institutions. Americans have acquired valuable economic assets in the form of oil concessions, the importance of which grows steadily, considering the depletion of United States oil reserves and the increasing demand for large supplies of oil for the reconstruction of Europe and the industrialization of Asia. The strategic considerations related to the area are no less important than economic interests. During the last war, the Middle East was a pivot of Allied operations. From this

4. *The Nation*, October 20, 1945.
5. Louis Bromfield in the Sunday *World-Herald Magazine*, December 1, 1946.

region, the defense of India, Africa, and to some extent Russia was conducted. Since the termination of the war, the eastern Mediterranean has come to be considered vital to the security of the United States itself. In fact the whole area extending from the Persian Gulf with its oil fields, to North Africa where the United States has acquired air and naval bases, has become involved in the American strategy directed at the containment of Russia.

Unlike the United States, Russia's political ambitions in the Middle East are not of recent date but extend back into the early part of the 19th century. At that time Great Britain was Russia's successful antagonist. She blocked Russia's expansion toward the Mediterranean by upholding the territorial integrity of the Ottoman Empire. In the Persian Gulf area, the British Government announced its intention to keep Russian influence out of the valley of the Tigris and Euphrates, and to prevent the concession to Russia of a port on the Persian Gulf; such concession, it affirmed, would be considered an international provocation to war.

Throughout the 19th century Russia hammered at the Ottoman Empire in an attempt to break it up and inherit some of the parts. When the break-up did come after the first World War, Russia herself had collapsed and was in the throes of a mighty revolution. During the inter-war period, Russia was occupied with her internal problems, so the disturbing shadow of the bear receded for a while from the international arena. When on occasion it emerged, it did so to assure the neighbors, Turkey and Persia and the rest of Asia, of Russia's sympathy and good intentions towards them, and to denounce Western imperialism which was exploiting the peoples of Asia and Africa.

The second World War lifted Russia from her isolation and raised her to the first rank of world powers—a position which she shares with one other power, the United States of America. Once more she is trying to push towards the southern seas, the Mediterranean in the west, and in the east the Persian Gulf and the Indian Ocean.

For Russia, the Middle East at her back door is vitally important. She covets its oil resources which, according to estimates of January 1953, constitute 53.46% of the world's known oil reserves. Its warm waters supply the deficiency of her land locked seas and frozen harbors. Above all, the Middle East is significant for strategic considerations, for it is an area from which attacks could be directed at particularly vulnerable points in Russian territory. Control of the area would place Russia in a preponderant position in the event of war.

The presence of large quantities of oil in the Arab countries has emphasized their economic and strategic importance and brought into still sharper focus the international rivalries for control of the region. To help understand this aspect of power conflict, a brief account is given of the oil situation in the Arab world.

There are two massive petroleum basins in the world. One is located around the Caribbean Sea and includes the United States, Mexico, Venezuela, and Colombia. The other takes in the Middle East from southern Russia to the Persian Gulf.

The Caribbean area was until recently by far the more developed of the two. But the Persian Gulf is rapidly becoming the center of world oil production. A decade ago, before many of the fields on the Arabian shore of the Gulf were discovered, a distinguished oil geologist, De Golyer, stated: "When one considers the great oil discoveries which have resulted from the meager exploitation thus far accomplished in the Middle East, the substantial number of known prospects not yet drilled, and the great areas still practically unexplored, the conclusion is inescapable that reserves of great magnitude remain to be discovered."[6] Most authorities quote upwards of a 100 billion barrels as the ultimate reserves to be discovered in the Persian Gulf area.[7] The extraordinary productivity of the fields—the yield of each well is entirely out of scale with normal experience in America or elsewhere—and the low cost of production, due among other things to the geological formation, cheap labor, and the small amount of wild-cat drilling, make the Arabian oil concessions a highly profitable venture.[8]

These concessions are wholly under Anglo-American control—with the exception of the Iraq Petroleum Company (IPC) in which French and Dutch interests have a share.

The IPC is the oldest concession operating in the Arab area of the Persian Gulf. Granted in 1925 for a period of 75 years, its terms were revised in 1931 and covered all Iraq except the vilayat of

6. De Golyer: Preliminary Report to the Technical Oil Mission to the Middle East, *Bulletin of the American Association of Petroleum Geologists,* vol. 28, 1944, p. 921.

7. Raymond F. Mikesell and Hollis B. Chenery: *Arabian Oil. America's Stake in the Middle East,* 1949, p. 28.

8. Sir Olaf Caroe: *Wells of Power,* p. 92; Mikesell and Chenery: *op. cit.,* pp. 20, 29.

Basra, subsequently granted to a subsidiary of IPC. The Company is formed by the British Anglo-Iranian, the Dutch-British Shell, the French Compagnie Française des Pétroles, and the Near East Development Corporation owned jointly and equally by Standard of New Jersey and Socony Vacuum. Each of the four partners owns 23.75% of the stocks. The remaining 5% are held by the original concessionaire under the Ottoman Empire. Production had come from one field, Kirkuk in northern Iraq, discovered in 1927, until the Zubair field, west of Basra, began producing in January 1952. Two pipelines twelve inches in diameter have since the beginning of 1935 connected the Kirkuk field with the Mediterranean, one line ending in Haifa,[9] the other in Tripoli. A duplicating 16-inch line has been laid from Kirkuk to Tripoli, and a 30-inch line, completed in 1952, connects Kirkuk with Banyas on the Syrian coast. A small refinery at Kirkuk meets local needs. The Tripoli refinery has been enlarged to an annual capacity of 500,000 tons. The Haifa refinery practically closed down when Iraq stopped the flow of oil to Israel in 1948.

Subsidiaries of the Iraq Petroleum Company hold 75-year concessions on the eastern shores of Arabia south of the Saudi Kingdom. Petroleum Development, Qatar, was established in 1935; Petroleum Development, Oman, in 1937. Petroleum Development, Trucial Coast, covers the Shaikhdoms of the coast under concessions granted between 1937 and 1945. Production began in Qatar early in 1950. None of the other areas is producing yet.

The Arabian American Oil Company—Aramco—is entirely American and operates in Saudi Arabia. The concession, covering eastern Saudi Arabia, was granted in 1933 to Standard of California for a period of 66 years. A supplemental agreement, concluded in 1939, extended the area leased to cover the entire kingdom and include the Saudi undivided half shares in the Kuwait and Iraq neutral zones respectively. Later the company relinquished its rights in the Kuwait neutral zone in return for the right to drill under the Gulf waters off the Saudi shore. In 1936, Standard of California, in need of marketing facilities, invited the Texas Company to hold an equal share in the concession. Texas, which had developed extensive facilities in Asia, Africa, and Europe, needed oil for its markets, and the two companies combined their interests. Standard of New Jersey and Socony Vacuum joined the combine in 1946, the reserves having proved of such magnitude as to call

9. Oil has not flowed through the Haifa line since the partition of Palestine.

for a vast capital outlay. Socony owns 10% of Aramco's stock, the other three own the 90% equally between them.

Aramco is the largest producer in the Middle East. Crude production averaged 840,000 barrels per day in 1952. The oil is pumped to the Mediterranean through Tapline—Trans-Arabian Pipeline—a 30-31-inch pipeline laid across 1,068 miles, mostly desert, between Dhahran on the Persian Gulf and Zahrani a few miles south of Sidon. Some oil is locally processed at Aramco's refinery in Ras Tanura, where the crude run during 1952 averaged 172,500 barrels daily, while a portion is pumped through an underwater pipeline to Bapeo's refinery on the island of Bahrain. Bapeo is the Bahrain Petroleum Company owned equally by Standard of California and Texas under a concession granted in 1930.

The Kuwait Oil Company (KOC) is an Anglo-American concern owned equally by Anglo-Iranian and the Gulf Exploration Corporation and incorporated as a British Company. The concession covers the whole area of Kuwait for a period of 75 years beginning December 1934. Oil was struck in 1936 in the Burgan field, the largest single oil structure yet found; its proven reserves are estimated at 14% of the world's known reserves. Commercial production began in 1946. Another field, Magwa, was opened in 1952. Already Kuwait rivals Saudi Arabia as largest producer. The KOC ships its crude by tankers loaded at Ahmadi, the oil port about 30 miles south of Kuwait city. The Ahmadi refinery, commissioned late in 1949, has a yearly capacity of one million tons.

Two American companies have prospecting rights in the Kuwait neutral zone. The American Independent Oil Company leased Kuwait's share in 1948; the share of Saudi Arabia was given in 1949 to Pacific Western Oil Corporation. Oil was found in the neutral zone early in 1953. An American group, the International Marine Oil Company,[10] in 1949 obtained the offshore concession around the peninsula of Qatar.

Since oil assumed importance as a strategic commodity closely linked with security, foreign oil concessions have become a matter of state policy. Great Britain, awake to the importance of oil in the Persian Gulf area, inserted in her treaties with the Persian Gulf chiefs clauses which reserved to the British government the right to make the oil grants in the territories covered by the treaties. The entry of American companies in the area was not welcomed by the

10. Owned by Superior Oil Company of California and Central Mining and Investment Corporation.

British. American interests were not allowed to participate in the development of Iraqi oil until the United States Government protested that Britain, then Mandatory over Iraq, had by excluding American Companies violated the open door policy under which the League of Nations mandates were to be operated. When the British Government had refused permission to Gulf Oil Corporation for a concession in Kuwait, the company appealed to the State Department which in turn protested to the Foreign Office, and the proceedings led to Britain's acquiescence in an Anglo-American partnership in the development of Kuwait oil. The American company operating in Bahrain is in a large measure under British control. The British Government refused concessions in Qatar and Trucial Oman to Standard of California, and leased the areas to subsidiaries of the IPC although the local Shaikhs would have preferred the American company.[11]

The expansion of American interests in Arabian oil nearly involved the United States Government in a dispute with France over the interpretation of what is known as the Red Line Agreement. This agreement, concluded in 1928 between the four participants in the IPC—of which France is one—stipulated that the oil resources within the area formerly comprised in the Turkish Empire and circumscribed by a red line would be developed by all four groups acting jointly, no separate action by any of the participants being sanctioned. In 1947, when Standard of New Jersey and Socony Vacuum decided to buy shares in Aramco, the French Government protested that their action was a violation of the Red Line Agreement. The State Department met the protest with the assertion that the Red Line Agreement had been invalidated by the British Trading-with-the-Enemy Act when France became allied with Germany during the occupation. France was assured, however, that the development of Saudi Arabian oil would not interfere with the expansion of the oil operations in Iraq.

The American Government was concerned enough about foreign oil to create in 1943 a Petroleum Reserves Corporation (PRC) with powers to acquire reserves of crude petroleum from sources outside the United States and to construct and operate refineries, pipelines, and other facilities abroad. The Secretary of the Interior was President of the PRC, and the Board of Directors included the

11. To regulate their relations with regard to the acquisition and distribution of Middle East Oil, the governments of Great Britain and the United States signed a Petroleum Agreement in 1944, amended the following year. But Congress has withheld ratification of the agreement.

Secretaries of State, War, and the Navy, and the head of the Foreign Economic Administration. The PRC negotiated for the purchase of the American concessions in Saudi Arabia and Bahrain, but the companies refused to sell, confident that the Government would protect the oil even if it did not own it. Another attempt at government ownership was made early in 1944 when the President of the PRC concluded a tentative agreement with Aramco and the Gulf Exploration Company whereby the Government proposed to construct and operate a pipeline connecting the fields of Saudi Arabia and Kuwait with the Mediterranean. But the project, opposed by the oil industry and by various sections of public opinion, was dropped, and the line was constructed by the companies comprised in Aramco.

In their relations with the Arab countries, the United States and Great Britain, however they may differ on particular issues, are united by a common purpose which prescribes a common overall policy. France moves in their orbit and is supported by them. The purpose of the three Western Powers is to keep Russia out of the area. Great Britain and France—the latter with far less flexibility than Britain—hold on tenaciously to their positions in the Arab world on the grounds which they have impressed upon the United States: that their withdrawal would create a vacuum into which Russia is ready to step. Hence their insistence on stability and security as the primary needs of the area, a view embodied in the Three Power Declaration and the Allied Command for Middle East Defense Project.

The Three Power Declaration, issued in May 1950 in London by the Foreign Ministers of France, Great Britain, and the United States, announced that arms would be available to the Arab states and Israel to meet their needs for internal security and defense. Should any of the states resort to the use of force to change the boundaries or truce lines, the Three Powers will take measures within or outside the United Nations to stop the aggression.

To the articulate Arab public, the Proclamation meant that the three Powers had constituted themselves trustees over the area. With regard to preventing the use of force, it was doubted that the Proclamation could check Israel's aggression any more than the decisions of the United Nations had done.

The answer of the Arab States, conveyed through the Arab League, expressed the apprehensions raised by the intention of the Three Powers to act outside the United Nations. On the question of arms the statement said that it was for the Arabs to decide what their needs were in relation to the extent of their territory, their extensive frontiers, and the size of their population. It sought assurance that the proclamation did not prejudice the final settlement of the Palestine question. And finally it affirmed that peace could be assured in the Middle East only if its problems are settled in accordance with the principles of justice and right.

The Middle East Defense Plan, offered to Egypt in the fall of 1951 by Great Britain in association with the United States, France, and Turkey, was intended to replace the Anglo-Egyptian treaty of 1936 which Egypt had just then abrogated. Egypt rejected the plan as substituting for the British occupation an international occupation.

Whether they act singly or jointly, the Western Powers have always subordinated the real needs of the area to their own interests. In the present world tension, the region is important as a base for defense and attack and as a source of oil. Its local problems and the legitimate interests and aspirations of its peoples are considered insignificant in relation to its place in the global strategy of the Western Powers.

While they continue to ignore Arab rights, the Western Powers assume that the Arabs will rally to their side in a future war as they had done in the past. To this effect, Mr. Morrison, former British Secretary of State for Foreign Affairs, spoke in the House of Commons in July 1951. It is precisely the experience of the first and second World Wars which makes the Arabs suspicious of Western projects for their defense.

The Arabs have been censured for not giving wholehearted support to the Allies during the second World War. The Arab attitude may be more sympathetically understood if compared to a similar situation in India. Both India and the Arab countries were under the domination of one or more of these Allies whose cause they were expected to espouse. Naturally neither Indians nor Arabs were enthusiastic about fighting one form of authoritarian rule when they were subjected to another, nor were they prepared to fight for liberty elsewhere as long as they were denied liberty in their own countries. To the Indians, there was not much difference between the fascist dictatorship which Britain was fighting in Europe and her authoritarian rule in India where her Viceroy wielded the unchecked powers of a dictator and was responsible to no one in India.[12] The Indians were not consulted about the war which they were expected to join. Nor were they free to determine their place and share in that war. All the while the British Government refused to give assurances about Indian freedom.

In these circumstances, and when Britain was engaged in a life and death struggle with fascism, the Indian people embarked on the "Quit India" campaign in the course of which scores of thousands of Indians were imprisoned or interned without trial, thousands were shot to death, and tens of thousands were driven out of schools and colleges. A reign of terror prevailed.[13] At the head of the Quit India Movement were Gandhi and Nehru. Now it is difficult to find anywhere in the world—whether in the East or in the West—greater men, men more sincerely and seriously devoted to the cause of freedom and democracy, or of a broader and more intense humanity than Gandhi and Nehru. And yet these two men —because their country had suffered long and the spirit of their people had been cramped by subjection to foreign rule, and because they had lost faith in England's promises—did not refrain from leading a movement which was bound to hinder the war effort of the Allies. This they did because they were convinced that it was their right and their first duty to free their own people before supporting wars for freedom elsewhere.

In the Arab countries there was nothing comparable to the "Quit India" movement. Not that the Arab grievances were less real than the Indian, but the Arabs lacked the leadership which in India identified itself with the masses and had worked for a generation to awaken the people's spirit and organize and direct their actions.

Among the Arab public in general there was an unfeigned hostility, provoked by the Palestine issue more than by any other wrong. Among the more thoughtful people, although they feared and abhorred fascism and were by tradition and education spiritually akin to the ideals of the democracies, there were forebodings about a post-war settlement to be effected by those powers who were in control of their countries. On the official level, however,— with the exception of the Kailani coup in Iraq—the Allied cause received all the aid which it was within the power of the local governments to extend. The economic resources of the Arab countries were controlled and directed to promote the war effort. Mili-

12. Jawaharlal Nehru: *The Discovery of India*, Calcutta, 1948, p. 2.
13. *Ibid.*, p. 1.

tary requirements were given priority in the use of all communications and ports. Egypt was the base of all operations in the Middle East, and Alexandria the headquarters of the east Mediterranean fleet. King Ibn Saud gave the Allies unwavering support throughout the war, and his moral influence carried weight among the Arabs outside his own kingdom. That the military power of the Arabs was negligible was due to the fact that in the case of Egypt and Iraq Great Britain, bound by treaty to train and equip their armies, had left them deplorably inadequate. The Arab Legion of Transjordan was as completely under British control as the Levant armies—Syrian and Lebanese troops—were under the French.

It was part of Britain's policy of keeping the Arab countries dependent upon her for their defense that the armies of Egypt and Iraq, entrusted to her, were left unfit. Britain's wartime Premier, Mr. Churchill, advised the Egyptian Government to stay out of the war, partly for lack of arms and partly because it was to Britain's advantage that Cairo, which had become the second capital of the British Empire, should remain an open city. But when Egypt reclaimed Britain's debts to her—to the amount of £400 million—the same Mr. Churchill, then in the opposition, declared in Parliament that these debts hardly paid for Britain's defense of Egypt.

It is this kind of defense imposed from the outside that Egypt and the other Arab countries are no longer prepared to accept. Such defense has its penalties in subverting the morale of a people and sacrificing their interest to those of the defending power. That the interests of the Arabs and of the Western Powers have been at variance has been amply demonstrated. The Korean war has brought home to the Arabs some sharp contrasts. Aggression of the North against the South Koreans evoked immediate action by the United Nations led by the United States. But in Palestine the aggression of an alien people against the indigenous population received the sanction of the United Nations, again led by the United States. In Korea, two strong armies were trained and equipped within a few years, while in Egypt and Iraq England left the local armies fit for little more than marching in parades. In the Korean war, among the forces which distinguished themselves were the Turkish troops, and for their bravery they received due admiration in the world press as their action was rewarded by the increase of United States aid to Turkey. Such just recognition contrasts painfully with the attitude towards the North African peoples, scores of thousands of whom fought equally bravely in two world wars on the side of the Allies. But because they fought as subject peoples their valor and their sacrifice were denied the recognition extended to a free people fighting for a cause. The inescapable moral is that valor and sacrifice count when backed by a national standing which gives them dignity and worth.

In their plans for Middle East defense the Western Powers consider the Arabs not as partners but as instruments of policy. They propose to secure a friendly territory and a passive people willing to place at their disposal resources, communications, bases, and labor as they had done in previous wars. They assume that the Arabs will acquiesce in these plans, the assumption being based on the belief that Arab society is fundamentally hostile to communism, that the Arab masses, conservative and apathetic, may be easily kept under control, and that the ruling classes whose vested interests lie in the maintenance of the status quo can be counted upon to do the bidding of the Western Powers.

This view can no longer be safely held. The masses are astir with ideas and emotions of various origins.[14] The ruling cliques have been discredited and are fast being removed from their position of control. New men, sprung from the masses or identified with them, are assuming power and conducting public affairs in the interests of the people above all other interests and considerations. Neither is it safe to rest upon Arab hostility to communism, however real that may be.

It is true that many considerations estrange the Arabs from communism. Communist ideology, based as it is upon a materialistic concept of history and of man's destiny, is the very antithesis of the Arab spiritual heritage according to which man is God's image created to fulfill His purpose upon the earth and destined to immortality in the world hereafter. Communist society, in which the individual and the family are subordinated to an exalted, all powerful and pervading state, is opposed to the basic concepts of Arab society where the family is the fundamental unit and basis of social solidarity in which the individual finds his security and self-fulfillment. Moreover, the Arab is an individualist and not easily regimented. He is attached to individual private property of which land is the most cherished possession. Next to his kin, the peasant Arab—and the vast majority of Arabs are peasants—is

14. "I have not seen a village between the Mediterranean and the Pacific that was not stirring uneasily." William O. Douglas: *Strange Lands and Friendly People,* 1951, p. 317.

attached to his land which represents not only wealth but prestige in his community and perpetuation and continued existence. For the land, inherited from ancestors, is to be faithfully kept and transmitted to descendants, thus assuring the continuation of the group around the ground to which it is linked. It is, however, necessary to qualify this statement by the reservation that since most of the Arab peasants do not actually own the land which they work, communism is not without attraction to them.

Thoughtful Arabs are not willing to see Communist indoctrination fill the minds of Arab youth and stir the masses at a time when Arab society is experiencing an inner crisis in trying to rediscover its own heritage, rethink this heritage in terms relevant to present day life, and become once again a creative force in world society. At such a time of intellectual and spiritual searching it is imperative that all the currents of thought be allowed to flow freely, that no one doctrine be imposed from the outside, and none of the trends which agitate the contemporary world be banned.

In so far as communism obstructs the right of the individual to fulfill his destiny, and in the measure that it seeks to undermine the Arab heritage and the fundamental bases of society, communism will be opposed by the Arabs.

This much said, it is necessary to state that, however communist ideology might be opposed to the essence of the Arab heritage, the foremost Communist State, Soviet Russia, is not the bogey that the Western Powers think it is or should be to the Arabs. For it is a fact that Russia is nowhere in the Arab world. She maintains no troops in any of the Arab countries, exercises no political control over them, and has no share in their economic exploitation. The danger of communist domination, however imminent, does not reconcile the Arabs to Western domination which is actual. Communist tyranny behind the Iron Curtain has a parallel in French oppression in North Africa. Whatever danger lurks behind Communism, the immediate and by far most ominous danger to the Arabs lies in the presence of Israel, the creation of Great Britain and the United States.

It is also worth remembering that the Western Democracies themselves have changed their attitude towards Soviet Russia, a change determined not so much by a conflict of principles and beliefs as by the power situation in the world, for Russia was as communist when she became the ally of the West in its struggle with fascism as she is today. Churchill's statement that he would join hands with the devil if that served his cause is not inspired by ideology but prompted by the natural urge to seek help wherever it may be found.

Russia's tactics in dealing with the Arab countries are clever. Almost invariably the Soviet Union has supported Arab independence—not out of solicitude for Arab freedom, to be sure, but with the purpose of ejecting France and Great Britain from the area. Nevertheless Russia's maneuvers left a favorable impression. The Soviet Union was the first power to give full recognition to the independence of Syria and Lebanon with no reservations as to special rights and privileges for any single power. In the dispute submitted to the United Nations in the winter of 1946 over the withdrawal of French and British troops from the two Levant States, the Soviet delegation forcefully backed the delegates of the two republics. When the Anglo-Egyptian controversy was brought before the Security Council in the summer of 1947, Russia supported Egypt's case. She has vetoed the admission of Jordan to the United Nations on the ground that the presence of British troops and dependence upon British financial help impair its qualification as a sovereign state. More recently the Soviet Union has voted with the Arab and other Asiatic states on the North African conflict with France, and its stand helped defeat the resolution which proposed direct negotiations between the Arabs and Israel without first calling upon Israel to put into effect previous resolutions of the United Nations. Although Russia voted for partition, her role in the Palestine issue was less onerous than that of Great Britain who created the Palestine problem and the United States who aggravated it.

It is not possible to speak with any degree of certainty about communists in the Arab countries, their numbers, strength, and organizations. In none of the Arab countries—except North Africa —are communist parties recognized. In North Africa some of the nationalists joined the Communist parties to air their views because the Communists were allowed greater freedom than the nationalists, but they soon broke away, founded nationalist parties, and became strongly anti-communist, like the Algerian leader Masali Al-Haj and his party the MTLD. In Tunisia where labor is well organized it is nationalist and definitely anti-communist. In Morocco, when the nationalist parties in April 1951 concluded the National Pact of Tangier, they pledged not to form a common front with the Morocco communists. In Egypt, prior to the army revolution, conditions—political, economic, and social—provided favorable soil for communism. Indiscriminate repression, especially as it was directed at all the liberal elements under the pretext of combating communism, intensified the resentment and bitterness. The fundamental reforms introduced by Mohammad Naguib and the new hope and exhilaration which he has infused into the nation are guarantees against the undermining effects of all subversive movements. In Lebanon, a section of organized labor is communist-oriented. In a cosmopolitan port city like Beirut, where uprooted and drifting elements abound, communist propaganda finds receptive ears. The remedy lies in social reforms such as are advocated by the Progressive Socialist Party, and in rooting the people in a cultural background which is real and meaningful to them. Syria in dealing with the communists has used both repression and the introduction of important economic and social reforms to increase general prosperity and spread a measure of social justice. Iraq continues the severe repression of communists, with what effect it is difficult to tell. But the most threatening hotbed of communism is found among the Palestine refugees who were torn away from their homes and their land and dumped in camps under wretched conditions which impair the health and undermine the morale, leaving the inmates to ponder their plight in despair. It is not conducive to a friendly attitude towards the West for these refugees to remember—as they very much do remember—that the two leading Western powers, Great Britain and the United States, were largely responsible for the loss of their country and the calamity which has befallen them.

Although communism as an ideology is repugnant to Arab tradition and Moslem religion, and although communist parties are outlawed in the Arab countries, yet because of conditions prevalent in many parts of the Arab world as a result of internal weakness or outside pressures, communism is not without prospects in this area.

Since the Western Powers are held responsible for much of the strain and stress under which the Arabs labor today, it does them little good to dangle the threat of communism over Arab heads. If they seriously wish to regain Arab confidence and good will they should rethink their whole policy in relation to the Arabs and be prepared to strike out on a new course of action.

It is essential for the West to realize at the outset that the Arab desire for liberty, their determination to free themselves from foreign control, their insistence on the right to equal partnership in freely contracted obligations are not communist inspired but are natural, indigenous stirrings and spring from an urge similar to that which prompted the American Revolution. Communist propaganda has not created Arab grievances against the Western Powers; it merely exploits these grievances which are real and basic and are deeply felt and resented throughout the Arab countries. In fact, communist propaganda trying to penetrate Arab society does not so much stress the dissemination of communist doctrines as it harps upon the wickedness of the imperialist West in its dealings with the Arabs. Neither does communism prop the vested interests and reactionary elements within Arab society which delay its internal liberation and reconstruction, but on the contrary it seeks to undermine their very existence, and in doing so is more in accord with the progressive elements than the Western powers who support anti-democractic governments just because they are anti-communist.

The Arabs know that western democracy in principle is very fine. They want to be convinced, however, by deeds and not only words, that the democracies mean what they profess. The western powers have made a very poor showing of democracy in their relations with the Arabs. The ideals of the French Revolution have been drowned in the waves of French oppression in North Africa. Britain's good name for integrity has suffered irretrievably as a result of British policy in the Arab countries, especially Palestine. And America in her recent relations with the Arabs has departed, with grievous consequences, from the heritage of the Pilgrim Fathers and the founders of the great Republic.

The West is confronted with the choice of initiating a "bold new policy" with regard to the Arab world, or acknowledging failure and defeat. The methods practised since the close of the first World War are doomed. Coercion and force defeat their purpose by aggravating the injustice and intensifying the feeling of resentment. "Divide and rule" and other forms of political intrigue are a double-edged weapon, for while they have kept the region divided and weak and therefore more easily held down by Great Britain and France, they have for this same reason left it exposed to the penetration of the subversive movements which the West—led by the United States—is trying to combat at the expense of great material and human cost. Neither is economic aid a reparation for political injury. Economic aid alone is at best a palliative, and at worst could be used, as indeed it has been used, against the forces of progress. The remedy and hope lie in a thorough revision of policy, in the light of realities intrinsic to the area, and in relation to the people whose home and land it is.

The foremost reality and the one that pervades all others is this: there can be no stability in the Arab world, no sound development within Arab society, and no healthy relations between the Arabs and the West, until the *political* atmosphere is cleared through the settlement of the area's problems in conformity with the rights and legitimate interests of the Arab people.

For it is a fact which cannot be overemphasized that political frustration is at the basis of instability in the region. It has led to a preoccupation with the political aspect of life which leaves to the crying need for social reconstruction only remnants of energy and thought. And finally it is this sense of frustration and injury that has estranged the Arabs from the Western Powers who are inseparably associated with the political set-up in the area, and with all the ills and evils which have sprung from it.

A satisfactory political settlement is a prerequisite to the kind of economic aid needed for such projects of development and reconstruction as would bring Arab society in tune with the liberal and progressive elements in the modern world. But no amount of material aid, however needed, can buy off the elemental urge and need of a people to be free and to order their lives in the light of what seems best to them.

A number of Arab countries have accepted aid under the Point Four program and are studying development projects in collaboration with U.S. experts. The main limitation of the program is its emphasis upon technical rather than financial aid, while there is greater need for large capital investment than for technical skill. To send foreign experts to an underdeveloped area without providing adequate means to put through the projects recommended is to expose these experts to frustration—their efforts are confined to blueprints rather than live projects—and to call forth disappointment among the local people who expect tangible results.

There is ample scope in the Arab countries for the investment of private capital on a large scale—provided such capital has in view legitimate profitmaking in conjunction with furthering the welfare of the country where it is invested. Too often in the past has foreign capital meant exploitation and political domination. These dangers are no longer what they once were, but even today foreign concessionary companies continue to believe that their interests are served by bribing corrupt governments and supporting reactionary regimes. In doing so they identify themselves with reaction, and forfeit the confidence and cooperation of the progressive elements. Foreign capital has the right to security and reasonable profit, and these can best be secured in a society whose stability rests upon the prosperity, liberty, and welfare of all classes of the population.

The Western Powers are concerned over the defense of the Middle East. Impelled by considerations of strategy they have come to view the area as a unit. But this view remains restricted to the place of the region in global strategy. In relation to its internal problems and the interests and wishes of its inhabitants it is not treated as a unit, but is regarded as a mosaic of insignificant states. A wholehearted support of Arab unity would strengthen the defense potentialities of the area and promote the purpose of the United Nations for close integration within homogeneous groups, leading to the integration of all free peoples in a just and enlightened world society.

The Arabs, too, are concerned over the defense of their area, but they are no longer willing to be used as instruments of policy. The defense of an area is the responsibility primarily of the people who inhabit it—and who will defend it to make their liberty secure but not to serve the interests of one power against another.

There is evidence—strong in Egypt and Syria—that the Arabs are seriously bent on strengthening their defense forces and building up their political and social solidarity, thereby fortifying their resistance to outside pressures and minimizing the effect of disruptive elements within. The Arabs need arms which the Western Powers, especially the United States, are in a position to supply. But the supply of arms, like the provision of economic aid, need not be tied to political strings if it is extended to free peoples who, because they are free, will use their strength—military, economic, and political—to defend their freedom and discharge their international obligations in a world where the cause of peace has become inseparably linked with the freedom of all peoples.

CHAPTER XVIII

The Greater Struggle

THE PROPHET Mohammad spoke to his comrades upon their return from battle saying: "You have come back from the lesser to the greater struggle." They asked: "What is the greater struggle, O Messenger of God?" And he answered: "The struggle within!"[1]

This greater struggle the Arabs are going through now. During the thirty years which followed the first World War, Arab energies were consumed in resistance to foreign rule, their efforts diverted to liberation from outside controls. This aspect of the fight has not been relinquished, nor can it be as long as some Arab countries remain under foreign rule and others only partially free. But the emphasis is beginning to shift to liberation from within. Signs of critical self-examination, of keen sensitiveness to the ills within Arab society, of thoughtful ponderings over conditions as they are in contrast to what they ought to be, of attempts to evaluate the Arab heritage and understand the relevancy and potentialities of Arab culture in relation to the contemporary world—these signs are beginning to delineate the Arab horizon which until recently was dominated by the aim of independence from foreign rule.

Independence, where it was achieved, did not usher in the millenium. In matters of efficiency, administrative ability, and probity in the conduct of public affairs, the independent regimes fell short of the standards that foreign administrations—and especially the British rather than the French—had set. The men to whom authority was transferred considered government more a private benefice than a public trust. They packed the administration with relatives and friends, and handed profitable transactions to their followers and associates. Those who had led the resistance gave up the fight once independence, however partial, was achieved. Some of the

1. Literally: with one's self.

leaders succumbed to a life of affluence and ease. They became more and more remote from the people who for a time had rallied around them in the struggle for independence. None sought to organize and prepare the people for the greater struggle. None had a constructive plan, nor the vision of the society which was to rise with the dawn of freedom. It had been one thing to say "No" to the foreign ruler; it was another to grapple with the problems which beset the building of a modern state.

Arab leadership during the past quarter of a century has been defective. And Arab leaders have shared with imperialism the blame for the ills which afflict Arab society. But since these leaders are the product of their society, their failures and their achievements are better understood if projected against their proper background. Arab society as it emerged from the first World War was basically medieval in structure. Its economy rested on an agriculture characterized by low productivity (except in Egypt), tenancy farming or share-cropping, and the concentration of agricultural land in the hands of a small absentee landowning class. Industry was represented by small shop handicrafts and domestic industry. With an under-developed economy, the means with which to finance adequate school systems, social services, and defense forces were deficient. The framework of a modern government was lacking: the tradition of public service was absent, and trained personnel, whether civil servants or experts and technicians, were too few to cope with the problems and needs.

Notwithstanding the basic unity of civilization, the homogeneity of the general pattern of culture, and the absence of class stratification, Arab society was nonetheless divided into three distinct sections: town-dwellers, peasants, and bedouins. The townspeople looked down upon the peasants whom they treated as milch cows. The peasants in turn mistrusted the townsmen, their exploiters, and suspected town life of wickedness and immorality. The bedouins, for their part, despised every form of life other than their own. They prized their desert freedom above the wealth of cities and the fruits of the soil. But they were a constant danger to the settled life whose bounties they coveted, and an ever present nuisance and challenge to any authority. The absence of a modern system of communications, the difficulty of moving from place to place because of the inadequacy of the means of transportation, kept these groups apart and their mutual suspicions unabated. The national uprisings, especially the Egyptian revolution of 1919 and the Iraqi revolt of 1920, brought for a time the various communities together in a common cause. But national consolidation was a slow process, and only lately has it been attempted methodically and with organized and serious effort.

The late king Faisal of Iraq, shortly before his death, gave a true picture of Iraqi society in a private memorandum which he distributed among a few leading statesmen. Iraq was a conglomeration of communal groups which lacked unity. The masses were ignorant and therefore an easy prey to all sorts of misleading ideas. The tribes were armed and opposed to every authority; they had to be paid to keep quiet. The government was weak by comparison with the various groups who despised it for its weakness and resented its interference. The state as Faisal saw, needed wise and able statesmanship to build up confidence in the government; an army to maintain order and authority in the presence of the armed communities; education for the masses; the delegation of greater authority to municipal and provincial councils to train people in government responsibility; and the settlement of the land problem.

Not only in Iraq, but among the Arabs in general, the attitude to the government was one of suspicion and mistrust. This was the legacy of centuries of foreign rule when the people felt the presence of the government only through the exactions it imposed upon them. Since the government was alien and oppressive, it had to be defied or tricked; and the law, imposed by an oppressor, had to be circumvented.

The centralization established under the mandates was maintained by the independent regimes. No adequate local public bodies were developed, to share the burden with the central administration and train the people in self-government. As a result, government became a heavily burdened, slow, and inefficient bureaucracy, and the people, who took little constructive interest in it, blamed it for their ills and at the same time came to rely upon it to do for them what they were not trained or organized to do themselves.

Centralization in government was accompanied by the concentration of all important activities—cultural or economic—in the big cities. Here were the universities, the libraries and museums, the printing presses, publishing houses, and newspapers. Professional men shunned the country and crowded themselves and their services in the cities. Wealth was concentrated in the hands of a few landowners, industrialists, and merchants who lived in the big cities, usually the capital of the country. The rest of the country, apart from the capital and perhaps one other principal town, remained politically, economically, and culturally a backwater.

Into this society, the Western parliamentary form of government was transplanted. No wonder it was not successful. An essential requisite for the successful working of the parliamentary system—organized political parties—was lacking. Political parties there were, but they revolved around individuals rather than principles and platforms. And if a program was formulated, it remained confined to paper, and the party activity limited to parlor talk. There was one exception, the Wafd in Egypt, a mammoth party, well organized; and in its earlier years it had had a mission and a message—to check the arbitrariness of the king and to free Egypt from the British—which made the nation rally around it. But with the years the Wafd lost its fighting spirit; corruption invaded its ranks and hit some of its foremost leaders; its leadership became dictatorial, keeping the young promising elements out of positions of orientation and direction, and withdrawing more and more from the popular base which had been its strength.

In the absence of genuine political parties with broad popular support, parliamentary government became a façade for autocratic rule. The parliamentary system of checks and balances did not function; instead, the head of the state—King, Regent, or President—who was supposed to reign and not rule, actually ruled pretty much as he pleased. He formed and dismissed governments, convened, prorogued, and annulled parliaments, suspended and abrogated the constitution. The political leaders from among whom the heads of governments and cabinet ministers were chosen, having no party support in parliament nor popular backing outside it, depended for their appointment and support upon the ruler, and were in actual practice responsible to him and not to parliament. The parliaments represented not so much the people as the vested interests of influential groups. The scales were heavily weighted on the side of the landowning class. The industrialists might have redressed the balance, but they soon merged their interests with those of the big landowners. Moreover, big industry was in large measure financed and controlled by foreign elements, and therefore it could not genuinely defend national interests. Labor and the peasants had no voice in parliament; those who presumed to speak in their name did not come from their rank and file, and were therefore not truly representative of them. Consequently, their interests were subordinated to the small but powerful groups.

It would be wrong to conclude from the foregoing that the parliamentary system of government is not suitable to the Arabs, or that Arab society is inherently opposed to it. On the contrary, the Arab heritage is essentially and basically democratic, and if parliamentary government has failed so far it is because the requisites for its proper functioning have not yet been provided. Even so, the parliamentary system as practiced during the past thirty years is far from being a complete failure. It was a necessary step for training in popular government and it established the principle of the people's sovereignty to which even autocratic rulers paid lip service. It will also be remembered that these parliaments, however inadequate and insufficiently democratic, were a stronghold for the defense of national rights against the dominating foreign power, and that they were at times the scene of vehement debates denouncing social injustice and government abuse.

Neither may it be assumed that foreign tutelage should have extended longer and that its early termination left the people unprepared for self-government. Foreign rule did not provide the opportunities for training in the responsibilities of democratic government. When the foreign power ruled directly, the people of the country were kept away from every position of real authority and responsibility. And when that power ruled behind a native façade, it joined hands with the vested interests and used its authority and influence to maintain the status quo. Moreover, no foreign administration, even if it were willing, could project itself into another people's background, grasp their real needs, and direct their efforts towards self-fulfillment. And finally, the independent governments, with all their failures, have to their credit important reforms—notably very creditable work in education—which would not have been possible of achievement had the foreign power remained in undisputed control.

The adoption of the Western form of government was one expression of the Arab efforts towards modernization and Westernization. Although Western influence was present in a number of Arab countries during the 19th Century, yet the full impact of the West was not felt until after the first World War. The impact was tremendous, and left the Arabs for a time dazzled and dazed. Quickly they tried to copy and imitate, to catch up with the wheel of progress. They copied laws and constitutions, school systems, patterns of behavior, thinking that in these lay the remedy and cure for the backward state in which they found themselves in relation to their foreign rulers. The efforts were bound to be superficial, limited as they were to the more obvious forms and expressions of Western civilization. It was not in the nature of this hurried and haphazard process to allow for an evaluation of that civilization, and a comprehension of its essence and of the attitude of mind and spirit which had created it. At the same time a precise knowledge of Arab society and its needs was wanting; nor was there a broad view and firm grasp of Arab culture and its meaning and message. The result was a loss of moorings, and of self-confidence and assurance. Perplexity and doubt were rampant, indifferences to fundamental values and a materialistic approach and evaluation prevailed. Frustration engendered by foreign rule, the inaptitude of native governments, the lack of opportunities for self-fulfillment, the failure of the leaders to inspire and win the confidence of youth and lead the people out of the morass in which they were stuck—all these led to excessive—seldom constructive—criticism, and at times close to despair.

It was not helpful that at this time of strain and stress the only type of leadership available was political leadership. Emphasis upon liberation from foreign rule and the political aspect of life marked out the political leader as the hero, the ideal, the person to look up to and rally around. The failure of political leaders left a sense of bitter disillusion, even cynicism, all the more alarming for lack of any other kind of leadership to fill the vacuum created by the disappointment at the performance of the political leaders. Religious leadership was ineffective; religion was losing its hold as a force in people's lives, and religious men had no message convincing and relevant to the issues of the time. The types of leaders at work in a modern dynamic society—scientists, explorers, industrialists, executives, and architects of great business enterprises—were still too few in Arab society. Even the intellectual leaders preferred to indulge in political life or to write hurriedly on a variety of subjects, in order to acquire quickly fame and possibly riches, rather than applying themselves with devotion to the study of their society and the task of guiding the nation out of its bafflement.

The effect of this bewilderment and confusion told most upon the nation's youth. In a fluid society, with its values changing fast, its religion no longer the bulwark it used to be; with the family—main-

stay of Arab society—threatened with disintegration; with no stable
civil institutions to rely on for guidance and support, and government a monopoly packed with favorites, youth felt unwanted, weak,
and insecure. In these circumstances, its pent up energy was spent
in political agitation: strikes, street demonstrations, and minor disturbances.

But there was also a constructive side, for the idealism and hope-
fulness of youth were not altogether overcome. Its sense of mission
was expressed in a number of organizations with a constructive social purpose. The Moslem Brothers, Al-Ikhwan al-Muslimun, most
influential of these movements, is here described in some detail.
The full weight of the Brothers was felt in Egypt, but there were
branches of the movement in other Arab countries.

The Moslem Brothers worked for social reform through religion.
Seeing the moral disintegration around them, the loss of faith, the
materialistic bent, the indifference and lack of self-confidence, they
set out to restore the lost moral values by the strict application of
the religious principles and regulations to daily conduct. Islam was
to be a living force in people's lives, a liberating force, and not an
opiate to dull the mind and spirit and keep the people in subjection.
In a society which had departed widely from the spirit and precepts
of religion, and had set up a variety of idols before which the mass of
the people were offering up their sweat and blood, the Brothers
taught anew that homage was due only to God, that none other
was to be feared but He alone, that all men were equal members of
a common brotherhood, and that moral strength and self-respect
were the hallmark of the believer.

The Brothers were not the fanatics and bigots their enemies
broadcast them to be. Their call not only found a hearing among
the downtrodden masses, but had a wide appeal to educated youth;
university students and professional men were prominent, by numbers and by influence, in the movement. For the Brothers, in their
zeal to restore the values of religion and strengthen its hold upon
people's lives, were not unaware of the demands of contemporary
life and of the scientific basis of a modern, progressive society. For
the scientific achievements of Western civilization they had great
respect and urged their adoption by Moslem society, but they
warned against the substitution of science for religion which in the
West had led to the abuse of the actual and potential results of
scientific discovery.

The Brothers were a well-organized movement. They spread

their teachings by social work and preaching, by founding of schools and economic establishments, and through a number of publications. These last included a daily paper—*The Moslem Brothers*, a weekly, and a monthly periodical—*Al-Shihab*. These were published in Cairo. *Al-Manar*, a daily paper, was the organ of the Ikhwan in Damascus, and another daily, *Liwa al-Haqq,* appeared in Mosul. There were 2000 branches of the Ikhwan in Egypt, and their meeting places were centers of religious and social education. In their schools they emphasized religious instruction and civic upbringing. Opportunities for physical training were provided in a number of sports clubs. A health section supervised the establishment of a hospital and several clinics where medical services were offered free. The Ikhwan were concerned with the development of economic resources for the general welfare of the people, not for the enrichment of a small group. To this end they established industrial companies and distributed their shares among thousands of holders including many workers. Their small spinning and weaving factory in a suburb of Cairo was a workshop where the principles of social justice were put into practice. The Ikhwan also tried their hand at the reclamation of wastelands; they bought 800 acres of state domain in the desert and converted it into productive soil. If the Ikhwan had confined their activities to social and religious work, they probably would have been allowed to continue their mission without interference from the authorities. But they became deeply involved in political action; yet it is difficult to see how they could have avoided this involvement when the political aspect dominated the life of the nation, and the political issues were considered the key to the other problems facing society.

The State, in the concept of the Ikhwan, was to be a theocracy, with the Koran its constitution. That the religious state may fulfill the purpose of religion, a long and arduous process of educating the people is necessary as a preparation. The partisan politics as practised by the existing political parties was destructive of national unity and of the oneness of purpose which should dominate public life while the country's problems, both external and internal, were still unsolved. The Ikhwan were vehement in their denunciation of the British occupation; and of all sections of the Egyptian population they were most keenly aware of the Zionist danger while Palestine was still under the Mandate.

The haste with which the Ikhwan wanted to assume power and control the state was incongruous with their view of the need for patient work to prepare the people for the coming of a just and righteous government. Moreover, they did not abstain from violence as a political method. They participated in terrorist acts and political assassination, although they were actually not guilty of many of the incidents which were attributed to them.

The Ikhwan were dissolved soon after the Palestine war, when all opposition to government was crushed and every form of freedom repressed. Their property and establishments were confiscated, and their work stopped. Many were cast in prison, others kept under strict surveillance, and a ban was placed upon any activity connected with them. The Ikhwan have since resumed their activity, but only as a religious organization.

The Ikhwan's concept of a theocratic state has not found wide acceptance even in religious circles. The violence of some of their political actions has been condemned. And there are many who think they are too stringent and meticulous about religious observances and general conduct. But, however people may differ with the Ikhwan, there is general admiration for their strength of character, resolute conviction, and seriousness of purpose. There is also wide recognition that the Ikhwan were conspicuous for their courage, honesty, and sense of dignity and human worth.

The impact of the West, however negative in some of its expressions and results, was a leavening force that caused a productive ferment of ideas and trends, and not only among those elements of Arab society who had studied and travelled in the West or attended European and American institutions in their own country; it also affected profoundly some thinkers whose background was entirely Arab. Three such men come to mind: one a Tunisian, the other a Najdi, and the third an Egyptian Azharite.

The Tunisian Al-Tahir al-Haddad was a product of his native environment. His education was of the traditional kind, acquired at the Zaitouna Mosque; he spent his whole life in his own country, laboring among his people—especially the working class—to improve their conditions and reform Tunisian society. Al-Tahir al-Haddad wrote two books: one, *Our Woman in the Religious Law and in Society,* brought him the anathema of the religious leaders because in it he stated that we should differentiate between the eternal truths which are the foundation of the Moslem faith, and certain laws and regulations which Islam laid down to meet temporary conditions, and which the passing of these conditions has rendered obsolete. For woman—the mother of mankind—and her place in society, woman who represents one half of the nation and therefore one half of its productive capacity, Al-Haddad had great concern, and he urged her emancipation and education, so that she might fulfill herself and discharge trust of bringing up the nation's youth. He believed that the basic ill of Tunisian society came from the degraded status of woman, and that salvation depended upon the proper education of woman and her active participation with man in the responsibilities of life.

In his other book—*Tunisian Workers*—Al-Haddad makes clear that Tunisian society is not a healthy organism, but one beset by many ills which foreign rule has aggravated. He urged a recognition of these ills, a deeper sense of social responsibility and compassion with the sorrows that afflict the mass of the people, as well as the need for economic development and productiveness through organized work. He stressed the importance of the cooperative movement, not only as a means to supply material needs, but as a training in mutual help and in a brotherly spirit. Cooperatives, by giving a sense of solidarity and strength to their members, would restore their courage, self-confidence, and capacity for independent action which native poverty and foreign exploitation had destroyed. Only when the people were organized in strong, active associations would their power be felt and the government forced to submit to their will. The fact that men like Al-Tahir Al-Haddad devoted their life to the cause of the toiling and trodden masses explains the vigor of the working class movement in Tunisia.

These Are the Chains of the Najdi Abdallah Ali Al-Qasimi, published in Cairo in 1946 and dedicated to King Abd-el-Aziz Ibn Saud, is a reasoned recognition of the merits of Western civilization, a denunciation of the mentality and habits which have kept Arab and Moslem society in chains, and a fervent plea for the wholehearted adoption of the spirit and attitude of mind which have made of Western civilization the dominant form of contemporary life.

Reviewing the state of the Arab and Moslem nations which are behind the West in everything—political freedom, economic and social development, and intellectual achievement—he asserts that the essence of the greatness and power of modern man is his daring knowledge which has subdued nature and conquered the enemies of mankind: poverty, disease, and ignorance. This intellectual daring has for centuries been atrophied in Moslem society. Through a perverted concept of religion, religious leaders have belittled man and taught that he was created a weak and ignorant being, and destined to remain so. And the people, indoctrinated with this defeatist concept of man, gave up the struggle with nature and with life, surrendered their natural right to independent judgment and freedom of thought, accepted authority without question and, resigned to their miserable lot in this world, hoped for a better life in the hereafter. But religion is not the annihilation of the human mind and will, nor does it sanction the subjection of man to self-imposed chains. It is a crime against religion to preach in its name acceptance of social injustice, opposition to progress, surrender, and resignation. The mission of Islam is the redemption of man: redemption from enslavement to the men of religion, to the tyranny of leaders, rulers, and any other created beings; redemption from submission to the evil systems of government which inflict poverty, distress and misery upon man; and redemption from the grip of doctrines and beliefs which are steeped in immobility, lead men astray, hinder their liberation, and muffle their creative and virtuous energies. To be a living force, religion must inspire and induce a forward-looking spirit which admits the reality of material progress, impels the acquisition of knowledge, instils faith in man and his unlimited possibilities, and builds up his inner resistance to all forms of danger that threaten his freedom and hinder his full development.

In his analysis of social problems, Qasimi emphasized the role of woman in society, and criticized severely man's tyranny and selfishness which deprived woman of freedom and education and then attributed the degraded status which he forced upon her to the teachings of religion. In Qasimi's opinion women's education should have priority over the education of men, for only the nation whose women are properly educated may hope that its men will have a sound and productive education.

And finally, the Azharite Khalid Mohammad Khalil, in his book *From Here We Begin*, pleads for religion as a social gospel and pours out a scathing denunciation of priestcraft which has poisoned religion and warped its meaning and mission. Religion is light, liberation, and love; it is a call to an abundant, joyous, and productive life. Priestcraft lives in darkness and is the enemy of knowledge which is light. It holds the people in the chains of superstition which it parades as religion, defends ignorance, poverty, and disease, instils dejection in the spirit, and upholds the interests of the mighty. How can love, the perfection of religion, exist in a society rent by conflict and hatred arising out of hunger, misery, and fear?

The toiling masses were for a long time a thing forgotten. But they are beginning to stir. Emissaries of various ideologies are busy offering their wares to the awakening masses. At no time was there a greater need of a living religion, a religion carved upon people's hearts and deep in their being because it answers their needs and is a friend and companion along the path of life. The message of liberty, freedom from fear, of social equality, and faith in themselves is what the people need to hear. A just socialism fulfills the purpose of religion and establishes a peace which rests upon inward security.

This book was denounced as anti-religious by a committee of ulama who demanded its confiscation. But the court before which the case came described it as glorifying God, honoring His Prophet, and defending the cause of the people.

A new generation grew up which, however troubled and perturbed, was more firm and self-assured than the generation that had reached manhood by the 1920's. The acquisition of independence restored self-respect, the beginning of large scale economic development through indigenous effort and enterprise opened hitherto untrodden paths, and the dissemination of education broadened the base of enlightened and articulate opinion.

Some new tones were discernible. Foreign rule was no longer blamed as the only cause of all the ills in Arab society. It was more widely realized that the Arab countries were subjected to foreign rule because they were internally weak, and that loss of independence was a punishment for a nation's failure to perform specific social duties. It was also realized that independence was not an end in itself but the means to a thorough, unhampered reconstruction of society. A new concept of government began to take shape, the concept that the primary mission of government was to ensure social justice through the full development of the country's resources for the welfare of the whole people, and to provide adequate social and educational services and equal opportunities for work and a decent livelihood to all citizens.

Serious social and economic studies, investigations into the conditions of labor and the peasants, and statistics on the distribution of wealth, on the expenditure of the national income, the earnings of the common man in relation to his barest needs, the state of health, housing, and general standard of living among the mass of the people revealed appalling conditions. Not that these conditions were unknown before, but now knowledge was supported by the weight of documented evidence which exposed to full view the stark ugliness of the facts. And this so devastating evidence was given wide publicity in the press.

Poverty was recognized as the chief evil; ignorance and disease were its offspring and could not be eradicated unless poverty was first uprooted. And the cause of poverty was not natural dearth and scarcity, but the inadequate development of national resources on the one hand, and on the other the concentration of wealth, land, and the means of production in the hands of a few, leaving the mass in destitution. What had the government done but support the vested interests? The burden of taxation fell upon the poor. In Egypt where the landowners were the all powerful class, the revenue from the land tax was less than the government expenditure on the Department of Irrigation whose benefits went largely to the owners of the big estates. Regressive tax systems were in force; indirect taxes—which, in proportion to income, hit the poor harder than the rich—provided most of the revenue. The same disregard for the general interest was evident in the expenditure of the public income; for example, the top level of the government service was paid out of proportion to the meager salaries of the lower ranks; in the apportionment of the educational budget among the various levels of education, the bulk of the appropriation—especially in Egypt—did not go where it was most needed—to the building up of the primary system which served the mass of the people—but to the higher stages which benefited a comparatively small number; and in public works—except in Egypt where the irrigation system was well developed and advanced—more money was spent on roads, streets, government buildings (which were needed and in themselves are good) than on productive projects—irrigation, land reclamation and development, utilization of the water resources for the production of power—or on social services.

The casual observer visiting the Arab countries after the second World War probably saw little evidence that far reaching changes were in the making. Those who observed more clearly could foresee the gathering storm. In Egypt, where social and political evil threatened to submerge the nation in chaos, warnings and alarms sounded from every quarter: from Parliament where reports warned of social and economic instability; from labor which expressed its anxiety and sense of insecurity through strikes and disturbances; from peasants who rose against their landlords; and from writers who kept the issues before the public. A number of thoughtful books were written which analyzed with care the social and economic data and charted reasonable and practicable plans for the building of a healthy social organism. Two small popularly written books by Taha Husain were widely read; one, the *Tormented Upon the Earth,* was a series of portraits of human misery in contemporary Egyptian society so vivid and convincing that even the most callous could hardly fail to be shaken. The other, *The True Promise,* was an account of the beginnings of the Moslem faith, the hardships and sufferings of which its first votaries were subjected, their steadfastness and heroism in the face of persecution, and their final triumph over the forces of evil. This little book was intended to fortify the people and raise their morale by bringing home to them the eternal truth that victory was for those who were strong in themselves and great in their cause, however lowly their position. *The True Promise* was made into a film which attracted large crowds.

Sections of the daily and periodical press in Egypt were outspoken, vigorous, and persistent in their attacks, which spared no form of evil and no person. They depicted a society rent into two hostile camps, one weighed down and embittered by toil and privation, the other hardened and depraved with surfeit. They warned that the masses which had toiled and suffered for so long had reached the point where they would no longer allow their sweat and blood to be transformed into the gold which the rich squandered in shameless extravagance. There was a foreboding that, unless drastic reforms were soon enacted, the seething anger and despair in the breast of the nation would at any time flare out in a raging fire which would consume everything before it.

This outspoken press worried the King who was a major source of evil and moral dissolution in the country. He intimidated the Wafd Government, which had lifted some of the restrictions previously imposed upon the press, and introduced new laws which amounted to a denial of freedom of expression. The press rose in unison against them, and in its fight it was supported by the majority party in Parliament—the Government's party, by all the professional groups, by business men and merchants, and by organized labor. Under the impact of this solid opposition the proposed bills were withdrawn.

Freedom of the press found a staunch supporter in the Council of State. This great state institution was independent of the Government and beyond the reach of any influence or pressure from whatever source. In freedom's darkest moments, when the country was under martial law, reaction in the saddle, and the liberal elements under surveillance, the Council of State stood as a bulwark defending personal and public freedom against Government encroachment or unwarranted attack. Many times when publications were confiscated or newspapers suspended, the Council of State pronounced resounding verdicts which released the publications and restored liberty to the threatened press.

The inevitable outburst came when the army assumed control on July 23rd, 1952. But it was a peaceful outburst, not the kind that would issue in a class or civil war, that would bring down the house upon the occupants before it raised a new construction. The army coup was quick and decisive. Its success was due partly to its admirable organization and preparation, and partly to the people's utter despair of the existing regime and their eager anticipation of any change.

The army struck at the King who had become the symbol of all that was evil in the state. Farouk was a dissolute despot, unrestrained by any inward checks or by respect for tradition, the Constitution, or the dignity of his office. His personal depravity and utter disregard of any moral values and public duties were capped by his treason to his country on two crucial occasions: in the Palestine war when his associates and agents supplied the army with deficient arms which killed the Egyptians instead of their enemies; and in the Anglo-Egyptian crisis of 1951-52 when he stabbed his Government in the back and plunged his country into internal disputes while the national cause hung in the balance. In the ultimatum demanding Farouk's abdication, Mohammad Naguib held the king, as the personification of those evils, responsible for undermining the structure of the nation, exposing it to chaos, and dishonoring Egypt's name abroad.

The abdication of the king removed the chief obstacle in the path of a clean public life, and of basic and thorough social reconstruction. But to effect such reform was an arduous task which required the mobilization of all the nations' human and material resources. Mohammed Naguib began with the hope that he could cooperate with the political parties if they purified their ranks, composed their personal antagonisms, and devoted themselves to the common task. But when they showed little readiness or ability to change their ways and grasp the fact that a new order was in force, the political parties were dissolved; Parliament had been dismissed before the army coup. The Constitution of 1923 was abrogated. The frequent suspensions of the Constitution had shown that it contained too many loopholes through which arbitrary authority found its way to enforcing its will. A three-year transition period was declared during which Mohammad Naguib assumed the responsibilities of rule, aided by a Council of the Revolution and a Cabinet of civilians responsible to him.

With military rule in Egypt and Syria, the question suggests itself: are the Arab countries veering toward military dictatorship? The answer may best be stated against the background of the regimes which were supplanted by military groups, and in the light of what these groups are trying to achieve.

The military coups in Syria and Egypt were not raised against democratic governments run in the interests of the people. In Syria, an oligarchy had monopolized power—though against the good intentions of President Al-Kuwatli; in Egypt the conduct of public life had sunk to the lowest abyss by the abuses of the King. The constitutions in these and other Arab countries had been drafted before foreign political control was lifted. Such being their origin, the constitutions aimed on the one hand to guarantee the interests of the controlling power, and on the other to strengthen the executive at the expense of the legislature. Parliament exercised a wholly insufficient control. Seldom, if ever, did a government resign because Parliament had withdrawn its confidence. And yet there was no stability but frequent changes of governments at the will of the head of the state. These changes only brought back the same old faces in new combinations, which intensified the rivalries among a few political leaders and debarred promising younger elements from participation in public life on a high level. The political parties—or what went by that name—paralyzed public life with the personal antagonisms among their leaders, instead of organizing and directing it. The public, whom the leaders had neither the courage to face with the truth, nor the strength or vision to serve and direct, was kept in a constant tension between the exaggerated promises and rabble-rousing harangues of the politicians, and the realities in which the people lived. In this maze, responsibility was lost. The people asked: Who rules? The Head of the State, the Government, Parliament, the street? Or perhaps the foreign power, however camouflaged its directing influence? Or maybe all these together, but pulling in divergent directions?

The military authorities have assumed full responsibility for the outcome of their assumption of rule. They know that they alone have to account for what becomes of the state under their direction.

They have brought a greater sense of seriousness and determination to public life. In Egypt, the motto of the new regime: Unity, Discipline, and Work, is being impressed by every possible means upon the entire population.

Strength, moral and material, is the keynote of the regimes both in Syria and Egypt. The lesson of the Palestine defeat was particularly poignant to the Army. To restore confidence to the nation and build up its strength, the army rose against those responsible for its humiliation and frustration in Palestine. Both the Syrian and the Egyptian Armies have already become a force to be reckoned with.

Productiveness is emphasized as the source of national strength and the basis of national well-being. In Syria, state planning has increased appreciably the country's wealth, and established its economy on a sound basis. In Egypt, the radical land reform, the irrigation projects for the reclamation of desert land, the determined trend towards industrialization, and the full development and utilization of the country's resources for the people's welfare, mark the military regime as a social revolution.

The military authorities claim that they rule in the name of the people and for their welfare, that in fact the army and the people are one. The peaceful revolution of the army came to fulfill the message of the liberal elements who though fully aware of the social needs did not command the force necessary to implement their plans. The army is therefore the nation's instrument for putting into effect social and political reforms.

The suspension of constitutional government is declared to be temporary, while the public is being inculcated with the spirit of the revolution; a new constitution is being drafted in harmony with its aims. Meanwhile long-awaited, overdue reforms are put through with a sense of urgency unhampered by partisan wranglings and endless parliamentary debates.

It is believed that while political parties are a necessity in a politically stabilized and mature society, the immediate need of Arab society is for unity and consolidation. The Liberation Movements launched in Syria and Egypt by the military authorities aim to achieve such a national consolidation by uniting all classes of the population in one strong front, in which all party affiliations shall

melt and all considerations shall be subordinated to the one task of
social reconstruction, complete political liberation, and the achievement of national strength.

In Egypt, the Liberation Movement is rapidly becoming a school
of civic virtues and character building. Military training camps
have been founded, and are even now turning out groups of young
volunteers, eager to die for their country. Other camps provide opportunities for workers, peasants, students, professional men and
any other groups to live, work, study, and play together, in an effort
to develop a common approach to problems and promote unity of
purpose. Camp and group leaders are trained with care. Spiritual
strength is the mark of the leader; faith in God, in himself, and in his
fellowmen is the directing force in his life; and his mission is to im-
part this faith and diffuse it so that a new generation may be formed
which is anchored in God, informed with a comprehension of its
rights and duties, and unshakable in its determination to achieve
the good and abundant life for the nation.

Mohammad Naguib and his associates are God-fearing men.
Their private and public lives, and their public utterances which
are frequent and addressed to a variety of audiences, reflect their
adherence to spiritual values and testify that God is the source of
their inspiration and the goal of their endeavor.

With God so real to these men, it is not likely that they will use
their authority and their present wide popularity to crush the individual under a dictatorship. On the contrary, they repeatedly emphasize their respect for and faith in the individual, and stress that
the cause of the individual and the nation is one, that there can be
no freedom for the nation until the individual is liberated from fear,
from weakness and a sense of abasement, from abject poverty and
the ignorance which leads men astray.

Whenever they meet with people, in camps, factories, and mass
meetings, in schools and universities, or in mosques during the Friday prayer, Mohammad Naguib and his officers stress anew the
country's need of every individual's effort, and try to impress upon
their hearers that every individual counts and is responsible for
building the nation. It is not only what the military leaders repeatedly state about the individual's importance, or what they are so
honestly and diligently trying to do to improve the lot of the common man; it is the fact that they—ordinary individuals from among
the lower ranks of the army, and with a background close to that of
the mass of the people—have shattered the idols which enslaved the

people and shaken the stronghold of wickedness to its foundations; it is this which has had a redeeming effect upon the spirit of the ordinary man. At the same time, they make no idle promises and arouse no exaggerated expectations. The problems and issues are kept before the people who are reminded with insistence that a long, hard struggle is ahead in which every citizen must share before a good and honorable life for the individual and the nation can be achieved.

Mohammad Naguib has become a name to conjure with, not only to the Egyptians but to all Arabs. He has all the marks of a genuine leader, foremost among them his oneness with the people. Whole-hearted response has come to him from a people long neglected and oppressed who have at last found a deliverer. Mohammad Naguib is always with them, never remote, never out of sight or reach. His love is all-embracing. Wherever there is sorrow, affliction, or catastrophe, he is there to share and make the burden light. His love for his fellowmen has brought out the best in people's hearts, as when the appeal was made to give for aid to the poor, for the Palestine refugees, and for the victims of the Palestine war. A sense of brotherhood pervaded the nation, and it gave abundantly and with joy. When he addresses soldiers, workers, and students as "my children," and confides to them their country's need and high expectations of them, he invariably wins their loving loyalty and cooperative response. He has a particular love for children, and they in turn have adopted him as their Santa Claus. He has the simplicity of true greatness. He carries the burden of office but none of its pomp. In fact, he and his comrades are almost ascetic in their habits. Geniality and kindliness are as characteristic as are his determination and strength of purpose. To his military training and discipline he has added an academic education in law and political economy. His mind is open and enlightened. He is realistic in his approach to problems, as his settlement of the Sudan question has shown, but his realism is not of the kind that hesitates before difficulties. He draws his strength from faith in God and from a truly religious spirit which finds self-fulfillment in dedication to a cause.

The crucial issue for the Arabs at the present moment is not the form of government under which they live, but the type of men responsible for the conduct of the state. As with other underdeveloped countries, a large measure of state planning and direction is required to achieve, within a reasonable time and on a large scale, the productivity necessary for a thorough social reconstruction. State control or supervision is needed for the launching of vast irrigation schemes, the reclamation and distribution of land, the establishment of industrialization on a firm basis, for afforestation, the control of soil erosion, the mechanization and modernization of agriculture, the development of mineral resources, in brief, for bringing to full fruition all the country's economic resources and possibilities. The national development of this wealth, conceived in the interests of the people, is conducive to the creation of a healthy and balanced society whose stability does not rest on external and therefore precarious considerations, but is firmly rooted in an inner sense of security and peace which springs from the fulfillment of basic needs.

The dangers of military rule are obvious. But it is a fact that in Syria and Egypt—both under military governments motivated by a vision of the public good, enjoying wide if not unanimous support, and commanding the power to act—substantial and far-reaching reforms have been put into effect or are in process of realization. The contrast is striking between the constructive determination evident here, and the hesitant action elsewhere in the Arab countries where efforts at reform are restricted and confined by a multitude of inhibitions and fears.

But military leadership is not the only kind of genuine, dynamic, and constructive leadership now at work in Arab society. The outstanding example, outside of military circles, of a people's leader is Kamal Jumblatt of Lebanon. Jumblatt is trying to build up a new society from the grass roots through the medium of his Progressive Socialist Party. This Party, launched in May, 1949 after long study and careful preparation, has won the loyalty and support of a large section of the Lebanese population. Its aim is the establishment of a socialist state where every citizen is an owner, and none are dispossessed, ownership to be understood as of three kinds, private, collective, and public; where every owner is a worker and no able-bodied person exempted from work; where every individual is assured of an honorable living through equal opportunity for work and education, and the provision of health and social insurance. On the political level, society is to be a disciplined democracy in which neither dictatorship nor chaos shall have a place. Progressiveness is the essential quality of this socialism, a forward looking spirit, never static, never satisfied with its achievements, but looking beyond to the perfection which is the goal of evolution and of creation. This progressive, socialist order is not to be imposed from above but must emanate from the people who have been trained and organized to know their rights, and to assume with confidence and joy their responsibilities.

In Lebanon, a small country divided against itself by communal antagonisms and suspicions, the Progressive Socialist Party has a message of especial significance and hope: the integration of individuals and groups, through mutual aid and cooperative effort, into one loving and creative society free of the bias and prejudice of any sectarian doctrine.

The PSP has already earned for itself a prominent place in the public life of Lebanon. It was primarily instrumental in organizing and consolidating the opposition to the regime that has been overthrown, and it was ready with a positive, carefully worked-out program of social and political reconstruction. The Party has resumed its vigorous campaign for reforms of a fundamental nature; it is not likely that the new regime will be allowed to rest on mere palliatives and half-measures.

Kamal Jumblatt, scion of a feudal family, has completely identified himself with the people. He has renounced a life of ease, inherited leadership, and prestige for a life of hardship, toil, and sacrifice. He has consecrated himself to fight the people's battle with them. There is much of the saint, and of the hero, in him. His complete mastery of himself has given him the qualities of an inspired man. He is deeply spiritual, very much of a mystic in his concept of religion and of man's relation to man. His love for his fellowmen is boundless, and finds expression in a passionate urge to advance their welfare. His wrath at evil and evildoers is devastating; his righteous indignation has spared no one. He has a thoroughly disciplined and enlightened mind, open to knowledge from any source. His study of Western thought, especially as it expressed itself in social movements, is serious and responsible. But he is not an imitator nor an unreserved admirer of the social experiences of the West. He believes that the East has a spiritual message for the contemporary world, and the socialism that he preaches and works for aims to achieve more than the material wellbeing of the individual. Jumblatt is deeply imbued with the life, work, and teachings of the world's spiritual leaders, among them the Hindu mystics. His own life is strikingly reminiscent of Gandhi's. To him, as to the great Indian leader, meditation is of the essence of mental and spiritual discipline; and after the crowded day's activity in the city or throughout the country, he retires to his ancestral mountain castle where, in quiet reflection and prayerful contemplation, he reviews the work accomplished and draws inspiration and strength for the work yet to be done. Like the Indian Master, Jumblatt abhors and condemns violence as a political weapon. In fact, to him, the means is as important as the end, and the moral law within him allows no compromise in matters of principle. His spiritual strength is reflected in his unflinching courage and determination, unruffled poise amidst the agitation of his surroundings, simplicity and humility. A man without fear and without reproach, he has become a symbol of moral force, and through him Lebanon may have a message of more than local significance.

The fight is on in several of the Arab countries—in some with much greater intensity and effectiveness than in others—against the ills that gnaw at the heart of society, cramp its growth, and deter its full liberation and the unhampered release of its energies and potentialities. Genuine native leadership of a high caliber is at work, building up the inner strength of the nation. The conviction that salvation must come from within, and with urgent immediacy, has taken hold of enough forceful and organized elements to bring its realization within reach. For the Arabs, isolation from the modern world and rejection of its achievements are no longer an issue—not even in remote regions and communities. Passed, also, has the phase of hurried imitation induced by superficial contacts with the West. Arab society has reached the stage where it is rediscovering its own values, and is sinking its roots deeper into its native heritage, always conscious of the need to maintain the closest relationship with the creative forces in the contemporary world.

The Arab movement for liberty, unity, and the recreation of society is on the march and cannot be arrested from the outside. External forces and pressures, whose destructive consequences have been amply shown in the preceding chapters, could, if they are allowed to continue, thwart the movement and warp its natural, constructive course. The Arabs would suffer, but not they alone in a world that has become closely interdependent.

There is much talk these days, and has been for some time, about Arab participation in a scheme for the defense of the free world. The scheme worked out in Washington and London, conceived in the light of current power politics, and remote from the needs of the Arabs, has failed to enlist their support. They ask—and it is the reality of their experience and relations with the Western Powers that makes the question appropriate and necessary: Freedom for whom, and of what kind, are the Arabs called upon to defend? Do the Powers really believe that they represent freedom to the Arabs when they have perpetrated in their midst one of the most ruthless acts of injustice which history records—the creation of Israel? Or the loss of what freedom should the people of North Africa fear? Can the North Africans apprehend a danger worse than the plight they actually find themselves in and which they have borne for generations? And the people of the small states of the Fertile Crescent, who were divided and consequently weakened to suit the interests of Great Britain and France—and for whom, because of the divisions forced upon them, Israel is a mortal danger—can these people adopt the cause of the Western Powers as their cause? Or Egypt, with its 20 million inhabitants, now astir with a new sense of national dignity and honor, and under a strong and honest government devoted to the cause of consolidating and strengthening the country, should Egypt continue to bear with the humiliation of a foreign occupation—however the name may change—because Great Britain and the United States want to keep the Suez Canal Zone for the defense of their oil possessions in the Arab countries and the safeguard of their strategic interests against Russia? Before the West may expect genuine cooperation from the Arabs, it should come to them with cleaner heart and hands than its past record shows. Any scheme imposed from the outside is doomed beforehand. Only a plan that is meaningful to them and is expressed and realized in terms that satisfy their yearning for the free and full life can win Arab loyalty.

It is not likely that a foreign ideology, any more than externally conceived political plans, can be imposed upon the Arabs against their will. Arab society represents an old, stable, and continuous civilization which has met successfully challenge and danger. Its power of adaptability, while preserving its identity, explains its permanence. It has within it the seeds of its growth, the ability to pass independent judgment upon contemporary trends, and the gift to select what is akin its genius and suitable to its needs.

Arab civilization, recreated, has a message which the modern world can ill afford to ignore. Because it has its roots in Western civilization no less than in the heritage of the East, and because its broad humanity has united in full equality a large variety of the races of mankind, its mediation is needed for a more complete cooperation between the peoples of East and West. Its spiritual basis and the emphasis upon ethics which Islam introduced into every subject—science, economics, politics—may redress the disequilibrium of modern civilization with its emphasis upon science. The doctrine of the "mean"—the even balance—, a cherished ideal of Arab tradition, is a safeguard against excess and exaggeration, and a steadying force against the impropriety of being swept away by extremes.

If stringent self-criticism is imperative for the Arabs as a preparation for the kind of grass roots reconstruction which their society needs, is not this kind of self-criticism the pressing, inescapable need of the West in its relation with the Arabs? If the Arabs have much to learn from the West, and need the strictest discipline, devotion, and awareness, to catch up with the march of time, is the need less urgent for the West to return to the best in its heritage, relive it, and make it a reality to the peoples of other cultures?

It is not political alliances and blocs—these are opportunistic and constantly fluctuating—that shall bring the peoples of the world together, but the discovery of the kindred, the good, and the strong in each other's culture. It is on the level of contacts with the best in their heritage that East and West shall really and permanently meet.

Index